THE HEATH INTRODUCTION TO POETRY

THE HEATH INTRODUCTION TO
POETRY

Third Edition

with a Preface on Poetry and a Brief History by

Joseph de Roche
Northeastern University

D. C. HEATH AND COMPANY
Lexington, Massachusetts / Toronto

International Standard Book Number: 0–669–14808–3

Library of Congress Catalog Card Number: 87–80256

ACKNOWLEDGMENTS

John Ashbery.   "City Afternoon" from *Self-Portrait in a Convex Mirror* by John Ashbery, copyright © 1972, 1973, 1974, 1975 by John Ashbery. "Paradoxes and Oxymorons" from *Shadow Train* by John Ashbery, copyright © 1980 by John Ashbery. Both reprinted by permission of Viking Penguin Inc.

Margaret Atwood.   "It Is Dangerous to Read Newspapers" from *The Animals in That Country* by Margaret Atwood. Reprinted by permission of the Oxford University Press, Canada.

W. H. Auden.   "The Unknown Citizen," Musée des Beaux Arts," "In Memory of W. B. Yeats," "Epitaph on a Tyrant," and "As I Walked Out One Evening" copyright 1940 and renewed 1968 by W. H. Auden. Reprinted from *Collected Shorter Poems 1927–1957*, by W. H. Auden, by permission of Random House, Inc. Also reprinted by permission of Faber and Faber Ltd. from *Collected Poems* by W. H. Auden.

Margaret Avison.   "The Nameless One" is reprinted from *The Dumbfounding, Poems* by Margaret Avison, copyright © 1966 by Margaret Avison. Reprinted by permission of W. W. Norton & Company, Inc.

Amiri Baraka (LeRoi Jones).   "W. W." from *Black Magic Poetry 1961–1967*, copyright © 1969 by LeRoi Jones. Reprinted by permission of The Sterling Lord Agency, Inc.

Beowulf.   From *Beowulf: The Oldest English Epic*, translated by Charles W. Kennedy, copyright 1940 by Oxford University Press, Inc., renewed 1968 by Charles W. Kennedy. Reprinted by permission.

Wendell Berry.   "The Peace of Wild Things," copyright © 1968 by Wendell Berry. Reprinted from his volume *Openings* by permission of Harcourt Brace Jovanovich, Inc.

John Berryman.   "A Professor's Song" from *Short Poems* by John Berryman, copyright 1946 by John Berryman, copyright renewed © 1974 by Kate Berryman. "Dream Song # 14" from *The Dream Songs* by John Berryman, copyright © 1959, 1962, 1963, 1964 by John Berryman. Reprinted by permission of Farrar, Straus and Giroux, Inc.

Earle Birney.   "Anglosaxon Street" (Toronto 1942), "Twenty-Third Flight" (Honolulu, 1958), "The Bear on the Delhi Road" (Srinagar, 1958—Ile des Porquerolles, 1959), and "From the Hazel Bough" (Military Hospital, Toronto, 1945—Vancouver, 1947) from *Collected Poems* by Earle Birney. Reprinted by permission of The Canadian Publishers, McClelland and Stewart Limited, Toronto.

Elizabeth Bishop.   "The Fish," "Sandpiper," and "In the Waiting Room" from *The Complete Poems 1927–1979* by Elizabeth Bishop, copyright © 1940, 1962, 1969, 1971, 1976, 1983 by Elizabeth Bishop. Reprinted by permission of Farrar, Straus and Giroux, Inc.

Robert Bly.   "Driving to Town" from *Silence in the Snowy Fields*, copyright © 1961 by Robert Bly, published by Wesleyan University Press, 1962. Reprinted by permission of the author.

Louise Bogan.   "The Crossed Apple" and "The Dragonfly" from *Blue Estuaries* by Louise Bogan, copyright © 1923, 1929, 1930, 1931, 1933, 1934, 1935, 1936, 1937, 1938, 1941, 1949, 1952, 1954 by Louise Bogan. "The Dragonfly"

v

copyright © 1963 by Steuben Glass, a division of Corning Glass Works. Reprinted by permission of Farrar, Straus and Giroux, Inc.

Rupert Brooke. "The Soldier" from *The Collected Poems of Rupert Brooke,* copyright 1915 by Dodd, Mead & Company. Copyright renewed 1943 by Edward Marsh. Reprinted by permission of Dodd, Mead & Company.

Gwendolyn Brooks. "The Bean Eaters" and "We Real Cool" from *The World of Gwendolyn Brooks* (1971), copyright 1959 by Gwendolyn Brooks. Reprinted by permission of the poet.

Robert Clayton Casto. "The Salt Pork" copyright © 1969 by Loyola University, New Orleans. Reprinted by permission of the *New Orleans Review.*

Lucille Clifton. "in the inner city" from *Good Times* by Lucille Clifton, copyright © 1969 by Lucille Clifton. Reprinted by permission of Random House, Inc.

Leonard Cohen. "Elegy" and "The Bus" are reprinted by permission of Leonard Cohen. All rights reserved.

Frances Cornford. "The Watch" from *Collected Poems* by Frances Cornford, published by Cresset Press, now a part of the Hutchinson Publishing Group. Reprinted by permission of the publisher.

Hart Crane. "Proem: To Brooklyn Bridge" is reprinted from *The Complete Poems and Selected Letters and Prose of Hart Crane,* edited by Brom Weber, by permission of Liveright Publishing Corporation. Copyright © 1933, 1958, 1966 by Liveright Publishing Corporation. "My Grandmother's Love Letters" from *The Collected Poems of Hart Crane,* copyright 1933, Liveright, Inc. Reprinted by permission of W. W. Norton, Inc.

Robert Creeley. "Oh No," and "Naughty Boy" from *For Love: Poems 1950–1960,* copyright © 1962 by Robert Creeley. Reprinted with the permission of Charles Scribner's Sons.

Countee Cullen. "For a Lady I Know" and "Heritage" from *On These I Stand: An Anthology of the Best Poems of Countee Cullen,* copyright 1925 by Harper & Row, Publishers, Inc., renewed 1953 by Ida M. Cullen. Reprinted by permission of Harper & Row, Publishers, Inc.

E. E. Cummings. "All in green went my love riding," "in Just-," "the Cambridge ladies who live in furnished souls" and "Buffalo Bill's" are reprinted from *Tulips & Chimneys* by E. E. Cummings by permission of Liveright Publishing Corporation. Copyright 1923, 1925 and renewed 1951, 1953 by E. E. Cummings. Copyright © 1973, 1976 by the Trustees for the E. E. Cummings Trust. Copyright © 1973, 1976 by George James Firmage. "may i feel said he" is reprinted from *No Thanks* by E. E. Cummings by permission of Liveright Publishing Corporation. Copyright © 1935 by E. E. Cummings. Copyright © 1968 by Marion Morehouse Cummings Trust. Copyright © 1973, 1978 by the Trustees for the E. E. Cummings Trust. Copyright © 1973, 1978 by George James Firmage. "my sweet old etcetera" is reprinted from *Is 5* by E. E. Cummings by permission of Liveright Publishing Corporation. Copyright 1926 by Horace Liveright. Copyright renewed 1953 by E. E. Cummings, "i sing of Olaf glad and big" is reprinted from *Viva* by E. E. Cummings by permission of Liveright Publishing Corporation. Copyright 1931, 1959 by E. E. Cummings. Copyright © 1979, 1973 by the Trustees for the E. E. Cummings Trust. Copyright © 1979, 1973 by George James Firmage.

Walter de la Mare. "The Listeners" reprinted by permission of The Literary Trustees of Walter de la Mare and The Society of Authors as their representatives.

Joseph de Roche. "Aunt Laura Moves Toward the Open Grave of Her Father," first published in *The Iowa Review,* and "Blond" are reprinted by permission of the poet.

James Dickey.   "The Animals of Heaven," copyright © 1961 by James Dickey, first appeared in *The New Yorker,* reprinted from *Drowning with Others.* "Buckdancer's Choice," copyright © 1965 by James Dickey, first appeared in *The New Yorker,* reprinted from *Buckdancer's Choice.* Both reprinted by permission of Wesleyan University Press.

Emily Dickinson.   All selections reprinted by permission of the publishers and the trustees of Amherst College from *The Poems of Emily Dickinson,* edited by Thomas H. Johnson, Cambridge, Mass.: The Belknap Press of Harvard University Press, copyright 1951, © 1955, 1979, 1983 by the President and Fellows of Harvard College.

Robert Duncan.   "Often I Am Permitted to Return to a Meadow" from *The Opening of the Field,* copyright © 1960 by Robert Duncan. Reprinted by permission of New Directions Publishing Corporation.

Richard Eberhart.   "The Fury of Aerial Bombardment" and "On a Squirrel Crossing the Road in Autumn, in New England" from *Collected Poems 1930–1976* by Richard Eberhart. Reprinted by permission of Oxford University Press, Inc.

T. S. Eliot.   "Preludes," "Rhapsody on a Windy Night," "Journey of the Magi," "La Figlia che Piange," "Marina," "Sweeney Among the Nightingales," and "The Love Song of J. Alfred Prufrock" from *Collected Poems 1909–1962* by T. S. Eliot, copyright 1936 by Harcourt Brace Jovanovich, Inc., copyright © 1963, 1964, by T. S. Eliot. Reprinted by permission of the publisher and Faber and Faber Ltd.

Kenneth Fearing.   "Dirge" from *New and Selected Poems,* copyright © 1956 by Kenneth Fearing. Reprinted by permission of Indiana University Press, Bloomington.

Lawrence Ferlinghetti.   "In Goya's greatest scenes we seem to see" and "The pennycandystore beyond the El" from *A Coney Island of the Mind,* copyright © 1958 by Lawrence Ferlinghetti. Reprinted by permission of New Directions Publishing Corporation.

Edward Field.   "The Bride of Frankenstein" is reprinted by permission of the poet.

Robert Francis.   "Catch," copyright © 1950 by Robert Francis, first appeared in *The Face Against the Glass* by Robert Francis. Reprinted from *The Orb Weaver* by permission of Wesleyan University Press.

Robert Frost.   "Mending Wall," "Out, Out—," "Birches," "The Oven Bird," "Once by the Pacific," "Design," "Stopping by Woods on a Snowy Evening," "Fire and Ice," "The Draft Horse," "In Winter in the Woods Alone," "The Road Not Taken," "Departmental," and "The Death of a Hired Man" from *The Poetry of Robert Forst,* edited by Edward Connery Lathem. Copyright © 1969 by Holt, Rinehart and Winston. Copyright © 1975 by Leslie Frost Ballantine. Reprinted by permission of Henry Holt and Company, Inc.

Allen Ginsberg.   "In back of the real," copyright © 1954 by Allen Ginsberg and "A Supermarket in California," copyright © 1955, by Allen Ginsberg from *Collected Poems: 1947–1980* by Allen Ginsberg. Reprinted by permission of Harper & Row, Publishers, Inc.

Nikki Giovanni.   "Nikki Rosa" reprinted by permission of Broadside Press.

Louise Glück.   "Gratitude" copyright © 1975 by Louise Glück, from *The House on Marshland,* published by The Ecco Press. Reprinted by permission.

Robert Graves.   "Down, Wanton, Down!" and "The Villagers and Death" from *Collected Poems* by Robert Graves, copyright © 1955 by Robert Graves. Reprinted by permission of A. P. Watt Ltd. on behalf of The Executors of the Estate of Robert Graves.

Arthur Guiterman.   "On the Vanity of Earthly Greatness" from *Gaily the*

Donald Justice. "Here in Katmandu," copyright © 1956 by Donald Justice, first appeared in *Poetry*. Reprinted from *The Summer Anniversaries* by permission of Wesleyan University Press. "Luxury" from *Departures* by Donald Justice, copyright © 1973 by Donald Justice. Reprinted with the permission of Atheneum Publishers. "Anonymous Drawing," copyright © 1961 by Donald Justice, reprinted from *Night Light* by permission of Wesleyan University Press.

A. M. Klein. "The Rocking Chair" and "Lone Bather" from *The Collected Poems of A. M. Klein*, edited by Miriam Waddington, copyright © McGraw-Hill Ryerson Limited, 1974. Reprinted by permission.

Etheridge Knight. "For Black Poets Who Think of Suicide" reprinted by permission of Broadside Press.

Kenneth Koch. "Mending Sump" copyright © 1960 by Kenneth Koch. Reprinted by permission of the author.

Philip Larkin. "The Whitsun Weddings" from *The Whitsun Weddings* by Philip Larkin. Reprinted by permission of Faber and Faber Ltd. "Church Going" from *The Less Deceived* by Philip Larkin. Reprinted by permission of The Marvell Press, England.

D. H. Lawrence. "Piano" and "Snake" from *The Complete Poems of D. H. Lawrence*, edited by Vivian de Sola Pinto and F. Warren Roberts, copyright © 1964, 1971 by Angelo Ravagli and C. M. Weekley, Executors of the Estate of Frieda Lawrence Ravagli. All rights reserved. Reprinted by permission of The Viking Press, Inc.

Irving Layton. "Berry Picking" from *A Wild Peculiar Joy*. Used by permission of Irving Layton. "Party at Hydra" from *The Unwavering Eye: Selected Poems 1969–1975* by Irving Layton. Reprinted by permission of The Canadian Publishers, McClelland and Stewart Limited, Toronto.

Denise Levertov. "Six Variations" (part iii), "Come into Animal Presence," "What Were They Like," and "Losing Track" from *Poems: 1960–1967* by Denise Levertov. Copyright © 1960, 1961, 1963, 1969 by Denise Levertov Goodman. "Six Variations" and "Losing Track" were first published in Poetry. Poems are reprinted by permission of New Directions Publishing Corporation.

Janet Lewis. "Girl Help" from *Poems Old and New 1918–1978* by Janet Lewis, 1981. Reprinted by permission of The Ohio University Press, Athens.

Amy Lowell. "Wind and Silver" from *The Complete Poetical Works of Amy Lowell*, copyright © 1955 by Houghton Mifflin Company. Reprinted by permission of Houghton Mifflin Company.

Robert Lowell. "Water" and "For the Union Dead" from *For the Union Dead* by Robert Lowell, copyright © 1960, 1962, 1964 by Robert Lowell. "Skunk Hour" from *Life Studies* by Robert Lowell, copyright © 1956, 1959 by Robert Lowell. All reprinted by permission of Farrar, Straus and Giroux, Inc. "Mr. Edwards and the Spider" from *Lord Weary's Castle*, copyright 1946, 1974 by Robert Lowell. Reprinted by permission of Harcourt Brace Jovanovich, Inc.

Archibald MacLeish. "Ars Poetica" and "You, Andrew Marvell" from *Collected Poems 1917–1952*, copyright © 1962 by Archibald MacLeish. Reprinted by permission of Houghton Mifflin Company.

Louis MacNeice. "London Rain" and "Sunday Morning" from *The Collected Poems of Louis MacNeice*. Reprinted by permission of Faber and Faber Ltd.

W. S. Merwin. "The River of Bees" and "The Moths" from *The Lice* by W. S. Merwin, copyright © 1967 by W. S. Merwin. Reprinted with the permission of Atheneum Publishers.

Edna St. Vincent Millay. "Love Is Not All: It Is Not Meat nor Drink," "What Lips My Lips Have Kissed, and Where, and Why," and "First Fig" by Edna St.

Vincent Millay. From *Collected Poems*, Harper & Row. Copyright © 1922, 1923, 1931, 1950, 1951, 1958 by Edna St. Vincent Millay and Norma Millay Ellis. Reprinted by permission.

Marianne Moore.   "Poetry" and "A Grave" reprinted with permission of Macmillan Publishing Co., Inc. from *Collected Poems* by Marianne Moore, copyright 1935 by Marianne Moore, renewed 1963 by Marianne Moore and T. S. Eliot. "The Mind Is an Enchanting Thing" reprinted with permission of Macmillan Publishing Co., Inc. from *Collected Poems* by Marianne Moore, copyright 1944, renewed 1972 by Marianne Moore.

Edwin Muir.   "Childhood," "The Animals," "The Brothers," and "The Horses" from *Collected Poems* by Edwin Muir. Copyright © 1960 by Willa Muir. Reprinted by permission of Oxford University Press, Inc. Also from *The Collected Poems of Edwin Muir*. Reprinted by permission of Faber and Faber Ltd.

Howard Nemerov.   "The Goose Fish" and "I Only Am Escaped Alone To Tell Thee" from *New and Selected Poems*, copyright 1960 by the University of Chicago. Reprinted by permission of the poet.

Michael Ondaatje.   "King Kong Meets Wallace Stevens," "Charles Darwin Pays a Visit, December 1971," and "Birth of Sound" by Michael Ondaatje. Copyright © by Michael Ondaatje from *There's A Trick With A Knife I'm Learning To Do: Poems 1968–83*, published by W. W. Norton. Reprinted by permission of the author.

Wilfred Owen.   "Strange Meeting," "Dulce et Decorum Est," and "Anthem for Doomed Youth" from *Collected Poems*, copyright © 1963 by Chatto & Windus, Ltd. Reprinted by permission of New Directions Publishing Corporation.

P. K. Page.   "The Stenographers" and "Schizophrenic" reprinted by permission of the author.

Dorothy Parker.   "Résumé" from *The Portable Dorothy Parker*, Revised and Enlarged Edition, edited by Brendan Gill, copyright 1926 by Dorothy Parker, copyright renewed 1954 by Dorothy Parker. Reprinted by permission of Viking Penguin Inc.

Donald Petersen.   "The Ballad of the Dead Yankees," copyright © 1958 by Donald Petersen. Reprinted from *The Spectral Boy*, by permission of Wesleyan University Press.

Sylvia Plath.   "Morning Song," "Daddy," and "Ariel" from *The Collected Poems of Sylvia Plath*, edited by Ted Hughes. "Morning Song" copyright © 1961 by Ted Hughes, "Daddy" copyright © 1963 by Ted Hughes, and "Ariel" copyright © 1965 by the Estate of Sylvia Plath. Reprinted by permission of Harper & Row, Publishers, Inc. Also from *Ariel* by Sylvia Plath, copyright 1965 by Ted Hughes, published by Faber and Faber, London. Reprinted by permission of Olwyn Hughes. "Medallion," copyright © 1962 by Sylvia Plath, from *The Colossus and Other Poems*, by Sylvia Plath. Reprinted by permission of Alfred A. Knopf, Inc. "Metaphors" from *The Collected Poems of Sylvia Plath*, edited by Ted Hughes, copyright © 1960 by Ted Hughes. Reprinted by permission of Harper & Row, Publishers, Inc. "Medallion" and "Metaphors" also from *The Colossus* by Sylvia Plath, copyright 1960 by Sylvia Plath, 1967 by Ted Hughes, published by Faber and Faber, London. Reprinted by permission of Olwyn Hughes.

Ezra Pound.   All selections are from *Personae*, copyright 1926 by Ezra Pound. Reprinted by permission of New Directions Publishing Corporation.

E. J. Pratt.   "The Prize Cat" by E. J. Pratt. Reprinted by permission of University of Toronto Press.

Alfred Purdy.   "Wilderness Gothic" from *Wild Grape Wine* by Al Purdy. "The Cariboo Horses" from *The Cariboo Horses* by Alfred Purdy. Both reprinted by permission of The Canadian Publishers, McClelland and Stewart Limited, Toronto.

Dudley Randall. "Ballad of Birmingham" reprinted by permission of Broadside Press.

John Crowe Ransom. "Old Mansion," "Spectral Lovers," and "Bells for John Whiteside's Daughter," copyright 1924 by Alfred A. Knopf, Inc., renewed 1952 by John Crowe Ransom, and "Piazza Piece," copyright 1927 by Alfred A. Knopf, Inc., renewed 1955 by John Crowe Ransom, from *Selected Poems, Third Edition, Revised and Enlarged*, by John Crowe Ransom. Reprinted by permission of Alfred A. Knopf, Inc.

Henry Reed. "Naming of Parts," "Judging Distances," and "Unarmed Combat" from *A Map of Verona* by Henry Reed. Reprinted by permission of Jonathan Cape Ltd. on behalf of the Estate of Henry Reed.

Adrienne Rich. "A Clock in the Square" copyright 1951 by Adrienne Rich. Reprinted by permission of the poet. "Aunt Jennifer's Tigers," "The Insusceptibles" and "Diving into the Wreck" are reprinted from *Poems, Selected and New, 1950–1974*, by Adrienne Rich, by permission of W. W. Norton & Company, Inc. Copyright © 1975, 1973, 1971, 1969, 1966 by W. W. Norton & Company, Inc., © 1951, 1955, 1973 by Adrienne Rich.

Edwin Arlington Robinson. "For a Dead Lady," copyright 1920 by Charles Scribner's Sons, and "Miniver Cheevy," copyright 1907 by Charles Scribner's Sons, from *The Town Down the River* by Edwin Arlington Robinson. Reprinted by permission of Charles Scribner's Sons. "Karma" and "New England" are reprinted with permission of Macmillan Publishing Company., Inc. from *Collected Poems* by Edwin Arlington Robinson, copyright 1925 by Edwin Arlington Robinson, renewed 1953 by Ruth Nivison and Barbara R. Holt. "Mr. Flood's Party" from *Collected Poems* by Edwin Arlington Robinson, copyright 1921 by Edwin Arlington Robinson, renewed 1949 by Ruth Nivison. "Eros Turannos" from *Collected Poems* by Edwin Arlington Robinson, copyright 1916 by Edwin Arlington Robinson, renewed 1944 by Ruth Nivison. Reprinted by permission of Macmillan Publishing Co., Inc.

Theodore Roethke. "Root Cellar" copyright 1943 by Modern Poetry Association; "The Waking" copyright 1953 by Theodore Roethke; "Dolor" copyright 1943 by Modern Poetry Association; "I Knew a Woman" copyright 1954 by Theodore Roethke; "In a Dark Time" copyright © 1960 by Beatrice Roethke as administratrix to the Estate of Theodore Roethke; "My Papa's Waltz" copyright 1942 by Hearst Magazines, Inc., "The Meadow Mouse" copyright © 1963 by Beatrice Roethke as administratrix to the Estate of Theodore Roethke. All selections from *The Collected Poems of Theodore Roethke*. Reprinted by permission of Doubleday and Company, Inc.

Carl Sandburg. "Early Copper" from *Honey and Salt*, copyright © 1963 by Carl Sandburg. "Fog" from *Chicago Poems* by Carl Sandburg, copyright 1916 by Holt, Rinehart and Winston, Inc.; copyright renewed 1944 by Carl Sandburg. "Cool Tombs" from *Cornhuskers* by Carl Sandburg, copyright 1918 by Holt, Rinehart and Winston, Inc., copyright renewed 1946 by Carl Sandburg. All reprinted by permission of Harcourt Brace Jovanovich, Inc.

Siegfried Sassoon. "Base Details" from *Collected Poems* by Siegfried Sassoon, copyright 1918 by E. P. Dutton & Co., renewed 1946 by Siegfried Sassoon. All rights reserved. Reprinted by permission of The Viking Press, Inc., and G. T. Sassoon.

Anne Sexton. "Her Kind" from *To Bedlam and Part Way Back*, copyright © 1960 by Anne Sexton. "Cinderella" from *Transformations*, copyright © 1971 by Anne Sexton. Both poems are reprinted by permission of Houghton Mifflin Company.

Kenneth Sherman. "My Father Kept His Cats Well Fed" from *The Cost of Living* by Kenneth Sherman, published by Mosaic Press. Reprinted by permission of the poet.

Louis Simpson. "My Father in the Night Commanding No" copyright © 1963 by Louis Simpson, first appeared in *The New Yorker*. Reprinted from *At the End of the Open Road* by permission of Wesleyan University Press.

Christopher Smart from *Rejoice in the Lamb* by Christopher Smart, with notes and introduction by William Force Stead. Reprinted by permission of Jonathan Cape Ltd. on behalf of the Executors of the William Force Stead Estate.

Stevie Smith. "Not Waving but Drowning" from *Not Waving but Drowning* by Stevie Smith. Reprinted by permission of the executor of Stevie Smith, James MacGibbon.

W. D. Snodgrass. "Mementos, 1" and "Lobsters in the Window" from *After Experience* by W. D. Snodgrass, copyright © 1960, 1963 by W. D. Snodgrass. "Lobsters in the Window" first appeared in *The New Yorker*.

Gary Snyder. "Before the Stuff Comes Down" from *Regarding Wave*, copyright © 1970 by Gary Snyder. Reprinted by permission of New Directions Publishing Corporation.

Raymond Souster. "Young Girls" from *Collected Poems of Raymond Souster*. Reprinted by permission of Oberon Press.

Stephen Spender. "I think continually of those who were truly great," and "The Express" by Stephen Spender. Copyright 1934 and renewed 1962 by Stephen Spender. Reprinted from *Collected Poems 1928–1953* by Stephen Spender, by permission of Random House, Inc. Also by permission of Faber and Faber Ltd.

William Stafford. "At the Un-National Monument Along the Canadian Border" and "Traveling Through the Dark" from *Stories That Could Be True: New and Collected Poems,* by William Stafford, copyright © 1960 by William Stafford. Reprinted by permission of Harper & Row, Publishers, Inc.

James Stephens. "The Wind" reprinted with permission of Macmillan Publishing Co., Inc. from *Collected Poems* by James Stephens, copyright 1915 by Macmillan Publishing Co., Inc., renewed 1943 by James Stephens.

Wallace Stevens. "Anecdote of the Jar," "Thirteen Ways of Looking at a Blackbird," and "Sunday Morning" copyright 1923, renewed 1951 by Wallace Stevens. "The Snow Man" copyright 1923, renewed 1951 by Alfred A. Knopf, Inc. "The Idea of Order at Key West" copyright 1936 by Wallace Stevens, renewed 1964 by Holly Stevens. All reprinted from *The Collected Poems of Wallace Stevens* by permission of Alfred A. Knopf, Inc.

Mark Strand. "The Dead" and "The Tunnel" from *Reasons for Moving* by Mark Strand, copyright © 1968 by Mark Strand. "The Dead" first appeared in *Atlantic Monthly;* "The Tunnel" first appeared in *Partisan Review*. Reprinted by permission of Atheneum Publishers. "Keeping Things Whole" from *Sleeping with One Eye Open,* copyright © 1964 by Mark Strand. Reprinted with the permission of Atheneum Publishers from *Selected Poems,* copyright © 1980 by Mark Strand.

May Swenson. "Question" from *New & Selected Things Taking Place* by May Swenson, copyright 1954, © renewed 1982 by May Swenson. By permission of Little, Brown and Company, in association with the Atlantic Monthly Press.

Allen Tate. "Ode to the Confederate Dead" from *Collected Poems 1919–1976* by Allen Tate, copyright © 1952, 1953, 1970, 1977 by Allen Tate; copyright 1931, 1932, 1937, 1948, by Charles Scribner's Sons; copyright renewed © 1959, 1960, 1965 by Allen Tate. Reprinted by permission of Farrar, Straus and Giroux, Inc.

Henry Taylor. "Riding a One-Eyed Horse" from *An Afternoon of Pocket Billiards: Poems* by Henry Taylor, copyright 1975 by Henry Taylor. Reprinted by permission of the author and the University of Utah Press.

Dylan Thomas. All selections from *The Poems of Dylan Thomas,* copyright 1946 by New Directions Publishing Corporation, 1952 by Dylan Thomas. Reprinted by permission of New Directions Publishing Corporation. Also from *The Poems* by Dylan Thomas, published by J. M. Dent. Reprinted by permission of David Higham Associates Ltd.

Edward Thomas. "Birds' Nests" and "The Gypsy" from *Collected Poems by Edward Thomas,* published by Faber and Faber Ltd. Reprinted by permission of Mrs. Myfanwy Thomas.

Derek Walcott. "Sea Canes" from *Sea Grapes* by Derek Walcott, copyright © 1971, 1973, 1974, 1975, 1976 by Derek Walcott. "A Far Cry from Africa" from *Selected Poems* by Derek Walcott, copyright © 1962, 1963, 1964 by Derek Walcott. Reprinted by permission of Farrar, Straus and Giroux Inc.

Richard Wilbur. "In a Churchyard," copyright © 1968 by Richard Wilbur, from his volume *Walking to Sleep.* "Place Pigale," copyright 1947, 1975 by Richard Wilbur, from *The Beautiful Changes and Other Poems.* "Exeunt," copyright 1952, 1980 by Richard Wilbur from *Things of This World.* "Love Calls Us to the Things of This World," copyright 1956, 1984 by Richard Wilbur, from *Things of This World.* All reprinted by permission of Harcourt Brace Jovanovich, Inc.

William Carlos Williams. "The Young Housewife," "The Yachts," and "The Red Wheelbarrow" from *Collected Earlier Poems of William Carlos Williams,* copyright 1938 by New Directions Publishing Corporation. "The Dance" from *Collected Later Poems,* copyright 1944 by William Carlos Williams. All reprinted by permission of New Directions Publishing Corporation.

Yvor Winters. "The Slow Pacific Swell," "To the Moon," and "At the San Francisco Airport" from *Collected Poems* by Yvor Winters, copyright 1960 by Yvor Winters. Reprinted with the permission of The Ohio University Press, Athens.

William Butler Yeats. All selections are from *Collected Poems* by William Butler Yeats. "The Wild Swans at Coole" and "An Irish Airman Foresees His Death," copyright 1919 by Macmillan Publishing Company, renewed by Bertha Georgie Yeats. "The Second Coming" and "Easter 1916," copyright 1924 by Macmillan Publishing Company, renewed 1952 by Bertha Georgie Yeats. "Leda and the Swan," "Sailing to Byzantium," and "Among School Children," copyright 1928 by Macmillan Publishing Company, renewed 1956 by Georgie Yeats. "After Long Silence," copyright 1933 by Macmillan Publishing Company, renewed 1961 by Bertha Georgie Yeats. "Politics" and "Lapis Lazuli," copyright 1940 by Georgie Yeats, renewed 1968 by Bertha Georgie Yeats, Michael Butler Yeats and Anne Yeats. "The Folly of Being Comforted," "When You Are Old," and "The Lake Isle of Innisfree" are from *Collected Poems of W. B. Yeats* (New York: Macmillan, 1956). Reprinted by permission of Macmillan Publishing Company. Also reprinted by permission of A. P. Watt Ltd. on behalf of Michael B. Yeats and Macmillan London Ltd.

Al Young. "Lemons, Lemons" copyright © 1969 by Al Young. Reprinted by permission of the poet.

⌒ CONTENTS

*Asterisk indicates excerpt.

~ FOREWORD

As with its predecessors, this third edition of *The Heath Introduction to Poetry* is designed to allow poets to speak for themselves to those who are learning to understand and appreciate their works. Joseph de Roche, in his *Preface—On Poetry* and *Brief History,* provides a survey of technical terms and major historical developments. He has also participated in the selection of contemporary poems.

We thank the many teachers of poetry at colleges throughout the United States and Canada for their helpful comments and suggestions. Valuable, detailed survey responses were provided by Sandra Bennett, Winona State University; Thomas E. Blom, University of British Columbia; Stavros Deligiorgis, University of Iowa; Fidel Fajardo, University of Iowa; Jane M. Flick, University of British Columbia; Donald W. Foster, University of California, Santa Barbara; Edward Geist, Hofstra University; Sheryll Luxton, Scott Community College; and Dan Morgan, Scott Community College. Ours, however, is the ultimate responsibility for the works chosen, their arrangement and editing.

Fifty-one selections are new to the third edition. Coverage of the English Romantics, including a complete "Rime of the Ancient Mariner," has been expanded. There are also longer poems by Poe, Whitman, and Swinburne, among others. Several important works by Yeats have been added. Included for the first time are E. J. Pratt, Edna St. Vincent Millay, Stephen Spender, Randall Jarrell, Seamus Heaney, and Michael Ondaatje.

To make things easier to find, each poem has been placed in general chronological sequence; however, nothing in the makeup of this volume compels a historical approach to its contents. Many poems, separated by time, were selected—among other reasons—because of their kinship, and can well be paired for comparison. Special emphasis has been given to the twentieth century; here Canadian poets, writing in English, join the British and American.

Various additional criteria guided our choices, as will become apparent to the reader. But in the final analysis, these are the poems that we felt others might enjoy as much as we do ourselves.

H. HOLTON JOHNSON, SENIOR EDITOR
D. C. Heath and Company

THE HEATH INTRODUCTION TO POETRY

⤳ PREFACE—ON POETRY

We value poetry for what it shows us about our inner and outer lives. We find pleasure in its music, admire the power of its language and imagery, take pride and comfort in what it says. We think of the poet as something between a witch doctor and a magician. Poetry, we believe, is special, magical, spontaneous. Lightning strikes, the muse comes down, the poet gets possessed by a fit of high emotion or a tidal wave of feeling and sensibility and presto! a poem falls out of his head the way a star falls out of the summer sky. True, poets have a special talent. Some poets manipulate language with a juggler's ease. Others see a likeness between two things where the rest of us see only a difference. Some poets can take the substance of an ordinary day and cast it in such stunning images that it is changed forever. But, for all of this, the foundations of a poem are as practical, demanding, and precise as any hard labor. Inside a poem are spinning parts—words running against and with each other, the counterparts of the valves, pistons, hinges and gears of more commonplace machinery.

Poems work like engines. The first thing to do with an automobile, for instance, is to turn the ignition key, engage the engine, and drive off. Most car drivers supposedly know how to shift the gears, understand how in some fashion or other the engine underneath the hood, if all is working well, will get them to where they want to go. On the other hand, most drivers don't know *how* the engine works. They know the engine has to be fed gasoline and lubricated with oil, but that's usually that. When anything goes wrong, the car goes to the garage where mechanics probe its mysterious innards and set things right again. The studying of the elements of poetry, in its way, seems much the same as examining a machine. If reading a poem is analogous to driving a car, then when we later discuss simile and metaphor, rhythm and meter, figures of speech and the other apparatus of poetry, we'll be doing what mechanics do—looking into the workings to see what parts are doing what job. When we analyze a poem, lay bare its parts, we do so to make the poem mean more to us, not less. In the same way that attacking an engine with a sledge hammer not only breaks down the engine but also destroys it, looking at some parts of a poem without realizing how they fit with other parts makes the analysis of a poem destructive. We examine a poem to delight in it. When we read a poem that excites us, knowing the skill that makes the poem work can make the poem more alive and lasting.

"Ah," you say, "but I like what a poem means, how it makes me feel, not all this business about metaphors and feet and meters." Fair enough. But what you are saying really is that you like the message of the poem, the propaganda, the pictures and ideas you agree with. But there is a trick here. If you like what the poem means, then you can boil it down into one sentence of prose and be just as pleased. The point is you *won't* be just as pleased. The idea will be there, but something will be missing: the poem will have vanished. For instance, take this thought: "I think my girlfriend Julia looks beautiful when she wears silks." Let's agree that this is true. But look what happens when the poet Herrick writes the same thing in a poem:

> Whenas in silks my Julia goes,
> Then, then, methinks, how sweetly flows
> That liquefaction of her clothes.

Or take a universal truth: "I like to be kissed." Wyatt puts it this way:

> When her loose gown from her shoulders did fall,
> And she me caught in her arms long and small,
> And therewith all sweetly did me kiss
> And softly said, "Dear heart, how like you this?"

Obviously something has happened to the idea in both cases. Rhyme has been added, meter and regularity. Julia's beauty, for its part, suddenly shares in the fluid motions of every liquid and flowing thing. Wyatt's lady delivers a kiss with a charm, grace, and courtesy that is as much a part of the movement of the rhythms within the lines as it is a part of her disarmingly bright, easy whisper.

When we analyze poems like these, we note how the poem moves, as well as how we are moved by the poem. When the excitement of reading a poem we like for the first time is over, when the transport and intoxication of surprise fades, what remains behind in the lines of a well-made poem are the careful devices of poetry that can bring us again and again to pleasure and delight.

Still, if poems are like engines, they are also like jewels. Hold a stone cut by a fine jeweler up to the light. The facets of the stone were cut to bring out of the stone a fire and beauty that otherwise would have been locked in. The same holds true for the craftsmanship a poet puts into a poem. When we have finished analyzing a poem foot by foot, line by line, we must still face up to the fact that not everything in a poem can be tucked away in some tidy mental cubbyhole. Why a poet chooses one word over another, one rhyme scheme over another, one subject over another, adds the erratic spectacle of human choice. We discover a distinct, individual voice even in the most formal poems. In short, if a poem may move like an engine with the power of its parts pushing and pulling together, then like a precious stone cut into its most flattering shape, a poem may also shine inside with the personality, emotions, and desires of the man or woman who made it. So if some of you are worrying, as some of you usually are, that by looking at the parts of a poem we are destroying its mystery and taking away its spontaneity, then you should be made happy by the realization that the poets in their grandeur or crankiness are beyond our grasp. After all is said and done, mystery remains.

From the far past of anonymous Anglo-Saxon poets to the present day, the single line of poetry, laid one upon another, has been the basic recognizable unit of a poem. We even say that a poem looks like a poem, meaning that we see lines standing individually apart and not, usually, running together as a prose paragraph would. On this frame, the various types and forms of poetry have been built. By examining lines of poetry, we can further break them down, a process we call **scanning** or **scansion,** into the common, small units that compose a poem: the consonant, the vowel, the syllable, the foot, the line. If for a time we can put aside all considerations such as what a poem means or what the poet is trying to say, we can find ourselves dealing with movement and sound on an extremely basic, almost abstract, level. While it is difficult to be objective and scientific about ideas, we can more easily lay claim to being scientific about units of sound and movement. Looking at individual lines, we can divide poetry historically and stylistically according to four types of line scansion: **accentual, syllabic, accentual-syllabic,** and **free verse.**

The earliest Anglo-Saxon English poetry was measured neither by rhyme nor meter. From its beginning, the English language has been an **accented** language. When we speak English, the language demands that certain words or syllables be stressed over others, receive more emphasis, and thus stand out from the words around them. Anglo-Saxon poets used the normal accents of the language to determine the length of their lines of poetry. In English, then, accents are an inescapable part of the measurement of poetry, and the **ictus** [´] over a syllable means that syllable is to be accented, while the **breve** [˘] means that syllable is not stressed and takes a secondary place within the line. Whenever possible, a reader should read a line of poetry slowly and in a *normal* tone of voice, letting the accents fall naturally. No reader should force a word to be accented that normally would be unstressed, unless in peculiar cases (e.g., Gerard Manley Hopkins) he is told to do so. Also, it's important to realize that some lines may be read in more than one way. A reader from Mississippi might read a line differently than a reader from Maine. Within reason and common sense, accenting a line leaves room for differences of opinion and pronunciation. In the following accentual passage from *Beowulf,* the beast Grendel creeps to the Dane's hall:

> When níght had fállen, the fiénd crépt near
> To the lófty háll, to leárn how the Dánes
> In Héorot faréd, when the feásting was dóne.

Notice how in the above passage, the first line has nine syllables; the second, ten; and the third line, ten or eleven. The syllable count of a line doesn't matter in accentual poetry; what matters is that each line have the same number of accents. In the first line, five words could possibly be accented, and only by progressing through the poem, line by line, would a reader new to the poem and to accentual verse be aware that a line of four accents should predominate. In fact, I have not accented the word "near," but have given it a secondary **stress,** an accent with less importance than a full stress but more than an unstressed syllable. But no matter how we read the lines, it should still be impossible for anyone reading normally to stress such words as "had," "the," "to," "in," etc.

Accentual verse, however, is not limited to Anglo-Saxon times. Coleridge's *Christabel,* for instance, is a Romantic experiment in accentuals. Gerard Manley Hopkins invented **sprung rhythm,** a 19th-century variation of accentual verse:

> Glóry bé to Gód for dáppled thíngs—
> For skíes of cóuple-cólor as a bríndled ców . . .

Modern poets have returned to accentual verse in an attempt to escape the more rigid, formal patterns of scansion that developed after the coming of **syllabic verse** into the English language.

Unlike English, the French language makes little use of heavily accented words. Counting out accents to determine the length of lines in French poetry seldom occurred. Instead, the French devised a system of counting out the number of syllables to fix the length of their lines of poetry. When William the Conqueror invaded England in 1066, he brought with him not only the French Norman court, but also French poets experienced in rhyme and syllabic rhythms. The next few centuries, culminating in Chaucer, witnessed the development of Old English to Middle English. Essentially what happened to the English language was a collision between Old English and French which eventually developed into an amalgam of the two; the language of the peasants and the language of the court came slowly together to create Middle English, a mid-point between Old and Modern English. For a relatively short period the English court spoke French and listened to French poets reciting a poetry with a strict syllabic length of line. Although syllabic poetry swiftly evolved into accentual-syllabic poetry, English, and later American, poets occasionally wrote poems in which the line length was determined solely by counting out syllables, lines in which the number of accents could vary as long as the number of syllables remained the same. Modern poets have been especially fascinated with the syllabic line. Syllabic poetry, like accentual poetry, allows a poet to escape the rhythms and demands of more regulated, often sing-song, verse. Such freedom can result in a more rugged type of poem.

Dylan Thomas's *In My Craft or Sullen Art* is an example of a syllabic poem:

> In my craft or sullen art
> Exercised in the still night
> When only the moon rages
> And the lovers lie abed . . .

Although the accents may change from line to line, both in their number and their placement, each line has seven syllables. Syllabic poems often have an odd number of syllables to a line and can be richly complicated. *Fern Hill* by Thomas and *Poetry* by Marianne Moore are syllabic poems where the line length differs within stanzas, but the stanzas match each other line by line.

But the kind of poetry that most people would instantly recognize as poetry, poetry that often rhymes, has a definite beat (or meter), and can move with a clock-like regularity—this is what we call **accentual-syllabic** poetry. From the 14th century to the 20th, accentual-syllabic poetry was predominant, becoming a convention and a tradition. Conventional poetry follows rules as strict as any laws, and the success of a poet has sometimes been measured by the skill with which he can manipulate words within the tightest of circumstances.

Accentual-syllabic poetry evolved normally enough when the counting of accents and the counting of syllables in a line happened at the same time, the marriage of Anglo-Saxon and French traditions. Poetry written like this sounds, of course, crafted and artificial. For centuries the fact that poetry sounded artificial bothered hardly anyone. Poetry was allied to music, was understood to be a progression of beautiful sounds—sometimes simple, sometimes intricate—but nonetheless an artifact, a work of craftsmanship. Now and again poets have rebelled against the demands of what they felt to be such exclusive structure and have questioned the value of highly ordered, traditional verse. One outcry has it that conventional verse is artificial and, therefore, either insincere or hopelessly out-of-date. Conventional verse gains much of its power from the tension that exists when a syntactical language like English, a language in which word order plays a commanding role in the sense of a sentence, gets molded by the poet into a formal poem that moves effortlessly. The comparison is often made between formal and free verse poems and horses. An untrained horse may be wild, free, and beautiful, but a trained horse, under a rider and a rein, gains in both purpose and power. Both have their virtues.

The counting out of accents and syllables together created the basic **foot** of English poetry. Because of the accentual base of the English language, when we divide syllables in a line into stressed and unstressed we soon discover that certain patterns keep recurring. As luck would have it, these patterns fit classical measures from Greek and Latin. Greek and Latin were quantitative languages. This means that instead of counting stresses, the two classical languages counted duration—the length of time (quantity) it took to say something. Their syllables were differentiated by whether they were longer than one another or shorter, not by whether they were louder or softer, stressed or unstressed. Long and short syllables were supposed to be the near equivalent of what in English, a qualitative language, we call stressed or unstressed—the quality of a syllable. Therefore, counting in accentual-syllabic verse became measured in feet.

The four basic feet in English poetry are:

Iamb [˘ ´]	**Anapest** [˘ ˘ ´]
Trochee [´ ˘]	**Dactyl** [´ ˘ ˘]

Notice that a foot is composed of either two or three syllables, no more or less, and that the type of foot is determined by the placement of the accent. Every sentence of the English language, all prose and all poetry, even free verse, is composed of these feet. They determine **rhythm** by the nature of how they are placed side by side. More important, they determine **meter,** the nature of the metrical regularity in an accentual-syllabic poem. One or another of these feet will predominate in a line of metrical verse.

The following lines show examples of the four basic English feet:

Iamb	Ĭ táste | ă líqu|ŏr név|ĕr bréwed
Trochee	Eárth, rĕ|céive ăn | hónŏred | guést
Anapest	Thĕ Ăssýr|iăn căme dówn | likĕ thĕ wólf | ŏn thĕ fóld
Dactyl	Oút ŏf thĕ | crádlĕ | éndlĕsslў | róckĭng

Note the divider [\|] which separates feet in a line.

The lines of a poem are seldom composed of only one kind of foot; this would sound as monotonous as a metronome. Substitutions are made, as in the dactyl above with its two trochees, in order to give a line a more interesting movement. Occasionally, rare feet, the **spondee** [´´] and the **pyrrhic** [˘˘], are interspersed with the four more common feet. An iambic line, therefore, can contain other feet, trochees, say, or anapests, just as a trochaic line could contain iambs. In lines like these where different feet are mixed together, whichever foot outnumbers the other determines the type of line. A line with four iambs and three trochees would become an iambic line.

Once we have discovered the predominant foot in a line by marking the accents and marking everything else as unstressed or secondary, then we count the number of feet in order to find the total length of the line. For instance:

Ĭ táste | ă líqu|ŏr név|ĕr bréwed

has four iambic feet. We call this **iambic tetrameter.** The following chart shows the relationship between the number of feet and the length of the line:

Number of Feet	Line Length	
one	mono	meter
two	di	meter
three	tri	meter
four	tetra	meter
five	penta	meter
six	hexa	meter
seven	hepta	meter

Theoretically the number of feet could go on to infinity, but for practical purposes a **heptameter**—a line from fourteen to twenty-one syllables long—approaches the outer length limits of most poems. The most common foot in the English language happens to be the iamb, probably because the use of articles (*the, a, an*) almost always ensures that an unstressed accent will show up in the position before a stress. Children's verse, by contrast, (*London Bridge is falling down, falling down, falling down*) often has trochaic feet dominating. Since children don't use as many articles in their speech as adults, their rhythms seem more primitive and emphatic. The most common line in English poetry is the **iambic pentameter,** probably because speaking anything longer than ten syllables in English usually requires an intake of breath, a pause, and often another line. In French, on the other hand, the most common line is one of twelve syllables, called in French, as in English, the **alexandrine.**

Precise as the measurement of an accentual-syllabic line can be, **elision** allows a poet to lengthen or shorten lines even within strict metrics. For instance, two vowels side by side can become a single syllable. Not only do we consider *a, e, i, o,* and *u* as vowels, but may also add *h, w,* and *v.* Look at these lines by Ralegh:

> The flowers do fade, and wanton fields
> To wayward winter reckoning yields;
> A honey tongue, a heart of gall,
> Is fancy's spring, but sorrow's fall.

The Nymph's Reply is written in iambic tetrameter, a poem which should have eight syllables to a line. The first two lines in the above stanza, however, count out to nine syllables apiece, while the second two lines count out to the anticipated eight syllables. We justify the extra syllable in the first line by noticing the word "flowers"; the vowels *o, w,* and *e* come together creating a **diphthong,** or two syllables which may be counted, and pronounced, as one syllable if the poet should so choose. In the second line, the word "reckoning" is commonly pronounced "reck'ning," thus compressing into two syllables what might have been, with more precise formal pronunciation, considered to be three syllables. In Milton's sonnet *On the Late Massacre* we see an example of an iambic pentameter line with eleven syllables instead of the normal ten:

> . . . and they
> To Heaven. Their martyred blood and ashes sow
> O'er all th'Italian fields where still doth sway
> The triple tyrant;

Elision takes place with the words "To Heaven" where the two-syllable word "Heaven" is technically considered to be one syllable. In the next line, "Over" is written "O'er," showing the elision in the spelling; likewise, in the same line, "the Italian fields" becomes "th'Italian fields." Modern poems do not show the elision outright by contracting words as Milton did in a 17th-century custom that is now felt to be old-fashioned. Elision, nevertheless, is present in modern accentual-syllabic poetry.

We can also use Milton to illustrate how another device, the **feminine ending,** allows a poet greater flexibility. A line is said to have a **masculine ending** when it ends on an accented syllable, a feminine ending when it ends on an unaccented syllable. The second

of these lines from Book IX of *Paradise Lost,* because of its feminine
ending, enjoys an extra syllable:

> Thus they in mutual accusation spent
> The fruitless hours, but neither self condemning

As an unaccented additional syllable at the close of the line, the
"ing" may be discounted. Thus a line that counts out to eleven
syllables may, at the poet's discretion, become technically a ten-
syllable line thanks to the feminine ending.

Accentual, syllabic, and accentual-syllabic poetry all find ways of
counting, ways of measuring the length of a line, and ways of controlling the movement of accents. Such poetry is formal, strict, and
demanding. The last type of poetry we consider here attempts to
break away from strictness and formality; we call this **free verse.**

We could not have free verse without formal verse; it would make
no sense. Free from what? we might well ask. Free from counting,
free from measuring, free from meter. Free from accentual, syllabic,
and accentual-syllabic verse. Free verse replaces the expected repetition of a particular foot with a looser movement we call rhythm. In
this respect free verse shares something, as we have seen, with accentual and syllabic poetry. But to be truly free, free verse must
also escape all predominant measurements—the placement of accents line to line must vary with no discernible pattern; the syllabic
count, too, must follow no measurable regularity. Likewise the device of rhyme is employed, if at all, with freedom and irregularity.
If, when we examine a poem, we can find no accentual or syllabic
pattern, then we can safely say we have a free verse poem. This
poem by E. E. Cummings. *In Just- spring,* though it has other
regularities, can serve as an example of a poem where the accents
and syllables in each line seem spontaneously and freely laid down:

> in Just-
> spring   when the world is mud-
> luscious the little
> lame balloonman
> whistles   far   and wee
>
> and eddieandbill come
> running from marbles and
> piracies and it's
> spring

In French, anything is free verse which simply doesn't conform to a regular syllabic count. English, because of its accentual base, complicates the issue. Indeed, by free verse, many contemporary poets simply mean poetry where no conscious effort has been made to make the lines of a poem conform to a regular pattern, whether or not these patterns do in fact occur. Often what on the page looks like free verse, some of the poems of T. S. Eliot and Dylan Thomas, for instance, under closer examination reveals itself to be syllabic or accentual verse. Other poems, like Ferlinghetti's *The pennycandy-store beyond the El,* move without discernible metric regularity but with plenty of rhythm.

Some poets have gone so far as to create poetry where the shape matters and the words do not, poems divorced sometimes even from words. These **concrete poems,** sometimes just repeating one letter of the alphabet, rely on the eye to capture a significant or pleasing shape, leaving the ear in a vacuum.

Although we've explored the importance of rhythm and accents, syllables and lines, more obvious poetic elements can strike us when we first look at a poem. Thus far we have looked at lines mainly as single units, but it's obvious that the lines in a poem are strung together. Often these groupings of lines, symmetrical on the left hand margin of the page and irregular on the right, arrange themselves in blocks of two lines, four lines, six lines, etc. Generally we then have a space, followed by an equal block of lines. We call these groupings of lines **stanzas,** the rough equivalent of a prose paragraph. Two-line stanzas are **couplets;** four-line, **quatrains;** six-line, **sextets,** eight-line, **octets;** and so forth. The eye catches this visual regularity, but the ear is at work, too. Besides recognizing accents, the ear hears sounds, the music of words and syllables. Rhyme is the most obvious of these sounds.

Rhyme is the repetition of the same or similar sounds often occurring at set intervals and most obviously appearing at the end of a line, where it is called **end rhyme.** For instance, the word "light" rhymes with "sight," "fight," "right," etc. To make the rhyme, the consonant "l" changes to "s" or another consonant. The rhyming constant is the sound "ight," on which constant echo the poet makes variations by changing the initial letter or letters. To some extent, the use of rhyme corresponds to the musical habit of returning to a familiar note or theme. In ancient folk poetry, before the widespread use of printing and the common ability to read, rhyme was an invaluable aid. Poetry could be more easily committed to memory when a consistent rhyme pattern jogged the mind. Thus, beyond pleasing the ear, rhyme may have had a very practical purpose. Today we can carry a transistor radio with us wherever we go. At the touch of our fingertips we can command music, poetry, or drama. In times past, men and women relied upon their own memories and the songs and poems they carried with them.

The following poem by Thom Gunn, *Black Jackets,* gives us examples of various kinds of rhymes.

True or **perfect rhyme** occurs when the initial consonants change, but succeeding vowels and consonants remain the same:

> In the silence that prolongs the span
> Rawly of music when the record ends,
> The red-haired boy who drove a van
> In weekday overalls but, like his friends,

In this first stanza, "span" and "van" are perfect rhymes as are "ends" and "friends."

Ear rhyme occurs when words are spelled differently but sound the same. To continue Gunn's poem:

> Wore cycle boots and jacket here
> To suit the Sunday hangout he was in,
> Heard, as he stretched back from his beer,
> Leather creak softly round his neck and chin.

The ear rhymes are "here" and "beer," "in" and "chin" being perfect rhymes.

Half-rhyme, near rhyme, or **slant rhyme,** occurs when there are changes within the vowel sounds of words meant to rhyme:

> Before him, on a coal-black sleeve
> Remote exertion had lined, scratched and burned
> Insignia that could not revive
> The heroic fall or climb where they were earned.

"Sleeve" and "revive" are half-rhymes where the initial vowel sound has changed from short to long, but the end "ve" sound has remained the same.

Assonance occurs when the vowels in a word agree, but the consonants do not; for instance, the words "seat" and "weak." **Consonance** occurs when the consonants agree but the vowels do not, as in the words "lick" and "luck." Assonance and consonance are both variations on half-rhyme. Within a line, the changing patterns of vowels add to the musical quality of a poem and are not necessarily occasions of rhyme. In this line of poetry, as the vowel "o" progresses in the line its sound quality changes and adds assonance:

> If all the world and love were young

Eye rhyme occurs when words are spelled the same and look alike but sound differently:

> These pretty pleasures might me move
> To live with thee and be thy love.

"Move" and "love" are eye rhymes. Such rhymes are also **historical rhymes** if, as in the above example by Ralegh, the pronunciation has changed over the years. The word "tea," for instance, once was an ear rhyme with "day"; today the two words are, at best, a half-rhyme.

Internal rhyme occurs when rhyme appears not only at the end of a line, but within it:

> In the sun that is young once only,
>   Time let me play and be
> Golden in the mercy of his means

In this example by Dylan Thomas, "sun" and "young" are internal rhymes; the last syllable of "mercy" is an internal rhyme with the end rhyme "be."

Masculine rhymes and **feminine rhymes** are the equivalents of masculine and feminine line endings. Rhymes that end on a stress, "van" and "span," are masculine rhymes; rhymes ending on an unstressed syllable, "falling" and "calling," are considered feminine.

Alliteration, the repetition of an initial sound, though not technically a form of rhyme, adds to the musical quality of any line or group of lines within a poem:

> About the lilting house and happy as the grass was green

The repetition of the "h" in "house" and "happy," and the "gr" in "grass" and "green," are both examples of alliteration. Accentual Anglo-Saxon poetry, already discussed, relied on alliteration as well as on accents, and not on rhyme, to create the music and balance of its lines.

Everything we have looked at so far may work simultaneously within any poem. An accentual-syllabic rhymed poem, for instance, may be filled with internal rhymes as well as with alliteration and assonance. One more element of sound, however, remains to be considered: *silence*. The punctuation marks in poems tell us when to fall silent and to pause. A period or exclamation mark can be thought of as a whole note in music—a full, heavy stop. A comma, on the other hand, gets perhaps a quarter note—a half stop. The clear, rhythmic reading of a poem depends on close attention to its punctuation marks.

Some readers, for instance, stop at the end of every line of poetry. There's no reason to do this unless a comma, period, or other punctuation mark tells us to come to a complete stop. Such readings are unnatural and damage the sense and flow of a poem.

> Farewell, too little, and too lately known,
> Whom I began to think and call my own;
> For sure our souls were near allied, and thine
> Cast in the same poetic mold with mine.

These first four lines of Dryden's *To the Memory of Mr. Oldham* show several uses of the pause in a tightly constructed accentual-syllabic poem. When a line of poetry has a pause at the end, as after "known," "own," and "mine," we say the line is **end-stopped.** But when there are pauses called for within the line, as after "little" and "allied," we call that pause a **caesura** (or cesura). When there is no pause at the end of a line, as after "thine," and one line should flow into another, we call that a **run-on line** or an **enjambment.** These effects, common in modern verse, can be illustrated by this last stanza of a poem by Robert Lowell:

> The Aquarium is gone. Everywhere,
> giant finned cars nose forward like fish;
> a savage servility
> slides by on grease.

The caesura after "gone" precedes the lines end-stopped after "everywhere" and "fish," while the last two lines are enjambed.

The examination of rhythm and sound within a poem can be the most difficult and demanding type of analysis. Such technical analysis requires close attention to the most minute parts of a poem and can remain independent of any meaning a poem may have—although punctuation goes hand in hand with a poem's meaning. When we isolate rhythms and meters we use basically only one of our five senses: *hearing.* Poems gather much of their power not just from our sense of hearing, but also from engaging our other four senses: *sight, touch, taste,* and *smell.* The objects, images, and sensations put into a line of poetry cause immediate reactions in a reader. **Imagism** builds on this reaction.

Imagist poetry, an early 20th-century movement fostered by Ezra Pound, attempted to shed excess words and create poems of concise, clear, concrete detail. There should be "no ideas but in things," as William Carlos Williams put it. Imagist poets avoided the old accentual-syllabic rhythms and depended on the poem's image and the mind's eye of the reader to create their effect. **Didactic poetry,** poems with an obviously spelled-out moral or message like much of Pope or Tennyson, was to be avoided. Oriental forms of poetry such as the **haiku,** a syllabic poem of seventeen syllables and three lines, were admired models. Imagist poems became prized for their subtleties. Pound's *In a Station of the Metro* is a famous example of an imagist poem:

> The apparition of these faces in the crowd;
> Petals on a wet, black bough.

This couplet, along with its title, is the entire poem. The title informs a reader that the poem is about a metro, a European subway, but the poem makes its statement without directly telling the reader what conclusions to make. The poem obviously means that the colorful faces of people in a dark subway are like flowers against dark branches. The poet selects his images and places them together, while the reader senses the relationships; the poem, like a small explosion, really occurs in the reader's brain.

The power of the haiku, its suggestiveness and directness of imagery, has been used by many modern poets to control and expand the limits of contemporary poetic forms. *Thirteen Ways of Looking at a Blackbird,* by Wallace Stevens, takes much of its form and structure from an understanding of, though not a slavish imitation of, the haiku. William Carlos Williams's *The Red Wheelbarrow* is a good example of the further development of the form in English, with its brief direct statement that "So much depends . . ."

Poems of all kinds contain **imagery,** the carefully described objects of the world. This horse by Auden performs unmistakably:

> . . . and the torturer's horse
> Scratches its innocent behind on a tree.

Or observe Roethke's woman:

> I knew a woman, lovely in her bones,
> When small birds sighed, she would sigh back at them . . .

The images are clear; the actions are clear. They mean what they say and, on one level, are no more or less than what we perceive them to be. These lines aren't difficult to understand; nothing is hidden or unrevealed. We know what a horse is, a tree, a woman, bones, a bird.

Poems also often refer to special knowledge, allude to something we may need to have explained. Auden's *Musée des Beaux Arts,* quoted above, contains specific **allusions.** The poem's title means "Museum of Fine Arts" in French. Within the poem, after Auden has described his itching horse, he immediately turns to a more specialized image: "In Breughel's Icarus..." Who is Breughel? Who is Icarus? Some of us will know this, others will not. Footnotes can help. But not everyone will know offhand that Breughel is a 16th-century European painter, that "Icarus" is one of his paintings, and that, further, Icarus was a classical figure from mythology who flew too close to the sun on wax wings. Poems may allude to very obscure information or to more simple information. If I know nothing of carpentry, for instance, a poem by a carpenter could be as mysterious and difficult for me as a poem like Auden's about a part of art history.

Images make **tropes—figures of speech** that show relationships between different things. In poems relationships occur that we would not ordinarily expect. Sometimes one object is transformed into another. These metamorphoses take place largely through **metaphor** and **simile,** two figures of speech often considered the heart of poetry. A poet's fame can rest on his imaginative use of tropes.

Metaphor implies a relationship, a similarity, between two different objects. Once established, this relationship changes our perception of both objects. In the simplest metaphors, such as "my love is a rose," both the idea "love" and the object "rose" become one and the same thing. Notice that love and rose are not *like* one another, they *are* one another; a magic change has taken place. The idea "love" has been made concrete—it is now not a vague internal feeling, an emotion, but a rose that theoretically could be picked, smelled, admired in a garden. We could make the identification even more exact, turn the rose red or white, describe the precise spicy quality of its smell. We call the subject of the comparison, in this case "love," the **tenor;** the figure that completes the metaphor, the "rose," we call the **vehicle.** In the metaphor below by John Donne, the poet's doctors become map-makers of the heavens, while Donne's body becomes the map wherein the ultimate destiny of his soul can be read:

> Whilst my physicians by their love are grown
>   Cosmographers, and I their map, who lie
> Flat on this bed . . .

When a metaphor becomes spun out, elaborated, complex, we call it an **extended metaphor.** When it extends itself beyond the original tenor and vehicle to other tenors and vehicles, we call it a **conceit.** In another example by Donne, the souls of two lovers become the same as the two legs of a draftsman's compass:

> If they be two, they are two so
>   As stiff twin compasses are two;
> Thy soul, the fixed foot, makes no show
> To move, but doth, if th'other do.

> And though it in the center sit,
>   Yet when the other far doth roam,
> It leans and harkens after it,
>   And grows erect, as that comes home.

A **simile** is a more direct comparison. If I say "my love is like a red, red rose," I construct a simile. *A Red, Red Rose,* by Robert Burns, is the classic example. By using the words "like," "as," or an equivalent, I precisely point out the relationship between the tenor and the vehicle. The identification is not as total as it is in a metaphor because "love" and "rose" are *not* one another, but merely *like* one another. The resemblance, though real, becomes superficial; similar parts are compared, but not the whole. The essential point to remember is that the obvious difference between a simile and a metaphor lies in the use of the words "like" and "as." When the relationship is pointed out directly we know we have a simile, as in these lines by Richard Wilbur:

> A cricket like a dwindled hearse
>   Crawls from the dry grass.

Or from Shakespeare:

> In me thou see'st the twilight of such day
> As after sunset fadeth in the west . . .

Along with metaphor and simile, other figures of speech work within a poem.

Allegory occurs when one object or idea is represented in the shape of another. In medieval morality plays and in some poems, abstract virtues or vices appear as people. In this way a moral or lesson can be made more easily concrete and dramatic. Samson, for instance, could be an allegorical example of strength. In Emily Dickinson's poem *Because I Could Not Stop For Death,* death appears as the allegorical figure of a coachman, a chauffeur driving her through life into the eternity of death.

Ambiguity gives richness to a poem by allowing more than one interpretation to the meaning of a word or metaphor. Ambiguity does not mean that a word or image is unclear; instead, it means that a reader can recognize more than one possible reading at a time. **Puns,** for instance, offer ambiguity. These lines from Wyatt's *They Flee From Me* may be read simultaneously two ways:

> But since that I so kindely am served
> I fain would know what she hath deserved.

The word "kindely" means both "served by a group" and "courteously."

Connotation, like ambiguity, offers an additional richness to a word's meaning. In the line from Theodore Roethke's *I Knew a Woman,*

> She was the sickle; I, poor I, the rake

the word "rake" has a **denotative,** or exact, dictionary meaning— a gardening tool designed to gather up the clippings on a lawn that a sickle might have cut down. In the context of the whole poem, however, and not just the line, "rake" has an added, **connotative,** meaning—a debauched man. The two meanings bounce off one another, giving the poem a scope it would not ordinarily have.

Contrast, the opposite of comparison, shows the difference between two objects:

> My mistress' eyes are nothing like the sun;
> Coral is far more red than her lips' red;
> If snow be white, why then her breasts are dun;
> If hairs be wires, black wires grow on her head.

These lines by Shakespeare show what Shakespeare's mistress cannot be compared to and therefore, by elimination, what she can be compared to.

Hyperbole is purposeful exaggeration to create a specific effect. In Shakespeare's *Sonnet 97,* he writes:

> How like a winter hath my absence been
> From thee, the pleasure of the fleeting year!
> What freezings have I felt, what dark days seen!
> What old December's bareness everywhere!

We know that Shakespeare did not literally freeze with real cold when he was separated from his mistress. We know the days did not literally turn dark, or June turn into December, but we feel through the poet's deliberate exaggeration the depth of his unhappiness.

Irony achieves its effect by stating things in one tone of voice when in fact the opposite meaning is meant. Auden's *Unknown Citizen* ends ironically by making a statement that the reader knows to be false. The whole poem is an ironic exercise in condemning the state by using the state's own terms of praise:

> Was he free? Was he happy? The question is absurd;
> Had anything been wrong, we should certainly have heard.

Metonymy occurs when a word that merely relates to an object describes the object itself. When Sidney wrote in his sonnet *With How Sad Steps, O Moon,*

> What, may it be that even in heav'nly place
> That busy archer his sharp arrows tries?

"That busy archer" refers to Cupid, the god of love, shooting arrows into the hearts of unsuspecting men and women. Thus an archer, by relating to the god of love, describes love without specifically using that word.

Onomatopoeia refers to the repetition of a sound meant to resemble what it is describing. The famous last lines of Tennyson's *Come Down, O Maid*

> The moan of doves in immemorial elms,
> And murmuring of innumerable bees

are intended to echo the sounds of birds and bees amongst ancient trees.

Oxymoron combines two words whose meanings should nullify each other; instead, when brought together, they make sense. An example would be "sweet pain" to describe "love."

Personification gives the attributes of human beings to ideas and objects. *Death, be not proud* by John Donne addresses death as if it were a person capable not only of hearing us but also of having the human emotion of pride. **Pathetic fallacy** is a form of personification where inanimate objects are given human attributes. When we call falling rain "heaven's tears," we indulge in the pathetic fallacy.

Symbolism occurs when an image stands for something entirely different. The "ocean" may symbolize "eternity"; the phrase "river to the sea" could symbolize "life flowing into death." Ordinarily, a symbol does not directly reveal what it stands for; the meaning must be deduced from a close reading of the poem and an understanding of conventional literary and cultural symbols. For instance, the Stars and Stripes is the flag of the United States, i.e., the symbol of the United States. We know this because we are told so, not because the flag in any way resembles the country. Without communal agreement, the flag of any country would merely be a colored piece of cloth.

Synecdoche takes a part of an object to describe the whole. In the stanza below by Emily Dickinson, "morning" and "noon," parts of the day, refer to the whole day. In the same way, the "Rafter of Satin" refers to a coffin by describing not the whole coffin, but merely part of its inner lining:

> Safe in their Alabaster Chambers—
> Untouched by Morning—
> And untouched by Noon—
> Lie the meek members of the Resurrection—
> Rafter of Satin—and Roof of Stone!

Synesthesia takes one of the five senses and creates an image or sensation perceived by another. For instance, "the golden cry of the trumpet" combines "golden," a sight, with "cry," hearing.

Understatement, the opposite of hyperbole, achieves its effect by deliberately saying less than could be said either to diminish or to enhance a subject. Auden's ironic poem *The Unknown Citizen* contains numerous examples of understatement showing how statistics cannot evaluate the ultimate happiness of a citizen's life.

These figures of speech and many others, subdivisions and refinements of those we have already defined, work singly or in groups to create the total imaginative effect of a poem.

Along with figures of speech, however, *types* of poems challenged poets. As we've seen, the earliest English poetry, the Anglo-Saxon, relied on alliteration and accent as the keystones of its formal structure. Rhyme arrived later with French forms, becoming firmly established when Old English made the linguistic transformation to Middle English. The arrangement of poems into rhymed stanzas became the concern not only of court poets but also of folk balladeers. Chaucer would later establish the iambic pentameter line and the rhymed couplet. Traditionally, poets were expected to write within established forms. Even within these forms, though, poetry evolved and poets experimented. The long history of conventional verse is not a history of static forms, but a history of generations of poets adding new perceptions and techniques to old certainties.

The **ballad,** genuine folk poetry, told simple dramatic stories. Handed down by memory, these anonymous poems passed from person to person. Set to music and sung from generation to generation, ballads, unlike written poetry, underwent change. Once a poem is written down, its form is usually established forever. But **folk ballads,** composed before the ordinary man or woman could read or write, were altered and enriched by the imaginations of unnamed men and women. The tradition of the ballad runs through English and American verse. The anonymous ballads of the 15th century have their counterparts in the ballads of 20th-century America, songs of social protest and the narratives of ordinary men and women. When professional poets write in ballad stanzas, as in Auden's *As I Walked Out One Evening,* we call these poems **literary ballads.**

The ballad stanza rhymes *a b c b*—the letters *a* and *c* standing for unrhymed word sounds, the letter *b* for rhymes. Ballads, too, very often contain **refrains,** the musical repetition of words or phrases. Some believe the ballad was originally a two-line rhyming song, thus explaining why there are only two rhymes in a four-line stanza. The demands of printing presses and page size may have forced the original couplets to be broken in two at their natural caesuras and refrains. Because early ballads were non-literary and came spontaneously from skilled, though unsophisticated, native poets, the rhymes are often half- and slant rhymes.

Epics—apparent fusions of myth and history—appear in the early stages of evolving cultures. *Beowulf* is the first English epic, a poem not of the common people but of cultural heroes involved in grand and significant adventures. Milton's *Paradise Lost* is a Christian epic, describing the expulsion of Adam and Eve from the Garden of Eden. Hart Crane's *The Bridge,* William Carlos Williams's *Patterson,* and Ezra Pound's *Cantos* are all attempts to create modern epics, in the first two cases for America, and in the latter case apparently for western civilization. Epics vary in structure; in *Beowulf* alliteration and accentual stress, not rhyme or stanza length, characterize the poem's structure.

Some poems receive their character from their **stanza patterns.** Two-line stanzas are called **couplets;** the iambic rhymed couplets of the Augustans Pope and Dryden, though not broken into separate stanzas, stand out as such forceful and integrated units that they are given the special name of **heroic couplets.** Three-line stanzas are **tercets** or, if they rhyme, **terza rima,** a term borrowed from the Italian. Four-line stanzas are called **quatrains.** A seven-line stanza, **rhyme royal,** *a b a b b c c,* introduced by Chaucer, determines the form of Wyatt's *They Flee From Me.* Many of the stanza forms, particularly the more complicated rhyming schemes, entered into English from Europe during the Renaissance. The most notable of these forms is the **sonnet.**

The **sonnet** was originally perfected in its **Italian** form by Petrarch. Normally a poem of fourteen lines, rhyming *a b b a a b b a* in its first eight lines, the **octet** (or octave), the sonnet concludes with a six-line **sestet** rhyming *c d c d c d* or *c d e c d e.* The eight-line octet presents the theme of the poem, traditionally love and romance, and elaborates upon it. The six-line sestet then reflects upon the theme and comes to a conclusion about it, tying everything together. Sidney's sonnets are English examples of the **Petrarchan sonnet,** while Spenser's sonnets with linked rhymes are a variation. Italian, however, is a language especially rich in rhymes; English is not. The search for four or five rhymes to be repeated in each sonnet, particularly difficult in English, may account for the development of the **Shakespearian sonnet.**

The **English** or **Shakespearian sonnet** is composed of three quatrains rhyming *a b a b, c d c d, e f e f,* and a concluding couplet *g g.* In the Shakespearian sonnet themes and recapitulations are developed in the same way as in the Petrarchan, but seven different rhymes are used instead of the more demanding four or five.

The **Miltonic sonnet** keeps the Petrarchan rhyme scheme, but another evolution takes place. Under Milton's refinement, the sonnet no longer breaks at the octet, but flows over, enjambs, from line to line and into the sestet. The sonnet appears to be more unified, structurally of one piece, beginning at one point and moving toward a seemingly inevitable controlled conclusion. Milton moves the theme of the sonnet away from love into larger intellectual and religious concerns, a development begun by Donne. Strict as its technical demands are, the sonnet shows, in its evolution and handling by different poets, the possibilities for change and variety within formal restraints. The sonnets of George Meredith from *Modern Love,* for instance, have sixteen lines instead of the traditional fourteen. Otherwise, in rhyme scheme and structure, the poems attempt to follow the traditional expectations of the sonnet. And succeed.

Gerard Manley Hopkins, for instance, attached his theories of accentual verse and sprung rhythm to the sonnet in *No Worse There Is None* and *(Carrion Comfort)*. Moreover, the way sonnets often turn themselves at their end, either in explanation, summation, or surprise, reflects a characteristic of a vast proportion of poetry, formal or otherwise, ancient or new. This ability of the sonnet to encapsulate in fourteen lines the function of so many other types of poetry may account in part for its recurring vitality and fascination. Used as a training ground for young poets, the sonnet offers the challenge of technical restraints. At the same time the sonnet can take images and ideas and open them up like flowers in the sun. The long poem *The Fish* by Elizabeth Bishop brings us at its end, as a superbly handled sonnet would, to a surprising refreshment which seems in retrospect inevitable.

The **ode** was originally a classic Greek and Roman poem composed for serious occasions. In English, the ode remains a poem on elevated and exalted themes. In the **Pindaric Ode,** named for the Greek poet Pindar, two structurally identical stanzas, the **strophe** and **antistrophe** (Greek for "turn" and "counterturn") are followed by a differently structured stanza, the **epode** (Greek for "stand"). The length of lines and the rhyming patterns are at the discretion of the poet. **Horatian Odes,** named after the Latin poet Horace, are composed of matched regular stanzas as in Keats' *Ode on a Grecian Urn.* The **Irregular Ode,** like Wordsworth's *Intimations on Immortality,* has stanzas of varying shapes, irregular rhyme schemes, and elaborate rhythms.

The **villanelle** not only rhymes but repeats lines in a predetermined manner, both as a refrain and as an integral part of the poem. Five stanzas of three lines each are followed by a quatrain. The first and third lines of the first stanza are repeated in a prescribed alter-nating order as the last lines of the remaining tercets, becoming the last two lines of the final quatrain. Dylan Thomas's poem, *Do Not Go Gentle Into That Good Night* is an example of a modern villanelle.

Emblematic poems, such as George Herbert's *Easter Wings,* take on the shape of the subject of the poem. An emblematic poem on swans, for instance, would have the shape of a swan.

Along with these forms, **blank verse** poems comprise a large body of poetry. Blank verse is simply poetry whose lines are composed of unrhymed iambic pentameter. Blank verse ranges all the way from Shakespeare's plays to a modern poem such as Wallace Stevens's *Sunday Morning.* And although these forms have their roots far in the past of English and European poetry, sonnets, villanelles, and blank verse stanzas, like accentual and syllabic verse, are still alive and vital.

Of course, we also define poems according to their subject matter. We've already mentioned the heroic sweep of the epic. Everyone knows that love poems are legion; many people first come to poetry when they fall in or out of love. **Elegies,** on the other hand, deal solemnly with death. When someone falls in love or someone dies, poems written specifically to reflect on the event are called **occa-sional poems.** Occasional poems commemorate battles, anniver-saries, coronations, the death of a goldfish; any occasion will do for an occasional poem.

Some poems are defined by the general manner in which they go about their task. **Narrative poems** tell a story, but, depending on how they tell it, narrative poems may be epics, ballads, or villanelles. A **satire** will hold up to ridicule or contempt anything the poet may despise, especially established institutions, attitudes, and people. **Parody,** a form of satire, closely imitates specific poems or poets in order to reveal their weaknesses and make light of them. Some poets, like Browning in *My Last Duchess,* wrote **dramatic monologues,** verse speeches delivered by a fictitious or historic person and de-signed to reveal character. Some of the greatest plays in the English language are, of course, poetry—poems to be delivered by actors and actresses from the stage. And alongside the poetic grandeur of a tragedy by Shakespeare exists the intensely personal **lyric,** usually a short, emotional poem meant to be sung or appreciated for its verbal music.

Harder to pin down, a poem's **tone** reveals the poet's attitude toward his subject and his reader. If a poet uses formal language, a strict meter, the restraints of a conventional stanza, tone will be affected one way. If, on the other hand, a poet uses street speech, loose or jazzy rhythms, if he finds his images in back alleys and under the lids of trash cans while letting his stanzas grow without rein or hindrance, then tone will be affected another way. Tone tells us whether a poet is solemn or comic about his subject, wheth r he is being serious or being a clown. How well or badly a poe handles his imagery, his technical effects, his language, in short everything he does in a poem establishes tone.

The poetry of our times often moves readers not necessarily by technical brilliance or control, but by the theme, attitude, and diction of the poet. The easygoing diction in Edward Field's *Bride of Frankenstein* and his use of cinematic images, familiar to a whole generation of moviegoers, allows the poem to make its point. So, too, Allen Ginsberg's use of a suburban setting in *A Supermarket in California* both engages and disarms the modern reader. Nikki Giovanni's *Nikki-Rosa* makes use of tone, diction, and readers' attitudes, black or white, to make its point. We thus move into a new era of didactic, or teaching, poetry, in which the message of the environment re-seen carries much of the power of the poem.

All that we have discussed, the scansions, metrics, and figures of speech, all of these are some of the supports we may discover in a poem. What we have looked at allows us to discuss the structure within a poem, but nowhere, I hope you've noticed, have I attempted to tell what a poem *is*. A poem may be any and all of these things, but none of them in themselves will make a poem successful. Only the poet and his imagination can do that. Flying buttresses may hold up the walls of a cathedral, but they are only part of the cathedral. Rocks may make mountains, but they are not the mountain scenery. When two pairs of lips meet we have a kiss, but to claim that that defines a kiss courts the ridiculous. Above everything, we care for poems because they move us. Whether in the face of life a poet is hysterical or thoughtful, serious or coy, he extends our awareness of our lives. If poems use regular rhythms, so do we. Within ourselves, our pulses can quicken or grow calm. If the images we see in poems are fanciful, we too daydream and alter reality. As men and women differ, so do poets. When poets tend to write alike, we say they belong to schools and some critics, preferring one school to another, promote one kind of poetry over another. The truth remains that different kinds of poets live side by side, like crows and sparrows. Twenty years after Alexander Pope had finally stopped worrying with stately logic and statelier meters about the proper study of mankind, Christopher Smart was busy considering his cat Jeoffrey. Just as the formal poet and the romantic have always lived side by side, some of our days are made memorable by how they are structured and some by how they are free.

The novelist E. M. Forster once suggested we should think of writers not as men and women locked into different centuries, but as men and women sitting around a table carrying on a living conversation. In every century we will find exciting poets, even if, for a time, their language and imagery seem strange. Although the horse and buggy gave way to the automobile, the ecstasies and laments, heroics and follies of men and women remained remarkably the same. When the automobile, in turn, gives way to something else, its drivers will not go out-of-date with it; they will only have to find another way to travel. They may choose to ride a horse again or they may learn to fly. As some of us prefer horses to cars or planes, we will naturally prefer some poets and poems to others. Not everyone, after all, becomes our close friend. Nonetheless, the more we open our lives to experience, the richer our lives become. The more poets and poems we come to understand, the livelier the world becomes, no matter what century they, or we, have been fated to live in.

Joseph de Roche

1

∼ A BRIEF HISTORY

Anglo-Saxon poetry was composed on the twin bases of alliterative sound and accentual beat; the separate lines were balanced in halves by a strong mid-line pause, the caesura. Early English poetry was also noted for its kennings, double-yoked metaphors—e.g., whales'-road = the ocean. Perfect rhyme, a somewhat later development, added a new music to anonymous lyrics and ballads: the folk poetry passed on by word of mouth and changed anew with each passing generation until it was finally fixed in written form. As Anglo-Saxon evolved with the French language to create Middle English, a syllabic count, carried over from French prosody, combined with the Anglo-Saxon accentual count to create accentual-syllabic poetry, a poetry of specific feet and meters, regulated line lengths, and stanzas of established, conventionally recognized structure. Through practice and tradition, accentual-syllabic poetry becomes the accepted norm of English verse; verse forms like the villanelle and the sonnet, the rondeau and the ballad stanza, the various quatrains and sestets become established. Once introduced by Chaucer, the iambic pentameter line shows its versatility by becoming the basic line of poems as diverse in shape and size as love lyrics, the rhymed couplet, and the sonnet. Rhyme becomes an expected element of a poem, more common than not. Poets such as Wyatt delight in elaborately conceived metaphors and similes. Pastoral poems, those by Ralegh and Marlowe, for instance, with rural scenery and characters, reflect older classical themes and traditional settings. Tichborne's *Elegy* is one example of a type of poem that reflects on mortality. The sonnet evolves from Sidney's obedience to the strict demands of the Petrarchan form to Shakespeare's use of the looser English sonnet. In the Petrarchan tradition, however, the sonnet concerns itself principally with love. Lyrics such as those from Shakespeare's plays represent the further development of poems meant to be sung and accompanied by music, but which also stand by themselves.

ANONYMOUS (8th Century)

The Seafarer (Modern version by Ezra Pound)

May I for my own self song's truth reckon,
Journey's jargon, how I in harsh days
Hardship endured oft.
Bitter breast-cares have I abided,
5 Known on my keel many a care's hold,
And dire sea-surge, and there I oft spent
Narrow nightwatch nigh the ship's head
While she tossed close to cliffs. Coldly afflicted,
My feet were by frost benumbed.
10 Chill its chains are; chafing signs
Hew my heart round and hunger begot.
Mere-weary mood. Lest man know not
That he on dry land loveliest liveth,
List how I, care-wretched, on ice-cold sea,
15 Weathered the winter, wretched outcast
Deprived of my kinsmen;
Hung with hard ice-flakes, where hail-scur flew,
There I heard naught save the harsh sea
And ice-cold wave, at whiles the swan cries,
20 Did for my games the gannet's clamor,
Sea-fowls' loudness was for me laughter,
The mews' singing all my mead-drink.
Storms, on the stone-cliffs beaten, fell on the stern
In icy feathers; full oft the eagle screamed
25 With spray on his pinion.
                           Not any protector
May make merry man faring needy.
This he little believes, who aye in winsome life
Abides 'mid burghers some heavy business,
Wealthy and wine-flushed, how I weary oft
30 Must bide above brine.
Neareth nightshade, snoweth from north,
Frost froze the land, hail fell on earth then,
Corn of the coldest. Nathless there knocketh now
The heart's thought that I on high streams
35 The salt-wavy tumult traverse alone.
Moaneth alway my mind's lust
That I fare forth, that I afar hence
Seek out a foreign fastness.
For this there's no mood-lofty man over earth's midst,

40 Not though he be given his good, but will have in his youth greed;
    Nor his deed to the daring, nor his king to the faithful
    But shall have his sorrow for sea-fare
    Whatever his lord will.
    He hath not heart for harping, nor in ring-having
45 Nor winsomeness to wife, nor world's delight
    Nor any whit else save the wave's slash,
    Yet longing comes upon him to fare forth on the water.
    Bosque taketh blossom, cometh beauty of berries,
    Fields to fairness, land fares brisker,
50 All this admonisheth man eager of mood,
    The heart turns to travel so that he then thinks
    On flood-ways to be far departing.
    Cuckoo calleth with gloomy crying,
    He singeth summerward, bodeth sorrow,
55 The bitter heart's blood. Burgher knows not—
    He the prosperous man—what some perform
    Where wandering them widest draweth.
    So that but now my heart burst from my breastlock,
    My mood 'mid the mere-flood,
60 Over the whale's acre, would wander wide.
    On earth's shelter cometh oft to me,
    Eager and ready, the crying lone-flyer,
    Whets for the whale-path the heart irresistibly,
    O'er tracks of ocean; seeing that anyhow
65 My lord deems to me this dead life
    On loan and on land, I believe not
    That any earth-weal eternal standeth
    Save there be somewhat calamitous
    That, ere a man's tide go, turn it to twain.
70 Disease or oldness or sword-hate
    Beats out the breath from doom-gripped body.
    And for this, every earl whatever, for those speaking after—
    Laud of the living, boasteth some last word,
    That he will work ere he pass onward,
75 Frame on the fair earth 'gainst foes his malice,
    Daring ado, . . .
    So that all men shall honor him after
    And his laud beyond them remain 'mid the English,
    Aye, for ever, a lasting life's-blast,
80 Delight 'mid the doughty.
                              Days little durable,
    And all arrogance of earthen riches,

There come now no kings nor Caesars
Nor gold-giving lords like those gone.
Howe'er in mirth most magnified,
85 Whoe'er lived in life most lordliest,
Drear all this excellence, delights undurable!
Waneth the watch, but the world holdeth.
Tomb hideth trouble. The blade is layed low.
Earthly glory ageth and seareth.
90 No man at all going the earth's gait,
But age fares against him, his face paleth,
Grey-haired he groaneth, knows gone companions,
Lordly men, are to earth o'ergiven,
Nor may he then the flesh-cover, whose life ceaseth,
95 Nor eat the sweet nor feel the sorry,
Nor stir hand nor think in mid heart,
And though he strew the grave with gold,
His born brothers, their buried bodies
Be an unlikely treasure hoard.

ANONYMOUS (8th Century)

From **Beowulf (Translation by C. W. Kennedy)**

"Oft in the hall I have heard my people,
Comrades and counsellors, telling a tale
Of evil spirits their eyes have sighted,
105 Two mighty marauders who haunt the moors.
One shape, as clearly as men could see,
Seemed woman's likeness, and one seemed man,
An outcast wretch of another world,
And huger far than a human form.
110 Grendel my countrymen called him, not knowing
What monster-brood spawned him, what sire begot.
Wild and lonely the land they live in,
Wind-swept ridges and wolf-retreats,
Dread tracts of fen where the falling torrent
115 Downward dips into gloom and shadow
Under the dusk of the darkening cliff.
Not far in miles lies the lonely mere
Where trees firm-rooted and hung with frost
Overshroud the wave with shadowing gloom.
120 And there a portent appears each night,

A flame in the water; no man so wise
Who knows the bound of its bottomless depth.
The heather-stepper, the horned stag,
The antlered hart hard driven by hounds,
125 Invading that forest in flight from afar
Will turn at bay and die on the brink
Ere ever he'll plunge in that haunted pool.
'Tis an eerie spot! Its tossing spray
Mounts dark to heaven when high winds stir
130 The driving storm, and the sky is murky,
And with foul weather the heavens weep."

ANONYMOUS—MIDDLE ENGLISH LYRICS
(13th & 14th Centuries)

Sumer Is Icumen In [1]

Sumer is icumen in,
    Lhude sing cuccu!
Groweth sed and bloweth med
    And springth the wude nu.
5   Sing cuccu!

Awe bleteth after lomb,
    Lhouth after calve cu,
Bulluc sterteth, bucke verteth;
    Murie sing cuccu!
10   Cuccu! cuccu!
Wel singes thu cuccu.
Ne swik thu naver nu!

Sing cuccu nu, Sing cuccu!
Sing cuccu, Sing cuccu nu!

---

[1] *Translation:*
Spring has come in,
    Loudly sing cuckoo!
Grows seed and blooms mead
    And springs the wood now.
        Sing cuckoo!

Ewe bleats after lamb,
    Lows after calf the cow,

Bullock starts, buck farts;
    Merrily sing cuckoo!
        Cuckoo! cuckoo!
Well sing thou cuckoo.
Cease thou never now!

Sing cuckoo now etc.

Alysoun[1]

Bytuene Mersh and Averil,
  When spray beginneth to springe,
The lutel foul hath hire wyl
  On hyre lud to synge.
5   Ich libbe in lovelonginge
  For semlokest of alle thynge;
  He may me blisse bringe:
Icham in hire baundoun.
  An hendy hap ichabbe yhent—
10   Ichot from hevene it is me sent:
  From alle wymmen mi love is lent
And lyht on Alysoun.

On heu hire her is fayr ynoh,
  Hire browe broune, hire eye blake;
15 With lossum chere he on me loh;
  With middel small and wel ymake.
  Bote he me wolle to hire take
  Forte buen hire owen make,
  Longe to lyven ichulle forsake
20 And feye fallen adoun.
  An hendy hap etc.

---

[1] *Translation:*
Between March and April
  When twigs begin to spring,
The little bird has a will
  In her tongue to sing.
I live in love-longing
  For the seemliest of all things;
  She may to me bliss bring:
I am in her power.
  A happy chance I have received—
  I know from heaven it is me sent:
  From all women my love is turned
And lights on Alison.

In hue her hair is fair enough,
  Her brow brown, her eye black;
With lovely face she on me laughed;
  With waist small and well-made.
  Unless she me will to her take
  To be her own mate,
  Long to live I shall forsake
And doomed fall down.
  A happy chance etc.

Nights when I turn and wake—
  So that my cheeks wax wan—
Lady, all for thy sake,
  Longing has come upon me,
  In the world there's not so wise a man
  That can all her goodness tell;
  Her neck is whiter than the swan,
And fairest maid in town.
  A happy chance etc.

I am from wooing all worn out,
  Weary as water on the beach;
Lest any take from me my mate
  Whom I have yearned for long.
  Better it is to suffer awhile sorely
  Than to mourn evermore.
  Fairest under gown,
Harken to my song.
  A happy chance etc.

Nihtes when y wende and wake—
    For-thi myn wonges waxeth won—
Levedi, al for thine sake,
25   Longinge is ylent me on.
    In world nis non so wyter mon
    That al hire bounte telle con;
    Hire swyre is whittore then the swon,
And feyrest may in toune.
30   An hendy hap etc.

Icham for wowyng al forwake,
    Wery so water in wore;
Lest eny reve me my make
    Ychabbe y-yyrned yore.
35   Betere is tholien whyle sore
    Then mournen evermore.
    Geynest under gore,
Herkne to my roun.
    An hendy hap etc.

All Night by the Rose

All night by the rose, rose—
    All night by the rose I lay;
Dared I not the rose steal,
    And yet I bore the flower away.

Western Wind

Western wind, when will thou blow,
    The small rain down can rain?
Christ, if my love were in my arms
    And I in my bed again.

The Lady Fortune

The lady Fortune is bothe freend and fo.
Of poure she maketh riche, of riche poure also;
She turneth wo al into wele, and wele al into wo.
Ne truste no man to this wele, the wheel it turneth so.

GEOFFREY CHAUCER (c.1343–1400)

From **The Legend of Good Women**

And as for me, though that I konne but lyte,[1]

30 On bokes for to rede I me delyte,
And to hem give I feyth and ful credence,
And in myn herte have hem in reverence
So hertely, that ther is game noon
That fro my bokes maketh me to goon,
35 But yt be seldom on the holy day,
Save, certeynly, whan that the monethe of May
Is comen, and that I here the foules[2] synge,
And that the floures gynnen for to sprynge,—
Fairewel my boke, and my devocioun!
40   Now have I thanne suche a condicioun,
That of alle the floures in the mede,
Thanne love I most thise floures white and rede,
Suche as men callen daysyes in her toune.
To hem have I so grete affeccioun,
45 As I seyde erst, whanne comen is the May,
That in my bed ther daweth me no day,
That I nam uppe and walkyng in the mede,
To seen this floure agein[3] the sonne sprede,
Whan it up rysith erly by the morwe;
50 That blisful sight softneth al my sorwe,
So glad am I, whan that I have presence
Of it, to doon it alle reverence,
As she that is of alle floures flour,
Fulfilled of al vertue and honour,
55 And evere ilike faire, and fresshe of hewe.
And I love it, and evere ylike newe,
And ever shal, til that myn herte dye;
Al swere I nat—of this I wol nat lye—
Ther lovede no wight hotter in his lyve.
60   And, whan that hit ys eve, I renne blyve,[4]
As sone as evere the sonne gynneth weste,[5]

---

[1] Know but little.
[2] Birds.
[3] Toward.
[4] Run quickly.
[5] Begins to go west.

To seen this flour, how it wol go to reste,
For fere of nyght, so hateth she derkenesse!
Hire chere[6] is pleynly sprad in the brightnesse
65 Of the sonne, for ther yt wol unclose.
Allas, that I ne had Englyssh, ryme or prose,
Suffisant this flour to preyse aryght!

ANONYMOUS—THE POPULAR BALLADS
(14th & 15th Centuries)

Get Up and Bar the Door

It fell about the Martinmas[1] time,
    And a gay time it was then,
When our good wife got puddings[2] to make,
    And she's boild them in the pan.

5 The wind sae cauld blew south and north,
    And blew into the floor;
Quoth our goodman to our goodwife,
    "Gae out and bar the door."

"My hand is in my hussyfskap,[3]
10   Goodman, as ye may see;
An it shoud nae be barrd this hundred year,
    It's no be barrd for me."

They made a paction tween them twa,
    They made it firm and sure,
15 That the first word whaeer shoud speak,
    Shoud rise and bar the door.

Then by there came two gentlemen,
    At twelve oclock at night,
And they could neither see house nor hall,
20   Nor coal nor candle-light.

"Now whether is this a rich man's house,
    Or whether is it a poor?"

---

[6] Countenance.

[1] November 11.
[2] Sausages.
[3] Household chores.

But neer a word wad ane o them speak,
    For barring of the door.

25 And first they ate the white puddings,
    And then they ate the black;
    Tho muckle[4] thought the goodwife to hersel,
      Yet neer a word she spake.

Then said the one unto the other,
30   "Here, man, tak ye my knife;
Do ye tak aff the auld man's beard,
    And I'll kiss the goodwife."

"But there's nae water in the house,
    And what shall we do than?"
35 "What ails ye at the pudding-broo,
    That boils into the pan?"

O up then started our goodman,
    An angry man was he:
"Will ye kiss my wife before my een,
40   And scad me wi pudding-bree?"

Then up and started our goodwife,
    Gied three skips on the floor:
"Goodman, you've spoken the foremost word,
    Get up and bar the door."

Lord Randal

"O where ha you been, Lord Randal, my son?
And where ha you been, my handsome young man?"
"I ha been at the greenwood; mother, mak my bed soon,
For I'm wearied wi hunting, and fain wad lie down."

5 "An wha met ye there, Lord Randal, my son?
An wha met you there, my handsome young man?"
"O I met wi my true-love; mother, mak my bed soon,
For I'm wearied wi huntin, and fain wad lie down."

"And what did she give you, Lord Randal, my son?
10 And what did she give you, my handsome young man?"

---

4 Much.

"Eels fried in a pan; mother, mak my bed soon,
For I'm wearied wi huntin, and fain wad lie down."

"And wha gat your leavins, Lord Randal, my son?
And wha gat your leavins, my handsome young man?"
15 "My hawks and my hounds; mother, mak my bed soon,
For I'm wearied wi hunting, and fain wad lie down."

"And what becam of them, Lord Randal, my son?
And what becam of them, my handsome young man?"
"They stretched their legs out and died; mother, mak my bed soon,
20 For I'm wearied wi huntin, and fain wad lie down."

"O I fear you are poisoned, Lord Randal, my son!
I fear you are poisoned, my handsome young man!"
"O yes, I am poisoned: mother, mak my bed soon,
For I'm sick at the heart, and I fain wad lie down."

25 "What d'ye leave to your mother, Lord Randal, my son?
What d'ye leave to your mother, my handsome young man?"
"Four and twenty milk kye;[1] mother, mak my bed soon,
For I'm sick at the heart, and I fain wad lie down."

"What d'ye leave to your sister, Lord Randal, my son?
30 What d'ye leave to your sister, my handsome young man?"
"My gold and my silver; mother, mak my bed soon,
For I'm sick at the heart, an I fain wad lie down."

"What d'ye leave to your brother, Lord Randal, my son?
What d'ye leave to your brother, my handsome young man?"
35 "My houses and my lands; mother, mak my bed soon,
For I'm sick at the heart, and I fain wad lie down."

"What d'ye leave to your true-love, Lord Randal, my son?
What d'ye leave to your true-love, my handsome young man?"
"I leave her hell and fire; mother, mak my bed soon,
40 For I'm sick at the heart, and I fain wad lie down."

The Three Ravens

There were three ravens sat on a tree,
    Downe a downe, hay down, hay downe,

---

[1] Kine = cows.

There were three ravens sat on a tree,
   With a downe,
5 There were three ravens sat on a tree,
They were as blacke as they might be,
   With a downe derrie, derrie, derrie, downe, downe.

The one of them said to his mate,
"Where shall we our breakfast take?" [1]

10 "Downe in yonder greene field,
There lies a knight slain under his shield.

"His hounds they lie downe at his feete,
So well they can their master keepe.

"His hawkes they flie so eagerly,[2]
15 There's no fowle dare him come nie."

Downe there comes a fallow doe,
As great with yong as she might goe.

She lift up his bloody hed,
And kist his wounds that were so red.

20 She got him up upon her back,
And carried him to earthen lake.[3]

She buried him before the prime,
She was dead herselfe ere evensong time.

God send every gentleman
25 Such hawkes, such hounds, and such a leman.[4]

The Cherry-Tree Carol

Joseph was an old man,
   and an old man was he,
When he wedded Mary,
   in the land of Galilee.

---

[1] The line pattern and refrain of the first stanza recur throughout.
[2] Fiercely.
[3] Grave.
[4] Lover.

5 Joseph and Mary walked
    through an orchard good,
Where was cherries and berries,
    so red as any blood.

Joseph and Mary walked
10   through an orchard green,
Where was berries and cherries,
    as thick as might be seen.

O then bespoke Mary,
    so meek and so mild:
15 "Pluck me one cherry, Joseph,
    for I am with child."

O then bespoke Joseph:
    with words most unkind:
"Let him pluck thee a cherry
20   that brought thee with child."

O then bespoke the babe,
    within his mother's womb:
"Bow down then the tallest tree,
    for my mother to have some."

25 Then bowed down the highest tree
    unto his mother's hand;
Then she cried, "See, Joseph,
    I have cherries at command."

O then bespoke Joseph:
30   "I have done Mary wrong;
But cheer up, my dearest,
    and be not cast down."

Then Mary plucked a cherry,
    as red as the blood,
35 Then Mary went home
    with her heavy load.

Then Mary took her babe,
    and sat him on her knee,
Saying, "My dear son, tell me
40   what this world will be."

"O I shall be as dead, mother,
    as the stones in the wall;
O the stones in the streets, mother,
    shall mourn for me all.

45 "Upon Easter-day, mother,
    my uprising shall be;
O the sun and the moon, mother,
    shall both rise with me."

The Unquiet Grave

"The wind doth blow today, my love,
    And a few small drops of rain;
I never had but one true-love,
    In cold grave she was lain.

5 "I'll do as much for my true-love
    As any young man may;
I'll sit and mourn all at her grave
    For a twelvemonth and a day."

The twelvemonth and a day being up,
10   The dead began to speak:
"Oh who sits weeping on my grave,
    And will not let me sleep?"

" 'Tis I, my love, sits on your grave,
    And will not let you sleep;
15 For I crave one kiss of your clay-cold lips,
    And that is all I seek."

"You crave one kiss of my clay-cold lips;
    But my breath smells earthy strong;
If you have one kiss of my clay-cold lips,
20   Your time will not be long.

" 'Tis down in yonder garden green,
    Love, where we used to walk,
The finest flower that e'er was seen
    Is withered to a stalk.

25 "The stalk is withered dry, my love,
    So will our hearts decay;

So make yourself content, my love,
    Till God calls you away."

Bonny Barbara Allan

It was in and about the Martinmas time,
    When the green leaves were a falling,
That Sir John Graeme, in the West Country,
    Fell in love with Barbara Allan.

5 He sent his man down through the town,
    To the place where she was dwelling:
"O haste and come to my master dear,
    Gin[1] ye be Barbara Allan."

O hooly,[2] hooly rose she up,
10   To the place where he was lying,
And when she drew the curtain by,
    "Young man, I think you're dying."

"O it's I'm sick, and very, very sick,
    And 'tis a' for Barbara Allan."
15 "O the better for me ye's never be,
    Tho your heart's blood were a spilling.

"O dinna ye mind,[3] young man," said she,
    "When ye was in the tavern a drinking,
That ye made the healths gae round and round,
20   And slighted Barbara Allan?"

He turnd his face unto the wall,
    And death was with him dealing:
"Adieu, adieu, my dear friends all,
    And be kind to Barbara Allan."

25 And slowly, slowly raise she up,
    And slowly, slowly left him,
And sighing said she could not stay,
    Since death of life had reft him.

---

[1] If.
[2] Slowly.
[3] Don't you remember.

> She had not gane a mile but twa.
> 30   When she heard the dead-bell ringing;
> And every jow[4] that the dead-bell geid,[5]
>   It cry'd "Woe to Barbara Allan!"

> "O mother, mother, make my bed!
>   O make it soft and narrow!
> 35 Since my love died for me today,
>   I'll die for him tomorrow."

JOHN SKELTON (1460?–1529)

To Mistress Margaret Hussey

> Merry Margaret,
>   As midsummer flower,
> Gentle as falcon
> Or hawk of the tower:
> 5 With solace and gladness,
> Much mirth and no madness,
> All good and no badness;
>   So joyously,
>   So maidenly,
> 10   So womanly
>   Her demeaning[1]
>   In every thing,
>   Far, far passing
>   That I can indite,
> 15   Or suffice to write
> Of Merry Margaret
>   As midsummer flower,
> Gentle as falcon
> Or hawk of the tower.
> 20   As patient and still
> And as full of good will
> As fair Isaphill,[2]
> Coriander,[3]

---

4 Stroke.
5 Gave.

1 Demeanor.
2 Hypsipyle, legendary princess of Lemnos who saved her father's life.
3 An aromatic herb.

Sweet pomander,[4]
25 Good Cassander,[5]
Steadfast of thought,
Well made, well wrought,
Far may be sought
Ere that ye can find
30 So courteous, so kind
As Merry Margaret,
This midsummer flower,
Gentle as falcon
Or hawk of the tower.

THOMAS WYATT (1503–1542)

The Lover Compareth His State to a Ship in Perilous Storm Tossed on the Sea

My galley chargèd with forgetfulness
Thorough sharp seas in winter nights doth pass
'Tween rock and rock; and eke[1] mine enemy, alas,
That is my lord, steereth with cruelness;
5 And every oar a thought in readiness,
As though that death were light in such a case.
An endless wind doth tear the sail apace,
Of forcèd sighs and trusty fearfulness.
A rain of tears, a cloud of dark disdain,
10 Hath done the wearied cords great hinderance,
Wreathed with error and eke with ignorance.
The stars be hid that led me to this pain;
Drownèd is reason that should me consort,
And I remain despairing of the port.

They Flee from Me

They flee from me that sometime did me seek
With naked foot stalking in my chamber.
I have seen them gentle tame and meek
That now are wild and do not remember
5 That sometime they put themself in danger

---

[4] A sachet of aromatics.
[5] Cassandra, legendary prophetess of Troy, symbolic of constancy and beauty.
[1] Also.

To take bread at my hand; and now they range
Busily seeking with a continual change.

Thanked be Fortune it hath been otherwise
Twenty times better; but once in special,
10 In thin array after a pleasant guise,
When her loose gown from her shoulders did fall,
And she me caught in her arms long and small;[1]
And therewith all sweetly did me kiss,
And softly said, "Dear heart, how like you this?"

15 It was no dream: I lay broad waking.
But all is turned thorough my gentleness
Into a strange fashion of forsaking;
And I have leave to go of her goodness,
And she also to use newfangleness.
20 But since that I so kindely[2] am served,
I fain would know what she hath deserved.

HENRY HOWARD, EARL OF SURREY (1517–1547)

The Soote[1] Season

The soote season that bud and bloom forth brings
With green hath clad the hill and eke the vale,
The nightingale with feathers new she sings,
The turtle to her make[2] hath told her tale.
5 Summer is come, for every spray now springs,
The hart hath hung his old head on the pale,[3]
The buck in brake his winter coat he flings,
The fishes float with new repairèd scale,
The adder all her slough away she slings,
10 The swift swallow pursueth the flyès smale,
The busy bee her honey now she mings,[4]—
Winter is worn, that was the flowers' bale:[5]
And thus I see, among these pleasant things
Each care decays—and yet my sorrow springs.

---

1 Slender.
2 In the manner of womankind; also "agreeably," in an ironic sense.

1 Sweet.
2 The turtledove to her mate.
3 Fence.
4 Mixes.
5 Woe.

Love That Doth Reign and Live
Within My Thought

Love that doth reign and live within my thought,
And built his seat within my captive breast,
Clad in the arms wherein with me he fought
Oft in my face he doth his banner rest.
5 But she that taught me love and suffer pain,
My doubtful hope and eke my hot desire
With shamefast look to shadow and refrain,
Her smiling grace converteth straight to ire.
And coward love then to the heart apace
10 Taketh his flight where he doth lurk and plain,[1]
His purpose lost, and dare not show his face.
For my lord's guilt thus faultless bide I pain;
   Yet from my lord shall not my foot remove.
   Sweet is the death that taketh end by love.

SIR WALTER RALEGH (1552?–1618)

The Nymph's Reply to the Shepherd

If all the world and love were young,
And truth in every shepherd's tongue,
These pretty pleasures might me move
To live with thee and be thy love.

5 Time drives the flocks from field to fold
When rivers rage and rocks grow cold,
And Philomel becometh dumb;
The rest complains of cares to come.

The flowers do fade, and wanton fields
10 To wayward winter reckoning yields;
A honey tongue, a heart of gall,
Is fancy's spring, but sorrow's fall.

Thy gowns, thy shoes, thy beds of roses,
Thy cap, thy kirtle, and thy posies

---

[1] Complain.

¹⁵ Soon break, soon wither, soon forgotten—
In folly ripe, in reason rotten.

Thy belt of straw and ivy buds,
Thy coral clasps and amber studs,
All these in me no means can move
²⁰ To come to thee and be thy love.

But could youth last and love still breed,
Had joys no date nor age no need,
Then these delights my mind might move
To live with thee and be thy love.

EDMUND SPENSER (1552?–1599)

From **Amoretti**

SONNET 15

Ye tradefull Merchants, that with weary toyle,
Do seeke most pretious things to make your gain,
And both the Indias of their treasure spoile,
What needeth you to seeke so farre in vaine?
5 For loe, my Love doth in her selfe containe
All this worlds riches that may farre be found:
If saphyres, loe her eies be saphyres plaine;
If rubies, loe hir lips be rubies sound;
If pearles, hir teeth be pearles both pure and round;
10 If yvorie, her forhead yvory weene;
If gold, her locks are finest gold on ground;
If silver, her faire hands are silver sheene:
    But that which fairest is but few behold:—
    Her mind, adornd with vertues manifold.

SONNET 67

Lyke as a huntsman, after weary chace,
Seeing the game from him escapt away,
Sits downe to rest him in some shady place,
With panting hounds beguilèd of their pray,
5 So after long pursuit and vaine assay,
When I all weary had the chace forsooke,
The gentle deere returned the selfe-same way,
Thinking to quench her thirst at the next brooke.
There she beholding me with mylder looke

10 Sought not to fly, but fearlesse still did bide,
   Till I in hand her yet halfe trembling tooke,
   And with her owne goodwill her fyrmely tyde.
      Strange thing, me seemd, to see a beast so wyld
      So goodly wonne, with her owne will beguyld.

SONNET 75

One day I wrote her name upon the strand,
But came the waves and washèd it away:
Agayne I wrote it with a second hand,
But came the tyde, and made my paynes his pray.
5 "Vayne man," sayd she, "that doest in vaine assay
A mortall thing so to immortalize;
For I my selve shall lyke to this decay,
And eek my name bee wypèd out lykewize."
"Not so," quod I, "let baser things devize[1]
10 To dy in dust, but you shall live by fame:
My verse your vertues rare shall eternize,
And in the hevens wryte your glorious name;
   Where, when as death shall all the world subdew,
   Our love shall live, and later life renew."

SONNET 82

Joy of my life, full oft for loving you
I blesse my lot, that was so lucky placed.
But then the more your owne mishap I rew,
That are so much by so meane love embased.
5 For, had the equall hevens so much you graced
In this as in the rest, ye mote invent[1]
Som hevenly wit, whose verse could have enchased
Your glorious name in golden moniment.
But since ye deignd so goodly to relent
10 To me, your thrall, in whom is little worth,
That little that I am shall all be spent
In setting your immortall prayses forth:
   Whose lofty argument, uplifting me,
   Shall lift you up unto an high degree.

---

[1] Contrive.
[1] Might find.

SIR PHILIP SIDNEY (1554–1586)

From **Astrophil and Stella**

SONNET 31

With how sad steps, O moon, thou climb'st the skies!
　How silently, and with how wan a face!
　What! may it be that even in heavenly place
　That busy archer his sharp arrows tries?
5 Sure, if that long-with-love-acquainted eyes
　Can judge of love, thou feel'st a lover's case;
　I read it in thy looks—thy languished grace
　To me, that feel the like, thy state descries.
Then, even of fellowship, O moon, tell me,
10　Is constant love deemed there but want of wit?
　Are beauties there as proud as here they be?
Do they above love to be loved, and yet
　Those lovers scorn whom that love doth possess?
　Do they call virtue there ungratefulness?

SONNET 74

I never drank of Aganippe well,[1]
　Nor ever did in shade of Tempe[2] sit,
　And muses scorn with vulgar brains to dwell;
　Poor layman I, for sacred rites unfit.
5 Some do I hear of poets' fury tell,
　But, God wot, wot not what they mean by it;
　And this I swear by blackest brook of hell,
　I am no pickpurse of another's wit.
How falls it then that with so smooth an ease
10　My thoughts I speak, and what I speak doth flow
　In verse, and that my verse best wits doth please?
Guess we the cause. What, is it thus? Fie, no.
　Or so? Much less. How then? Sure thus it is,
　My lips are sweet, inspired with Stella's kiss.

Thou Blind Man's Mark

Thou blind man's mark,[1] thou fool's self-chosen snare,
Fond fancy's scum, and dregs of scattered thought,

---

[1] Fountain of the Muses, at the foot of Mount Helicon.
[2] A valley in Greece, symbol of idyllic nature.
[1] Target.

Bands of all evils, cradle of causeless care,
Thou web of will whose end is never wrought;

5 Desire, Desire, I have too dearly bought
With prize of mangled mind thy worthless ware!
Too long, too long asleep thou hast me brought
Who should my mind to higher things prepare.

But yet in vain thou hast my ruin sought;
10 In vain thou madest me to vain things aspire;
In vain thou kindlest all thy smoky fire.

For Virtue hath this better lesson taught:
Within myself to seek my only hire,
Desiring nought but how to kill desire.

Leave Me, O Love

Leave me, O Love, which reachest but to dust,
And thou, my mind, aspire to higher things.
Grow rich in that which never taketh rust.
Whatever fades but fading pleasure brings.

5 Draw in thy beams and humble all thy might
To that sweet yoke where lasting freedoms be,
Which breaks the clouds and opens forth the light
That doth both shine and give us sight to see.

O take fast hold; let that light be thy guide
10 In this small course which birth draws out to death,
And think how evil becometh him to slide
Who seeketh heaven and comes of heavenly breath.
   Then farewell, world! The uttermost I see!
   Eternal Love, maintain thy life in me.

JOHN LYLY (1554–1606)

Cupid and My Campaspe

Cupid and my Campaspe played
At cards for kisses; Cupid paid.
He stakes his quiver, bow, and arrows,
His mother's doves and team of sparrows;

5 Loses them, too. Then down he throws
  The coral of his lip, the rose
  Growing on's cheek (but none knows how) ;
  With these, the crystal of his brow,
  And then the dimple of his chin:
10 All these did my Campaspe win.
  At last he set her both his eyes;
  She won, and Cupid blind did rise.
      O Love, has she done this to thee?
      What shall, alas! become of me?

GEORGE PEELE (1557–1596)

His Golden Locks Time Hath to Silver Turned

His golden locks time hath to silver turned;
  Oh, time too swift, oh, swiftness never ceasing!
His youth 'gainst time and age hath ever spurned,
  But spurned in vain; youth waneth by increasing.
5 Beauty, strength, youth, are flowers but fading seen;
Duty, faith, love, are roots, and ever green.

His helmet now shall make a hive for bees,
  And lover's sonnets turned to holy psalms,
A man-at-arms must now serve on his knees,
10   And feed on prayers, which are age his alms;
But though from court to cottage he depart,
His saint is sure of his unspotted heart.

And when he saddest sits in homely cell,
  He'll teach his swains this carol for a song:
15 Blest be the hearts that wish my sovereign well,
  Cursed be the souls that think her any wrong!
Goddess, allow this agèd man his right,
To be your beadsman now, that was your knight.

CHIDIOCK TICHBORNE (1558?–1586)

Tichborne's Elegy

*Written with His Own Hand in the Tower
Before His Execution*

My prime of youth is but a frost of cares,
My feast of joy is but a dish of pain,

My crop of corn is but a field of tares,
And all my good is but vain hope of gain;
5 The day is past, and yet I saw no sun,
And now I live, and now my life is done.

My tale was heard and yet it was not told,
My fruit is fallen and yet my leaves are green,
My youth is spent and yet I am not old,
10 I saw the world and yet I was not seen;
My thread is cut and yet it is not spun,
And now I live, and now my life is done.

I sought my death and found it in my womb,
I looked for life and saw it was a shade,
15 I trod the earth and knew it was my tomb,
And now I die, and now I was but made;
My glass is full, and now my glass is run,
And now I live, and now my life is done.

ROBERT SOUTHWELL (1561?–1595)

The Burning Babe

As I in hoary winter's night stood shivering in the snow,
Surprised I was with sudden heat which made my heart to glow;
And lifting up a fearful eye to view what fire was near,
A pretty babe all burning bright did in the air appear;
5 Who, scorchèd with excessive heat, such floods of tears did shed
As though his floods should quench his flames which with his tears
were fed.
"Alas," quoth he, "but newly born in fiery heats I fry,
Yet none approach to warm their hearts or feel my fire but I!
My faultless breast the furnace is, the fuel wounding thorns,
10 Love is the fire, and sighs the smoke, the ashes shame and scorns;
The fuel justice layeth on, and mercy blows the coals,
The metal in this furnace wrought are men's defilèd souls,
For which, as now on fire I am to work them to their good,
So will I melt into a bath to wash them in my blood."
15 With this he vanished out of sight and swiftly shrunk away,
And straight I callèd unto mind that it was Christmas day.

SAMUEL DANIEL (1562?–1619)

From **Delia**

SONNET 31

Look, Delia, how we 'steem the half-blown rose,
The image of thy blush and summer's honor,
Whilst in her tender green she doth inclose
That pure sweet beauty Time bestows upon her.
5 No sooner spreads her glory in the air
But straight her full-blown pride is in declining.
She then is scorned that late adorned the fair;
So clouds thy beauty after fairest shining.
No April can revive thy withered flowers,
10 Whose blooming grace adorns thy glory now;
Swift speeding Time, feathered with flying hours,
Dissolves the beauty of the fairest brow.
    Oh let not then such riches waste in vain,
    But love whilst that thou mayst be loved again.

MICHAEL DRAYTON (1563–1631)

From **Idea**

SONNET 6

How many paltry, foolish, painted things
That now in coaches trouble every street
Shall be forgotten, whom no poet sings,
Ere they be well wrapped in their winding-sheet!
5 Where I to thee eternity shall give
When nothing else remaineth of these days,
And queens hereafter shall be glad to live
Upon the alms of thy superfluous praise.
Virgins and matrons, reading these my rimes,
10 Shall be so much delighted with thy story
That they shall grieve they lived not in these times
To have seen thee, their sex's only glory.
    So shalt thou fly above the vulgar throng
    Still to survive in my immortal song.

SONNET 7

Since there's no help, come, let us kiss and part.
Nay, I have done, you get no more of me,

And I am glad, yea glad with all my heart
That thus so cleanly I myself can free;
5　Shake hands forever, cancel all our vows,
And when we meet at any time again
Be it not seen in either of our brows
That we one jot of former love retain.
Now at the last gasp of Love's latest breath,
10　When, his pulse failing, Passion speechless lies,
When Faith is kneeling by his bed of death
And Innocence is closing up his eyes,
　　　Now if thou would'st, when all have given him over,
　　　From death to life thou might'st him yet recover.

CHRISTOPHER MARLOWE (1564–1593)

From **Doctor Faustus**

ACT V, SCENE I

FAUST. Was this the face that launched a thousand ships,
And burnt the topless towers of Ilium?
Sweet Helen, make me immortal with a kiss.—
100　Her lips suck forth my soul; see where it flies!—
Come, Helen, come, give me my soul again.
Here will I dwell, for heaven be in these lips,
And all is dross that is not Helena.
I will be Paris, and for love of thee,
105　Instead of Troy shall Wittenberg be sacked;
And I will combat with weak Menelaus,
And wear thy colors on my plumèd crest;
Yea, I will wound Achilles in the heel,
And then return to Helen for a kiss.
110　O, thou art fairer than the evening air
Clad in the beauty of a thousand stars;
Brighter art thou than flaming Jupiter
When he appeared to hapless Semele;
More lovely than the monarch of the sky
115　In wanton Arethusa's azured arms;
And none but thou shalt be my paramour.

ACT V, SCENE II

FAUST. Ah, Faustus,
Now hast thou but one bare hour to live,

And then thou must be damned perpetually!
Stand still, you ever-moving spheres of heaven,
75 That time may cease and midnight never come!
Fair Nature's eye, rise, rise again and make
Perpetual day; or let this hour be but
A year, a month, a week, a natural day,
That Faustus may repent and save his soul!
80 *O lente, lente, currite noctis equi!* [1]
The stars move still, time runs, the clock will strike,
The Devil will come, and Faustus must be damned.
O, I'll leap up to my God! Who pulls me down?
See, see where Christ's blood streams in the firmament!
85 One drop would save my soul—half a drop! ah, my Christ!—
Ah, rend not my heart for naming of my Christ!—
Yet will I call on him!—O, spare me, Lucifer!—
Where is it now? 'T is gone; and see where God
Stretcheth out his arm, and bends his ireful brows!—
90 Mountains and hills, come, come and fall on me,
And hide me from the heavy wrath of God!
No! no!—
Then will I headlong run into the earth!—
Earth, gape!—O no, it will not harbor me!—
95 You stars that reigned at my nativity,
Whose influence hath allotted death and hell,
Now draw up Faustus like a foggy mist
Into the entrails of yon lab'ring cloud,
That when you vomit forth into the air,
100 My limbs may issue from their smoky mouths,
So that my soul may but ascend to heaven.

[*The watch strikes*

Ah, half the hour is past! 'T will all be past anon!—
O God,
If thou wilt not have mercy on my soul,
105 Yet for Christ's sake, whose blood hath ransomed me,
Impose some end to my incessant pain:
Let Faustus live in hell a thousand years,
A hundred thousand, and at last be saved!—
O, no end is limited to damnèd souls!
110 Why wert thou not a creature wanting soul?
Or why is this immortal that thou hast?
Ah, Pythagoras' metempsychosis! were that true,

---

[1] Run slowly, slowly, horses of the night—adapted from Ovid's *Amores.*

This soul should fly from me, and I be changed
Unto some brutish beast! All beasts are happy,
115 For when they die
Their souls are soon dissolved in elements;
But mine must live, still to be plagued in hell.
Cursed be the parents that engend'red me!
No, Faustus, curse thyself, curse Lucifer,
120 That hath deprived thee of the joys of heaven.

> [*The clock striketh twelve*

O, it strikes, it strikes! Now, body, turn to air,
Or Lucifer will bear thee quick to hell!

> [*Thunder and lightning*

O soul, be changed into little water-drops,
And fall into the ocean—ne're be found!—
125 My God, my God, look not so fierce on me!
>   *Enter* DEVILS
Adders and serpents, let me breathe awhile!—
Ugly hell, gape not!—Come not, Lucifer!—
I'll burn my books!—Ah, Mephistophilis!

The Passionate Shepherd to His Love

Come live with me, and be my love,
And we will all the pleasures prove
That hills and valleys, dales and fields,
And all the craggy mountains yields.

5 And we will sit upon the rocks,
Seeing the shepherds feed their flocks,
By shallow rivers, to whose falls
Melodious birds sing madrigals.

And I will make thee beds of roses
10 And a thousand fragrant posies,
A cap of flowers, and a kirtle
Embroidered all with leaves of myrtle;

A gown made of the finest wool,
Which from our pretty lambs we pull,
15 Fair linèd slippers, for the cold,
With buckles of the purest gold;

A belt of straw and ivy-buds
With coral clasps and amber studs.

And if these pleasures may thee move,
20 Come live with me, and be my love.

The shepherds' swains shall dance and sing
For thy delight each May morning.
If these delights thy mind may move,
Then live with me, and be my love.

WILLIAM SHAKESPEARE (1564–1616)

From **The Sonnets**

SONNET 18

Shall I compare thee to a summer's day?
Thou art more lovely and more temperate:
Rough winds do shake the darling buds of May,
And summer's lease hath all too short a date:
5 Sometime too hot the eye of heaven shines,
And often is his gold complexion dimmed;
And every fair from fair sometime declines,
By chance or nature's changing course untrimmed:
But thy eternal summer shall not fade
10 Nor lose possession of that fair thou ow'st,[1]
Nor shall Death brag thou wand'rest in his shade,
When in eternal lines to time thou grow'st.
   So long as men can breathe or eyes can see,
   So long lives this, and this gives life to thee.

SONNET 29

When, in disgrace with Fortune and men's eyes,
I all alone beweep my outcast state,
And trouble deaf heaven with my bootless cries,
And look upon myself and curse my fate,
5 Wishing me like to one more rich in hope,
Featured like him, like him with friends possessed,
Desiring this man's art, and that man's scope,
With what I most enjoy contented least;
Yet in these thoughts myself almost despising,
10 Haply I think on thee, and then my state,
Like to the lark at break of day arising

---

[1] Ownest.

From sullen earth, sings hymns at heaven's gate;
  For thy sweet love remembered such wealth brings
  That then I scorn to change my state with kings.

SONNET 55

Not marble nor the gilded monuments
Of princes shall outlive this powerful rime;
But you shall shine more bright in these contents
Than unswept stone, besmeared with sluttish time.
5 When wasteful war shall statues overturn,
And broils root out the work of masonry,
Nor Mars his sword nor war's quick fire shall burn
The living record of your memory.
'Gainst death and all oblivious enmity
10 Shall you pace forth; your praise shall still find room
Even in the eyes of all posterity
That wear this world out to the ending doom.
  So, till the Judgment that yourself arise,
  You live in this, and dwell in lovers' eyes.

SONNET 64

When I have seen by Time's fell hand defaced
The rich proud cost of outworn buried age;
When sometime lofty towers I see down-rased,
And brass eternal slave to mortal rage;
5 When I have seen the hungry ocean gain
Advantage on the kingdom of the shore,
And the firm soil win of the wat'ry main,
Increasing store with loss and loss with store;
When I have seen such interchange of state,
10 Or state itself confounded to decay,
Ruin hath taught me thus to ruminate,
That Time will come and take my love away.
  This thought is as a death, which cannot choose
  But weep to have that which it fears to lose.

SONNET 73

That time of year thou mayst in me behold
When yellow leaves, or none, or few, do hang
Upon those boughs which shake against the cold,
Bare ruined choirs where late the sweet birds sang.

5 In me thou see'st the twilight of such day
As after sunset fadeth in the west,
Which by and by black night doth take away,
Death's second self that seals up all in rest.
In me thou see'st the glowing of such fire
10 That on the ashes of his youth doth lie,
As the deathbed whereon it must expire,
Consumed with that which it was nourished by.
    This thou perceiv'st, which makes thy love more strong
    To love that well which thou must leave ere long.

SONNET 104

To me, fair friend, you never can be old,
For as you were when first your eye I eyed,
Such seems your beauty still. Three winters cold
Have from the forests shook three summers' pride,
5 Three beauteous springs to yellow autumn turned
In process of the seasons have I seen,
Three April perfumes in three hot Junes burned,
Since first I saw you fresh which yet are green.
Ah yet doth beauty like a dial hand
10 Steal from his figure, and no pace perceived!
So your sweet hue, which methinks still doth stand,
Hath motion, and mine eye may be deceived;
    For fear of which, hear this thou age unbred:
    Ere you were born was beauty's summer dead.

SONNET 116

Let me not to the marriage of true minds
Admit impediments. Love is not love
Which alters when it alteration finds,
Or bends with the remover to remove.
5 O no! it is an ever-fixèd mark
That looks on tempests and is never shaken;
It is the star to every wand'ring bark,
Whose worth's unknown, although his height be taken.
Love's not Time's fool, though rosy lips and cheeks
10 Within his bending sickle's compass come.
Love alters not with his brief hours and weeks,
But bears it out even to the edge of doom.
    If this be error, and upon me proved,
    I never writ, nor no man ever loved.

SONNET 129

Th' expense of spirit in a waste of shame
Is lust in action; and, till action, lust
Is perjured, murd'rous, bloody, full of blame,
Savage, extreme, rude, cruel, not to trust;
5 Enjoyed no sooner but despisèd straight;
Past reason hunted, and no sooner had,
Past reason hated, as a swallowed bait
On purpose laid to make the taker mad;
Mad in pursuit, and in possession so;
10 Had, having, and in quest to have, extreme;
A bliss in proof—and proved, a very woe;
Before, a joy proposed; behind, a dream.
    All this the world well knows; yet none knows well
    To shun the heaven that leads men to this hell.

SONNET 151

Love is too young to know what conscience is,—
Yet who knows not conscience is born of love?
Then, gentle cheater, urge not my amiss,
Lest guilty of my faults thy sweet self prove.
5 For, thou betraying me, I do betray
My nobler part to my gross body's treason;
My soul doth tell my body that he may
Triumph in love: flesh stays no farther reason,
But rising at thy name doth point out thee
10 As his triumphant prize. Proud of this pride,
He is contented thy poor drudge to be,
To stand in thy affairs, fall by thy side.
    No want of conscience hold it that I call
    Her "love" for whose dear love I rise and fall.

Songs from the Plays

Love's Labor's Lost

SPRING

When daisies pied and violets blue
    And lady-smocks[1] all silver-white

---

[1] Cuckoo-flowers.

And cuckoo-buds of yellow hue
   Do paint the meadows with delight,
5 The cuckoo then, on every tree,
   Mocks married men; for thus sings he:
          "Cuckoo!
Cuckoo, cuckoo!"—O word of fear,
Unpleasing to a married ear!

10 When shepherds pipe on oaten straws,
   And merry larks are plowmen's clocks,
When turtles tread,[2] and rooks and daws,
   And maidens bleach their summer smocks,
The cuckoo then, on every tree,
15 Mocks married men; for thus sings he:
          "Cuckoo!
Cuckoo, cuckoo!"—O word of fear,
Unpleasing to a married ear!

WINTER

When icicles hang by the wall,
   And Dick the shepherd blows his nail,
And Tom bears logs into the hall,
   And milk comes frozen home in pail,
5 When blood is nipped, and ways be foul,
Then nightly sings the staring owl:
          "To-who!
Tu-whit, tu-who!" a merry note,
While greasy Joan doth keel [1] the pot.

10 When all aloud the wind doth blow,
   And coughing drowns the parson's saw,[2]
And birds sit brooding in the snow,
   And Marian's nose looks red and raw,
When roasted crabs[3] hiss in the bowl,
15 Then nightly sings the staring owl:
          "To-who!
Tu-whit, tu-who!" a merry note,
While greasy Joan doth keel the pot.

---

[2] Turtledoves mate.
[1] Cool by stirring.
[2] Wise saying.
[3] Crab apples.

As You Like It

UNDER THE GREENWOOD TREE

Under the greenwood tree
Who loves to lie with me,
And turn his merry note
Unto the sweet bird's throat,
5 Come hither, come hither, come hither!
          Here shall he see
          No enemy
But winter and rough weather.

          Who doth ambition shun,
10   And loves to live i' th' sun,
Seeking the food he eats
And pleased with what he gets,
Come hither, come hither, come hither!
          Here shall he see
15   No enemy
But winter and rough weather.

BLOW, BLOW, THOU WINTER WIND

Blow, blow, thou winter wind!
Thou art not so unkind
     As man's ingratitude.

Thy tooth is not so keen,
5   Because thou art not seen,
          Although thy breath be rude.

Heigh-ho, sing heigh-ho, unto the green holly!
Most friendship is feigning, most loving mere folly:
          Then, heigh-ho, the holly!
10   This life is most jolly.

Freeze, freeze, thou bitter sky!
That dost not bite so nigh
          As benefits forgot.
Though thou the waters warp,
15   Thy sting is not so sharp
          As friend rememb'red not.

Heigh-ho, sing heigh ho! &c.

IT WAS A LOVER AND HIS LASS

It was a lover and his lass,
    With a hey, and a ho, and a hey nonino,
That o'er the green corn field did pass
    In springtime, the only pretty ring time,
5 When birds do sing, hey ding a ding, ding:
Sweet lovers love the spring.

Between the acres of the rye,
    With a hey, and a ho, and a hey nonino,
These pretty country folks would lie,
10   In springtime, etc.

This carol they began that hour,
    With a hey, and a ho, and a hey nonino,
How that a life was but a flower
    In springtime, etc.

15 And therefore take the present time,
    With a hey, and a ho, and a hey nonino;
For love is crownèd with the prime
    In springtime, etc.

Twelfth Night

O MISTRESS MINE

O mistress mine, where are you roaming?
O, stay and hear! your true-love's coming,
    That can sing both high and low.
Trip no further, pretty sweeting;
5 Journeys end in lovers meeting,
    Every wise man's son doth know.

What is love? 'Tis not hereafter;
Present mirth hath present laughter;
    What's to come is still unsure:
10 In delay there lies no plenty;
Then come kiss me, sweet and twenty!
    Youth's a stuff will not endure.

WHEN THAT I WAS AND A LITTLE TINY BOY

When that I was and a little tiny boy,
    With hey, ho, the wind and the rain,

A foolish thing was but a toy,
    For the rain it raineth every day.

5 But when I came to man's estate,
    With hey, ho, the wind and the rain,
  'Gainst knaves and thieves men shut their gate,
    For the rain it raineth every day.

But when I came, alas! to wive,
10   With hey, ho, the wind and the rain,
By swaggering could I never thrive,
    For the rain it raineth every day.

But when I came unto my beds,
    With hey, ho, the wind and the rain,
15 With tosspots still had drunken heads,
    For the rain it raineth every day.

A great while ago the world begun,
    With hey, ho, the wind and the rain;
But that's all one, our play is done,
20   And we'll strive to please you every day.

Measure for Measure

TAKE, O TAKE THOSE LIPS AWAY

Take, O take those lips away,
    That so sweetly were forsworn;
And those eyes, the break of day,
    Lights that do mislead the morn;
5 But my kisses bring again, bring again,
Seals of love, but sealed in vain, sealed in vain.

Cymbeline

HARK, HARK! THE LARK

Hark, hark! the lark at heaven's gate sings,
    And Phoebus[1] 'gins arise,
His steeds to water at those springs
    On chaliced flowers that lies;

---

[1] Apollo.

5 And winking Mary-buds[2] begin
 To ope their golden eyes,
With every thing that pretty is,
 My lady sweet, arise!
  Arise, arise!

FEAR NO MORE THE HEAT O' TH' SUN

Fear no more the heat o' th' sun,
 Nor the furious winter's rages;
Thou thy worldly task hast done,
 Home art gone, and ta'en thy wages.
5 Golden lads and girls all must,
As chimney-sweepers, come to dust.

Fear no more the frown o' th' great;
 Thou art past the tyrant's stroke.
Care no more to clothe and eat;
10 To thee the reed is as the oak.
The scepter, learning, physic, must
All follow this, and come to dust.

Fear no more the lightning flash,
 Nor th' all-dreaded thunder-stone;
15 Fear not slander, censure rash;
 Thou hast finished joy and moan.
All lovers young, all lovers must
Consign to thee, and come to dust.

No exorciser harm thee!
20 Nor no witchcraft charm thee!
Ghost unlaid forbear thee!
Nothing ill come near thee!
Quiet consummation have,
And renownèd be thy grave!

The Tempest

COME UNTO THESE YELLOW SANDS

Come unto these yellow sands,
 And then take hands.

---

2 Sleeping marigolds.

Curtsied when you have and kissed,
　　The wild waves whist,[1]
5　Foot it featly[2] here and there;
　And, sweet sprites, the burthen[3] bear.
　　　Hark, hark!
　　　　(*Burthen, dispersedly.*) Bow-wow!
　　　The watchdogs bark!
10　　　　(*Burthen, dispersedly.*) Bow-wow!
　　　Hark, hark! I hear
　　　The strain of strutting chanticleer
　　　　Cry cock-a-diddle-dow!

FULL FADOM FIVE

Full fadom five thy father lies;
　　Of his bones are coral made;
Those are pearls that were his eyes;
　　Nothing of him that doth fade
5　But doth suffer a sea-change
Into something rich and strange.
Sea nymphs hourly ring his knell:
　　　　(*Burthen.*) Ding-dong!
Hark! now I hear them—Ding-dong, bell!

WHERE THE BEE SUCKS, THERE SUCK I

Where the bee sucks, there suck I;
　　In a cowslip's bell I lie;
　There I couch when owls do cry.
　On the bat's back I do fly
5　　After summer merrily.
Merrily, merrily shall I live now
Under the blossom that hangs on the bough.

ANONYMOUS—ELIZABETHAN LYRICS
(16th & 17th Centuries)

Back and Side Go Bare

Back and side go bare, go bare,
　　Both foot and hand go cold;

---

1 Quiet.
2 Nimbly.
3 The drone.

But, belly, God send thee good ale enough,
　　Whether it be new or old.

5 I cannot eat but little meat,
　　My stomach is not good;
But sure I think that I can drink
　　With him that wears a hood.
Though I go bare, take ye no care,
10　I am nothing a-cold;
I stuff my skin so full within
　　Of jolly good ale and old.
　　　　Back and side go bare, go bare, &c.

I love no roast but a nutbrown toast,
15　And a crab laid in the fire;
A little bread shall do me stead,
　　Much bread I not desire.
No frost nor snow, no wind, I trow,
　　Can hurt me if I would,
20 I am so wrapt, and throughly lapt
　　Of jolly good ale and old.
　　　　Back and side go bare, go bare, &c.

And Tib my wife, that as her life
　　Loveth well good ale to seek,
25 Full oft drinks she, till ye may see
　　The tears run down her cheek.
Then doth she troll to me the bowl,
　　Even as a maltworm should;
And saith, "Sweetheart, I took my part
30　Of this jolly good ale and old."
　　　　Back and side go bare, go bare, &c.

Now let them drink, till they nod and wink,
　　Even as good fellows should do;
They shall not miss to have the bliss
35　Good ale doth bring men to.
And all poor souls that have scourèd bowls,
　　Or have them lustily trolled,
God save the lives of them and their wives,
　　Whether they be young or old.
40　　Back and side go bare, go bare,
　　　Both foot and hand go cold;
　　But, belly, God send thee good ale enough,
　　　Whether it be new or old.

April Is in My Mistress' Face

April is in my mistress' face,
And Jùly in her eyes hath place,
Within her bosom is September,
But in her heart a cold December.

My Love in Her Attire

My love in her attire doth show her wit,
   It doth so well become her.
For every season she hath dressings fit,
   For winter, spring, and summer.
5 No beauty she doth miss
   When all her robes are on;
But Beauty's self she is
   When all her robes are gone.

There Is a Lady Sweet and Kind

There is a lady sweet and kind,
Was never face so pleased my mind;
I did but see her passing by,
And yet I love her till I die.

5 Her gesture, motion and her smiles,
Her wit, her voice, my heart beguiles,
Beguiles my heart, I know not why,
And yet I love her till I die.

Her free behavior, winning looks,
10 Will make a lawyer burn his books.
I touched her not, alas, not I,
And yet I love her till I die.

Had I her fast betwixt mine arms,
Judge you that think such sports were harms,
15 Were't any harm? No, no, fie, fie!
For I will love her till I die.

Should I remain confinèd there,
So long as Phoebus in his sphere,
I to request, she to deny,
20 Yet would I love her till I die.

Cupid is wingèd and doth range;
Her country so my love doth change,
But change she earth, or change she sky,
Yet will I love her till I die.

The Silver Swan

The silver swan, who living had no note,
When death approached, unlocked her silent throat;
Leaning her breast against the reedy shore,
Thus sung her first and last, and sung no more:
5 "Farewell, all joys; Oh death, come close mine eyes;
More geese than swans now live, more fools than wise."

THOMAS NASHE (1567–1601)

Spring, the Sweet Spring

Spring, the sweet spring, is the year's pleasant king;
Then blooms each thing, then maids dance in a ring,
Cold doth not sting, the pretty birds do sing,
   "Cuckoo, jug-jug, pu-we, to-witta-woo!"

5 The palm[1] and may[2] make country houses gay,
Lambs frisk and play, the shepherds pipe all day,
And we hear aye birds tune this merry lay,
   "Cuckoo, jug-jug, pu-we, to-witta-woo."

The fields breathe sweet, the daisies kiss our feet,
10 Young lovers meet, old wives a-sunning sit,
In every street these tunes our ears do greet,
   "Cuckoo, jug-jug, pu-we, to-witta-woo!"
   Spring, the sweet spring!

Adieu, Farewell Earth's Bliss

Adieu, farewell earth's bliss!
This world uncertain is;
Fond are life's lustful joys:
Death proves them all but toys.

---

[1] Pussywillow.
[2] Hawthorn.

5 None from his darts can fly;
  I am sick, I must die.
    Lord, have mercy on us!

  Rich men, trust not in wealth;
  Gold cannot buy you health;
10 Physic himself must fade.
  All things to end are made;
  The plague full swift goes by;
  I am sick, I must die.
    Lord, have mercy on us!

15 Beauty is but a flower,
  Which wrinkles will devour;
  Brightness falls from the air;
  Queens have died young and fair;
  Dust hath closed Helen's eye.
20 I am sick, I must die.
    Lord, have mercy on us!

  Strength stoops unto the grave;
  Worms feed on Hector brave;
  Swords may not fight with fate;
25 Earth still holds ope her gate;
  "Come, come!" the bells do cry.
  I am sick, I must die.
    Lord, have mercy on us!

  Wit with his wantonness
30 Tasteth death's bitterness;
  Hell's executioner
  Hath no ears for to hear
  What vain art can reply.
  I am sick, I must die.
35   Lord, have mercy on us!

  Haste, therefore, each degree,
  To welcome destiny!
  Heaven is our heritage,
  Earth but a player's stage;
40 Mount we unto the sky.
  I am sick, I must die.
    Lord, have mercy on us!

THOMAS CAMPION (1567–1620)

My Sweetest Lesbia

My sweetest Lesbia, let us live and love;
And though the sager sort our deeds reprove,
Let us not weigh them: heaven's great lamps do dive
Into their west, and straight again revive;
5 But soon as once set is our little light,
Then must we sleep one ever-during night.

If all would lead their lives in love like me,
Then bloody swords and armor should not be;
No drum nor trumpet peaceful sleeps should move,
10 Unless alarm came from the camp of love.
But fools do live, and waste their little light,
And seek with pain their ever-during night.

When timely death my life and fortune ends,
Let not my hearse be vexed with mourning friends;
15 But let all lovers, rich in triumph, come
And with sweet pastimes grace my happy tomb;
And, Lesbia, close up thou my little light,
And crown with love my ever-during night.

Now Winter Nights Enlarge

Now winter nights enlarge
  The number of their hours,
And clouds their storms discharge
  Upon the airy towers.
5 Let now the chimneys blaze
  And cups o'erflow with wine;
Let well-tuned words amaze
  With harmony divine.
Now yellow waxen lights
10   Shall wait on honey love,
While youthful revels, masques, and courtly sights
  Sleep's leaden spells remove.

This time doth well dispense
  With lovers' long discourse;
15 Much speech hath some defense,
  Though beauty no remorse.

All do not all things well;
 Some measures comely tread,
Some knotted riddles tell,
20 Some poems smoothly read.
The summer hath his joys,
 And winter his delights;
Though love and all his pleasures are but toys,
 They shorten tedious nights.

There Is a Garden in Her Face

There is a garden in her face,
 Where roses and white lilies grow;
A heavenly paradise is that place,
 Wherein all pleasant fruits do flow.
5 There cherries grow, which none may buy
Till "Cherry ripe!" themselves do cry.

Those cherries fairly do enclose
 Of orient pearl a double row,
Which when her lovely laughter shows,
10 They look like rose-buds filled with snow.
Yet them nor peer nor prince can buy,
Till "Cherry ripe!" themselves do cry.

Her eyes like angels watch them still;
 Her brows like bended bows do stand,
15 Threat'ning with piercing frowns to kill
 All that attempt with eye or hand
Those sacred cherries to come nigh,
Till "Cherry ripe!" themselves do cry.

2

~ A BRIEF HISTORY

The works of John Donne give numerous famous examples of tropes, figures of speech, which lend his poetry the elaborate quality of the conceit. Along with extended metaphors, devices such as personification, alliteration, and apostrophe combine with complicated meters, irregular line lengths, and eccentric stanza structure. Another Metaphysical poet, Herbert, not only creates conceits for his effects, but sometimes uses visual shapes as well. His *Easter Wings* is an example of an emblematic poem. Earth-bound metaphors allow the Metaphysical poets to arrive at supernatural, religious, and emotional visions ordinarily beyond the five senses. The sonnets of John Donne concern themselves not only with love, their traditional mode, but also with religion and mortality. Milton's sonnets break away from the usual octet and sestet divisions to create a poem which seems to be a more unified whole. Poems continue to be written on classical models from the Greek and Latin. Ben Jonson composes his *Pindaric Ode*. Some poets write on classical themes. Robert Herrick's *To the Virgins, to Make Much of Time* and Andrew Marvell's *To His Coy Mistress* are examples of poems built up not only on elaborate conceits, but also on the ancient idea of *carpe diem,* "seize the day." John Milton composes his epic *Paradise Lost* in blank verse and uses technical devices such as elision to lengthen and shorten individual lines of otherwise standardized length. Alexander Pope shows another way to avoid monotony in a long poem when he varies the rhythm of his heroic couplets by moving the caesura to various positions within individual lines. The poems of John Dryden and Pope are often didactic—poems written not only to entertain, but also to teach and instruct the reader. Such poems appeal directly to the intellect as well as to the five senses: the life of the mind is considered equal to the emotional and sensational life.

JOHN DONNE (1572–1631)

Song

Go and catch a falling star,
  Get with child a mandrake[1] root,
Tell me where all past years are
  Or who cleft the devil's foot,
5 Teach me to hear mermaids singing
Or to keep off envy's stinging,
     And find
     What wind
Serves to advance an honest mind.

10 If thou be'st born to strange sights,
  Things invisible to see,
Ride ten thousand days and nights
  Till age snow white hairs on thee.
Thou, when thou return'st, wilt tell me
15 All strange wonders that befell thee,
     And swear
     No where
Lives a woman true, and fair.

If thou find'st one, let me know;
20   Such a pilgrimage were sweet.
Yet do not; I would not go,
  Though at next door we might meet.
Though she were true, when you met her,
 And last, till you write your letter,
25   Yet she
     Will be
False ere I come, to two, or three.

The Sun Rising

  Busy old fool, unruly sun,
    Why dost thou thus
Through windows and through curtains call on us?
Must to thy motions lovers' seasons run?

---

[1] The large forked root of the mandrake was often credited with human attributes, because of its fancied resemblance to the human body.

5   Saucy, pedantic wretch, go chide
           Late schoolboys and sour 'prentices,
       Go tell court huntsmen that the king will ride,
       Call country ants to harvest offices.
       Love, all alike, no season knows nor clime,
10 Nor hours, days, months, which are the rags of time.

           Thy beams, so reverend and strong
               Why shouldst thou think?
       I could eclipse and cloud them with a wink,
       But that I would not lose her sight so long.
15   If her eyes have not blinded thine,
           Look, and tomorrow late tell me
       Whether both th' Indias of spice and mine
       Be where thou left'st them, or lie here with me;
       Ask for those kings whom thou saw'st yesterday,
20 And thou shalt hear: All here in one bed lay.

           She's all states, and all princes I;
               Nothing else is.
       Princes do but play us; compared to this,
       All honor's mimic, all wealth alchemy.
25   Thou, sun, art half as happy as we,
           In that the world's contracted thus;
       Thine age asks ease, and since thy duties be
       To warm the world, that's done in warming us.
       Shine here to us, and thou art everywhere;
30 This bed thy center is, these walls thy sphere.

Song

       Sweetest love, I do not go
           For weariness of thee,
       Nor in hope the world can show
           A fitter love for me;
5   But since that I
       Must die at last, 'tis best
       To use myself in jest
           Thus by feigned deaths to die.

       Yesternight the sun went hence,
10   And yet is here today;
       He hath no desire nor sense,
           Nor half so short a way.

Then fear not me,
But believe that I shall make
15 Speedier journeys, since I take
More wings and spurs than he.

O how feeble is man's power,
That, if good fortune fall,
Cannot add another hour
20 Nor a lost hour recall!
But come bad chance,
And we join to it our strength,
And we teach it art and length,
Itself o'er us to advance.

25 When thou sigh'st thou sigh'st not wind,
But sigh'st my soul away;
When thou weep'st, unkindly kind,
My life's blood doth decay.
It cannot be
30 That thou lov'st me as thou say'st,
If in thine my life thou waste:
That art the best of me.

Let not thy divining heart
Forethink me any ill;
35 Destiny may take thy part,
And may thy fears fulfil.
But think that we
Are but turned aside to sleep:
They who one another keep
40 Alive, ne'er parted be.

A Valediction: Of Weeping

Let me pour forth
My tears before thy face whilst I stay here,
For thy face coins them, and thy stamp they bear,
And by this mintage they are something worth,
5 For thus they be
Pregnant of thee;
Fruits of much grief they are, emblems of more—
When a tear falls, that Thou falls which it bore,
So thou and I are nothing then, when on a divers shore.

10   On a round ball
A workman that hath copies by can lay
An Europe, Afrique, and an Asia,
And quickly make that which was nothing, all;
    So doth each tear
15   Which thee doth wear,
A globe, yea world, by that impression grow,
Till thy tears mixed with mine do overflow
This world; by waters sent from thee, my heaven dissolvèd so.

    O more than moon,
20 Draw not up seas to drown me in thy sphere;
Weep me not dead in thine arms, but forbear
To teach the sea what it may do too soon;
    Let not the wind
    Example find,
25 To do me more harm than it purposeth;
Since thou and I sigh one another's breath,
Whoe'er sighs most is cruelist, and hastes the other's death.

The Apparition

When by thy scorn, O murd'ress, I am dead,
And that thou think'st thee free
From all solicitation from me,
Then shall my ghost come to thy bed,
 5 And thee, feigned vestal, in worse arms shall see:
Then thy sick taper will begin to wink,
And he, whose thou art then, being tired before,
Will, if thou stir, or pinch to wake him, think
   Thou call'st for more,
10 And in false sleep, will from thee shrink:
And then, poor aspen wretch, neglected thou
Bathed in a cold quicksilver sweat wilt lie
   A verier ghost than I.
What I will say, I will not tell thee now,
15 Lest that preserve thee; and since my love is spent,
I'd rather thou shouldst painfully repent,
Than by my threat'nings rest still innocent.

A Valediction: Forbidding Mourning

As virtuous men pass mildly away,
And whisper to their souls to go,

Whilst some of their sad friends do say,
"The breath goes now," and some say, "No,"

5 So let us melt and make no noise,
No tear-floods, nor sigh-tempests move;
'Twere profanation of our joys
To tell the laity our love.

Moving of th' earth brings harm and fears;
10 Men reckon what it did and meant.
But trepidation of the spheres,
Though greater far, is innocent.

Dull sùblunary lovers' love
(Whose soul is sense) cannot admit
15 Absence, because it doth remove
Those things which elemented it.

But we by a love so much refined
That ourselves know not what it is,
Inter-assurèd of the mind,
20 Care less eyes, lips, and hands to miss.

Our two souls, therefore, which are one,
Though I must go, endure not yet
A breach, but an expansion,
Like gold to airy thinness beat.

25 If they be two, they are two so
As stiff twin compasses are two;
Thy soul, the fixed foot, makes no show
To move, but doth if th' other do.

And though it in the center sit,
30 Yet when the other far doth roam,
It leans and hearkens after it,
And grows erect as that comes home.

Such wilt thou be to me, who must,
Like th' other foot, obliquely run;
35 Thy firmness makes my circle just,
And makes me end where I begun.

The Funeral

Whoever comes to shroud me, do not harm
   Nor question much
That subtle wreath of hair which crowns mine arm:
The mystery, the sign, you must not touch,
5   For 'tis my outward soul,
Viceroy to that which, then to heaven being gone,
   Will leave this to control
And keep these limbs, her provinces, from dissolutiön.

For if the sinewy thread my brain lets fall
10   Through every part
Can tie those parts, and make me one of all,
These hairs which upward grew, and strength and art
   Have from a better brain,
Can better do't—except she meant that I
15   By this should know my pain,
As prisoners then are manacled when they're condemned to die.

Whate'er she meant by it, bury it with me;
   For since I am
Love's martyr, it might breed idolatry
20 If into others' hands these relics came.
   As 'twas humility
To afford to it all that a soul can do,
   So, 'tis some bravery,
That since you would have none of me, I bury some of you.

From **Holy Sonnets**

SONNET 7

At the round earth's imagined corners, blow
Your trumpets, angels, and arise, arise
From death, you numberless infinities
Of souls, and to your scattered bodies go;
5 All whom the flood did, and fire shall o'erthrow;
All whom war, dearth, age, agues, tyrannies,
Despair, law, chance, hath slain, and you whose eyes
Shall behold God, and never taste death's woe.
But let them sleep, Lord, and me mourn a space,
10 For if above all these my sins abound,
   'Tis late to ask abundance of thy grace
When we are there; here on this lowly ground

Teach me how to repent; for that's as good
As if thou hadst sealed my pardon with thy blood.

SONNET 10

Death, be not proud, though some have callèd thee
Mighty and dreadful, for thou art not so;
For those whom thou think'st thou dost overthrow
Die not, poor Death, nor yet canst thou kill me.
5 From rest and sleep, which but thy pictures be,
Much pleasure; then from thee much more must flow;
And soonest our best men with thee do go,
Rest of their bones and souls' delivery.
Thou'rt slave to fate, chance, kings, and desperate men,
10 And dost with poison, war, and sickness dwell;
And poppy or charms can make us sleep as well
And better than thy stroke. Why swell'st thou then?
One short sleep past, we wake eternally,
And Death shall be no more: Death, thou shalt die.

SONNET 13

What if this present were the world's last night?
Mark in my heart, O soul, where thou dost dwell,
The picture of Christ crucified, and tell
Whether that countenance can thee affright,
5 Tears in His eyes quench the amazing light,
Blood fills His frowns, which from His pierced head fell.
And can that tongue adjudge thee unto hell,
Which prayed forgiveness for His foes' fierce spite?
No, no; but as in my idolatry
10 I said to all my profane mistresses,
Beauty, of pity, foulness only is
A sign of rigor: so I say to thee,
To wicked spirits are horrid shapes assigned,
This beauteous form assures a piteous mind.

SONNET 14

Batter my heart, three-personed God; for you
As yet but knock, breathe, shine, and seek to mend;
That I may rise, and stand, o'erthrow me, and bend
Your force, to break, blow, burn, and make me new.
5 I, like an usurped town, to another due,

Labor to admit you, but Oh, to no end,
Reason your viceroy in me, me should defend,
But is captived, and proves weak or untrue.
Yet dearly I love you, and would be loved fain,
10 But am betrothed unto your enemy:
Divorce me, untie, or break that knot again,
Take me to you, imprison me, for I
Except you enthral me, never shall be free,
Nor ever chaste, except you ravish me.

Hymm to God My God, in My Sickness

Since I am coming to that holy room,
    Where, with thy choir of Saints for evermore,
I shall be made thy music; as I come
    I tune the instrument here at the door,
5   And what I must do then, think now before.

Whilst my physicians by their love are grown
    Cosmographers, and I their map, who lie
Flat on this bed, that by them may be shown
    That this is my Southwest discovery
10   *Per fretum febris*,[1] by these straits to die,

I joy, that in these straits, I see my west;[2]
    For, though their currents yield return to none,
What shall my west hurt me? As west and east
    In all flat maps (and I am one) are one,
15   So death doth touch the Resurrection.

Is the Pacific Sea my home? Or are
    The eastern riches? Is Jerusalem?
Anyan,[3] and Magellan, and Gibraltàr,
    All straits, and none but straits, are ways to them,
20   Whether where Japhet dwelt, or Cham, or Shem.[4]

We think that Paradise and Calvary,
    Christ's Cross, and Adam's tree, stood in one place;

---

1 Through the straits of fever.
2 My death.
3 Modern Annam, then thought of as a strait between Asia and America.
4 Sons of Noah, said to have settled Europe, Asia, and Africa after the flood.

Look Lord, and find both Adams met in me;
   As the first Adam's sweat surrounds my face,
25   May the last Adam's blood my soul embrace.

So, in his purple wrapped receive me, Lord,
   By these his thorns give me his other crown;
And as to others' souls I preached thy word,
   Be this my text, my sermon to mine own,
30   Therefore that he may raise, the Lord throws down.

BEN JONSON (1572–1637)

On My First Son[1]

Farewell, thou child of my right hand, and joy;
My sin was too much hope of thee, loved boy,
Seven years thou wert lent to me, and I thee pay,
Exacted by thy fate, on the just day.
5 O, could I lose all father now. For why
Will man lament the state he should envy?
To have so soon 'scaped world's and flesh's rage,
And, if no other misery, yet age?
Rest in soft peace, and, asked, say, "Here doth lie
10 Ben Jonson his best piece of poetry."
For whose sake henceforth all his vows be such,
As what he loves may never like too much.

Fragmentum Petronius Arbiter, Translated

Doing a filthy pleasure is and short;
And done we straight repent us of the sport:
Let us not then rush blindly on unto it,
Like lustful beasts, that only know to do it,
5 For lust will languish and that heat decay;
But thus, thus, keeping endless holiday,
Let us together closely lie and kiss;
There is no labor, nor no shame in this.
This hath pleased, doth please, and long will please; never
10 Can this decay, but is beginning ever.

---

[1] Jonson's son died of the plague on his seventh birthday in 1603.

Epitaph on S. P.,[1] a Child of Queen Elizabeth's Chapel

Weep with me, all you that read
    This little story;
And know, for whom a tear you shed
    Death's self is sorry.
5 'Twas a child that so did thrive
    In grace and feature,
As heaven and nature seemed to strive
    Which owned the creature.
Years he numbered scarce thirteen
10   When fates turned cruel,
Yet three filled zodiacs[2] had he been
    The stage's jewel;
And did act, what now we moan,
    Old men so duly,
15 As, sooth, the Parcae[3] thought him one,
    He played so truly.
So, by error, to his fate
    They all consented;
But viewing him since, alas, too late!
20   They have repented,
And have sought, to give new birth,
    In baths to steep him;
But being so much too good for earth,
    Heaven vows to keep him.

Epitaph on Elizabeth, L. H.

Wouldst thou hear what man can say
In a little? Reader, stay.
Underneath this stone doth lie
As much beauty as could die;
5 Which in life did harbor give
To more virtue than doth live.
If at all she had a fault,
Leave it buried in this vault.
One name was Elizabeth;
10 The other, let it sleep with death:

---

1 Salomon Pavy, a child actor who had performed in Jonson's plays.
2 Three years.
3 The three Fates.

Fitter, where it died, to tell,
Than that it lived at all. Farewell!

Queen and Huntress

Queen and huntress, chaste and fair,
Now the sun is laid to sleep,
Seated in thy silver chair,
State in wonted manner keep:
5   Hesperus entreats thy light,
    Goddess excellently bright.

Earth, let not thy envious shade
Dare itself to interpose;
Cynthia's shining orb was made
10 Heaven to clear when day did close:
    Bless us, then, with wishèd sight,
    Goddess excellently bright.

Lay thy bow of pearl apart,
And thy crystal-shining quiver;
15 Give unto the flying hart
Space to breathe, how short soever;
    Thou that mak'st a day of night,
    Goddess excellently bright.

Come, My Celia

Come, my Celia, let us prove,
While we can, the sports of love;
Time will not be ours forever,
He, at length, our goods will sever.
5 Spend not then his gifts in vain:
Suns that set may rise again;
But if once we lose this light,
'Tis with us perpetual night.
Why should we defer our joys?
10 Fame and rumor are but toys.
Cannot we delude the eyes
Of a few poor household spies?
Or his easier ears beguile,
So removèd by our wile?
15 'Tis no sin love's fruits to steal,
But the sweet thefts to reveal;

To be taken, to be seen,
These have crimes accounted been.

Still to be Neat

Still to be neat, still to be dressed,
As you were going to a feast;
Still to be powdered, still perfumed:
Lady, it is to be presumed,
5 Though art's hid causes are not found,
All is not sweet, all is not sound.

Give me a look, give me a face,
That makes simplicity a grace;
Robes loosely flowing, hair as free:
10 Such sweet neglect more taketh me
Than all the adulteries of art;
They strike mine eyes, but not my heart.

Song: To Celia

Drink to me only with thine eyes,
 And I will pledge with mine;
Or leave a kiss but in the cup,
 And I'll not look for wine.
5 The thirst that from the soul doth rise
 Doth ask a drink divine;
But might I of Jove's nectar sup,
 I would not change for thine.

I sent thee late a rosy wreath,
10 Not so much honoring thee
As giving it a hope, that there
 It could not withered be.
But thou thereon didst only breathe,
 And sent'st it back to me;
15 Since when it grows, and smells, I swear,
 Not of itself but thee.

From A Pindaric Ode

It is not growing like a tree
 In bulk, doth make man better be;
Or standing long an oak, three hundred year,

To fall a log at last, dry, bald, and sear:
5   A lily of a day
        Is fairer far, in May,
      Although it fall and die that night;
      It was the plant and flower of light.
      In small proportions we just beauties see,
10   And in short measures life may perfect be.

To the Memory of My Beloved, the Author, Mr. William Shakespeare, and What He Hath Left Us

To draw no envy, Shakespeare, on thy name,
    Am I thus ample to thy book and fame;
While I confess thy writings to be such
    As neither man nor Muse can praise too much.
5 'Tis true, and all men's suffrage. But these ways
    Were not the paths I meant unto thy praise:
For seeliest ignorance on these may light,
    Which, when it sounds at best, but echoes right;
Or blind affection, which doth ne'er advance
10   The truth, but gropes, and urgeth all by chance;
Or crafty malice might pretend this praise,
    And think to ruin where it seemed to raise.
These are as some infàmous bawd or whore
    Should praise a matron. What could hurt her more?
15 But thou art proof against them, and indeed
    Above th' ill fortune of them, or the need.
I therefore will begin. Soul of the age!
    The applause! delight! the wonder of our stage!
My Shakespeare, rise; I will not lodge thee by
20   Chaucer or Spenser, or bid Beaumont lie
A little further, to make thee a room:[1]
    Thou art a monument, without a tomb;
And art alive still while thy book doth live,
    And we have wits to read and praise to give
25 That I not mix thee so, my brain excuses;
    I mean with great, but disproportioned Muses:
For, if I thought my judgment were of years,
    I should commit thee surely with thy peers,
And tell how far thou didst our Lyly outshine,

---

[1] In Westminster Abbey.

30   Or sporting Kyd, or Marlowe's mighty line.
    And though thou hadst small Latin, and less Greek,
       From thence to honor thee I would not seek
    For names, but call forth thundering Aeschylus,
       Euripides, and Sophocles to us,
35 Pacuvius, Accius,[2] him of Cordova dead,[3]
       To life again, to hear thy buskin[4] tread
    And shake a stage; or, when thy socks were on,[5]
       Leave thee alone for the comparison
    Of all that insolent Greece or haughty Rome
40   Sent forth, or since did from their ashes come.
       Triumph, my Britain; thou hast one to show
       To whom all scenes of Europe homage owe.
    He was not of an age, but for all time!
    And all the Muses still were in their prime
45 When like Apollo he came forth to warm
       Our ears, or like a Mercury to charm!
    Nature herself was proud of his designs,
       And joyed to wear the dressing of his lines!
    Which were so richly spun, and woven so fit,
50   As, since, she will vouchsafe no other wit.
    The merry Greek, tart Aristophanes,
       Neat Terence, witty Plautus, now not please,
    But antiquated and deserted lie,
       As they were not of Nature's family.
55 Yet must I not give Nature all: thy art,
       My gentle Shakespeare, must enjoy a part.
    For though the poet's matter Nature be,
       His art doth give the fashion; and that he
    Who casts[6] to write a living line must sweat
60   (Such as thine are) and strike the second heat
    Upon the Muse's anvil, turn the same,
       And himself with it, that he thinks to frame,
    Or for the laurel he may gain a scorn;
       For a good poet's made, as well as born.
65 And such wert thou. Look how the father's face

---

2 Roman tragedians.
3 Seneca.
4 High boot worn by Greek tragic actors.
5 Low shoes worn in comedy.
6 Aspires.

Lives in his issue; even so the race
Of Shakespeare's mind and manners brightly shines
    In his well-turnèd and true-filèd lines,
In each of which he seems to shake a lance,
70   As brandished at the eyes of ignorance.
Sweet swan of Avon, what a sight it were
    To see thee in our waters yet appear,
And make those flights upon the banks of Thames
    That so did take Eliza and our James!
75 But stay, I see thee in the hemisphere
    Advanced, and made a constellation there!
Shine forth, thou star of poets, and with rage
    Or influence chide or cheer the drooping stage,
Which, since thy flight from hence, hath mourned like night
80   And dèspairs day, but for thy volume's light.

JOHN WEBSTER (1580?–1625)

Call for the Robin Redbreast and the Wren

Call for the robin redbreast and the wren,
    Since o'er shady groves they hover
    And with leaves and flowers do cover
The friendless bodies of unburied men.
5   Call unto his funeral dole
    The ant, the fieldmouse, and the mole,
To rear him hillocks that shall keep him warm,
And (when gay tombs are robbed) sustain no harm;
But keep the wolf far thence, that's foe to men;
10 For with his nails he'll dig them up again.

ROBERT HERRICK (1591–1674)

From **Hesperides**

THE ARGUMENT[1] OF HIS BOOK

I sing of brooks, of blossoms, birds, and bowers:
Of April, May, of June, and July flowers.

---

1 "Argument" is the term formerly used for a brief summary of the contents of a book.

I sing of May-poles, hock-carts, wassails, wakes,
Of bridegrooms, brides, and of their bridal cakes.
5 I write of youth, of love, and have access
By these, to sing of cleanly wantonness.
I sing of dews, of rains, and piece by piece
Of balm, of oil, of spice, and ambergris.
I sing of times trans-shifting; and I write
10 How roses first came red, and lilies white.
I write of groves, of twilights, and I sing
The court of Mab, and of the Fairy King.
I write of hell; I sing (and ever shall)
Of heaven, and hope to have it after all.

Delight in Disorder

A sweet disorder in the dress
Kindles in clothes a wantonness:
A lawn[1] about the shoulders thrown
Into a fine distraction,
5 An erring lace which here and there
Enthralls the crimson stomacher,[2]
A cuff neglectful and thereby
Ribbands to flow confusedly,
A winning wave (deserving note)
10 In the tempestuous petticoat,
A careless shoestring in whose tie
I see a wild civility,
Do more bewitch me than when art
Is too precise in every part.

Another Grace for a Child

Here a little child I stand,
Heaving up my either hand;
Cold as paddocks[1] though they be,
Here I lift them up to thee,
5 For a benison to fall
On our meat, and on us all. Amen.

---

[1] A scarf of fine linen.
[2] Bodice.
[1] Toads or frogs.

Upon Julia's Clothes

Whenas in silks my Julia goes,
Then, then, methinks, how sweetly flows
That liquefaction of her clothes.

Next, when I cast mine eyes and see
5 That brave vibration each way free,
O how that glittering taketh me!

To the Virgins, to Make Much of Time

Gather ye rosebuds while ye may:
    Old Time is still a-flying;
And this same flower that smiles today,
    Tomorrow will be dying.

5 The glorious lamp of heaven, the sun,
    The higher he's a-getting,
The sooner will his race be run,
    And nearer he's to setting.

That age is best which is the first,
10   When youth and blood are warmer;
But being spent, the worse, and worst
    Times, still succeed the former.

Then be not coy, but use your time;
    And while ye may, go marry:
15 For, having lost but once your prime,
    You may for ever tarry.

GEORGE HERBERT (1593–1633)

The Pulley

When God at first made man,
Having a glass of blessings standing by,
    "Let us," said he, "pour on him all we can:
Let the world's riches, which dispersèd lie,
5   Contract into a span."

So Strength first made a way;
Then Beauty flowed; then Wisdom, Honor, Pleasure.
    When almost all was out, God made a stay,

Perceiving that alone of all his treasure
10   Rest in the bottom lay.

"For if I should," said he,
"Bestow this jewel also on my creature,
   He would adore my gifts instead of me,
And rest in Nature, not the God of Nature;
15   So both should losers be.

"Yet let him keep the rest,
But keep them with repining restlessness:
   Let him be rich and weary, that at least,
If goodness lead him not, yet weariness
20   May toss him to my breast."

The Collar[1]

I struck the board [2] and cried, "No more!
      I will abroad!
What, shall I ever sigh and pine?
My lines and life are free: free as the road,
5   Loose as the wind, as large as store.
      Shall I be still in suit? [3]
Have I no harvest but a thorn
To let me blood, and not restore
What I have lost with cordial [4] fruit?
10   Sure there was wine
Before my sighs did dry it; there was corn
      Before my tears did drown it.
Is the year only lost to me?
      Have I no bays[5] to crown it,
15 No flowers, no garlands gay? all blasted?
      All wasted?
Not so, my heart; but there is fruit,
      And thou hast hands.
Recover all thy sigh-blown age
20 On double pleasures. Leave thy cold dispute

---

1 The iron band encircling the neck of a prisoner or slave; also perhaps a pun on "choler" as "rebellious anger."
2 Dining table.
3 Always petitioning.
4 Restorative.
5 Laurels.

Of what is fit and not. Forsake thy cage,
       Thy rope of sands,
Which petty thoughts have made and made to thee
   Good cable, to enforce and draw,
25   And be thy law,
While thou didst wink and wouldst not see.
        Away! take heed!
        I will abroad!
Call in thy death's-head there! Tie up thy fears!
30   He that forbears
   To suit and serve his need,
      Deserves his load."
But as I raved, and grew more fierce and wild
      At every word,
35 Methought I heard one calling, "Child!"
     And I replied, "My Lord."

Easter Wings

Lord, who createdst man in wealth and store,
   Though foolishly he lost the same,
     Decaying more and more,
       Till he became
5   Most poor:
        With thee
        O let me rise
     As larks, harmoniously,
   And sing this day thy victories:
10 Then shall the fall further the flight in me.

My tender age in sorrow did begin:
   And still with sicknesses and shame
     Thou didst so punish sin,
       That I became
15   Most thin.
        With thee
       Let me combine,
    And feel this day thy victory:
   For, if I imp[1] my wing on thine,
20 Affliction shall advance the flight in me.

---

[1] In falconry, to graft feathers on a damaged wing.

Virtue

Sweet day, so cool, so calm, so bright,
The bridal of the earth and sky,
The dew shall weep thy fall tonight,
　　For thou must die.

5 Sweet rose, whose hue, angry and brave,
Bids the rash gazer wipe his eye,
Thy root is ever in its grave,
　　And thou must die.

Sweet spring, full of sweet days and roses,
10 A box where sweets compacted lie,
My music shows ye have your closes,[1]
　　And all must die.

Only a sweet and virtuous soul,
Like seasoned timber, never gives;
15 But though the whole world turn to coal,
　　Then chiefly lives.

Love (III)

Love bade me welcome; yet my soul drew back,
　　Guilty of dust and sin.
But quick-eyed Love, observing me grow slack
　　From my first entrance in,
5 Drew nearer to me, sweetly questioning
　　If I lacked anything.

"A guest," I answered, "worthy to be here."
　　Love said, "You shall be he."
"I, the unkind, ungrateful? Ah my dear,
10　　I cannot look on Thee."
Love took my hand, and smiling, did reply,
　　"Who made the eyes but I?"

"Truth, Lord, but I have marred them; let my shame
　　Go where it doth deserve."
15 "And know you not," says Love, "who bore the blame?"

---

[1] Musical cadences.

"My dear, then I will serve."
"You must sit down," says Love, "and taste my meat."
So I did sit and eat.

THOMAS CAREW (1594?–1639?)

A Song

Ask my no more where Jove bestows,
When June is past, the fading rose;
For in your beauty's orient deep
These flowers, as in their causes, sleep.

5 Ask me no more whither do stray
The golden atoms of the day;
For in pure love heaven did prepare
Those powders to enrich your hair.

Ask me no more whither doth haste
10 The nightingale, when May is past;
For in your sweet dividing throat
She winters, and keeps warm her note.

Ask me no more where those stars light,
That downwards fall in dead of night;
15 For in your eyes they sit, and there
Fixèd become, as in their sphere.

Ask me no more if east or west
The phoenix builds her spicy nest;
For unto you at last she flies,
20 And in your fragrant bosom dies.

EDMUND WALLER (1606–1687)

On a Girdle

That which her slender waist confined
Shall now my joyful temples bind;
No monarch but would give his crown
His arms might do what this has done.

5 It was my heaven's extremest sphere,
The pale which held that lovely deer;

My joy, my grief, my hope, my love
Did all within this circle move.

A narrow compass, and yet there
10 Dwelt all that's good and all that's fair:
Give me but what this ribband bound,
Take all the rest the sun goes round!

Go, Lovely Rose

Go, lovely rose,
Tell her that wastes her time and me,
That now she knows,
When I resemble her to thee,
5   How sweet and fair she seems to be.

Tell her that's young,
And shuns to have her graces spied,
That hadst thou sprung
In deserts, where no men abide,
10   Thou must have uncommended died.

Small is the worth
Of beauty from the light retired;
Bid her come forth,
Suffer herself to be desired,
15   And not blush so to be admired.

Then die, that she
The common fate of all things rare
May read in thee;
How small a part of time they share,
20   That are so wondrous sweet and fair.

JOHN MILTON (1608–1674)

How Soon Hath Time

How soon hath Time, the subtle thief of youth,
Stolen on his wing my three-and-twentieth year!
My hasting days fly on with full career,
But my late spring no bud or blossom shew'th.
5 Perhaps my semblance might deceive the truth
That I to manhood am arrived so near;

And inward ripeness doth much less appear,
That some more timely-happy spirits endu'th.[1]
Yet be it less or more, or soon or slow,
10 It shall be still in strictest measure even
To that same lot, however mean or high,
Toward which Time leads me, and the will of Heaven;
All is, if I have grace to use it so,
As ever in my great Taskmaster's eye.

On His Blindness

When I consider how my light is spent,
Ere half my days, in this dark world and wide,
And that one talent which is death to hide
Lodged with me useless, though my soul more bent
5 To serve therewith my Maker, and present
My true account, lest he returning chide,
"Doth God exact day labor, light denied?"
I fondly ask; but Patience, to prevent
That murmur, soon replies: "God doth not need
10 Either man's work or his own gifts; who best
Bear his mild yoke, they serve him best. His state
Is kingly: thousands at his bidding speed
And post o'er land and ocean without rest.
They also serve who only stand and wait."

At a Solemn Music

Blest pair of Sirens, pledges of Heaven's joy,
Sphere-born harmonious sisters, Voice and Verse,
Wed your divine sounds, and mixed power employ
Dead things with inbreathed sense able to pierce,
5 And to our high-raised fantasy present
That undisturbed song of pure consent,[1]
Aye sung before the sapphire-colored throne
To him that sits thereon
With saintly shout and solemn jubilee,
10 Where the bright seraphim in burning row
Their loud uplifted angel-trumpets blow,
And the cherubic host in thousand choirs

---

1 Endoweth.
1 Harmony.

Touch their immortal harps of golden wires,
With those just spirits that wear victorious palms,
15 Hymns devout and holy psalms
Singing everlastingly;
That we on earth with undiscording voice
May rightly answer that melodious noise;
As once we did, till disproportioned sin
20 Jarred against nature's chime, and with harsh din
Broke the fair music that all creatures made
To their great Lord, whose love their motion swayed
In perfect diapason,[2] whilst they stood
In first obedience, and their state of good.
25 O may we soon again renew that song,
And keep in tune with Heaven, till God ere long
To his celestial consort us unite.
To live with him, and sing in endless morn of light.

On the Late Massacre in Piedmont

Avenge, O Lord, thy slaughtered saints, whose bones
Lie scattered on the Alpine mountains cold;
Even them who kept thy truth so pure of old
When all our fathers worshipped stocks and stones,
5 Forget not: in thy book record their groans
Who were thy sheep and in their ancient fold
Slain by the bloody Piemontese, that rolled
Mother with infant down the rocks. Their moans
The vales redoubled to the hills, and they
10 To heaven. Their martyred blood and ashes sow
O'er all the Italian fields where still doth sway
The triple tyrant;[1] that from these may grow
A hundredfold, who, having learnt thy way,
Early may fly the Babylonian woe.[2]

From Paradise Lost, Book XII

He[1] ended; and thus Adam last replied:
"How soon hath thy prediction, seer blest,

---

[2] Concord.

[1] The Pope, whose tiara has three crowns.

[2] The Roman Catholic Church was identified by the Puritans with the Babylon of Revelation 17-18.

[1] The Angel Michael.

Measured this transient world, the race of time,
Till time stand fixed! Beyond is all abyss,
555 Eternity, whose end no eye can reach.
Greatly instructed I shall hence depart,
Greatly in peace of thought, and have my fill
Of knowledge, what this vessel can contain,
Beyond which was my folly to aspire.
560 Henceforth I learn that to obey is best,
And love with fear the only God, to walk
As in his presence, ever to observe
His providence, and on him sole depend,
Merciful over all his works, with good
565 Still overcoming evil, and by small
Accomplishing great things, by things deemed weak
Subverting worldly strong, and worldly wise
By simply meek; that suffering for truth's sake
Is fortitude to highest victory,
570 And to the faithful death the gate of life,
Taught this by his example whom I now
Acknowledge my Redeemer ever blest."
    To whom thus also the angel last replied:
"This having learned, thou hast attained the sum
575 Of wisdom; hope no higher, though all the stars
Thou knew'st by name, and all the ethereal powers,
All secrets of the deep, all Nature's works,
Or works of God in heaven, air, earth, or sea,
And all the riches of this world enjoy'dst,
580 And all the rule, one empire. Only add
Deeds to thy knowledge answerable; add faith;
Add virtue, patience, temperance; add love,
By name to come called charity, the soul
Of all the rest: then wilt thou not be loath
585 To leave this Paradise, but shalt possess
A paradise within thee, happier far.
Let us descend now, therefore, from this top
Of speculation; for the hour precise
Exacts our parting hence; and, see, the guards,
590 By me encamped on yonder hill, expect
Their motion, at whose front a flaming sword
In signal of remove waves fiercely round.
We may no longer stay. Go, waken Eve;
Her also I with gentle dreams have calmed,
595 Portending good, and all her spirits composed
To meek submission: thou at season fit

Let her with thee partake what thou hast heard,
Chiefly what may concern her faith to know,
The great deliverance by her seed to come
600 (For by the woman's seed) on all mankind,
That ye may live, which will be many days,
Both in one faith unanimous; though sad
With cause for evils past, yet much more cheered
With meditation on the happy end."
605   He ended, and they both descend the hill;
Descended, Adam to the bower where Eve
Lay sleeping ran before, but found her waked;
And thus with words not sad she him received:
     "Whence thou return'st and whither went'st I know;
610 For God is also in sleep, and dreams advise,
Which he hath sent propitious, some great good
Presaging, since, with sorrow and heart's distress
Wearied, I fell asleep: but now lead on;
In me is no delay; with thee to go,
615 Is to stay here; without thee here to stay,
Is to go hence unwilling; thou to me
Art all things under heaven, all places thou,
Who for my willful crime art banished hence.
This further consolation yet secure
620 I carry hence: though all by me is lost,
Such favor I unworthy am vouchsafed,
By me the promised seed shall all restore."
     So spake our mother Eve, and Adam heard
Well pleased, but answered not; for now too nigh
625 The Archangel stood, and from the other hill
To their fixed station, all in bright array,
The Cherubim descended, on the ground
Gliding metèorous, as evening mist
Risen from a river o'er the marish glides
630 And gathers ground fast at the laborer's heel
Homeward returning. High in front advanced,
The brandished sword of God before them blazed
Fierce as a comet, which with torrid heat,
And vapor as the Libyan air adust,
635 Began to parch that temperate clime; whereat
In either hand the hastening Angel caught
Our lingering parents, and to the eastern gate
Led them direct, and down the cliff as fast
To the subjected plain; then disappeared.
640 They, looking back, all the eastern side beheld

Of Paradise, so late their happy seat,
Waved over by that flaming brand, the gate
With dreadful faces thronged and fiery arms.
Some natural tears they dropped, but wiped them soon;
645 The world was all before them, where to choose
Their place of rest, and Providence their guide:
They hand in hand, with wandering steps and slow,
Through Eden took their solitary way.

THE END

SIR JOHN SUCKLING (1609–1642)

Song

Why so pale and wan, fond lover?
　　Prithee, why so pale?
Will, when looking well can't move her,
　　Looking ill prevail?
5　Prithee, why so pale?

Why so dull and mute, young sinner?
　　Prithee, why so mute?
Will, when speaking well can't win her,
　　Saying nothing do't?
10　Prithee, why so mute?

Quit, quit, for shame; this will not move,
　　This cannot take her.
If of herself she will not love,
　　Nothing can make her:
15　The devil take her!

The Constant Lover

Out upon it! I have loved
　　Three whole days together;
And am like to love three more,
　　If it prove fair weather!

5 Time shall moult away his wings,
　　Ere he shall discover
In the whole wide world again
　　Such a constant lover.

But the spite on't is, no praise
10   Is due at all to me:
Love with me had made no stays,
    Had it any been but she.

Had it any been but she,
    And that very face,
15 There had been at least ere this
    A dozen dozen in her place!

ANNE BRADSTREET (1612?–1672)

To My Dear and Loving Husband

If ever two were one, then surely we.
If ever man were lov'd by wife, then thee;
If ever wife was happy in a man,
Compare with me ye women if you can.
5 I prize thy love more then whole Mines of gold,
Or all the riches that the East doth hold.
My love is such that Rivers cannot quench,
Nor ought but love from thee, give recompence.
Thy love is such I can no way repay,
10 The heavens reward thee manifold I pray.
Then while we live, in love lets so persever,
That when we live no more, we may live ever.

A Letter to Her Husband, Absent upon Publick Employment

My head, my heart, mine Eyes, my life, nay more,
My joy, my Magazine of earthly store,
If two be one, as surely thou and I,
How stayest thou there, whilst I at *Ipswich* lye?
5 So many steps, head from the heart to sever
If but a neck, soon should we be together:
I like the earth this season, mourn in black,
My Sun is gone so far in's Zodiack,
Whom whilst I 'joy'd, nor storms, nor frosts I felt,
10 His warmth such frigid colds did cause to melt.
My chilled limbs now nummed lye forlorn;
Return, return sweet *Sol* from *Capricorn;*

In this dead time, alas, what can I more
Then view those fruits which through thy heat I bore?
15 Which sweet contentment yield me for a space,
True living Pictures of their Fathers face.
O strange effect! now thou art *Southward* gone,
I weary grow, the tedious day so long;
But when thou *Northward* to me shalt return,
20 I wish my Sun may never set, but burn
Within the Cancer of my glowing breast,
The welcome house of him my dearest guest.
Where ever, ever stay, and go not thence,
Till natures sad decree shall call thee hence;
25 Flesh of thy flesh, bone of thy bone,
I here, thou there, yet both but one.

ABRAHAM COWLEY (1618–1667)

From **Anacreontics**

Or some copies of verses translated
paraphrastically out of Anacreon

DRINKING

The thirsty earth soaks up the rain,
And drinks, and gapes for drink again.
The plants suck in the earth, and are
With constant drinking fresh and fair.
5 The sea itself, which one would think
Should have but little need of drink,
Drinks ten thousand rivers up,
So filled that they o'erflow the cup.
The busy sun—and one would guess
10 By's drunken, fiery face no less—
Drinks up the sea, and when he's done,
The moon and stars drink up the sun.
They drink and dance by their own light;
They drink and revel all the night.
15 Nothing in nature's sober found,
But an eternal health goes round.
Fill up the bowl, then, fill it high,
Fill all the glasses there, for why
Should every creature drink but I?
20 Why, man of morals, tell me why?

RICHARD LOVELACE (1618–1657?)

To Althea, From Prison

When Love with unconfinèd wings
  Hovers within my gates,
And my divine Althea brings
  To whisper at the grates;
5 When I lie tangled in her hair
  And fettered to her eye:
The gods that wanton in the air
  Know no such liberty.

When flowing cups run swiftly round,
10 With no allaying Thames,
Our careless heads with roses bound,
  Our hearts with loyal flames;
When thirsty grief in wine we steep,
  When healths and draughts go free:
15 Fishes that tipple in the deep
  Know no such liberty.

When, like committed linnets, I
  With shriller throat shall sing
The sweetness, mercy, majesty,
20 And glories of my King;
When I shall voice aloud how good
  He is, how great should be:
Enlargèd winds that curl the flood
  Know no such liberty.

25 Stone walls do not a prison make,
  Nor iron bars a cage;
Minds innocent and quiet take
  That for an hermitage.
If I have freedom in my love,
30 And in my soul am free,
Angels alone, that soar above,
  Enjoy such liberty.

To Lucasta, Going to the Wars

Tell me not, sweet, I am unkind,
  That from the nunnery

Of thy chaste breast and quiet mind
   To war and arms I fly.

5 True, a new mistress now I chase,
   The first foe in the field;
And with a stronger faith embrace
   A sword, a horse, a shield.

Yet this inconstancy is such
10   As you too shall adore;
I could not love thee, dear, so much,
   Loved I not honor more.

ANDREW MARVELL (1621–1678)

The Nymph Complaining for the Death of Her Fawn

The wanton troopers riding by
Have shot my fawn, and it will die.
Ungentle men! they cannot thrive
Who killed thee. Thou ne'er didst alive
5 Them any harm, alas! nor could
Thy death yet do them any good.
I'm sure I never wished them ill:
Nor do I for all this, nor will:
But, if my simple prayers may yet
10 Prevail with Heaven to forget
Thy murder, I will join my tears,
Rather than fail. But, O my fears!
It cannot die so. Heaven's king
Keeps register of everything,
15 And nothing may we use in vain;
Even beasts must be with justice slain,
Else men are made their deodands.[1]
Though they should wash their guilty hands
In this warm life-blood which doth part
20 From thine, and wound me to the heart,
Yet could they not be clean; their stain

---

[1] In English law, a deodand was a personal chattel which, having occasioned the death of a human, was forfeited to the Crown to be applied to pious uses.

Is dyed in such a purple grain.
There is not such another in
The world, to offer for their sin.
25 Unconstant Sylvio, when yet
I had not found him counterfeit,
One morning (I remember well),
Tied in this silver chain and bell,
Gave it to me: nay, and I know
30 What he said then, I'm sure I do:
Said he, "Look how your huntsman here
Hath taught a fawn to hunt his dear."
But Sylvio soon had me beguiled;
This waxèd tame, while he grew wild,
35 And quite regardless of my smart,
Left me his fawn, but took his heart.
    Thenceforth I set myself to play
My solitary time away
With this; and, very well content,
40 Could so mine idle life have spent;
For it was full of sport, and light
Of foot and heart, and did invite
Me to its game: it seemed to bless
Itself in me; how could I less
45 Than love it? O, I cannot be
Unkind to a beast that loveth me.
    Had it lived long, I do not know
Whether it too might have done so
As Sylvio did; his gifts might be
50 Perhaps as false, or more, than he;
But I am sure, for aught that I
Could in so short a time espy,
Thy love was far more better than
The love of false and cruel men.
55 With sweetest milk and sugar first
I it at my own fingers nursed;
And as it grew, so every day
It waxed more white and sweet than they.
It had so sweet a breath! And oft
60 I blushed to see its foot more soft
And white, shall I say than my hand?
Nay, any lady's of the land.
    It is a wondrous thing how fleet
'Twas on those little silver feet;
65 With what a pretty skipping grace

It oft would challenge me the race;
And, when't had left me far away,
'Twould stay, and run again, and stay;
For it was nimbler much than hinds,
70 And trod as if on the fòur winds.
     I have a garden of my own,
But so with roses overgrown,
And lilies, that you would it guess
To be a little wilderness;
75 And all the spring-time of the year
It only lovèd to be there.
Among the beds of lilies I
Have sought it oft, where it should lie,
Yet could not, till itself would rise,
80 Find it, although before mine eyes;
For, in the flaxen lilies' shade,
It like a bank of lilies laid.
Upon the roses it would feed,
Until its lips e'en seemed to bleed.
85 And then to me 'twould boldly trip,
And print those roses on my lip.
But all its chief delight was still
On roses thus itself to fill,
And its pure virgin limbs to fold
90 In whitest sheets of lilies cold:
Had it lived long, it would have been
Lilies without, roses within.
     O help! O help! I see it faint
And die as calmly as a saint!
95 See how it weeps! the tears do come
Sad, slowly dropping like a gum.
So weeps the wounded balsam; so
The holy frankincense doth flow;
The brotherless Heliades[2]
100 Melt in such amber tears as these.
     I in a golden vial will
Keep these two crystal tears, and fill
It till it do o'erflow with mine,
Then place it in Diana's shrine.
105   Now my sweet fawn is vanished to

---

[2] Daughters of the sun-god (Helios or Apollo), who mourned their brother
Phaethon until they were turned into poplars, and their tears into amber.

Whither the swans and turtles[3] go;
In fair Elysium to endure,
With milk-like lambs and ermines pure.
O do not run too fast; for I
110 Will but bespeak thy grave, and die.
First, my unhappy statue shall
Be cut in marble, and withal,
Let it be weeping too; but there
The engraver sure his art may spare;
115 For I so truly thee bemoan,
That I shall weep, though I be stone,
Until my tears, still dropping, wear
My breast, themselves engraving there;
There at my feet shalt thou be laid,
120 Of purest alabaster made;
For I would have thine image be
White as I can, though not as thee.

To His Coy Mistress

Had we but world enough, and time,
This coyness, lady, were no crime.
We would sit down, and think which way
To walk, and pass our long love's day.
5 Thou by the Indian Ganges' side
Shouldst rubies find; I by the tide
Of Humber would complain. I would
Love you ten years before the Flood,
And you should, if you please, refuse
10 Till the conversion of the Jews.
My vegetable love should grow
Vaster than empires, and more slow;
An hundred years should go to praise
Thine eyes and on thy forehead gaze,
15 Two hundred to adore each breast,
But thirty thousand to the rest:
An age at least to every part,
And the last age should show your heart.
For, lady, you deserve this state,
20 Nor would I love at lower rate.
But at my back I always hear
Time's wingèd chariot hurrying near;

---

3 Turtledoves.

And yonder all before us lie
Deserts of vast eternity.
25 Thy beauty shall no more be found,
Nor in thy marble vault shall sound
My echoing song; then worms shall try
That long preserved virginity,
And your quaint honor turn to dust,
30 And into ashes all my lust.
 The grave's a fine and private place,
But none, I think, do there embrace.
  Now, therefore, while the youthful hue
Sits on thy skin like morning dew,
35 And while thy willing soul transpires
At every pore with instant fires,
Now let us sport us while we may,
And now, like am'rous birds of prey,
Rather at once our time devour
40 Than languish in his slow-chapped power.
Let us roll all our strength and all
Our sweetness up into one ball,
And tear our pleasures with rough strife
Through the iron gates of life.
45 Thus, though we cannot make our sun
Stand still, yet we will make him run.

HENRY VAUGHAN (1622?–1695)

The Retreat

Happy those early days! when I
Shined in my angel-infancy;
Before I understood this place
Appointed for my second race,
5 Or taught my soul to fancy aught
But a white, celestial thought;
When yet I had not walked above
A mile, or two, from my first love,
And looking back at that short space
10 Could see a glimpse of His bright face;
When on some gilded cloud or flower
My gazing soul would dwell an hour,
And in those weaker glories spy
Some shadows of eternity;
15 Before I taught my tongue to wound

My conscience with a sinful sound,
Or had the black art to dispense
A several ¹ sin to every sense;
But felt through all this fleshly dress
20 Bright shoots of everlastingness.
   O, how I long to travel back,
And tread again that ancient track!
That I might once more reach that plain,
Where first I left my glorious train;
25 From whence th' enlightened spirit sees
That shady city of palm trees—
But ah! my soul with too much stay
Is drunk, and staggers in the way!
Some men a forward motion love,
30 But I by backward steps would move,
And when this dust falls to the urn,
In that state I came, return.

The World

I saw eternity the other night
Like a great ring of pure and endless light,
   All calm, as it was bright;
And round beneath it, time, in hours, days, years,
5   Driven by the spheres,¹
Like a vast shadow moved, in which the world
   And all her train were hurled.
The doting lover in his quaintest strain
   Did there complain;
10 Near him, his lute, his fancy, and his flights,
   Wit's sour delights,
With gloves and knots, the silly snares of pleasure.
   Yet his dear treasure,
All scattered lay, while he his eyes did pour
15   Upon a flower.

The darksome statesman, hung with weights and woe
Like a thick midnight fog, moved there so slow
   He did not stay, nor go.

---

¹ Separate.
¹ Of the Ptolemaic universe.

Condemning thoughts, like sad eclipses, scowl
20   Upon his soul;
And clouds of crying witnesses without
        Pursued him with one shout.
Yet digged the mole and, lest his ways be found,
        Worked underground,
25 Where he did clutch his prey; but One did see
        That policy.
Churches and altars fed him; perjuries
        Were[2] gnats and flies;
It rained about him blood and tears, but he
30   Drank them as free.[3]

The fearful miser on a heap of rust
Sat pining all his life there, did scarce trust
        His own hands with the dust,
Yet would not place one piece above,[4] but lives
35   In fear of thieves.
Thousands there were as frantic as himself,
        And hugged each one his pelf;
The downright epicure placed heaven in sense,
        And scorned pretence;
40 While others, slipped into a wide excess,
        Said little less.
The weaker sort slight, trivial wares enslave,
        Who think them brave;[5]
And poor, despisèd Truth sat counting by[6]
45   Their victory.

Yet some, who all this while did weep and sing,
And sing and weep, soared up into the ring;
        But most would use no wing.
"O fools," said I, "thus to prefer dark night
50   Before true light!
To live in grots and caves, and hate the day
        Because it shows the way,

---

2 Were as insignificant as.
3 As freely as they rained about him.
4 In heaven.
5 Splendid.
6 Observing.

The way which from this dead and dark abode
    Leads up to God,
55 A way where you might tread the sun, and be
    More bright than he!"
But, as I did their madness so discuss,
    One whispered thus:
"This ring the Bridegroom did for none provide
60   But for his bride." [7]

They Are All Gone

They are all gone into the world of light!
    And I alone sit lingering here;
Their very memory is fair and bright,
    And my sad thoughts doth clear.

5 It glows and glitters in my cloudy breast
    Like stars upon some gloomy grove,
Or those faint beams in which this hill is dressed,
    After the sun's remove.

I see them walking in an air of glory,
10   Whose light doth trample on my days:
My days, which are at best but dull and hoary,
    Mere glimmering and decays.

O holy hope! and high humility,
    High as the heavens above!
15 These are your walks, and you have showed them me
    To kindle my cold love.

Dear, beauteous death! The jewel of the just,
    Shining nowhere but in the dark;
What mysteries do lie beyond thy dust,
20   Could man outlook that mark! [1]

He that hath found some fledged bird's nest may know
    At first sight if the bird be flown;
But what fair well or grove he sings in now,
    That is to him unknown.

---

[7] The marriage of Christ and the Church.
[1] Boundary.

²⁵ And yet, as angels in some brighter dreams
    Call 'to the soul when man doth sleep,
So some strange thoughts transcend our wonted themes,
    And into glory peep.

If a star were confined into a tomb,
³⁰   Her captive flames must needs burn there;
But when the hand that locked her up gives room,
    She'll shine through all the sphere.

O Father of eternal life, and all
    Created glories under thee!
³⁵ Resume thy spirit² from this world of thrall
    Into true liberty.

Either disperse these mists, which blot and fill
    My pèrspective³ still as they pass,
Or else remove me hence unto that hill
⁴⁰   Where I shall need no glass.

JOHN DRYDEN (1631–1700)

Lines Printed under the Engraved Portrait of Milton

Three poets, in three distant ages born,
Greece, Italy, and England did adorn.
The first in loftiness of thought surpassed,
The next in majesty, in both the last:
5 The force of Nature could no farther go;
To make a third she joined the former two.

Why Should a Foolish Marriage Vow

Why should a foolish marriage vow,
    Which long ago was made,
Oblige us to each other now
    When passion is decayed?
5 We loved, and we loved, as long as we could,
    Till our love was loved out in us both;

---

² Take back my soul.
³ Telescope.

But our marriage is dead when the pleasure is fled:
   'Twas pleasure first made it an oath.

If I have pleasures for a friend,
10   And farther love in store,
What wrong has he whose joys did end,
   And who could give no more?
'Tis a madness that he should be jealous of me,
   Or that I should bar him of another:
15 For all we can gain is to give ourselves pain,
   When neither can hinder the other.

To the Memory of Mr. Oldham[1]

Farewell, too little and too lately known,
Whom I began to think and call my own:
For sure our souls were near allied, and thine
Cast in the same poetic mold with mine.
5 One common note on either lyre did strike,
And knaves and fools we both abhorred alike.
To the same goal did both our studies drive;
The last set out the soonest did arrive.
Thus Nisus[2] fell upon the slippery place,
10 While his young friend performed and won the race.
O early ripe! to thy abundant store
What could advancing age have added more?
It might (what nature never gives the young)
Have taught the numbers of thy native tongue.
15 But satire needs not those, and wit will shine
Through the harsh cadence of a rugged line.
A noble error, and but seldom made,
When poets are by too much force betrayed.
Thy gen'rous fruits, though gathered ere their prime,
20 Still showed a quickness; and maturing time
But mellows what we write to the dull sweets of rime.
Once more, hail, and farewell! farewell, thou young,
But ah! too short, Marcellus[3] of our tongue!
Thy brows with ivy and with laurels bound;
25 But fate and gloomy night encompass thee around.

---

1 John Oldham, a writer of satire.
2 In the *Aeneid*, V., Nisus slips in the blood of a sacrifice, allowing his friend
   Euryalus to win the race.
3 Nephew of the emperor Augustus; he died at twenty.

JONATHAN SWIFT (1667–1745)

A Description of the Morning

Now hardly here and there an hackney-coach
Appearing, showed the ruddy morn's approach.
Now Betty from her master's bed had flown,
And softly stole to discompose her own.
5 The slipshod 'prentice from his master's door,
Had pared the dirt, and sprinkled round the floor.
Now Moll had whirled her mop with dext'rous airs,
Prepared to scrub the entry and the stairs.
The youth with broomy stumps began to trace
10 The kennel edge, where wheels had worn the place.
The small-coal man was heard with cadence deep,
'Till drowned in shriller notes of chimney sweep,
Duns at his lordship's gate began to meet,
And brickdust Moll had screamed through half a street.
15 The turnkey now his flock returning sees,
Duly let out a-nights to steal for fees.
The watchful bailiffs take their silent stands;
And schoolboys lag with satchels in their hands.

A Description of a City Shower

Careful observers may foretell the hour
(By sure prognostics) when to dread a show'r.
While rain depends, the pensive cat gives o'er
Her frolics, and pursues her tail no more.
5 Returning home at night, you'll find the sink
Strike your offended sense with double stink.
If you be wise, then go not far to dine;
You'll spend in coach-hire more than save in wine.
A coming show'r your shooting corns presage,
10 Old a-ches throb, your hollow tooth will rage:
Saunt'ring in coffee-house is Dulman seen;
He damns the climate, and complains of spleen.
    Meanwhile the South, rising with dabbled wings,
A sable cloud athwart the welkin flings,
15 That swill'd more liquor than it could contain,
And, like a drunkard, gives it up again.
Brisk Susan whips her linen from the rope,
While the first drizzling show'r is borne aslope:
Such is that sprinkling, which some careless quean
20 Flirts on you from her mop, but not so clean:

You fly, invoke the gods; then turning, stop
To rail; she singing, still whirls on her mop.
Not yet the dust had shunn'd th' unequal strife,
But, aided by the wind, fought still for life,
25 And wafted with its foe by vi'lent gust,
'Twas doubtful which was rain, and which was dust.
Ah! where must needy poet seek for aid,
When dust and rain at once his coat invade?
Sole coat, where dust cemented by the rain
30 Erects the nap, and leaves a cloudy stain.
Now in contiguous drops the flood comes down,
Threat'ning with deluge this *devoted* town.
To shops in crowds the daggled females fly,
Pretend to cheapen goods, but nothing buy.
35 The Templar spruce, while ev'ry spout's abroach,
Stays till 'tis fair, yet seems to call a coach.
The tuck'd-up sempstress walks with hasty strides,
While streams run down her oil'd umbrella's sides.
Here various kinds, by various fortunes led,
40 Commence acquaintance underneath a shed.
Triumphant Tories, and desponding Whigs,
Forget their feuds, and join to save their wigs.
Box'd in a chair the beau impatient sits,
While spouts run clatt'ring o'er the roof by fits,
45 And ever and anon with frightful din
The leather sounds; he trembles from within.
So when Troy chairmen bore the wooden steed,
Pregnant with Greeks impatient to be freed
(Those bully Greeks, who, as the moderns do,
50 Instead of paying chairmen, ran them through),
Laocoön struck the outside with his spear,
And each imprison'd hero quak'd for fear.
Now from all parts the swelling kennels flow,
And bear their trophies with them as they go:
55 Filth of all hues and odor seem to tell
What street they sail'd from, by their sight and smell.
They, as each torrent drives with rapid force,
From Smithfield to St. Pulchre's shape their course,
And in huge confluence join'd at Snowhill ridge,
60 Fall from the conduit prone to Holborn bridge.
— Sweeping from butcher's stalls, dung, guts, and blood,
Drown'd puppies, stinking sprats, all drench'd in mud,
Dead cats, and turnip-tops, come tumbling down the flood.

JOSEPH ADDISON (1672–1719)

Ode

The spacious firmament on high,
With all the blue ethereal sky,
And spangled heav'ns, a shining frame,
Their great Original proclaim:
5 Th' unwearied sun, from day to day,
Does his Creator's power display,
And publishes to every land
The work of an Almighty Hand.

Soon as the evening shades prevail,
10 The moon takes up the wondrous tale,
And nightly to the listening earth
Repeats the story of her birth:
Whilst all the stars that round her burn,
And all the planets, in their turn,
15 Confirm the tidings as they roll,
And spread the truth from pole to pole.

What though, in solemn silence, all
Move round the dark terrestrial ball?
What though nor real voice nor sound
20 Amid their radiant orbs be found?
In reason's ear they all rejoice,
And utter forth a glorious voice,
Forever singing, as they shine,
"The Hand that made us is divine."

JOHN GAY (1685–1732)

Songs from The Beggar's Opera

IF THE HEART OF A MAN

If the heart of a man is depressed with cares,
The mist is dispelled when a woman appears;
    Like the notes of a fiddle, she sweetly, sweetly
Raises the spirits, and charms our ears.
5   Roses and lilies her cheeks disclose,
    But her ripe lips are more sweet than those.

                    Press her,
                    Caress her
                    With blisses,
10   Her kisses
          Dissolve us in pleasure, and soft repose.

THE MODES OF THE COURT

The modes of the court so common are grown
    That a true friend can hardly be met;
Friendship for interest is but a loan,
    Which they let out for what they can get.
5   'Tis true, you find
        Some friends so kind,
Who will give you good counsel themselves to defend.
        In sorrowful ditty,
        They promise, they pity,
10 But shift you, for money, from friend to friend.

ALEXANDER POPE (1688–1744)

Ode on Solitude

Happy the man whose wish and care
    A few paternal acres bound,
Content to breathe his native air,
                    In his own ground.

5 Whose herds with milk, whose fields with bread,
    Whose flocks supply him with attire,
Whose trees in summer yield him shade,
                    In winter fire.

    Blest, who can unconcernedly find
10   Hours, days, and years slide soft away,
    In health of body, peace of mind,
                    Quiet by day,

    Sound sleep by night; study and ease,
        Together mixed; sweet recreation;
15 And innocence, which most does please
                    With meditation.

Thus let me live, unseen, unknown;
 Thus unlamented let me die;
Steal from the world, and not a stone
20   Tell where I lie.

From **An Essay on Man**

 VI. What would this Man? Now upward will he soar,
And, little less than angel, would be more;
175 Now, looking downwards, just as grieved appears
To want the strength of bulls, the fur of bears.
Made for his use all creatures if he call,
Say what their use, had he the powers of all?
Nature to these without profusion kind,
180 The proper organs, proper pow'rs assigned;
Each seeming want compènsated of course,
Here with degrees of swiftness, there of force;
All in exact proportion to the state;
Nothing to add, and nothing to abate.
185 Each beast, each insect, happy in its own:
Is heav'n unkind to man, and man alone?
Shall he alone, whom rational we call,
Be pleased with nothing if not blessed with all?
 The bliss of man (could pride that blessing find)
190 Is not to act or think beyond mankind;
No pow'rs of body or of soul to share,
But what his nature and his state can bear.
Why has not man a microscopic eye?
For this plain reason, man is not a fly.
195 Say what the use, were finer optics giv'n,
T' inspect a mite, not comprehend the heav'n?
Or touch, if tremblingly alive all o'er,
To smart and agonize at ev'ry pore?
Or, quick effluvia darting through the brain,
200 Die of a rose in aromatic pain?
If nature thundered in his op'ning ears,
And stunned him with the music of the spheres,
How would he wish that heav'n had left him still
The whisp'ring zephyr and the purling rill!
205 Who finds not Providence all good and wise,
Alike in what it gives and what it denies?
 VII. Far as creation's ample range extends,
The scale of sensual, mental pow'rs ascends:

Mark how it mounts to man's imperial race
210 From the green myriads in the peopled grass;
What modes of sight betwixt each wide extreme,
The mole's dim curtain and the lynx's beam:
Of smell, the headlong lioness between,
And hound sagacious on the tainted green:
215 Of hearing, from the life that fills the flood
To that which warbles through the vernal wood:
The spider's touch, how exquisitely fine!
Feels at each thread, and lives alone the line:
In the nice[1] bee what sense, so subtly true,
220 From pois'nous herbs extracts the healing dew?
How instinct varies in the grov'ling swine,
Compared, half-reas'ning elephant, with thine!
'Twixt that and reason what a nice[2] barrièr!
For ever sep'rate, yet for ever near!
225 Remembrance and reflection how allied;
What thin partitions sense from thought divide:
And middle natures how they long to join,
Yet never pass th' insuperable line!
Without this just gradation could they be
230 Subjected, these to those, or all to thee?

SAMUEL JOHNSON (1709–1784)

The Vanity of Human Wishes

Let observation with extensive view,
Survey mankind, from China to Peru;
Remark each anxious toil, each eager strife,
And watch the busy scenes of crowded life;
5 Then say how hope and fear, desire and hate,
O'erspread with snares the clouded maze of fate,
Where wav'ring man, betrayed by vent'rous pride,
To tread the dreary paths without a guide,
As treach'rous phantoms in the mist delude,
10 Shuns fancied ills, or chases airy good;
How rarely reason guides the stubborn choice,
Rules the bold hand, or prompts the suppliant voice;
How nations sink, by darling schemes oppressed,

---

1 Discriminating.
2 Fine.

When vengeance listens to the fool's request.
15 Fate wings with ev'ry wish th' afflictive dart,
Each gift of nature, and each grace of art,
With fatal heat impetuous courage glows,
With fatal sweetness elocution flows,
Impeachment stops the speaker's pow'rful breath,
20 And restless fire precipitates on death.
    But scarce observed, the knowing and the bold
Fall in the gen'ral massacre of gold;
Wide-wasting pest! that rages unconfined,
And crowds with crimes the records of mankind;
25 For gold his sword the hireling ruffian draws,
For gold the hireling judge distorts the laws;
Wealth heaped on wealth, nor truth nor safety buys,
The dangers gather as the treasures rise.
    Let hist'ry tell where rival kings command,
30 And dubious title shakes the madded land,
When statutes glean the refuse of the sword,
How much more safe the vassal than the lord;
Low skulks the hind beneath the rage of pow'r,
And leaves the wealthy traitor in the Tow'r,
35 Untouched his cottage, and his slumbers sound,
Though confiscation's vultures hover round.
    The needy traveler, serene and gay,
Walks the wild heath, and sings his toil away.
Does envy seize thee? crush th' upbraiding joy,
40 Increase his riches and his peace destroy;
Now fears in dire vicissitude invade,
The rustling brake alarms, and quiv'ring shade,
Nor light nor darkness bring his pain relief,
One shows the plunder, and one hides the thief.
45   Yet still one gen'ral cry the skies assails,
And gain and grandeur load the tainted gales;
Few know the toiling statesman's fear or care,
Th' insidious rival and the gaping heir.
    Once more, Democritus, arise on earth,
50 With cheerful wisdom and instructive mirth,
See motley life in modern trappings dressed,
And feed with varied fools th' eternal jest:
Thou who couldst laugh where want enchained caprice,
Toil crushed conceit, and man was of a piece;
55 Where wealth unloved without a mourner died,
And scarce a sycophant was fed by pride;
Where ne'er was known the form of mock debate,

Or seen a new-made mayor's unwieldy state;
Where change of fav'rites made no change of laws,
60 And senates heard before they judged a cause;
How wouldst thou shake at Britain's modish tribe,
Dart the quick taunt, and edge the piercing gibe?
Attentive truth and nature to descry,
And pierce each scene with philosophic eye.
65 To thee were solemn toys or empty show,
The robes of pleasure and the veils of woe:
All aid the farce, and all thy mirth maintain,
Whose joys are causeless, or whose griefs are vain.
　　Such was the scorn that filled the sage's mind,
70 Renewed at ev'ry glance on humankind;
How just that scorn ere yet thy voice declare,
Search every state, and canvass ev'ry prayer,
　　Unnumbered suppliants crowd Preferment's gate,
Athirst for wealth, and burning to be great;
75 Delusive Fortune hears th' incessant call,
They mount, they shine, evaporate, and fall.
On ev'ry stage the foes of peace attend,
Hate dogs their flight, and insult mocks their end.
Love ends with hope, the sinking statesman's door
80 Pours in the morning worshiper no more;
For growing names the weekly scribbler lies,
To growing wealth the dedicator flies,
From every room descends the painted face,
That hung the bright Palladium of the place,
85 And smoked in kitchens, or in auctions sold,
To better features yields the frame of gold;
For now no more we trace in ev'ry line
Heroic worth, benevolence divine:
The form distorted justifies the fall,
90 And detestation rids th' indignant wall.
　　But will not Britain hear the last appeal,
Sign her foes' doom, or guard her fav'rites' zeal?
Through Freedom's sons no more remonstrance rings,
Degrading nobles and controlling kings;
95 Our supple tribes repress their patriot throats,
And ask no questions but the price of votes;
With weekly libels and septennial ale,
Their wish is full to riot and to rail.
　　In full-blown dignity, see Wolsey stand,
100 Law in his voice, and fortune in his hand:
To him the church, the realm, their pow'rs consign,

Through him the rays of regal bounty shine,
Turn'd by his nod the stream of honor flows,
His smile alone security bestows:
105 Still to new heights his restless wishes tow'r,
Claim leads to claim, and pow'r advances pow'r;
Till conquest unresisted ceased to please,
And rights submitted, left him none to seize.
At length his sov'reign frowns—the train of state
110 Mark the keen glance, and watch the sign to hate.
Where'er he turns he meets a stranger's eye,
His suppliants scorn him, and his followers fly;
At once is lost the pride of aweful state,
The golden canopy, the glitt'ring plate,
115 The regal palace, the luxurious board,
The liv'ried army, and the menial lord.
With age, with cares, with maladies oppressed,
He seeks the refuge of monastic rest.
Grief aids disease, remembered folly stings,
120 And his last sighs reproach the faith of kings.
    Speak thou, whose thoughts at humble peace repine,
Shall Wolsey's wealth, with Wolsey's end be thine?
Or liv'st thou now, with safer pride content,
The wisest justice on the banks of Trent?
125 For why did Wolsey near the steeps of fate,
On weak foundations raise th' enormous weight?
Why but to sink beneath misfortune's blow,
With louder ruin to the gulfs below?
    What gave great Villiers to th' assassin's knife,
130 And fixed disease on Harley's closing life?
What murdered Wentworth, and what exiled Hyde,
By kings protected, and to kings allied?
What but their wish indulged in courts to shine,
And pow'r too great to keep, or to resign?
135   When first the college rolls receive his name,
The young enthusiast quits his ease for fame;
Through all his veins the fever of renown
Burns from the strong contagion of the gown;
O'er Bodley's dome his future labors spread,
140 And Bacon's mansion trembles o'er his head.
Are these thy views? proceed, illustrious youth,
And virtue guard thee to the throne of Truth!
Yet should thy soul indulge the gen'rous heat,
Till captive Science yields her last retreat;
145 Should Reason guide thee with her brightest ray,

And pour on misty Doubt resistless day;
Should no false Kindness lure to loose delight,
Nor Praise relax, nor Difficulty fright;
Should tempting Novelty thy cell refrain,
150 And Sloth effuse her opiate fumes in vain;
Should Beauty blunt on fops her fatal dart,
Nor claim the triumph of a lettered heart;
Should no Disease thy torpid veins invade,
Nor Melancholy's phantoms haunt thy shade;
155 Yet hope not life from grief or danger free,
Nor think the doom of man reversed for thee:
Deign on the passing world to turn thine eyes,
And pause awhile from letters, to be wise;
There mark what ills the scholar's life assail,
160 Toil, envy, want, the patron, and the jail.
See nations slowly wise, and meanly just,
To buried merit raise the tardy bust.
If dreams yet flatter, once again attend,
Hear Lydiat's life, and Galileo's end.
165   Nor deem, when learning her last prize bestows,
The glitt'ring eminence exempt from foes;
See when the vulgar 'scape, despised or awed,
Rebellion's vengeful talons seize on Laud.
From meaner minds, though smaller fines content,
170 The plundered palace or sequestered rent;
Marked out by dangerous parts he meets the shock,
And fatal Learning leads him to the block:
Around his tomb let Art and Genius weep,
But hear his death, ye blockheads, hear and sleep.
175   The festal blazes, the triumphal show,
The ravished standard, and the captive foe,
The senate's thanks, the gàzette's pompous tale,
With force resistless o'er the brave prevail.
Such bribes the rapid Greek[1] o'er Asia whirled,
180 For such the steady Romans shook the world;
For such in distant lands the Britons shine,
And stain with blood the Danube or the Rhine;
This pow'r has praise, that virtue scarce can warm,
Till fame supplies the universal charm.
185 Yet Reason frowns on War's unequal game,
Where wasted nations raise a single name,

---

[1] Alexander the Great.

And mortgaged states their grandsires' wreaths regret,
From age to age in everlasting debt;
Wreaths which at last the dear-bought right convey
190 To rust on medals, or on stones decay.
　　　On what foundation stands the warrior's pride,
How just his hopes let Swedish Charles[2] decide;
A frame of adamant, a soul of fire,
No dangers fright him, and no labors tire;
195 O'er love, o'er fear, extends his wide domain,
Unconquered lord of pleasure and of pain;
No joys to him pacific scepters yield,
War sounds the trump, he rushes to the field;
Behold surrounding kings their pow'r combine,
200 And one capitulate, and one resign;
Peace courts his hand, but spreads her charms in vain;
"Think nothing gained," he cries, " 'till nought remain,
On Moscow's walls till Gothic standards fly,
And all be mine beneath the polar sky."
205 The march begins in military state,
And nations on his eye suspended wait;
Stern Famine guards the solitary coast,
And Winter barricades the realms of Frost;
He comes, not want and cold his course delay;—
210 Hide, blushing Glory, hide Pultowa's day:
The vanquished hero leaves his broken bands,
And shows his miseries in distant lands;
Condemned a needy supplicant to wait,
While ladies interpose, and slaves debate.
215 But did not Chance at length her error mend?
Did no subverted empire mark his end?
Did rival monarchs give the fatal wound?
Or hostile millions press him to the ground?
His fall was destined to a barren strand,
220 A petty fortress, and a dubious hand;
He left the name, at which the world grew pale,
To point a moral, or adorn a tale.
　　　All times their scenes of pompous woes afford,
From Persia's tyrant [3] to Bavaria's lord.[4]

---

2 Charles XII of Sweden, defeated by Peter the Great at Pultowa in 1709.
3 Xerxes.
4 Charles Albert, Elector of Bavaria, whose claim to the title of Holy Roman
  Emperor in opposition to Maria Theresa led to the War of the Austrian Succes-
  sion, 1740–1748.

225 In gay hostility, and barb'rous pride,
    With half mankind embattled at his side,
    Great Xerxes comes to seize the certain prey,
    And starves exhausted regions in his way;
    Attendant Flatt'ry counts his myriads o'er,
230 Till counted myriads sooth his pride no more;
    Fresh praise is tried till madness fires his mind,
    The waves he lashes, and enchains the wind;
    New pow'rs are claimed, new pow'rs are still bestowed,
    Till rude resistance lops the spreading god;
235 The daring Greeks deride the martial show,
    And heap their valleys with the gaudy foe;
    Th' insulted sea with humbler thoughts he gains,
    A single skiff to speed his flight remains;
    Th' incumbered oar scarce leaves the dreaded coast
240 Through purple billows and a floating host.
       The bold Bavarian, in a luckless hour,
    Tries the dread summits of Caesarean pow'r,
    With unexpected legions bursts away,
    And sees defenseless realms receive his sway;
245 Short sway! fair Austria spreads her mournful charms,
    The queen, the beauty, sets the world in arms;
    From hill to hill the beacons rousing blaze
    Spreads wide the hope of plunder and of praise;
    The fierce Croatian, and the wild Hussar,
250 And all the sons of ravage crowd the war;
    The baffled prince in honor's flatt'ring bloom
    Of hasty greatness finds the fatal doom,
    His foes derision, and his subjects blame,
    And steals to death from anguish and from shame.
255   "Enlarge my life with multitude of days,"
    In health, in sickness, thus the suppliant prays;
    Hides from himself his state, and shuns to know,
    That life protracted is protracted woe.
    Time hovers o'er, impatient to destroy,
260 And shuts up all the passages of joy:
    In vain their gifts the bounteous seasons pour,
    The fruit autumnal, and the vernal flow'r,
    With listless eyes the dotard views the store,
    He views, and wonders that they please no more;
265 Now pall the tasteless meats, and joyless wines,
    And Luxury with sighs her slave resigns.
    Approach, ye minstrels, try the soothing strain,
    Diffuse the tuneful lenitives of pain:

No sounds alas would touch th' impervious ear,
270 Though dancing mountains witnessed Orpheus near;
Nor lute nor lyre his feeble pow'rs attend,
Nor sweeter music of a virtuous friend,
But everlasting dictates crowd his tongue,
Perversely grave, or positively wrong.
275 The still returning tale, and ling'ring jest,
Perplex the fawning niece and pampered guest,
While growing hopes scarce awe the gath'ring sneer,
And scarce a legacy can bribe to hear;
The watchful guests still hint the last offence,
280 The daughter's petulance, the son's expence,
Improve his heady rage with treach'rous skill,
And mold his passions till they make his will.
    Unnumbered maladies his joints invade,
Lay siege to life and press the dire blockade;
285 But unextinguished avarice still remains,
And dreaded losses aggravate his pains;
He turns, with anxious heart and crippled hands,
His bonds of debt, and mortgages of lands;
Or views his coffers with suspicious eyes,
290 Unlocks his gold, and counts it till he dies.
    But grant, the virtues of a temp'rate prime
Bless with an age exempt from scorn or crime;
An age that melts with unperceived decay,
And glides in modest innocence away;
295 Whose peaceful day Benevolence endears,
Whose night congratulating Conscience cheers;
The gen'ral fav'rite as the gen'ral friend:
Such age there is, and who shall wish its end?
    Yet ev'n on this her load Misfortune flings,
300 To press the weary minutes' flagging wings:
New sorrow rises as the day returns,
A sister sickens, or a daughter mourns.
Now kindred Merit fills the sable bier,
Now lacerated Friendship claims a tear.
305 Year chases year, decay pursues decay,
Still drops some joy from with'ring life away;
New forms arise, and diff'rent views engage,
Superfluous lags the vet'ran on the stage,
Till pitying Nature signs the last release,
310 And bids afflicted worth retire to peace.
    But few there are whom hours like these await,
Who set unclouded in the gulfs of fate.

From Lydia's monarch[5] should the search descend,
By Solon cautioned to regard his end,
315 In life's last scene what prodigies surprise,
Fears of the brave, and follies of the wise?
From Marlb'rough's eyes the streams of dotage flow,
And Swift expires a driv'ler and a show.
   The teeming mother, anxious for her race,
320 Begs for each birth the fortune of a face:
Yet Vane[6] could tell what ills from beauty spring;
And Sedley[7] cursed the form that pleased a king.
Ye nymphs of rosy lips and radiant eyes,
Whom pleasure keeps too busy to be wise,
325 Whom joys with soft varieties invite,
By day the frolic, and the dance by night,
Who frown with vanity, who smile with art,
And ask the latest fashion of the heart,
What care, what rules your heedless charms shall save,
330 Each nymph your rival, and each youth your slave?
Against your fame with fondness hate combines,
The rival batters, and the lover mines.
With distant voice neglected Virtue calls,
Less heard and less, the faint remonstrance falls;
335 Tired with contempt, she quits the slipp'ry reign,
And Pride and Prudence take her seat in vain.
In crowd at once, where none the pass defend,
The harmless Freedom, and the private Friend.
The guardians yield, by force superior plied;
340 By Int'rest, Prudence; and by Flatt'ry, Pride.
Now beauty falls betrayed, despised, distressed,
And hissing Infamy proclaims the rest.
   Where then shall Hope and Fear their objects find?
Must dull Suspense corrupt the stagnant mind?
345 Must helpless man, in ignorance sedate,
Roll darkling down the torrent of his fate?
Must no dislike alarm, no wishes rise,
No cries attempt the mercies of the skies?
Enquirer, cease, petitions yet remain,
350 Which heav'n may hear, nor deem religion vain.

---

[5] Croesus.
[6] Anne Vane, deserted mistress of Frederick, Prince of Wales.
[7] Catherine Sedley, mistress of the Duke of York, abandoned when he became James II.

Still raise for good the supplicating voice,
But leave to heav'n the measure and the choice,
Safe in his pow'r, whose eyes discern afar
The secret ambush of a specious prayer.
355 Implore his aid, in his decisions rest,
Secure whate'er he gives, he gives the best.
Yet when the sense of sacred presence fires,
And strong devotion to the skies aspires,
Pour forth thy fervors for a healthful mind,
360 Obedient passions, and a will resigned;
For love, which scarce collective man can fill;
For patience sov'reign o'er transmuted ill;
For faith, that panting for a happier seat,
Counts death kind Nature's signal of retreat:
365 These goods for man the laws of heav'n ordain,
These goods he grants, who grants the pow'r to gain;
With these celestial wisdom calms the mind,
And makes the happiness she does not find.

On the Death of Mr. Robert Levet

Condemned to hope's delusive mine,
　　As on we toil from day to day,
By sudden blasts, or slow decline,
　　Our social comforts drop away.

5 Well tried through many a varying year,
　　See Levet to the grave descend;
Officious, innocent, sincere,
　　Of ev'ry friendless name the friend.

Yet still he fills affection's eye,
10　　Obscurely wise, and coarsely kind;
Nor, lettered arrogance, deny
　　Thy praise to merit unrefined.

When fainting nature called for aid,
　　And hov'ring death prepared the blow,
15 His vig'rous remedy displayed
　　The power of art without the show.

In misery's darkest cavern known,
　　His useful care was ever nigh,

Where hopeless anguish poured his groan,
20   And lonely want retired to die.

No summons mocked by chill delay,
    No petty gain disdained by pride,
The modest wants of ev'ry day
    The toil of ev'ry day supplied.

25 His virtues walked their narrow round,
    Nor made a pause, nor left a void;
And sure th' Eternal Master found
    The single talent well employed.

The busy day, the peaceful night,
30   Unfelt, uncounted, glided by;
His frame was firm, his powers were bright,
    Though now his eightieth year was nigh.

Then with no throbbing fiery pain,
    No cold gradations of decay,
35 Death broke at once the vital chain,
    And freed his soul the nearest way.

3

~ A BRIEF HISTORY

Some Romantic poets experimented within established forms. Other poets worked in more irregular and personal veins. In Christopher Smart's *Rejoice in the Lamb* the lines are composed roughly as sentences arranged in parallels. Gray's *Elegy,* on the other hand, combines a sober relective tone with a pastoral English churchyard setting to create a conventionally rhymed and structured poem. Thus the sonnet, ode, and elegy continue to be written side by side with more experimental and evolutionary poetry. Wordsworth's irregular ode, *Intimations of Immortality,* and Keats's Horatian *Ode on a Grecian Urn* may be contrasted with the personal symbolism of William Blake's *The Sick Rose* or *The Tyger.* Blake is also an example of a poet who turns his attention to subjects not previously considered to be poetic: *The Little Black Boy* and *The Chimney Sweeper.* While Coleridge creates a drug-induced landscape in the exotic pleasure dome of *Kubla Khan,* a lyric poet like Robert Burns will write about a subject as simple as a mouse. The older poetic dictions, dictions in which the language of poetry was ordinarily different from that of prose or the marketplace, begin to give up their exclusive hold. Instead of using formal language, some poets— like their anonymous forebears the balladeers—find a language closer to home. The poems of the Scot, Burns, echo the sounds of ordinary speech. Even while poets are writing about their contemporary scene, however, they also hark back to other times. In a 19th-century poem,

Wordsworth's sonnet *Composed Upon Westminster Bridge* alludes to the classic myths and the ancient pagan gods Proteus and Triton. Keats, of course, turns to an antique artifact to buttress his ode to beauty and truth—a case again of anchoring an idea, beauty, to the reality of an image, the Grecian Urn.

THOMAS GRAY (1716–1771)

Ode on a Distant Prospect of Eton College

Ye distant spires, ye antique towers,
    That crown the wat'ry glade,
Where grateful Science still adores
    Her Henry's holy shade;[1]
5 And ye, that from the stately brow
Of Windsor's heights th' expanse below
    Of grove, of lawn, of mead survey,
Whose turf, whose shade, whose flowers among
Wanders the hoary Thames along
10   His silver-winding way;

Ah, happy hills! ah, pleasing shade!
    Ah, fields beloved in vain,
Where once my careless childhood strayed
    A stranger yet to pain!
15 I feel the gales that from ye blow
A momentary bliss bestow,
    As waving fresh their gladsome wing,
My weary soul they seem to sooth,
And, redolent of joy and youth,
20   To breathe a second spring.

Say, Father Thames, for thou hast seen
    Full many a sprightly race
Disporting on thy margent green
    The paths of pleasure trace,
25 Who foremost now delight to cleave
With pliant arm thy glassy wave?
    The captive linnet which enthrall?
What idle progeny succeed
To chase the rolling circle's speed,
30   Or urge the flying ball?

While some on earnest business bent
    Their murm'ring labors ply
'Gainst graver hours, that bring constraint
    To sweeten liberty:
35 Some bold adventurers disdain

---

1 Henry VI, founder of Eton.

133

The limits of their little reign,
    And unknown regions dare descry;
Still as they run they look behind,
They hear a voice in every wind,
40   And snatch a fearful joy.

Gay hope is theirs by fancy fed,
    Less pleasing when possest;
The tear forgot as soon as shed,
    The sunshine of the breast:
45 Theirs buxom health of rosy hue,
Wild wit, invention ever-new,
    And lively cheer of vigor born;
The thoughtless day, the easy night,
The spirits pure, the slumbers light,
50   That fly th' approach of morn.

Alas, regardless of their doom,
    The little victims play!
No sense have they of ills to come,
    Nor care beyond today:
55 Yet see how all around 'em wait
The ministers of human fate,
    And black Misfortune's baleful train!
Ah, show them where in ambush stand
To seize their prey the murth'rous band!
60   Ah, tell them they are men!

These shall the fury Passions tear,
    The vultures of the mind,
Disdainful Anger, pallid Fear,
    And Shame that skulks behind;
65 Or pining Love shall waste their youth,
Or Jealousy with rankling tooth,
    That inly gnaws the secret heart,
And Envy wan, and faded Care,
Grim-visaged comfortless Despair,
70   And Sorrow's piercing dart.

Ambition this shall tempt to rise,
    Then whirl the wretch from high,
To bitter Scorn a sacrifice,
    And grinning Infamy.
75 The stings of Falsehood those shall try,

And hard Unkindness' altered eye,
   That mocks the tear it forced to flow;
And keen Remorse with blood defiled,
And moody Madness laughing wild
80   Amid severest woe.

Lo, in the vale of years beneath
   A grisly troop are seen,
The painful family of Death,
   More hideous than their Queen:
85 This racks the joints, this fires the veins,
That every laboring sinew strains,
   Those in the deeper vitals rage:
Lo, Poverty, to fill the band,
That numbs the soul with icy hand,
90   And slow-consuming Age.

To each his suff'rings: all are men,
   Condemned alike to groan,
The tender for another's pain,
   Th' unfeeling for his own.
95 Yet, ah! why should they know their fate?
Since sorrow never comes too late,
   And happiness too swiftly flies.
Thought would destroy their paradise.
No more; where ignorance is bliss,
100   'Tis folly to be wise.

Elegy Written in a Country Churchyard

The curfew tolls the knell of parting day;
The lowing herd wind slowly o'er the lea;
The plowman homeward plods his weary way,
And leaves the world to darkness and to me.

5 Now fades the glimmering landscape on the sight,
And all the air a solemn stillness holds,
Save where the beetle wheels his droning flight,
And drowsy tinklings lull the distant folds;

Save that from yonder ivy-mantled tow'r,
10 The moping owl does to the moon complain
Of such as, wand'ring near her secret bow'r,
Molest her ancient solitary reign.

Beneath those rugged elms, that yew tree's shade,
Where heaves the turf in many a mold'ring heap,
15 Each in his narrow cell for ever laid,
The rude forefathers of the hamlet sleep.

The breezy call of incense-breathing Morn,
The swallow twitt'ring from the straw-built shed,
The cock's shrill clarion, or the echoing horn,
20 No more shall rouse them from their lowly bed.

For them no more the blazing hearth shall burn,
Or busy housewife ply her evening care;
No children run to lisp their sire's return,
Or climb his knees the envied kiss to share.

25 Oft did the harvest to their sickle yield;
Their furrow oft the stubborn glebe has broke;
How jocund did they drive their team afield!
How bowed the woods beneath their sturdy stroke!

Let not Ambition mock their useful toil,
30 Their homely joys, and destiny obscure;
Nor Grandeur hear with a disdainful smile,
The short and simple annals of the poor.

The boast of heraldry, the pomp of pow'r,
And all that beauty, all that wealth, e'er gave
35 Awaits alike th' inevitable hour.
The paths of glory lead but to the grave.

Nor you, ye proud, impute to these the fault
If Mem'ry o'er their tomb no trophies raise,
Where, through the long-drawn aisle and fretted vault,
40 The pealing anthem swells the note of praise.

Can storied urn¹ or animated ² bust
Back to its mansion call the fleeting breath?
Can Honor's voice provoke³ the silent dust,
Or Flattery soothe the dull cold ear of Death?

---

¹ Funeral urn.
² Lifelike.
³ Call forth.

45 Perhaps in this neglected spot is laid
Some heart once pregnant with celestial fire;
Hands that the rod of empire might have swayed,
Or waked to ecstasy the living lyre.

But Knowledge to their eyes her ample page,
50 Rich with the spoils of time, did ne'er unroll;
Chill Penury repressed their noble rage,[4]
And froze the genial [5] current of the soul.

Full many a gem of purest ray serene
The dark unfathomed caves of ocean bear;
55 Full many a flower is born to blush unseen,
And waste its sweetness on the desert air.

Some village Hampden,[6] that with dauntless breast
The little tyrant of his fields withstood;
Some mute inglorious Milton here may rest,
60 Some Cromwell guiltless of his country's blood.

Th' applause of list'ning senates to command,
The threats of pain and ruin to despise,
To scatter plenty o'er a smiling land,
And read their hist'ry in a nation's eyes,

65 Their lot forbade: nor circumscribed alone
Their growing virtues, but their crimes confined;
Forbade to wade through slaughter to a throne
And shut the gates of mercy on mankind,

The struggling pangs of conscious truth to hide,
70 To quench the blushes of ingenuous shame,
Or heap the shrine of Luxury and Pride
With incense kindled at the Muse's flame.

Far from the madding crowd's ignoble strife,
Their sober wishes never learned to stray;
75 Along the cool sequestered vale of life
They kept the noiseless tenor of their way.

---

4 Inspiration.
5 Creative.
6 John Hampden, leader of the opposition to the tyranny of Charles I.

Yet ev'n these bones from insult to protect,
Some frail memorial still erected nigh,
With uncouth rimes and shapeless sculpture decked,
80 Implores the passing tribute of a sigh.

Their name, their years, spelt by th' unlettered Muse,
The place of fame and elegy supply;
And many a holy text around she strews,
That teach the rustic moralist to die.

85 For who, to dumb Forgetfulness a prey,
This pleasing anxious being e'er resigned,
Left the warm precincts of the cheerful day,
Nor cast one longing ling'ring look behind?

On some fond breast the parting soul relies,
90 Some pious drops the closing eye requires;
Ev'n from the tomb the voice of Nature cries,
Ev'n in our ashes live their wanted fires.

For thee who, mindful of th' unhonored dead,
Dost in these lines their artless tale relate,
95 If chance, by lonely contemplation led,
Some kindred spirit shall inquire thy fate,

Haply some hoary-headed swain may say,
"Oft have we seen him at the peep of dawn
Brushing with hasty steps the dews away
100 To meet the sun upon the upland lawn.

"There at the foot of yonder nodding beech
That wreathes its old fantastic roots so high,
His listless length at noontide would he stretch,
And pore upon the brook that babbles by.

105 "Hard by yon wood, now smiling as in scorn,
Mutt'ring his wayward fancies he would rove,
Now drooping, woeful wan, like one forlorn,
Or crazed with care, or crossed in hopeless love.

"One morn I missed him on the customed hill,
110 Along the heath and near his fav'rite tree;

Another came; nor yet beside the rill,
Nor up the lawn, nor at the wood was he;

"The next, with dirges due in sad array
Slow through the church-way path we saw him borne.
115 Approach and read (for thou canst read) the lay,
Graved on the stone beneath yon aged thorn."

THE EPITAPH

Here rests his head upon the lap of Earth
A youth to fortune and to fame unknown.
Fair Science frowned not on his humble birth,
120 And Melancholy marked him for her own.

Large was his bounty, and his soul sincere,
Heav'n did a recompense as largely send:
He gave to Misery all he had, a tear;
He gained from heav'n ('twas all he wished) a friend.

125 No farther seek his merits to disclose,
Or draw his frailties from their dread abode
(There they alike in trembling hope repose),
The bosom of his Father and his God.

WILLIAM COLLINS (1721–1759)

Ode Written in the Beginning of the Year 1746

How sleep the brave who sink to rest
By all their country's wishes blest!
When Spring, with dewy fingers cold,
Returns to deck their hallowed mold,
5 She there shall dress a sweeter sod
Than Fancy's feet have ever trod.

By fairy hands their knell is rung,
By forms unseen their dirge is sung;
There Honor comes, a pilgrim gray,
10 To bless the turf that wraps their clay,
And Freedom shall awhile repair,
To dwell a weeping hermit there!

CHRISTOPHER SMART (1722–1771)

From **Rejoice in the Lamb**

For I will consider my Cat Jeoffry.
For he is the servant of the Living God, duly and daily serving him.
For at the first glance of the glory of God in the East he worships in
    his way.
For is this done by wreathing his body seven times round with elegant
    quickness.
5 For then he leaps up to catch the musk, which is the blessing of God
    upon his prayer.
For he rolls upon prank to work it in.
For having done duty and received blessing he begins to consider
    himself.
For this he performs in ten degrees.
For first he looks upon his forepaws to see if they are clean.
10 For secondly he kicks up behind to clear away there.
For thirdly he works it upon stretch with the forepaws extended.
For fourthly he sharpens his paws by wood.
For fifthly he washes himself.
For sixthly he rolls upon wash.
15 For seventhly he fleas himself, that he may not be interrupted upon
    the beat.[1]
For eighthly he rubs himself against a post.
For ninthly he looks up for his instructions.
For tenthly he goes in quest of food.
For having considered God and himself he will consider his neighbor.
20 For if he meets another cat he will kiss her in kindness.
For when he takes his prey he plays with it to give it chance.
For one mouse in seven escapes by his dallying.
For when his day's work is done his business more properly begins.
For he keeps the Lord's watch in the night against the adversary.
25 For he counteracts the powers of darkness by his electrical skin and
    glaring eyes.
For he counteracts the Devil, who is death, by brisking about the life.
For in his morning orisons he loves the sun and the sun loves him.
For he is of the tribe of Tiger.
For the Cherub Cat is a term of the Angel Tiger.
30 For he has the subtlety and hissing of a serpent, which in goodness
    he suppresses.

---

[1] On his daily rounds.

For he will not do destruction, if he is well-fed, neither will he spit without provocation.

For he purrs in thankfulness, when God tell him he's a good Cat.

For he is an instrument for the children to learn benevolence upon.

For every house is incomplete without him and a blessing is lacking in the spirit.

35 For the Lord commanded Moses concerning the cats at the departure of the Children of Israel from Egypt.

For every family had one cat at least in the bag.

For the English Cats are the best in Europe.

For he is the cleanest in the use of his forepaws of any quadruped.

For the dexterity of his defense is an instance of the love of God to him exceedingly.

40 For he is the quickest to his mark of any creature.

For he is tenacious of his point.

For he is a mixture of gravity and waggery.

For he knows that God is his Saviour.

For there is nothing sweeter than his peace when at rest.

45 For there is nothing brisker than his life when in motion.

For he is of the Lord's poor and so indeed is he called by benevolence perpetually—Poor Jeoffry! poor Jeoffry! the rat has bit thy throat.

For I bless the name of the Lord Jesus that Jeoffry is better.

For the divine spirit comes about his body to sustain it in complete cat.

For his tongue is exceeding pure so that it has in purity what it wants in music.

50 For he is docile and can learn certain things.

For he can set up with gravity, which is patience upon approbation.

For he can fetch and carry, which is patience in employment.

For he can jump over a stick, which is patience upon proof positive.

For he can spraggle upon waggle at the word of command.

55 For he can jump from an eminence into his master's bosom.

For he can catch the cork and toss it again.

For he is hated by the hypocrite and miser.

For the former is afraid of detection.

For the latter refuses the charge.

60 For he camels his back to bear the first notion of business.

For he is good to think on, if a man would express himself neatly.

For he made a great figure in Egypt for his signal services.

For he killed the ichneumon-rat[2] very pernicious by land.

---

[2] Mongoose. It was, however, generally regarded as beneficial.

For his ears are so acute that they sting again.
65 For from this proceeds the passing quickness of his attention.
For by stroking him I have found out electricity.
For I perceived God's light about him both wax and fire.
For the electrical fire is the spiritual substance, which God sends
    from heaven to sustain the bodies both of man and beast.
For God has blessed him in the variety of his movements.
70 For, though he cannot fly, he is an excellent clamberer.
For his motions upon the face of the earth are more than any other
    quadruped.
For he can tread to all the measures upon the music.
For he can swim for life.
For he can creep.

OLIVER GOLDSMITH (1730–1774)

When Lovely Woman Stoops to Folly

When lovely woman stoops to folly,
    And finds too late that men betray,
What charm can soothe her melancholy,
    What art can wash her guilt away?

5 The only art her guilt to cover,
    To hide her shame from every eye,
To give repentance to her lover,
    And wring his bosom—is to die.

WILLIAM COWPER (1731–1800)

Light Shining Out of Darkness

God moves in a mysterious way,
    His wonders to perform;
He plants his footsteps in the sea,
    And rides upon the storm.

5 Deep in unfathomable mines
    Of never failing skill,
He treasures up his bright designs,
    And works his sovereign will.

Ye fearful saints fresh courage take;
10   The clouds ye so much dread

Are big with mercy, and shall break
    In blessings on your head.

Judge not the Lord by feeble sense,
    But trust him for his grace;
15 Behind a frowning providence,
    He hides a smiling face.

His purposes will ripen fast,
    Unfolding every hour;
The bud may have a bitter taste,
20   But sweet will be the flower.

Blind unbelief is sure to err,
    And scan his work in vain;
God is his own interpreter,
    And he will make it plain.

Epitaph on a Hare

Here lies, whom hound did ne'er pursue,
    Nor swifter greyhound follow,
Whose foot ne'er tainted morning dew,
    Nor ear heard huntsman's halloo;

5 Old Tiney, surliest of his kind,
    Who, nursed with tender care,
And to domestic bounds confined,
    Was still a wild jack hare.

Though duly from my hand he took
10   His pittance every night;
He did it with a jealous look,
    And, when he could, would bite.

His diet was of wheaten bread
    And milk, and oats, and straw;
15 Thistles, or lettuces instead,
    With sand to scour his maw.

On twigs of hawthorn he regaled,
    On pippins' russet peel;
And, when his juicy salads failed,
20   Sliced carrot pleased him well.

A Turkey carpet was his lawn,
  Whereon he loved to bound,
To skip and gambol like a fawn,
  And swing his rump around.

25 His frisking was at evening hours,
  For then he lost his fear;
But most before approaching showers,
  Or when a storm drew near.

Eight years and five round-rolling moons
30   He thus saw steal away,
Dozing out all his idle noons,
  And every night at play.

I kept him for his humor's sake,
  For he would oft beguile
35 My heart of thoughts that made it ache,
  And force me to a smile.

But now beneath this walnut shade
  He finds his long last home,
And waits, in snug concealment laid,
40   Till gentler Puss[1] shall come.

He, still more aged, feels the shocks,
  From which no care can save,
And, partner once of Tiney's box,
  Must soon partake his grave.

The Castaway

Obscurest night involved the sky,
  Th' Atlantic billows roared,
When such a destined wretch as I,
  Washed headlong from on board,
5 Of friends, of hope, of all bereft,
His floating home forever left.

No braver chief could Albion boast
  Than he with whom he went,

---

[1] Another pet hare.

Nor ever ship left Albion's coast,
10   With warmer wishes sent.
He loved them both, but both in vain,
Nor him beheld, nor her again.

Not long beneath the whelming brine,
Expert to swim, he lay;
15 Nor soon he felt his strength decline,
Or courage die away;
But waged with death a lasting strife,
Supported by despair of life.

He shouted; nor his friends had failed
20   To check the vessel's course,
But so the furious blast prevailed,
That, pitiless perforce,
They left their outcast mate behind,
And scudded still before the wind.

25 Some succor yet they could afford;
And, such as storms allow,
The cask, the coop, the floated cord,
Delayed not to bestow.
But he (they knew) nor ship, nor shore,
30 Whate're they gave, should visit more.

Nor, cruel as it seemed, could he
Their haste himself condemn,
Aware that flight, in such a sea,
Alone could rescue them;
35 Yet bitter felt it still to die
Deserted, and his friends so nigh.

He long survives, who lives an hour
In ocean, self-upheld;
And so long he, with unspent power,
40   His destiny repelled;
And ever, as the minutes flew,
Entreated help, or cried, "Adieu!"

At length, his transient respite past,
His comrades, who before
45 Had heard his voice in every blast,
Could catch the sound no more.

For then, by toil subdued, he drank
The stifling wave, and then he sank.

No poet wept him: but the page
50   Of narrative sincere,
That tells his name, his worth, his age,
    Is wet with Anson's[1] tear.
And tears by bards or heroes shed
Alike immortalize the dead.

55 I therefore purpose not, or dream,
    Descanting on his fate,
To give the melancholy theme
    A more enduring date:
But misery still delights to trace
60 Its semblance in another's case.

No voice divine the storm allayed,
    No light propitious shone;
When, snatched from all effectual aid,
    We perished, each alone:
65 But I beneath a rougher sea,
And whelmed in deeper gulfs than he.

PHILIP FRENEAU (1752–1832)

The Indian Burying Ground

In spite of all the learned have said,
    I still my opinion keep;
The posture, that we give the dead,
    Points out the soul's eternal sleep.

5 Not so the ancients of these lands—
    The Indian, when from life released,
Again is seated with his friends,
    And shares again the joyous feast.

His imaged birds, and painted bowl,
10   And venison, for a journey dressed,
Bespeak the nature of the soul,
    Activity, that knows no rest.

---

[1] The poem was inspired by an incident related by George Anson, a British admiral.

His bow, for action ready bent,
  And arrows, with a head of stone,
15 Can only mean that life is spent,
  And not the old ideas gone.

Thou, stranger, that shalt come this way,
  No fraud upon the dead commit—
Observe the swelling turf, and say
20 They do not lie, but here they sit.

Here still a lofty rock remains,
  On which the curious eye may trace
(Now wasted, half, by wearing rains)
  The fancies of a ruder race.

25 Here still an aged elm aspires,
  Beneath whose far-projecting shade
(And which the shepherd still admires)
  The children of the forest played!

There oft a restless Indian queen
30 (Pale Shebah, with her braided hair)
And many a barbarous form is seen
  To chide the man that lingers there.

By midnight moons, o'er moistening dews;
  In habit for the chase arrayed,
35 The hunter still the deer pursues,
  The hunter and the deer, a shade!

And long shall timorous fancy see
  The painted chief, and pointed spear,
And Reason's self shall bow the knee
40 To shadows and delusions here.

PHILLIS WHEATLEY (1753?–1784)

On Being Brought from Africa to America

'Twas mercy brought me from my *Pagan* land,
Taught my benighted soul to understand
That there's a God, that there's a *Saviour* too:
Once I redemption neither sought nor knew.
5 Some view our sable race with scornful eye,

"Their color is a diabolic die."
Remember, *Christians, Negroes,* black as *Cain,*
May be refin'd, and join th' angelic train.

WILLIAM BLAKE (1757–1827)

From **Songs of Innocence**

INTRODUCTION

Piping down the valleys wild
Piping songs of pleasant glee
On a cloud I saw a child,
And he laughing said to me,

5 "Pipe a song about a Lamb";
So I piped with merry chear;
"Piper pipe that song again"—
So I piped, he wept to hear.

"Drop thy pipe thy happy pipe
10 Sing thy songs of happy chear";
So I sung the same again
While he wept with joy to hear.

"Piper sit thee down and write
In a book that all may read"—
15 So he vanish'd from my sight.
And I pluck'd a hollow reed,

And I made a rural pen,
And I stain'd the water clear,
And I wrote my happy songs
20 Every child may joy to hear.

THE LAMB

Little Lamb, who made thee?
Dost thou know who made thee?
Gave thee life & bid thee feed,
By the stream & o'er the mead;
5 Gave thee clothing of delight,
Softest clothing wooly bright;

Gave thee such a tender voice,
Making all the vales rejoice!
 Little Lamb who made thee?
10   Dost thou know who made thee?

 Little Lamb I'll tell thee,
 Little Lamb I'll tell thee!
He is callèd by thy name,
For he calls himself a Lamb:
15 He is meek & he is mild,
He became a little child:
I a child & thou a lamb,
We are callèd by his name.
 Little Lamb God bless thee.
20   Little Lamb God bless thee.

THE CHIMNEY SWEEPER

When my mother died I was very young,
And my father sold me while yet my tongue
Could scarcely cry " 'weep! 'weep! 'weep! 'weep!"
So your chimneys I sweep & in soot I sleep.

5 There's little Tom Dacre, who cried when his head
That curl'd like a lambs back, was shav'd, so I said,
"Hush, Tom! never mind it, for when your head's bare,
You know that the soot cannot spoil your white hair."

And so he was quiet, & that very night,
10 As Tom was a-sleeping he had such a sight!
That thousands of sweepers, Dick, Joe, Ned, & Jack,
Were all of them lock'd up in coffins of black;

And by came an Angel who had a bright key,
And he open'd the coffins & set them all free;
15 Then down a green plain, leaping, laughing they run,
And wash in a river and shine in the Sun;

Then naked & white, all their bags left behind,
They rise upon clouds, and sport in the wind.
And the Angel told Tom, if he'd be a good boy,
20 He'd have God for his father & never want joy.

And so Tom awoke; and we rose in the dark
And got with our bags & our brushes to work.
Tho' the morning was cold, Tom was happy & warm;
So if all do their duty, they need not fear harm.

THE LITTLE BLACK BOY

My mother bore me in the southern wild,
And I am black, but O! my soul is white;
White as an angel is the English child:
But I am black as if bereav'd of light.

5 My mother taught me underneath a tree,
And sitting down before the heat of day,
She took me on her lap and kissèd me,
And pointing to the east, began to say:

"Look on the rising sun: there God does live,
10 And gives his light, and gives his heat away;
And flowers and trees and beasts and men receive
Comfort in morning, joy in the noon day.

"And we are put on earth a little space,
That we may learn to bear the beams of love,
15 And these black bodies and this sun-burnt face
Is but a cloud, and like a shady grove.

"For when our souls have learn'd the heat to bear,
The cloud will vanish; we shall hear his voice,
Saying, 'Come out from the grove, my love & care,
20 And round my golden tent like lambs rejoice.' "

Thus did my mother say, and kissèd me;
And thus I say to little English boy:
When I from black and he from white cloud free,
And round the tent of God like lambs we joy,

25 I'll shade him from the heat till he can bear
To lean in joy upon our father's knee;
And then I'll stand and stroke his silver hair,
And be like him, and he will then love me.

From **Songs of Experience**

THE SICK ROSE

O Rose, thou art sick.
The invisible worm
That flies in the night
In the howling storm

5 Has found out thy bed
Of crimson joy,
And his dark secret love
Does thy life destroy.

THE TYGER

Tyger! Tyger! burning bright
In the forests of the night,
What immortal hand or eye
Could frame thy fearful symmetry?

5 In what distant deeps or skies
Burnt the fire of thine eyes?
On what wings dare he aspire?
What the hand, dare seize the fire?

And what shoulder, & what art,
10 Could twist the sinews of thy heart?
And when thy heart began to beat,
What dread hand? & what dread feet?

What the hammer? what the chain?
In what furnace was thy brain?
15 What the anvil? what dread grasp
Dare its deadly terrors clasp?

When the stars threw down their spears,
And water'd heaven with their tears,
Did he smile his work to see?
20 Did he who made the Lamb make thee?

Tyger! Tyger! burning bright
In the forests of the night,
What immortal hand or eye
Dare frame thy fearful symmetry?

LONDON

I wander thro' each charter'd street,
Near where the charter'd Thames does flow,
And mark in every face I meet
Marks of weakness, marks of woe.

5 In every cry of every Man,
In every Infant's cry of fear,
In every voice, in every ban,
The mind-forg'd manacles I hear.

How the Chimney-sweeper's cry
10 Every blackning Church appalls;
And the hapless Soldier's sigh
Runs in blood down Palace walls.

But most thro' midnight streets I hear
How the youthful Harlot's curse
15 Blasts the new-born Infant's tear,
And blights with plagues the Marriage hearse.

To the Muses

Whether on Ida's shady brow,
Or in the chambers of the East,
The chambers of the sun, that now
From antient melody have ceased;

5 Whether in Heaven ye wander fair,
Or the green corners of the earth,
Or the blue regions of the air
Where the melodious winds have birth;

Whether on chrystal rocks ye rove,
10 Beneath the bosom of the sea
Wandering in many a coral grove,
Fair Nine, forsaking Poetry!

How have you left the antient love
That bards of old enjoyed in you!
15 The languid strings do scarcely move!
The sound is forced, the notes are few!

From **Milton**

And did those feet in ancient time
Walk upon England's mountains green?
And was the holy Lamb of God
On England's pleasant pastures seen?

5 And did the Countenance Divine
Shine forth upon our clouded hills?
And was Jerusalem builded here,
Among these dark Satanic Mills?

Bring me my Bow of burning gold:
10 Bring me my Arrows of desire:
Bring me my Spear: O clouds unfold!
Bring me my Chariot of fire!

I will not cease from Mental Fight,
Nor shall my Sword sleep in my hand,
15 Till we have built Jerusalem
In England's green & pleasant Land.

ROBERT BURNS (1759–1796)

To a Mouse

*On Turning Her Up in Her Nest with
the Plough, November 1785*

Wee, sleekit,[1] cow'rin', tim'rous beastie,
O, what a panic's in thy breastie!
Thou need na start awa sae hasty,
   Wi' bickering brattle! [2]
5 I wad be laith to rin[3] an' chase thee,
   Wi' murdering pattle! [4]

I'm truly sorry man's dominion
Has broken Nature's social union,
An' justifies that ill opinion
10   Which makes thee startle

---

[1] Sleek.
[2] Hasty scamper.
[3] Loath to run.
[4] Plowstaff.

At me, thy poor earth-born companion,
        An' fellow-mortal!

I doubt na, whyles,[5] but thou may thieve;
What then? poor beastie, thou maun live!
15 A daimen icker in a thrave[6]
        'S a sma' request;
I'll get a blessin wi' the lave,[7]
        And never miss 't!

Thy wee-bit housie, too, in ruin!
20 Its silly wa's the win's are strewin'!
An' naething, now, to big[8] a new ane,
        O' foggage[9] green!
An' bleak December's win's ensuin',
        Baith snell [10] an' keen!

25 Thou saw the fields laid bare an' waste,
An' weary winter comin' fast,
An' cozie here, beneath the blast,
        Thou thought to dwell,
Till crash! the cruel coulter past
30   Out thro' thy cell.

That wee bit heap o' leaves an' stibble
Has cost thee monie a weary nibble!
Now thou's turned out, for a' thy trouble,
        But house or hald,[11]
35 To thole[12] the winter's sleety dribble,
        An' cranreuch[13] cauld!

But, Mousie, thou art no thy lane,[14]
In proving foresight may be vain:
The best-laid schemes o' mice an' men
40   Gang aft agley,[15]

---

[5] Sometimes.
[6] An occasional ear in 24 sheaves.
[7] Remainder.
[8] Build.
[9] Moss.
[10] Harsh.
[11] Without house or hold.
[12] Endure.
[13] Hoarfrost.
[14] Not alone.
[15] Go oft awry.

An' lea'e us nought but grief an' pain,
For promis'd joy!

Still thou art blest, campared wi' me!
The present only toucheth thee:
45 But och! I backward cast my e'e,
On prospects drear!
An' forward, tho' I canna see,
I guess an' fear!

John Anderson, My Jo

John Anderson my jo,[1] John,
When we were first acquent,
Your locks were like the raven,
Your bonie brow was brent,[2]
5 But now your brow is beld, John,
Your locks are like the snow;
But blessings on your frosty pow,[3]
John Anderson, my jo.

John Anderson my jo, John,
10 We clamb the hill thegither;
And mony a canty[4] day, John,
We've had wi' ane anither:
Now we maun totter down, John,
And hand in hand we'll go,
15 And sleep thegither at the foot,
John Anderson, my jo.

A Red, Red Rose

O my luve's like a red, red rose,
That's newly sprung in June;
O my luve's like the melodie
That's sweetly played in tune.

---

[1] Joy.
[2] Straight.
[3] Poll.
[4] Merry.

5 As fair art thou, my bonnie lass,
    So deep in luve am I;
And I will luve thee still, my dear,
    Till a' the seas gang dry.

Till a' the seas gang dry, my dear,
10   And the rocks melt wi' the sun:
O I will love thee still, my dear,
    While the sands o' life shall run.

And fare thee weel, my only luve,
    And fare thee weel awhile!
15 And I will come again, my luve,
    Though it were ten thousand mile.

O, Wert Thou in the Cauld Blast

O, wert thou in the cauld blast
    On yonder lea, on yonder lea,
My plaidie[1] to the angry airt,[2]
    I'd shelter thee, I'd shelter thee.
5 Or did Misfortune's bitter storms
    Around thee blaw, around thee blaw,
Thy bield [3] should be my bosom,
    To share it a', to share it a'.

Or were I in the wildest waste,
10   Sae black and bare, sae black and bare,
The desert were a Paradise,
    If thou wert there, if thou wert there.
Or were I monarch o' the globe,
    Wi' thee to reign, wi' thee to reign,
15 The brightest jewel in my crown
    Wad be my queen, wad be my queen.

---

[1] Plaid.
[2] Direction of the wind.
[3] Shelter.

Afton Water

Flow gently, sweet Afton! among thy green braes,
Flow gently, I'll sing thee a song in thy praise;
My Mary's asleep by thy murmuring stream,
Flow gently, sweet Afton, disturb not her dream.

5 Thou stock dove whose echo resounds through the glen,
Ye wild whistling blackbirds in yon thorny den,
Thou green-crested lapwing, thy screaming forbear,
I charge you, disturb not my slumbering fair.

How loftly, sweet Afton, thy neighboring hills,
10 Far marked with the courses of clear, winding rills;
There daily I wander as noon rises high,
My flocks and my Mary's sweet cot in my eye.

How pleasant thy banks and green valleys below,
Where, wild in the woodlands, the primroses blow;
15 There oft, as mild ev'ning weeps over the lea,
The sweet-scented birk shades my Mary and me.

Thy crystal stream, Afton, how lovely it glides,
And winds by the cot where my Mary resides;
How wanton thy waters her snowy feet lave,
20 As, gathering sweet flowerets, she stems thy clear wave.

Flow gently, sweet Afton, among thy green braes,
Flow gently, sweet river, the theme of my lays;
My Mary's asleep by thy murmuring stream,
Flow gently, sweet Afton, disturb not her dream.

WILLIAM WORDSWORTH (1770–1850)

Lines

*Composed a Few Miles above Tintern Abbey
on Revisiting the Banks of the Wye
During a Tour. July 13, 1798*

Five years have passed; five summers, with the length
Of five long winters! and again I hear
These waters, rolling from their mountain-springs
With a soft inland murmur.—Once again
5 Do I behold these steep and lofty cliffs,

That on a wild secluded scene impress
Thoughts of more deep seclusion; and connect
The landscape with the quiet of the sky.
The day is come when I again repose
10 Here, under this dark sycamore, and view
These plots of cottage-ground, these orchard-tufts,
Which at this season, with their unripe fruits,
Are clad in one green hue, and lose themselves
'Mid groves and copses. Once again I see
15 These hedge-rows, hardly hedge-rows, little lines
Of sportive wood run wild: these pastoral farms,
Green to the very door; and wreaths of smoke
Sent up, in silence, from among the trees!
With some uncertain notice, as might seem
20 Of vagrant dwellers in the houseless woods,
Or of some Hermit's cave, where by his fire
The Hermit sits alone.
                                    These beauteous forms,
Through a long absence, have not been to me
As is a landscape to a blind man's eye:
25 But oft, in lonely rooms, and 'mid the din
Of towns and cities, I have owed to them,
In hours of weariness, sensations sweet,
Felt in the blood, and felt along the heart;
And passing even into my purer mind,
30 With tranquil restoration:—feelings too
Of unremembered pleasure: such, perhaps,
As have no slight or trivial influence
On that best portion of a good man's life,
His little, nameless, unremembered, acts
35 Of kindness and of love. Nor less, I trust,
To them I may have owed another gift,
Of aspect more sublime; that blessèd mood,
In which the burthen of the mystery,
In which the heavy and the weary weight
40 Of all this unintelligible world,
Is lightened:—that serene and blessèd mood,
In which the affections gently lead us on,—
Until, the breath of this corporeal frame
And even the motion of our human blood
45 Almost suspended, we are laid asleep
In body, and become a living soul:
While with an eye made quiet by the power
Of harmony, and the deep power of joy,

We see into the life of things.
If this

50 Be but a vain belief, yet, oh! how oft—
In darkness and amid the many shapes
Of joyless daylight; when the fretful stir
Unprofitable, and the fever of the world,
Have hung upon the beatings of my heart—
55 How oft, in spirit, have I turned to thee,
O sylvan Wye! thou wanderer thro' the woods,
How often has my spirit turned to thee!

And now, with gleams of half-extinguished thought,
With many recognitions dim and faint,
60 And somewhat of a sad perplexity,
The picture of the mind revives again:
While here I stand, not only with the sense
Of present pleasure, but with pleasing thoughts
That in this moment there is life and food
65 For future years. And so I dare to hope,
Though changed, no doubt, from what I was when first
I came among these hills; when like a roe
I bounded o'er the mountains, by the sides
Of the deep rivers, and the lonely streams,
70 Wherever nature led: more like a man
Flying from something that he dreads than one
Who sought the thing he loved. For nature then
(The coarser pleasures of my boyish days,
And their glad animal movements all gone by)
75 To me was all in all.—I cannot paint
What then I was. The sounding cataract
Haunted me like a passion: the tall rock,
The mountain, and the deep and gloomy wood,
Their colors and their forms, were then to me
80 An appetite; a feeling and a love,
That had no need of a remoter charm,
By thought supplied, nor any interest
Unborrowed from the eye.—That time is past,
And all its aching joys are now no more,
85 And all its dizzy raptures. Not for this
Faint I, nor mourn nor murmur; other gifts
Have followed; for such loss, I would believe,
Abundant recompense. For I have learned
To look on nature, not as in the hour
90 Of thoughtless youth; but hearing oftentimes

The still, sad music of humanity,
Nor harsh nor grating, though of ample power
To chasten and subdue. And I have felt
A presence that disturbs me with the joy
95 Of elevated thoughts; a sense sublime
Of something far more deeply interfused,
Whose dwelling is the light of setting suns,
And the round ocean and the living air,
And the blue sky, and in the mind of man:
100 A motion and a spirit, that impels
All thinking things, all objects of all thought,
And rolls through all things. Therefore am I still
A lover of the meadows and the woods,
And mountains; and of all that we behold
105 From this green earth; of all the mighty world
Of eye, and ear,—both what they half create,
And what perceive; well pleased to recognise
In nature and the language of the sense
The anchor of my purest thoughts, the nurse,
110 The guide, the guardian of my heart, and soul
Of all my moral being.
　　　　　　　　Nor perchance,
If I were not thus taught, should I the more
Suffer my genial spirits to decay:
For thou[1] art with me here upon the banks
115 Of this fair river; thou my dearest Friend,
My dear, dear Friend; and in thy voice I catch
The language of my former heart, and read
My former pleasures in the shooting lights
Of thy wild eyes. Oh! yet a little while
120 May I behold in thee what I was once,
My dear, dear Sister! and this prayer I make,
Knowing that Nature never did betray
The heart that loved her; 'tis her privilege,
Through all the years of this our life, to lead
125 From joy to joy: for she can so inform
The mind that is within us, so impress
With quietness and beauty, and so feed
With lofty thoughts, that neither evil tongues,
Rash judgments, nor the sneers of selfish men,
130 Nor greetings where no kindness is, nor all

---

1 Wordsworth's sister Dorothy.

The dreary intercourse of daily life,
Shall e'er prevail against us, or disturb
Our cheerful faith, that all which we behold
Is full of blessings. Therefore let the moon
135 Shine on thee in thy solitary walk;
And let the misty mountain-winds be free
To blow against thee: and, in after years,
When these wild ecstasies shall be matured
Into a sober pleasure; when thy mind
140 Shall be a mansion for all lovely forms,
Thy memory be as a dwelling-place
For all sweet sounds and harmonies; oh! then,
If solitude, or fear, or pain, or grief,
Should be thy portion, with what healing thoughts
145 Of tender joy wilt thou remember me,
And these my exhortations! Nor, perchance—
If I should be where I no more can hear
Thy voice, nor catch from thy wild eyes these gleams
Of past existence—wilt thou then forget
150 That on the banks of this delightful stream
We stood together; and that I, so long
A worshipper of Nature, hither came
Unwearied in that service: rather say
With warmer love—oh! with far deeper zeal
155 Of holier love. Nor wilt thou then forget
That after many wanderings, many years
Of absence, these steep woods and lofty cliffs,
And this green pastoral landscape, were to me
More dear, both for themselves and for thy sake!

She Dwelt Among the Untrodden Ways

She dwelt among the untrodden ways
    Beside the springs of Dove.
A Maid whom there were none to praise
    And very few to love;

5 A violet by a mossy stone
    Half hidden from the eye!
—Fair as a star, when only one
    Is shining in the sky.

She lived unknown, and few could know
10   When Lucy ceased to be;

But she is in her grave, and, oh,
    The difference to me!

A Slumber Did My Spirit Seal

A slumber did my spirit seal;
    I had no human fears:
She seemed a thing that could not feel
    The touch of earthly years.

5 No motion has she now, no force;
    She neither hears nor sees;
Rolled round in earth's diurnal course,
    With rocks, and stones, and trees.

It Is a Beauteous Evening

It is a beauteous evening, calm and free,
The holy time is quiet as a Nun
Breathless with adoration; the broad sun
Is sinking down in its tranquillity;
5 The gentleness of heaven broods o'er the Sea:
Listen! the mighty Being is awake,
And doth with his eternal motion make
A sound like thunder—everlastingly.
Dear Child! dear Girl! that walkest with me here,
10 If thou appear untouched by solemn thought,
Thy nature is not therefore less divine:
Thou liest in Abraham's bosom all the year;
And worshipp'st at the Temple's inner shrine,
God being with thee when we know it not.

London, 1802

Milton! thou shouldst be living at this hour:
England hath need of thee: she is a fen
Of stagnant waters: altar, sword, and pen,
Fireside, the heroic wealth of hall and bower,
5 Have forfeited their ancient English dower
Of inward happiness. We are selfish men;
Oh! raise us up, return to us again;
And give us manners, virtue, freedom, power.
Thy soul was like a Star, and dwelt apart;

10 Thou hadst a voice whose sound was like the sea:
  Pure as the naked heavens, majestic, free,
  So didst thou travel on life's common way,
  In cheerful godliness; and yet thy heart
  The lowliest duties on herself did lay.

Composed upon Westminster Bridge, September 3, 1802

Earth has not anything to show more fair:
Dull would he be of soul who could pass by
A sight so touching in its majesty;
This City now doth, like a garment, wear
5 The beauty of the morning; silent, bare,
Ships, towers, domes, theaters, and temples lie
Open unto the fields, and to the sky;
All bright and glittering in the smokeless air.
Never did sun more beautifully steep
10 In his first splendor, valley, rock, or hill;
Ne'er saw I, never felt, a calm so deep!
The river glideth at his own sweet will:
Dear God! the very houses seem asleep;
And all that mighty heart is lying still!

Ode

Intimations of Immortality from Recollections of Early Childhood

The Child is father of the Man;
And I could wish my days to be
Bound each to each by natural piety.

1

There was a time when meadow, grove, and stream,
The earth, and every common sight,
    To me did seem
    Apparelled in celestial light,
5 The glory and the freshness of a dream.
It is not now as it hath been of yore;—
    Turn wheresoe'er I may,
        By night or day,
The things which I have seen I now can see no more.

2

¹⁰ The Rainbow comes and goes,
And lovely is the Rose,
The Moon doth with delight
Look round her when the heavens are bare;
Waters on a starry night
¹⁵ Are beautiful and fair;
The sunshine is a glorious birth;
But yet I know, where'er I go,
That there hath past away a glory from the earth.

3

Now, while the birds thus sing a joyous song,
²⁰ And while the young lambs bound
As to the tabor's sound,
To me alone there came a thought of grief:
A timely utterance gave that thought relief,
And I again am strong:
²⁵ The cataracts blow their trumpets from the steep;
No more shall grief of mine the season wrong;
I hear the Echoes through the mountains throng,
The Winds come to me from the fields of sleep,
And all the earth is gay;
³⁰ Land and sea
Give themselves up to jollity,
And with the heart of May
Doth every Beast keep holiday;—
Thou Child of Joy,
³⁵ Shout round me, let me hear thy shouts, thou happy Shepherd-boy!

4

Ye blessèd Creatures, I have heard the call
Ye to each other make; I see
The heavens laugh with you in your jubilee;
My heart is at your festival,
⁴⁰ My head hath its coronal,
The fulness of your bliss, I feel—I feel it all.
Oh evil day! if I were sullen
While Earth herself is adorning,
This sweet May-morning,
⁴⁵ And the Children are culling
On every side,

In a thousand valleys far and wide,
Fresh flowers; while the sun shines warm,
And the Babe leaps up on his Mother's arm:—
50   I hear, I hear, with joy I hear!
—But there's a Tree, of many, one,
A single Field which I have looked upon,
Both of them speak of something that is gone:
The Pansy at my feet
55   Doth the same tale repeat:
Whither is fled the visionary gleam?
Where is it now, the glory and the dream?

5

Our birth is but a sleep and a forgetting:
The Soul that rises with us, our life's Star,
60   Hath had elsewhere its setting,
And cometh from afar:
Not in entire forgetfulness,
And not in utter nakedness,
But trailing clouds of glory do we come
65   From God, who is our home:
Heaven lies about us in our infancy!
Shades of the prison-house begin to close
Upon the growing Boy,
But He
70 Beholds the light, and whence it flows,
He sees it in his joy;
The Youth, who daily farther from the east
Must travel, still is Nature's Priest,
And by the vision splendid
75   Is on his way attended;
At length the Man perceives it die away,
And fade into the light of common day.

6

Earth fills her lap with pleasures of her own;
Yearnings she hath in her own natural kind,
80 And, even with something of a Mother's mind,
And no unworthy aim,
The homely Nurse doth all she can
To make her Foster-child, her Inmate Man,
Forget the glories he hath known,
85 And that imperial palace whence he came.

7

Behold the Child among his new-born blisses,
A six years' Darling of a pigmy size!
See, where 'mid work of his own hand he lies,
Fretted by sallies of his mother's kisses,
90 With light upon him from his father's eyes!
See, at his feet, some little plan or chart,
Some fragment from his dream of human life,
Shaped by himself with newly-learnèd art;
 A wedding or a festival,
95 A mourning or a funeral;
  And this hath now his heart,
  And unto this he frames his song:
  Then will he fit his tongue
To dialogues of business, love, or strife;
100 But it will not be long
 Ere this be thrown aside,
 And with new joy and pride
The little Actor cons another part;
Filling from time to time his "humorous stage"
105 With all the Persons, down to palsied Age,
That Life brings with her in her equipage;
 As if his whole vocation
 Were endless imitation.

8

Thou, whose exterior semblance doth belie
110 Thy Soul's immensity;
Thou best Philosopher, who yet dost keep
Thy heritage, thou Eye among the blind,
That, deaf and silent, read'st the eternal deep,
Haunted for ever by the eternal mind,—
115 Mighty Prophet! Seer blest!
  On whom those truths do rest,
Which we are toiling all our lives to find,
In darkness lost, the darkness of the grave;
Thou, over whom thy Immortality
120 Broods like the Day, a Master o'er a Slave,
A Presence which is not to be put by;
Thou little Child, yet glorious in the might
Of heaven-born freedom on thy being's height,
Why with such earnest pains dost thou provoke
125 The years to bring the inevitable yoke,

Thus blindly with thy blessedness at strife?
Full soon thy Soul shall have her earthly freight,
And custom lie upon thee with a weight,
Heavy as frost, and deep almost as life!

9

130   O joy! that in our embers
        Is something that doth live,
        That nature yet remembers
        What was so fugitive!
The thought of our past years in me doth breed
135 Perpetual benediction: not indeed
For that which is most worthy to be blest;
Delight and liberty, the simple creed
Of Childhood, whether busy or at rest,
With new-fledged hope still fluttering in his breast:—
140   Not for these I raise
            The song of thanks and praise;
        But for those obstinate questionings
        Of sense and outward things,
        Falling from us, vanishings;
145   Blank misgivings of a Creature
Moving about in worlds not realised,
High instincts before which our mortal Nature
Did tremble like a guilty Thing surprised:
            But for those first affections,
150   Those shadowy recollections,
        Which, be they what they may,
Are yet the fountain-light of all our day,
Are yet a master-light of all our seeing;
        Uphold us, cherish, and have power to make
155 Our noisy years seem moments in the being
Of the eternal Silence: truths that wake,
            To perish never:
Which neither listlessness, nor mad endeavor,
            Nor Man nor Boy,
160 Nor all that is at enmity with joy,
Can utterly abolish or destroy!
        Hence in a season of calm weather
            Though inland far we be,
Our Souls have sight of that immortal sea
165   Which brought us hither,
        Can in a moment travel thither,

And see the Children sport upon the shore,
And hear the mighty waters rolling evermore.

10

Then sing, ye Birds, sing, sing a joyous song!
170 And let the young Lambs bound
  As to the tabor's sound!
We in thought will join your throng,
  Ye that pipe and ye that play,
  Ye that through your hearts to-day
175 Feel the gladness of the May!
What though the radiance which was once so bright
Be now for ever taken from my sight,
 Though nothing can bring back the hour
Of splendor in the grass, of glory in the flower;
180 We will grieve not, rather find
  Strength in what remains behind;
  In the primal sympathy
  Which having been must ever be;
  In the soothing thoughts that spring
185 Out of human suffering;
  In the faith that looks through death,
In years that bring the philosophic mind.

11

And O, ye Fountains, Meadows, Hills, and Groves,
Forebode not any severing of our loves!
190 Yet in my heart of hearts I feel your might;
I only have relinquished one delight
To live beneath your more habitual sway.
I love the Brooks which down their channels fret,
Even more than when I tripped lightly as they;
195 The innocent brightness of a new-born Day
  Is lovely yet;
The Clouds that gather round the setting sun
Do take a sober coloring from an eye
That hath kept watch o'er man's mortality;
200 Another race hath been, and other palms are won.
Thanks to the human heart by which we live,
Thanks to its tenderness, its joys, and fears,
To me the meanest flower that blows can give
Thoughts that do often lie too deep for tears.

She Was a Phantom of Delight

She was a Phantom of delight
When first she gleamed upon my sight;
A lovely Apparition, sent
To be a moment's ornament;
5 Her eyes as stars of Twilight fair;
Like Twilight's, too, her dusky hair;
But all things else about her drawn
From May-time and the cheerful Dawn;
A dancing Shape, an Image gay,
10 To haunt, to startle, and way-lay.

I saw her upon nearer view,
A Spirit, yet a Woman too!
Her household motions light and free,
And steps of virgin-liberty;
15 A countenance in which did meet
Sweet records, promises as sweet;
A Creature not too bright or good
For human nature's daily food;
For transient sorrows, simple wiles,
20 Praise, blame, love, kisses, tears, and smiles.

And now I see with eye serene
The very pulse of the machine;
A Being breathing thoughtful breath,
A Traveller between life and death;
25 The reason firm, the temperate will,
Endurance, foresight, strength, and skill;
A perfect Woman, nobly planned,
To warn, to comfort, and command;
And yet a Spirit still, and bright
30 With something of angelic light.

The World Is Too Much with Us

The world is too much with us; late and soon,
Getting and spending, we lay waste our powers:
Little we see in Nature that is ours;
We have given our hearts away, a sordid boon!
5 This Sea that bares her bosom to the moon;
The winds that will be howling at all hours,

And are up-gathered now like sleeping flowers;
For this, for everything, we are out of tune;
It moves us not.—Great God! I'd rather be
10 A Pagan suckled in a creed outworn;
So might I, standing on this pleasant lea,
Have glimpses that would make me less forlorn;
Have sight of Proteus rising from the sea;
Or hear old Triton blow his wreathèd horn.

I Wandered Lonely as a Cloud

I wandered lonely as a cloud
That floats on high o'er vales and hills,
When all at once I saw a crowd,
A host, of golden daffodils;
5 Beside the lake, beneath the trees,
Fluttering and dancing in the breeze.

Continuous as the stars that shine
And twinkle on the milky way,
They stretched in never-ending line
10 Along the margin of a bay:
Ten thousand saw I at a glance,
Tossing their heads in sprightly dance.

The waves beside them danced; but they
Outdid the sparkling waves in glee;
15 A poet could not but be gay,
In such a jocund company;
I gazed—and gazed—but little thought
What wealth the show to me had brought:

For oft, when on my couch I lie
20 In vacant or in pensive mood,
They flash upon that inward eye
Which is the bliss of solitude;
And then my heart with pleasure fills,
And dances with the daffodils.

The Solitary Reaper

Behold her, single in the field,
Yon solitary Highland Lass!

Reaping and singing by herself;
Stop here, or gently pass!
5 Alone she cuts and binds the grain,
And sings a melancholy strain;
O listen! for the Vale profound
Is overflowering with the sound.

No Nightingale did ever chaunt
10 More welcome notes to weary bands
Of travelers in some shady haunt,
Among Arabian sands;
A voice so thrilling ne'er was heard
In springtime from the Cuckoo bird,
15 Breaking the silence of the seas
Among the farthest Hebrides.

Will no one tell me what she sings?—
Perhaps the plaintive numbers flow
For old, unhappy, far-off things,
20 And battles long ago;
Or is it some more humble lay,
Familiar matter of today?
Some natural sorrow, loss, or pain,
That has been, and may be again?

25 Whate'er the theme, the Maiden sang
As if her song could have no ending;
I saw her singing at her work,
And o'er the sickle bending—
I listened, motionless and still;
30 And, as I mounted up the hill,
The music in my heart I bore,
Long after it was heard no more.

Mutability

From low to high doth dissolution climb,
And sink from high to low, along a scale
Of awful notes, whose concord shall not fail;
A musical but melancholy chime,
5 Which they can hear who meddle not with crime,
Nor avarice, nor over-anxious care.
Truth fails not; but her outward forms that bear
The longest date do melt like frosty rime,

That in the morning whitened hill and plain
10 And is no more; drop like the tower sublime
Of yesterday, which royally did wear
His crown of weeds, but could not even sustain
Some casual shout that broke the silent air,
Or the unimaginable touch of Time.

Scorn Not the Sonnet

Scorn not the sonnet; critic, you have frowned,
Mindless of its just honors; with this key
Shakespeare unlocked his heart; the melody
Of this small lute gave ease to Petrarch's wound;
5 A thousand times this pipe did Tasso sound;
With it Camöens soothed an exile's grief;
The sonnet glittered a gay myrtle leaf
Amid the cypress with which Dante crowned
His visionary brow; a glow-worn lamp,
10 It cheered mild Spenser, called from Faeryland
To struggle through dark ways; and, when a damp
Fell round the path of Milton, in his hand
The thing became a trumpet; whence he blew
Soul-animating strains—alas, too few!

SAMUEL TAYLOR COLERIDGE (1772–1834)

Kubla Khan

In Xanadu did Kubla Khan
A stately pleasure-dome decree:
Where Alph, the sacred river, ran
Through caverns measureless to man
5   Down to a sunless sea.
So twice five miles of fertile ground
With walls and towers were girdled round:
And there were gardens bright with sinuous rills,
Where blossomed many an incense-bearing tree;
10 And here were forests ancient as the hills,
Enfolding sunny spots of greenery.

But oh! that deep romantic chasm which slanted
Down the green hill athwart a cedarn cover!
A savage place! as holy and enchanted

15 As e'er beneath a waning moon was haunted
   By woman wailing for her demon-lover!
   And from this chasm, with ceaseless turmoil seething,
   As if this earth in fast thick pants were breathing,
   A mighty fountain momently was forced:
20 Amid whose swift half-intermitted burst
   Huge fragments vaulted like rebounding hail,
   Or chaffy grain beneath the thresher's flail:
   And 'mid these dancing rocks at once and ever
   It flung up momently the sacred river.
25 Five miles meandering with a mazy motion
   Through wood and dale the sacred river ran,
   Then reached the caverns measureless to man,
   And sank in tumult to a lifeless ocean:
   And 'mid this tumult Kubla heard from far
30 Ancestral voices prophesying war!

   The shadow of the dome of pleasure
   Floated midway on the waves;
   Where was heard the mingled measure
   From the fountain and the caves.

35 It was a miracle of rare device,
   A sunny pleasure-dome with caves of ice!

   A damsel with a dulcimer
   In a vision once I saw:
   It was an Abyssinian maid,
40 And on her dulcimer she played,
   Singing of Mount Abora.
   Could I revive within me
   Her symphony and song,
   To such a deep delight 'twould win me,

45 That with music loud and long,
   I would build that dome in air,
   That sunny dome! those caves of ice!
   And all who heard should see them there,
   And all should cry, Beware! Beware!
50 His flashing eyes, his floating hair!
   Weave a circle round him thrice,
   And close your eyes with holy dread,
   For he on honey-dew hath fed,
   And drunk the milk of Paradise.

This Lime-Tree Bower My Prison

Well, they are gone, and here must I remain,
This lime-tree bower my prison! I have lost
Beauties and feelings, such as would have been
Most sweet to my remembrance even when age
5 Had dimm'd mine eyes to blindness! They, meanwhile,
Friends, whom I never more may meet again,
On springy heath, along the hill-top edge,
Wander in gladness, and wind down, perchance,
To that still roaring dell, of which I told;
10 The roaring dell, o'erwooded, narrow, deep,
And only speckled by the mid-day sun;
Where its slim trunk the ash from rock to rock
Flings arching like a bridge;—that branchless ash,
Unsunn'd and damp, whose few poor yellow leaves
15 Ne'er tremble in the gale, yet tremble still,
Fann'd by the water-fall! and there my friends
Behold the dark green file of long lank weeds,
That all at once (a most fantastic sight!)
Still nod and drip beneath the dripping edge
20 Of the blue clay-stone.
                              Now, my friends emerge
Beneath the wide wide Heaven—and view again
The many-steepled tract magnificent
Of hilly fields and meadows, and the sea,
With some fair bark, perhaps, whose sails light up
25 The slip of smooth clear blue betwixt two Isles
Of purple shadow! Yes! they wander on
In gladness all; but thou, methinks, most glad,
My gentle-hearted Charles! [1] for thou hast pined
And hunger'd after Nature, many a year,
30 In the great City pent, winning thy way
With sad yet patient soul, through evil and pain
And strange calamity! Ah! slowly sink
Behind the western ridge, thou glorious Sun!
Shine in the slant beams of the sinking orb,
35 Ye purple heath-flowers! richlier burn, ye clouds!
Live in the yellow light, ye distant groves!

---

[1] Charles Lamb.

And kindle, thou blue Ocean! So my friend
Struck with deep joy may stand, as I have stood,
Silent with swimming sense; yea, gazing round
40 On the wide landscape, gaze till all doth seem
Less gross than bodily; and of such hues
As veil the Almighty Spirit, when yet he makes
Spirits perceive his presence.

                        A delight
Comes sudden on my heart, and I am glad
45 As I myself were there! Nor in this bower,
This little lime-tree bower, have I not mark'd
Much that has sooth'd me. Pale beneath the blaze
Hung the transparent foliage; and I watch'd
Some broad and sunny leaf, and lov'd to see
50 The shadow of the leaf and stem above
Dappling its sunshine! And that walnut-tree
Was richly ting'd, and a deep radiance lay
Full on the ancient ivy, which usurps
Those fronting elms, and now, with blackest mass
55 Makes their dark branches gleam a lighter hue·
Through the late twilight: and though now the bat
Wheels silent by, and not a swallow twitters,
Yet still the solitary humble-bee
Sings in the bean-flower! Henceforth I shall know
60 That Nature ne'er deserts the wise and pure;
No plot so narrow, be but Nature there,
No waste so vacant, but may well employ
Each faculty of sense, and keep the heart
Awake to Love and Beauty! and sometimes
65 'Tis well to be bereft of promis'd good,
That we may lift the soul, and contemplate
With lively joy the joys we cannot share.
My gentle-hearted Charles! when the last rook
Beat its straight path along the dusky air
70 Homewards, I blest it! deeming its black wing
(Now a dim speck, now vanishing in light)
Had cross'd the mighty Orb's dilated glory,
While thou stood'st gazing; or, when all was still,
Flew creeking o'er thy head, and had a charm
75 For thee, my gentle-hearted Charles, to whom
No sound is dissonant which tells of Life.

The Rime of the Ancient Mariner

Facile credo, plures esse Naturas invisibiles quam visibiles in rerum universitate. Sed horum omnium familiam quis nobis enarrabit? et gradus et cognationes et discrimina et singulorum munera? Quid agunt? quae loca habitant? Harum rerum notitiam semper ambivit ingenium humanum, nunquam attigit. Juvat, interea, non diffiteor, quandoque in animo, tanquam in tabulà, majoris et melioris mundi imaginem contemplari: ne mens assuefacta hodiernae vitae minutiis se contrahat nimis, et tota subsidat in pusillas cogitationes. Sed veritati interea invigilandum est, modusque servandus, ut certa ab incertis, diem a nocte, distinguamus.

T. BURNET, *Archaeol. Phil.* p. 68.[1]

ARGUMENT

How a Ship, having first sailed to the Equator, was driven by Storms to the cold Country towards the South Pole; how the Ancient Mariner cruelly and in contempt of the laws of hospitality killed a Seabird and how he was followed by many and strange Judgements: and in what manner he came back to his own Country. [*Lyrical Ballads.* ed. of 1800.]

PART I

It is an ancient Mariner,
And he stoppeth one of three.
"By thy long grey beard and glittering eye,
Now wherefore stopp'st thou me?

An ancient Mariner meeteth three Gallants bidden to a wedding-feast, and detaineth one.

5 The Bridegroom's doors are opened wide,
And I am next of kin;
The guests are met, the feast is set:
May'st hear the merry din."

He holds him with his skinny hand,
10 "There was a ship," quoth he.
"Hold off! unhand me, grey-beard loon!"
Eftsoons his hand dropt he.

---

[1] I readily believe that there are more invisible than visible things in the universe. But who will tell us of their families, ranks, similarities and differences? What do they do? Where do they live? Human knowledge has always circled around the understanding of these things but has never achieved it. It is pleasant, however, to contemplate at times, as in a picture, the image of a greater and better world lest the mind, too accustomed to the details of everyday life, become contracted and dwell completely on trivial things. But meanwhile we must be watchful of truth and keep within certain limits so that we may distinguish truth from opinion, day from night.

He holds him with his glittering eye—
The Wedding-Guest stood still,
15 And listens like a three years' child:
The Mariner hath his will.

The Wedding-Guest is
spellbound by the eye
of the old seafaring
man, and constrained
to hear his tale.

The Wedding-Guest sat on a stone:
He cannot choose but hear;
And thus spake on that ancient man,
20 The bright-eyed Mariner.

"The ship was cheered, the harbour cleared,
Merrily did we drop
Below the kirk, below the hill,
Below the lighthouse top.

25 The Sun came up upon the left,
Out of the sea came he!
And he shone bright, and on the right
Went down into the sea.

The Mariner tells how
the ship sailed south-
ward with a good
wind and fair weather,
till it reached the line.

Higher and higher every day,
30 Till over the mast at noon—"
The Wedding-Guest here beat his breast,
For he heard the loud bassoon.

The bride hath paced into the hall,
Red as a rose is she;
35 Nodding their heads before her goes
The merry minstrelsy.

The Wedding-Guest
heareth the bridal
music; but the Mari-
ner continueth his
tale.

The Wedding-Guest he beat his breast,
Yet he cannot choose but hear;
And thus spake on the ancient man,
40 The bright-eyed Mariner.

"And now the STORM-BLAST came, and he
Was tyrannous and strong:
He struck with his o'ertaking wings,
And chased us south along.

The ship driven by a
storm toward the
south pole.

45 With sloping masts and dipping prow,
As who pursued with yell and blow
Still treads the shadow of his foe,

And forward bends his head,
The ship drove fast, loud roared the blast,
50 And southward aye we fled.

And now there came both mist and snow,
And it grew wondrous cold:
And ice, mast-high, came floating by,
As green as emerald.

55 And through the drifts the snowy clifts
Did send a dismal sheen:
Nor shapes of men nor beasts we ken—
The ice was all between.

The ice was here, the ice was there,
60 The ice was all around:
It cracked and growled, and roared and howled,
Like noises in a swound!¹

At length did cross an Albatross,
Thorough the fog it came;
65 As if it had been a Christian soul,
We hailed it in God's name.

It ate the food it ne'er had eat,
And round and round it flew.
The ice did split with a thunder-fit;
70 The helmsman steered us through!

And a good south wind sprung up behind;
The Albatross did follow,
And every day, for food or play,
Came to the mariners' hollo!

75 In mist or cloud, on mast or shroud,²
It perched for vespers nine;
Whiles all the night, through fog-smoke white,
Glimmered the white Moon-shine."

The land of ice, and of fearful sounds where no living thing was to be seen.

Till a great sea-bird, called the Albatross, came through the snow-fog, and was received with great joy and hospitality.

And lo! the Albatross proveth a bird of good omen, and followeth the ship as it returned northward through fog and floating ice.

---

¹ Swoon.
² The rope that supports the masthead.

"God save thee, ancient Mariner!
80 From the fiends, that plague thee thus!—
Why look'st thou so?"—With my cross-bow
I shot the ALBATROSS.

The ancient Mariner
inhospitably killeth
the pious bird of good
omen.

PART II

The Sun now rose upon the right:
Out of the sea came he,
85 Still hid in mist, and on the left
Went down into the sea.

And the good south wind still blew behind,
But no sweet bird did follow,
Nor any day for food or play
90 Came to the mariners' hollo!

And I had done a hellish thing,
And it would work 'em woe:
For all averred, I had killed the bird
That made the breeze to blow.
95 Ah wretch! said they, the bird to slay,
That made the breeze to blow!

His shipmates cry out
against the ancient
Mariner, for killing
the bird of good luck.

Nor dim nor red, like God's own head,
The glorious Sun uprist:
Then all averred, I had killed the bird
100 That brought the fog and mist.
'Twas right, said they, such birds to slay,
That bring the fog and mist.

But when the fog
cleared off, they jus-
tify the same, and thus
make themselves ac-
complices in the
crime.

The fair breeze blew, the white foam flew,
The furrow followed free;
105 We were the first that ever burst
Into that silent sea.

The fair breeze con-
tinues; the ship enters
the Pacific Ocean, and
sails northward, even
till it reaches the Line.

Down dropt the breeze, the sails dropt down,
'Twas sad as sad could be;
And we did speak only to break
110 The silence of the sea!

The ship hath been
suddenly becalmed.

All in a hot and copper sky,
The bloody Sun, at noon,
Right up above the mast did stand,
No bigger than the Moon.

115 Day after day, day after day,
We stuck, nor breath nor motion;
As idle as a painted ship
Upon a painted ocean.

Water, water, every where,
120 And all the boards did shrink;
Water, water, every where,
Nor any drop to drink.

And the Albatross be-
gins to be avenged.

The very deep did rot: O Christ!
That ever this should be!
125 Yea, slimy things did crawl with legs
Upon the slimy sea.

About, about, in reel and rout
The death-fires danced at night;
The water, like a witch's oils,
130 Burnt green, and blue and white.

A Spirit had followed
them; one of the invis-
ible inhabitants of this
planet, neither de-
parted souls nor
angels; concerning
whom the learned
Jew, Josephus,
and the Platonic
Constantinopolitan,
Michael Psellus, may
be consulted. They
are very numerous,
and there is no climate
or element without
one or more.

And some in dreams assurèd were
Of the Spirit that plagued us so;
Nine fathom deep he had followed us
From the land of mist and snow.

135 And every tongue, through utter drought,
Was withered at the root;
We could not speak, no more than if
We had been choked with soot.

Ah! well a-day! what evil looks
140 Had I from old and young!
Instead of the cross, the Albatross
About my neck was hung.

The shipmates, in
their sore distress,
would fain throw the
whole guilt on the an-
cient Mariner: in sign
whereof they hang the
dead sea-bird round
his neck.

PART III

There passed a weary time. Each throat
Was parched, and glazed each eye.
145 A weary time! a weary time!
How glazed each weary eye,
When looking westward, I beheld
A something in the sky.

The ancient Mariner
beholdeth a sign in
the element afar off.

At first it seemed a little speck,
150 And then it seemed a mist;
It moved and moved, and took at last
A certain shape, I wist.

A speck, a mist. a shape, I wist!
And still it neared and neared:
155 As if it dodged a water-sprite,
It plunged and tacked and veered.

With throats unslaked, with black lips baked,
We could nor laugh nor wail;
Through utter drought all dumb we stood!
160 I bit my arm, I sucked the blood,
And cried, A sail! a sail!

> At its nearer approach, it seemeth him to be a ship; and at a dear ransom he freeth his speech from the bonds of thirst.

With throats unslaked, with black lips baked,
Agape they heard me call:
Gramercy! they for joy did grin,
165 And all at once their breath drew in,
As they were drinking all.

> A flash of joy;

See! see! (I cried) she tacks no more!
Hither to work us weal;
Without a breeze, without a tide,
170 She steadies with upright keel!

> And horror follows. For can it be a ship that comes onward without wind or tide?

The western wave was all a-flame.
The day was well nigh done!
Almost upon the western wave
Rested the broad bright Sun;
175 When that strange shape drove suddenly
Betwixt us and the Sun.

And straight the Sun was flecked with bars,
(Heaven's Mother send us grace!)
As if through a dungeon-grate he peered
180 With broad and burning face.

> It seemeth him but the skeleton of a ship.

Alas! (thought I, and my heart beat loud)
How fast she nears and nears!
Are those *her* sails that glance in the Sun,
Like restless gossameres?

> And its ribs are seen as bars on the face of the setting Sun.

185 Are those *her* ribs through which the Sun
    Did peer, as through a grate?
    And is that Woman all her crew?
    Is that a DEATH? and are there two?
    Is DEATH that woman's mate?

190 *Her* lips were red, *her* looks were free,
    Her locks were yellow as gold:
    Her skin was as white as leprosy,
    The Night-mare LIFE-IN-DEATH was she,
    Who thicks man's blood with cold.

195 The naked hulk alongside came,
    And the twain were casting dice;
    "The game is done! I've won! I've won!"
    Quoth she, and whistles thrice.

    The Sun's rim dips; the stars rush out:
200 At one stride comes the dark;
    With far-heard whisper, o'er the sea,
    Off shot the spectre-bark.

    We listened and looked sideways up!
    Fear at my heart, as at a cup,
205 My life-blood seemed to sip!
    The stars were dim, and thick the night,
    The steersman's face by his lamp gleamed white;
    From the sails the dew did drip—
    Till clomb above the eastern bar
210 The hornèd Moon, with one bright star
    Within the nether tip.

    One after one, by the star-dogged Moon,
    Too quick for groan or sigh,
    Each turned his face with a ghastly pang,
215 And cursed me with his eye.

    Four times fifty living men,
    (And I heard nor sigh nor groan)
    With heavy thump, a lifeless lump,
    They dropped down one by one.

220 The souls did from their bodies fly,—
    They fled to bliss or woe!

The Spectre-Woman and her Deathmate, and no other on board the skeleton ship.

Like vessel, like crew!

Death and Life-in-Death have diced for the ship's crew, and she (the latter) winneth the ancient Mariner.

No twilight within the courts of the Sun.

At the rising of the Moon,

One after another,

His shipmates drop down dead.

But Life-in-Death begins her work on the ancient Mariner.

And every soul, it passed me by,
Like the whizz of my cross-bow!

PART IV

"I fear thee, ancient Mariner!
225 I fear thy skinny hand!
And thou art long, and lank, and brown,
As is the ribbed sea-sand.[3]

The Wedding-Guest
feareth that a Spirit is
talking to him;

I fear thee and thy glittering eye,
And thy skinny hand, so brown."—
230 Fear not, fear not, thou Wedding-Guest!
This body dropt not down.

Alone, alone, all, all alone,
Alone on a wide wide sea!
And never a saint took pity on
235 My soul in agony.

But the ancient Mari-
ner assureth him of
his bodily life, and
proceedeth to relate
his horrible penance.

The many men, so beautiful!
And they all dead did lie:
And a thousand thousand slimy things
Lived on; and so did I.

He despiseth the crea-
tures of the calm,

240 I looked upon the rotting sea,
And drew my eyes away;
I looked upon the rotting deck,
And there the dead men lay.

And envieth that *they*
should live, and so
many lie dead.

I looked to heaven, and tried to pray;
245 But or ever a prayer had gusht,
A wicked whisper came, and made
My heart as dry as dust.

I closed my lids, and kept them close,
And the balls like pulses beat;
250 For the sky and the sea, and the sea and the sky
Lay like a load on my weary eye,
And the dead were at my feet.

---

[3] For the last two lines of this stanza I am indebted to Mr. Wordsworth. It was on a delightful walk from Nether Stowey to Dulverton, with him and his sister, in the Autumn of 1797, that this poem was planned, and in part composed (Coleridge).

The cold sweat melted from their limbs,
Nor rot nor reek did they:
255 The look with which they looked on me
Had never passed away.

But the curse liveth
for him in the eye of
the dead men.

An orphan's curse would drag to hell
A spirit from on high;
But oh! more horrible than that
260 Is the curse in a dead man's eye!
Seven days, seven nights, I saw that curse,
And yet I could not die.

In his loneliness and
fixedness he yearneth
towards the journey-
ing Moon, and the
stars that still sojourn,
yet still move onward;
and every where the
blue sky belongs to
them, and is their ap-
pointed rest, and their
native country and
their own natural
homes, which they en-
ter unannounced, as
lords that are certainly
expected and yet
there is a silent joy at
their arrival.

The moving Moon went up the sky,
And no where did abide:
265 Softly she was going up,
And a star or two beside—

Her beams bemocked the sultry main,
Like April hoar-frost spread;
But where the ship's huge shadow lay,
270 The charmèd water burnt alway
A still and awful red.

Beyond the shadow of the ship,
I watched the water-snakes:
They moved in tracks of shining white,
275 And when they reared, the elfish light
Fell off in hoary flakes.

By the light of the
Moon he beholdeth
God's creatures of the
great calm.

Within the shadow of the ship
I watched their rich attire:
Blue, glossy green, and velvet black,
280 They coiled and swam; and every track
Was a flash of golden fire.

O happy living things! no tongue
Their beauty might declare:
A spring of love gushed from my heart,
285 And I blessed them unaware:
Sure my kind saint took pity on me,
And I blessed them unaware.

Their beauty and
their happiness.

He blesseth them in
his heart.

The self-same moment I could pray;
And from my neck so free

The spell begins to
break.

290 The Albatross fell off, and sank
    Like lead into the sea.

PART V

Oh sleep! it is a gentle thing,
Beloved from pole to pole!
To Mary Queen the praise be given!
295 She sent the gentle sleep from Heaven,
That slid into my soul.

The silly buckets on the deck,   By grace of the holy
That had so long remained,   Mother, the ancient
I dreamt that they were filled with dew;   Mariner is refreshed
300 And when I awoke, it rained.   with rain.

My lips were wet, my throat was cold,
My garments all were dank;
Sure I had drunken in my dreams,
And still my body drank.

305 I moved, and could not feel my limbs:
I was so light—almost
I thought that I had died in sleep,
And was a blessèd ghost.

And soon I heard a roaring wind: He heareth sounds
310 It did not come anear;   and seeth strange
But with its sound it shook the sails,   sights and commo-
That were so thin and sere.   tions in the sky and
                                   the element.

The upper air burst into life!
And a hundred fire-flags sheen,
315 To and fro they were hurried about!
And to and fro, and in and out,
The wan stars danced between.

And the coming wind did roar more loud,
And the sails did sigh like sedge;
320 And the rain poured down from one black cloud;
The Moon was at its edge.

The thick black cloud was cleft, and still
The Moon was at its side:
Like waters shot from some high crag,

325 The lightning fell with never a jag,
    A river steep and wide.

    The loud wind never reached the ship,
    Yet now the ship moved on!
    Beneath the lightning and the Moon
330 The dead men gave a groan.

    They groaned, they stirred, they all uprose,
    Nor spake, nor moved their eyes;
    It had been strange, even in a dream,
    To have seen those dead men rise.

335 The helmsman steered, the ship moved on;
    Yet never a breeze up-blew;
    The mariners all 'gan work the ropes,
    Where they were wont to do;
    They raised their limbs like lifeless tools—
340 We were a ghastly crew.

    The body of my brother's son
    Stood by me, knee to knee:
    The body and I pulled at one rope,
    But he said nought to me.

The bodies of the ship's crew are inspired and the ship moves on;

345 "I fear thee, ancient Mariner!"
    Be calm, thou Wedding-Guest!
    'Twas not those souls that fled in pain,
    Which to their corses came again,
    But a troop of spirits blest:

350 For when it dawned—they dropped their arms,
    And clustered round the mast;
    Sweet sounds rose slowly through their mouths,
    And from their bodies passed.

But not by the souls of the men, nor by daemons of earth or middle air, but by a blessed troop of angelic spirits, sent down by the invocation of the guardian saint.

    Around, around, flew each sweet sound,
355 Then darted to the Sun;
    Slowly the sounds came back again,
    Now mixed, now one by one.

    Sometimes a-dropping from the sky
    I heard the sky-lark sing;
360 Sometimes all little birds that are,
    How they seemed to fill the sea and air
    With their sweet jargoning!

And now 'twas like all instruments,
Now like a lonely flute;
365 And now it is an angel's song,
That makes the heavens be mute.

It ceased; yet still the sails made on
A pleasant noise till noon,
A noise like of a hidden brook
370 In the leafy month of June,
That to the sleeping woods all night
Singeth a quiet tune.

Till noon we quietly sailed on,
Yet never a breeze did breathe:
375 Slowly and smoothly went the ship,
Moved onward from beneath.

Under the keel nine fathom deep,
From the land of mist and snow,
The spirit slid: and it was he
380 That made the ship to go.
The sails at noon left off their tune,
And the ship stood still also.

The lonesome Spirit from the south-pole carries on the ship as far as the Line, in obedience to the angelic troop, but still requireth vengeance.

The Sun, right up above the mast,
Had fixed her to the ocean:
385 But in a minute she 'gan stir,
With a short uneasy motion—
Backwards and forwards half her length
With a short uneasy motion.

Then like a pawing horse let go,
390 She made a sudden bound:
It flung the blood into my head,
And I fell down in a swound.

How long in that same fit I lay,
I have not to declare;
395 But ere my living life returned,
I heard and in my soul discerned
Two voices in the air.

"Is it he?" quoth one, "Is this the man?
By him who died on cross,
400 With his cruel bow he laid full low
The harmless Albatross.

The Polar Spirit's fellow-daemons, the invisible inhabitants of the element, take part in his wrong; and two of them relate, one to the other, that penance long and heavy for the ancient Mariner hath been accorded to the Polar Spirit, who returneth southward.

The spirit who bideth by himself
In the land of mist and snow,
He loved the bird that loved the man
405 Who shot him with his bow."

The other was a softer voice,
As soft as honey-dew:
Quoth he, "The man hath penance done,
And penance more will do."

PART VI

FIRST VOICE

410 "But tell me, tell me! speak again,
Thy soft response renewing—
What makes that ship drive on so fast?
What is the ocean doing?"

SECOND VOICE

"Still as a slave before his lord,
415 The ocean hath no blast;
His great bright eye most silently
Up to the Moon is cast—

If he may know which way to go;
For she guides him smooth or grim.
420 See, brother, see! how graciously
She looketh down on him."

FIRST VOICE

"But why drives on that ship so fast,
Without or wave or wind?"

The Mariner hath been cast into a trance; for the angelic power causeth the vessel to drive northward faster than human life could endure.

SECOND VOICE

"The air is cut away before,
425 And closes from behind.

Fly, brother, fly! more high, more high!
Or we shall be belated:
For slow and slow that ship will go,
When the Mariner's trance is abated."

430 I woke, and we were sailing on
As in a gentle weather:
'Twas night, calm night, the moon was high;
The dead men stood together.

All stood together on the deck,
435 For a charnel-dungeon fitter:
All fixed on me their stony eyes,
That in the Moon did glitter.

The pang, the curse, with which they died,
Had never passed away:
440 I could not draw my eyes from theirs,
Nor turn them up to pray.

And now this spell was snapt: once more
I viewed the ocean green,
And looked far forth, yet little saw
445 Of what had else been seen—

Like one, that on a lonesome road
Doth walk in fear and dread,
And living once turned round walks on,
And turns no more his head;
450 Because he knows, a frightful fiend
Doth close behind him tread.

But soon there breathed a wind on me,
Nor sound nor motion made:
Its path was not upon the sea,
455 In ripple or in shade.

It raised my hair, it fanned my cheek
Like a meadow-gale of spring—
It mingled strangely with my fears,
Yet it felt like a welcoming.

460 Swiftly, swiftly flew the ship,
Yet she sailed softly too:
Sweetly, sweetly blew the breeze—
On me alone it blew.

Oh! dream of joy! is this indeed
465 The light-house top I see?

Is this the hill? is this the kirk?
Is this mine own countree?

We drifted o'er the harbour-bar,
And I with sobs did pray—
470 O let me be awake, my God!
Or let me sleep alway.

The harbour-bay was clear as glass,
So smoothly it was strewn!
And on the bay the moonlight lay,
475 And the shadow of the Moon.

The rock shone bright, the kirk no less,
That stands above the rock:
The moonlight steeped in silentness
The steady weathercock.

480 And the bay was white with silent light,
Till rising from the same,
Full many shapes, that shadows were,   The angelic spirits
In crimson colours came.   leave the dead bodies,

A little distance from the prow   And appear in their
485 Those crimson shadows were: own forms of light.
I turned my eyes upon the deck—
Oh, Christ! what saw I there!

Each corse lay flat, lifeless and flat,
And, by the holy rood!
490 A man all light, a seraph-man,
On every corse there stood.

This seraph-band, each waved his hand:
It was a heavenly sight!
They stood as signals to the land,
495 Each one a lovely light;

This seraph-band, each waved his hand,
No voice did they impart—
No voice; but oh! the silence sank
Like music on my heart.

500 But soon I heard the dash of oars,
I heard the Pilot's cheer;

My head was turned perforce away
And I saw a boat appear.

The Pilot and the Pilot's boy,
505 I heard them coming fast:
Dear Lord in Heaven! it was a joy
The dead men could not blast.

I saw a third—I heard his voice:
It is the Hermit good!
510 He singeth loud his godly hymns
That he makes in the wood.
He'll shrieve my soul, he'll wash away
The Albatross's blood.

PART VII

This Hermit good lives in that wood
515 Which slopes down to the sea.
How loudly his sweet voice he rears!
He loves to talk with marineres
That come from a far countree.

The Hermit of the
Wood,

He kneels at morn, and noon, and eve—
520 He hath a cushion plump:
It is the moss that wholly hides
The rotted old oak-stump.

The skiff-boat neared: I heard them talk,
"Why, this is strange, I trow!
525 Where are those lights so many and fair,
That signal made but now?"

"Strange, by my faith!" the Hermit said—
"And they answered not our cheer!
The planks looked warped! and see those sails,
530 How thin they are and sere!
I never saw aught like to them,
Unless perchance it were

Approacheth the ship
with wonder.

Brown skeletons of leaves that lag
My forest-brook along;
535 When the ivy-tod[4] is heavy with snow,

---

[4] ivy-bush.

And the owlet whoops to the wolf below,
That eats the she-wolf's young."

"Dear Lord! it hath a fiendish look—
(The Pilot made reply)
540 I am a-feared"—"Push on, push on!"
Said the Hermit cheerily.

The boat came closer to the ship,
But I nor spake nor stirred;
The boat came close beneath the ship,
545 And straight a sound was heard.

Under the water it rumbled on,
Still louder and more dread:
It reached the ship, it split the bay;
The ship went down like lead.

The ship suddenly sinketh.

550 Stunned by that loud and dreadful sound,
Which sky and ocean smote,
Like one that hath been seven days drowned
My body lay afloat;
But swift as dreams myself I found
555 Within the Pilot's boat.

The ancient Mariner is saved in the Pilot's boat.

Upon the whirl, where sank the ship,
The boat spun round and round;
And all was still, save that the hill
Was telling of the sound.

560 I moved my lips—the Pilot shrieked
And fell down in a fit;
The holy Hermit raised his eyes,
And prayed where he did sit.

I took the oars: the Pilot's boy,
565 Who now doth crazy go,
Laughed loud and long, and all the while
His eyes went to and fro.
"Ha! ha!" quoth he, "full plain I see,
The Devil knows how to row."

570 And now, all in my own countree,
I stood on the firm land!

The Hermit stepped forth from the boat,
And scarcely he could stand.

"O shrieve me, shrieve me, holy man!'
575 The Hermit crossed his brow.
"Say quick," quoth he, "I bid thee say—
What manner of man art thou?"

The ancient Mariner
earnestly entreateth
the Hermit to shrieve
him; and the penance
of life falls on him.

Forthwith this frame of mine was wrenched
With a woeful agony,
580 Which forced me to begin my tale;
And then it left me free.

Since then, at an uncertain hour,
That agony returns:
And till my ghastly tale is told,
585 This heart within me burns.

And ever and anon
through out his future
life an agony con-
straineth him to travel
from land to land;

I pass, like night, from land to land;
I have strange power of speech;
That moment that his face I see,
I know the man that must hear me:
590 To him my tale I teach.

What loud uproar bursts from that door!
The wedding-guests are there:
But in the garden-bower the bride
And bride-maids singing are:
595 And hark the little vesper bell,
Which biddeth me to prayer!

O Wedding-Guest! this soul hath been
Alone on a wide wide sea:
So lonely 'twas that God himself
600 Scarce seemèd there to be.

O sweeter than the marriage-feast,
'Tis sweeter far to me,
To walk together to the kirk
With a goodly company!—

605 To walk together to the kirk,
And all together pray,
While each to his great Father bends,

Old men, and babes, and loving friends
And youths and maidens gay!

610 Farewell, farewell! but this I tell
To thee, thou Wedding-Guest!
He prayeth well, who loveth well
Both man and bird and beast.

He prayeth best, who loveth best
615 All things both great and small;
For the dear God who loveth us,
He made and loveth all.

The Mariner, whose eye is bright,
Whose beard with age is hoar,
620 Is gone: and now the Wedding-Guest
Turned from the bridegroom's door.

He went like one that hath been stunned,
And is of sense forlorn:
A sadder and a wiser man,
625 He rose the morrow morn.

And to teach, by his own example, love and reverence to all things that God made and loveth.

Dejection: An Ode

WRITTEN APRIL 4, 1802

Late, late yestreen I saw the new Moon,
With the old Moon in her arms;
And I fear, I fear, my Master dear!
We shall have a deadly storm.
BALLAD OF SIR PATRICK SPENCE

I

Well! If the Bard was weather-wise, who made
    The grand old ballad of Sir Patrick Spence,
    This night, so tranquil now, will not go hence
Unroused by winds, that ply a busier trade
5 Than those which mould yon cloud in lazy flakes,
Or the dull sobbing draft, that moans and rakes
Upon the strings of this Æolian lute,
        Which better far were mute.
    For lo! the New-moon winter-bright!
10   And overspread with phantom light,
    (With swimming phantom light o'erspread
    But rimmed and circled by a silver thread)

I see the old Moon in her lap, foretelling
  The coming-on of rain and squally blast.
15 And oh! that even now the gust were swelling,
  And the slant night-shower driving loud and fast!
Those sounds which oft have raised me, whilst they awed,
    And sent my soul abroad,
Might now perhaps their wonted impulse give,
20 Might startle this dull pain, and make it move and live!

II

A grief without a pang, void, dark, and drear,
  A stifled, drowsy, unimpassioned grief,
  Which finds no natural outlet, no relief,
    In word, or sigh, or tear—
25 O lady! in this wan and heartless mood,
To other thoughts by yonder throstle woo'd,
  All this long eve, so balmy and serene,
Have I been gazing on the western sky,
  And its peculiar tint of yellow green:
30 And still I gaze—and with how blank an eye!
And those thin clouds above, in flakes and bars,
That give away their motion to the stars;
Those stars, that glide behind them or between,
Now sparkling, now bedimmed, but always seen:
35 Yon crescent Moon, as fixed as if it grew
In its own cloudless, starless lake of blue;
I see them all so excellently fair,
I see, not feel, how beautiful they are!

III

  My genial spirits fail;
40   And what can these avail
To lift the smothering weight from off my breast?
  It were a vain endeavour,
  Though I should gaze for ever
On that green light that lingers in the west:
45 I may not hope from outward forms to win
The passion and the life, whose fountains are within.

IV

O Lady! we receive but what we give,
And in our life alone does Nature live:
Ours is her wedding garment, ours her shroud!
50   And would we aught behold, of higher worth,

Than that inanimate cold world allowed
To the poor loveless ever-anxious crowd,
   Ah! from the soul itself must issue forth
A light, a glory, a fair luminous cloud
55   Enveloping the Earth—
And from the soul itself must there be sent
   A sweet and potent voice, of its own birth,
Of all sweet sounds the life and element!

V

O pure of heart! thou need'st not ask of me
60 What this strong music in the soul may be!
What, and wherein it doth exist,
This light, this glory, this fair luminous mist,
This beautiful and beauty-making power.
   Joy, virtuous Lady! Joy that ne'er was given,
65 Save to the pure, and in their purest hour,
Life, and Life's effluence, cloud at once and shower,
Joy, Lady! is the spirit and the power,
Which wedding Nature to us gives in dower
   A new Earth and new Heaven,
70 Undreamt of by the sensual and the proud—
Joy is the sweet voice, Joy the luminous cloud—
     We in ourselves rejoice!
And thence flows all that charms or ear or sight,
   All melodies the echoes of that voice,
75 All colours a suffusion from that light.

VI

There was a time when, though my path was rough,
   This joy within me dallied with distress,
And all misfortunes were but as the stuff
   Whence Fancy made me dreams of happiness:
80 For hope grew round me, like the twining vine,
And fruits, and foliage, not my own, seemed mine.
But now afflictions bow me down to earth:
Nor care I that they rob me of my mirth;
     But oh! each visitation
85 Suspends what nature gave me at my birth,
   My shaping spirit of Imagination.

For not to think of what I needs must feel,
   But to be still and patient, all I can;
And haply by abstruse research to steal

90   From my own nature all the natural man—
      This was my sole resource, my only plan:
      Till that which suits a part infects the whole,
      And now is almost grown the habit of my soul.

VII

      Hence, viper thoughts, that coil around my mind,
95   Reality's dark dream!
      I turn from you, and listen to the wind,
          Which long has raved unnoticed. What a scream
      Of agony by torture lengthened out
      That lute sent forth! Thou Wind, that rav'st without,
100   Bare crag, or mountain-tairn, or blasted tree,
      Or pine-grove whither woodman never clomb,
      Or lonely house, long held the witches' home,
          Methinks were fitter instruments for thee,
      Mad Lutanist! who is this month of showers,
105 Of dark-brown gardens, and of peeping flowers,
      Mak'st Devils' yule, with worse than wintry song,
      The blossoms, buds, and timorous leaves among.
          Thou Actor, perfect in all tragic sounds!
      Thou mighty Poet, e'en to frenzy bold!
110   What tell'st thou now about?
          'Tis of the rushing of an host in rout,
          With groans, of trampled men, with smarting wounds—
      At once they groan with pain, and shudder with the cold!
      But hush! there is a pause of deepest silence!
115   And all that noise, as of a rushing crowd,
      With groans, and tremulous shudderings—all is over—
          It tells another tale, with sounds less deep and loud!
              A tale of less affright,
              And tempered with delight,
120 As Otway's self had framed the tender lay,—
              'Tis of a little child
              Upon a lonesome wild,
      Not far from home, but she hath lost her way:
      And now moans low in bitter grief and fear,
125 And now screams loud, and hopes to make her mother hear.[1]

VIII

      'Tis midnight, but small thoughts have I of sleep:
      Full seldom may my friend such vigils keep!

---

[1] Lines 121–125 tell the story of Wordsworth's *Lucy Gray*.

Visit her, gentle Sleep! with wings of healing,
   And may this storm be but a mountain-birth,
130 May all the stars hang bright above her dwelling,
   Silent as though they watched the sleeping Earth!
     With light heart may she rise,
     Gay fancy, cheerful eyes,
   Joy lift her spirit, joy attune her voice;
135 To her may all things live, from pole to pole,
   Their life the eddying of her living soul!
    O simple spirit, guided from above,
   Dear Lady! friend devoutest of my choice,
   Thus mayest thou ever, evermore rejoice.

WALTER SAVAGE LANDOR (1775–1864)

Rose Aylmer

Ah what avails the sceptered race,
   Ah what the form divine!
What every virtue, every grace!
   Rose Aylmer, all were thine.
5 Rose Aylmer, whom these wakeful eyes
   May weep, but never see,
A night of memories and of sighs
   I consecrate to thee.

Past Ruined Ilion Helen Lives

Past ruined Ilion Helen lives,
   Alcestis rises from the shades;
Verse calls them forth; 'tis verse that gives
   Immortal youth to mortal maids.

5 Soon shall Oblivion's deepening veil
   Hide all the peopled hills you see,
The gay, the proud, while lovers hail
   In distant ages you and me.

The tear for fading beauty check,
10   For passing glory cease to sigh;
One form shall rise above the wreck,
   One name, Ianthe, shall not die.

Dying Speech of an Old Philosopher

I strove with none, for none was worth my strife:
   Nature I loved, and, next to Nature, Art:
I warmed both hands before the fire of Life;
   It sinks; and I am ready to depart.

GEORGE GORDON, LORD BYRON (1788–1824)

So We'll Go No More A-Roving

So we'll go no more a-roving
   So late into the night,
Though the heart be still as loving,
   And the moon be still as bright.

5 For the sword outwears its sheath,
      And the soul wears out the breast,
   And the heart must pause to breathe,
      And Love itelf have rest.

   Though the night was made for loving,
10   And the day returns too soon,
   Yet we'll go no more a-roving
      By the light of the moon.

She Walks in Beauty

She walks in beauty, like the night
   Of cloudless climes and starry skies;
And all that's best of dark and bright
   Meet in her aspect and her eyes:
5 Thus mellowed to that tender light
   Which heaven to gaudy day denies.

One shade the more, one ray the less,
   Had half impaired the nameless grace
Which waves in every raven tress,
10   Or softly lightens o'er her face;
Where thoughts serenely sweet express
   How pure, how dear their dwelling place.

And on that cheek, and o'er that brow,
   So soft, so calm, yet eloquent,

15 The smiles that win, the tints that glow,
    But tell of days in goodness spent,
  A mind at peace with all below,
    A heart whose love is innocent!

The Destruction of Sennacherib[1]

The Assyrian came down like the wolf on the fold,
And his cohorts were gleaming in purple and gold;
And the sheen of their spears was like stars on the sea,
When the blue wave rolls nightly on deep Galilee.

5 Like the leaves of the forest when summer is green,
  That host with their banners at sunset were seen:
  Like the leaves of the forest when autumn hath blown,
  That host on the morrow lay wither'd and strown.

For the Angel of Death spread his wings on the blast,
10 And breathed in the face of the foe as he pass'd
  And the eyes of the sleepers wax'd deadly and chill,
  And their hearts but once heaved, and forever grew still!

And there lay the steed with his nostril all wide,
But through it there roll'd not the breath of his pride;
15 And the foam of his gasping lay white on the turf,
  And cold as the spray of the rock-beating surf.

And there lay the rider distorted and pale,
With the dew on his brow, and the rust on his mail:
And the tents were all silent, the banners alone,
20 The lances unlifted, the trumpet unblown.

And the widows of Ashur are loud in their wail,
And the idols are broke in the temple of Baal;
And the might of the Gentile, unsmote by the sword,
Hath melted like snow in the glance of the Lord!

Prometheus

Titan! to whose immortal eyes
  The sufferings of mortality,
  Seen in their sad reality,

---

[1] For an account of the episode see II Kings 18–19.

Were not as things that gods despise;
5 What was thy pity's recompense?
A silent suffering, and intense;
The rock, the vulture, and the chain,
All that the proud can feel of pain,
The agony they do not show,
10 The suffocating sense of woe,
    Which speaks but in its loneliness,
And then is jealous lest the sky
Should have a listener, nor will sigh
    Until its voice is echoless.

15 Titan! to thee the strife was given
    Between the suffering and the will,
    Which torture where they cannot kill;
And the inexorable Heaven,
And the deaf tyranny of Fate,
20 The ruling principle of Hate,
Which for its pleasure doth create
The things it may annihilate,
Refused thee even the boon to die:
The wretched gift eternity
25 Was thine—and thou hast borne it well.

All that the Thunderer[1] wrung from thee
Was but the menace which flung back
On him the torments of thy rack;
The fate thou didst so well foresee,[2]
30 But would not to appease him tell;
And in thy silence was his sentence,
And in his soul a vain repentance,
And evil dread so ill dissembled,
That in his hand the lightnings trembled.

35 Thy Godlike crime was to be kind,
    To render with thy precepts less
    The sum of human wretchedness,
And strengthen man with his own mind;
But baffled as thou wert from high, .
40 Still in thy patient energy,

---

[1] Zeus, hurler of thunderbolts.
[2] Prometheus held the secret of what would ultimately bring about the downfall of Zeus.

In the endurance, and repulse
　Of thine impenetrable spirit,
Which Earth and Heaven could not convulse,
　A mighty lesson we inherit:
45 Thou art a symbol and a sign
　To mortals of their fate and force;
Like thee, man is in part divine,
　A troubled stream from a pure source;
And man in portions can foresee
50 His own funereal destiny;
His wretchedness, and his resistance,
And his sad unallied existence:
To which his spirit may oppose
Itself—and equal to all woes,
55 　And a firm will, and a deep sense,
Which even in torture can descry
　Its owns concenter'd recompense,
Triumphant where it dares defy,
And making death a victory.

PERCY BYSSHE SHELLEY (1792–1822)

Hymn to Intellectual Beauty

The awful shadow of some unseen Power
　Floats though unseen among us,—visiting
　This various world with as inconstant wing
As summer winds that creep from flower to flower,—
5 Like moonbeams that behind some piny mountain shower,
　　It visits with inconstant glance
　　Each human heart and countenance;
Like hues and harmonies of evening,—
　　Like clouds in starlight widely spread,—
10 　　Like memory of music fled,—
　　Like aught that for its grace may be
Dear, and yet dearer for its mystery.

Spirit of BEAUTY, that dost consecrate
　With thine own hues all thou dost shine upon
15 　Of human thought or form,—where art thou gone?
Why dost thou pass away and leave our state,
This dim vast vale of tears, vacant and desolate?
　　Ask why the sunlight not for ever
　　Weaves rainbows o'er yon mountain-river,

²⁰ Why aught should fail and fade that once is shown,
    Why fear and dream and death and birth
    Cast on the daylight of this earth
    Such gloom,—why man has such a scope
For love and hate, despondency and hope?

²⁵ No voice from some sublimer world hath ever
    To sage or poet these responses given—
    Therefore the names of Demon, Ghost, and Heaven,
Remain the records of their vain endeavor,
Frail spells—whose uttered charm might not avail to sever,
³⁰   From all we hear and all we see,
    Doubt, chance, and mutability.
Thy light alone—like mist o'er mountains driven,
    Or music by the night-wind sent
    Through strings of some still instrument,
³⁵   Or moonlight on a midnight stream,
Gives grace and truth to life's unquiet dream.

Love, Hope, and Self-esteem, like clouds depart
    And come, for some uncertain moments lent.
    Man were immortal, and omnipotent,
⁴⁰ Didst thou, unknown and awful as thou art,
Keep with thy glorious train firm state within his heart.
    Thou messenger of sympathies,
    That wax and wane in lovers' eyes—
Thou— that to human thought art nourishment,
⁴⁵   Like darkness to a dying flame!
    Depart not as thy shadow came,
    Depart not—lest the grave should be,
Like life and fear, a dark reality.

While yet a boy I sought for ghosts, and sped
⁵⁰   Through many a listening chamber, cave and ruin,
    And starlight wood, with fearful steps pursuing
Hopes of high talk with the departed dead.
I called on poisonous names with which our youth is fed;
    I was not heard—I saw them not—
⁵⁵   When musing deeply on the lot
Of life, at that sweet time when winds are wooing
    All vital things that wake to bring
    News of birds and blossoming,—
    Sudden, thy shadow fell on me;
⁶⁰ I shrieked, and clasped my hands in ecstasy!

I vowed that I would dedicate my powers
    To thee and thine—have I not kept the vow?
    With beating heart and streaming eyes, even now
I call the phantoms of a thousand hours
65 Each from his voiceless grave: they have in visioned bowers
      Of studious zeal or love's delight
      Outwatched with me the envious night—
They know that never joy illumed my brow
      Unlinked with hope that thou wouldst free
70   This world from its dark slavery,
      That thou—O awful LOVELINESS,
Wouldst give whate'er these words cannot express.

The day becomes more solemn and serene
    When noon is past—there is a harmony
75   In autumn, and a lustre in its sky,
Which through the summer is not heard or seen,
As if it could not be, as if it had not been!
      Thus let thy power, which like the truth
      Of nature on my passive youth
80 Descended, to my onward life supply
      Its calm—to one who worships thee,
      And every form containing thee,
      Whom, SPIRIT, thy spells did bind
To fear himself, and love all human kind.

Ozymandias

I met a traveler from an antique land
Who said: Two vast and trunkless legs of stone
Stand in the desert . . . Near them, on the sand,
Half sunk, a shattered visage lies, whose frown,
5 And wrinkled lip, and sneer of cold command,
Tell that its sculptor well those passions read
Which yet survive, stamped on these lifeless things,
The hand that mocked them, and the heart that fed:
And on the pedestal these words appear:
10 "My name is Ozymandias, king of kings:
Look on my works, ye Mighty, and despair!"
Nothing beside remains. Round the decay
Of that colossal wreck, boundless and bare
The lone and level sands stretch far away.

Ode to the West Wind

1

O wild West Wind, thou breath of Autumn's being,
Thou, from whose unseen presence the leaves dead
Are driven, like ghosts from an enchanter fleeing,

Yellow, and black, and pale, and hectic red,
5 Pestilence-stricken multitudes: O thou,
Who chariotest to their dark wintry bed

The wingèd seeds, where they lie cold and low,
Each like a corpse within its grave, until
Thine azure sister of the Spring shall blow

10 Her clarion o'er the dreaming earth, and fill
(Driving sweet buds like flocks to feed in air)
With living hues and odors plain and hill:

Wild Spirit, which art moving everywhere;
Destroyer and preserver; hear, oh, hear!

2

15 Thou on whose stream, mid the steep sky's commotion,
Loose clouds like earth's decaying leaves are shed,
Shook from the tangled boughs of Heaven and Ocean,

Angels of rain and lightning: there are spread
On the blue surface of thine aery surge,
20 Like the bright hair uplifted from the head

Of some fierce Maenad, even from the dim verge
Of the horizon to the zenith's height,
The locks of the approaching storm. Thou dirge

Of the dying year, to which this closing night
25 Will be the dome of a vast sepulcher,
Vaulted with all thy congregated might

Of vapors, from whose solid atmosphere
Black rain, and fire, and hail will burst: oh, hear!

3

Thou who didst waken from his summer dreams
30 The blue Mediterranean, where he lay,
Lulled by the coil of his crystàlline streams,

Beside a pumice isle in Baiae's bay,
And saw in sleep old palaces and towers
Quivering within the wave's intenser day,

35 All overgrown with azure moss and flowers
So sweet, the sense faints picturing them! Thou
For whose path the Atlantic's level powers

Cleave themselves into chasms, while far below
The sea-blooms and the oozy woods which wear
40 The sapless foliage of the ocean, know
Thy voice, and suddenly grow gray with fear,
And tremble and despoil themselves: oh, hear!

4

If I were a dead leaf thou mightest bear;
If I were a swift cloud to fly with thee;
45 A wave to pant beneath thy power, and share

The impulse of thy strength, only less free
Than thou, O uncontrollable! If even
I were as in my boyhood, and could be

The comrade of thy wanderings over Heaven,
50 As then, when to outstrip thy skiey speed
Scarce seem a vision; I would ne'er have striven

As thus with thee in prayer in my sore need.
Oh, lift me as a wave, a leaf, a cloud!
I fall upon the thorns of life! I bleed!

55 A heavy weight of hours has chained and bowed
One too like thee: tameless, and swift, and proud.

5

Make me thy lyre, even as the forest is:
What if my leaves are falling like its own!
The tumult of thy mighty harmonies

60 Will take from both a deep, autumnal tone,
Sweet though in sadness. Be thou, Spirit fierce,
My spirit! Be thou me, impetuous one!

Drive my dead thoughts over the universe
Like withered leaves to quicken a new birth!
65 And, by the incantation of this verse,

Scatter, as from an unextinguished hearth
Ashes and sparks, my words among mankind!
Be through my lips to unawakened earth

The trumpet of a prophecy! O Wind,
70 If Winter comes, can Spring be far behind?

To ————

Music, when soft voices die,
Vibrates in the memory—
Odors, when sweet violets sicken,
Live within the sense they quicken.

Rose leaves, when the rose is dead,
5 Are heaped for the belovèd's bed;
And so thy thoughts, when thou art gone,
Love itself shall slumber on.

From **Hellas: Two Choruses**

WORLDS ON WORLDS

Worlds on worlds are rolling ever
    From creation to decay,
Like the bubbles on a river
    Sparkling, bursting, borne away.
5   But they are still immortal
    Who, through birth's orient portal
And death's dark chasm hurrying to and fro,
    Clothe their unceasing flight
    In the brief dust and light
10 Gathered around their chariots as they go;
    New shapes they still may weave,
    New gods, new laws receive,

Bright or dim are they as the robes they last
   On Death's bare ribs had cast.

15   A power from the unknown God,
    A Promethean conqueror, came;
  Like a triumphal path he trod
    The thorns of death and shame.
    A mortal shape to him
    Was like the vapor dim
20 Which the orient planet animates with light;
    Hell, Sin, and Slavery came,
    Like bloodhounds mild and tame,
  Nor preyed, until their Lord had taken flight;
25   The moon of Mahomet
    Arose, and it shall set:
  While blazoned as on Heaven's immortal noon
    The cross leads generations on.
    Swift as the radiant shapes of sleep
30   From one whose dreams are Paradise
  Fly, when the fond wretch wakes to weep,
    And Day peers forth with her blank eyes;
    So fleet, so fain, so fair,
    The Powers of earth and air
35 Fled from the folding-star of Bethlehem:
    Apollo, Pan, and Love,
    And even Olympian Jove
  Grew weak, for killing Truth had glared on them;
40   Our hills and seas and streams,
    Dispeopled of their dreams,
  Their waters turned to blood, their dew to tears,
    Wailed for the golden years.

THE WORLD'S GREAT AGE

The world's great age begins anew,
  The golden years return,
The earth doth like a snake renew
  Her winter weeds outworn:
5 Heaven smiles, and faiths and empires gleam,
Like wrecks of a dissolving dream.

A brighter Hellas rears its mountains
  From waves serener far;

A new Peneus rolls his fountains
10   Against the morning star.
Where fairer Tempes[1] bloom, there sleep
Young Cyclads[2] on a sunnier deep.

A loftier Argo[3] cleaves the main,
    Fraught with a later prize;
15 Another Orpheus sings again,
    And loves, and weeps, and dies.
A new Ulysses leaves once more
Calypso for his native shore.

Oh, write no more the tale of Troy,
20   If earth Death's scroll must be!
Nor mix with Laian[4] rage the joy
    Which dawns upon the free:
Although a subtler Sphinx renew
Riddles of death Thebes never knew.

25 Another Athens shall arise,
    And to remoter time
Bequeath, like sunset to the skies,
    The splendor of its prime;
And leave, if nought so bright may live,
30 All earth can take or Heaven can give.

Saturn and Love their long repose
    Shall burst, more bright and good
Than all who fell, than One who rose,
    Than many unsubdued:
35 Not gold, not blood, their altar dowers,
But votive tears and symbol flowers.

Oh, cease! must hate and death return?
    Cease! must men kill and die?
Cease! drain not to its dregs the urn
40   Of bitter prophecy.
The world is weary of the past,
Oh, might it die or rest at last!

---

1 The vale of Tempe in Thessaly, through which the river Peneus flows.
2 Islands in the Aegean.
3 The ship in which Jason sailed in quest of the Golden Fleece.
4 Laius, father of Oedipus.

WILLIAM CULLEN BRYANT (1794–1878)

An Indian at the Burial-Place of His Fathers

It is the spot I came to seek—
    My father's ancient burial-place,
Ere from these vales, ashamed and weak,
    Withdrew our wasted race.
5 It is the spot—I know it well—
Of which our old traditions tell.

For here the upland bank sends out
    A ridge toward the riverside;
I know the shaggy hills about,
10   The meadows smooth and wide,
The plains, that toward the southern sky,
Fenced east and west by mountains lie.

A white man, gazing on the scene,
    Would say a lovely spot was here,
15 And praise the lawns, so fresh and green,
    Between the hills so sheer.
I like it not—I would the plain
Lay in its tall old groves again.

The sheep are on the slopes around,
20   The cattle in the meadows feed,
And laborers turn the crumbling ground,
    Or drop the yellow seed,
And prancing steeds, in trappings gay,
Whirl the bright chariot o'er the way.

25 Methinks it were a nobler sight
    To see these vales in woods arrayed,
Their summits in the golden light,
    Their trunks in grateful shade,
And herds of deer that bounding go
30 O'er hills and prostrate trees below.

And then to mark the lord of all,
    The forest hero, trained to wars,
Quivered and plumed, and lithe and tall,
    And seamed with glorious scars,
35 Walk forth, amid his reign, to dare
The wolf, and grapple with the bear.

This bank, in which the dead were laid,
   Was sacred when its soil was ours;
Hither the silent Indian maid
40   Brought wreaths of beads and flowers,
And the gray chief and gifted seer
Worshipped the god of thunders here.

But now the wheat is green and high
   On clods that hid the warrior's breast,
45 And scattered in the furrows lie
   The weapons of his rest;
And there, in the loose sand, is thrown
Of his large arm the mouldering bone.

Ah, little thought the strong and brave
50   Who bore their lifeless chieftain forth—
Or the young wife that weeping gave
   Her first-born to the earth,
That the pale race who waste us now
Among their bones should guide the plough.

55 They waste us—ay—like April snow
   In the warm noon, we shrink away;
And fast they follow, as we go
   Toward the setting day—
Till they shall fill the land, and we
60 Are driven into the Western sea.

But I behold a fearful sign,
   To which the white men's eyes are blind;
Their race may vanish hence, like mine,
   And leave no trace behind,
65 Save ruins o'er the region spread,
And the white stones above the dead.

Before these fields were shorn and tilled,
   Full to the brim our rivers flowed;
The melody of waters filled
70   The fresh and boundless wood;
And torrents dashed and rivulets played,
And fountains spouted in the shade.

Those grateful sounds are heard no more,
   The springs are silent in the sun;

75 The rivers, by the blackened shore,
　　With lessening current run;
　The realm our tribes are crushed to get
　May be a barren desert yet.

JOHN KĒATS (1795–1821)

On First Looking into Chapman's Homer[1]

Much have I travelled in the realms of gold,
　　And many goodly states and kingdoms seen;
　　Round many western islands have I been
　Which bards in fealty to Apollo hold.
5 Oft of one wide expanse had I been told
　　That deep-browed Homer ruled as his demesne;
　　Yet did I never breathe its pure serene
　Till I heard Chapman speak out loud and bold:
　Then felt I like some watcher of the skies
10　　When a new planet swims into his ken;
　Or like stout Cortez[2] when with eagle eyes
　　He stared at the Pacific—and all his men
　Looked at each other with a wild surmise—
　　Silent, upon a peak in Darien.

When I Have Fears

When I have fears that I may cease to be
　Before my pen has gleaned my teeming brain,
Before high-piled books, in charactery,[1]
　Hold like rich garners the full ripened grain;
5 When I behold, upon the night's starred face,
　Huge cloudy symbols of a high romance,
And think that I may never live to trace
　Their shadows, with the magic hand of chance;
And when I feel, fair creature of an hour,
10　That I shall never look upon thee more,
Never have relish in the faery power
　Of unreflecting love;—then on the shore

---

1 A translation by George Chapman, a contemporary of Shakespeare.
2 It was actually Balboa who discovered the Pacific in 1513.

1 Characters, writing.

Of the wide world I stand alone, and think
Till love and fame to nothingness do sink.

Ode to a Nightingale

1

My heart aches, and a drowsy numbness pains
  My sense, as though of hemlock I had drunk,
Or emptied some dull opiate to the drains
  One minute past, and Lethe-wards[1] had sunk:
5 'Tis not through envy of thy happy lot,
  But being too happy in thine happiness—
    That thou, light-wingèd Dryad of the trees,
      In some melodious plot
Of beechen green, and shadows numberless,
10   Singest of summer in full-throated ease.

2

O, for a draught of vintage! that hath been
  Cooled a long age in the deep-delvèd earth,
Tasting of Flora[2] and the country green,
  Dance, and Provençal song, and sunburnt mirth!
15 O for a beaker full of the warm South,
  Full of the true, the blushful Hippocrene,[3]
    With beaded bubbles winking at the brim,
      And purple-stainèd mouth;
That I might drink, and leave the world unseen,
20   And with thee fade away into the forest dim:

3

Fade far away, dissolve, and quite forget
  What thou among the leaves hast never known,
The weariness, the fever, and the fret
  Here, where men sit and hear each other groan;
25 Where palsy shakes a few, sad, last gray hairs,
  Where youth grows pale, and spectre-thin, and dies,

---

[1] Towards the river Lethe, in the underworld.
[2] Goddess of flowers.
[3] Fountain of the Muses on Mt. Helicon.

Where but to think is to be full of sorrow
And leaden-eyed despairs,
Where Beauty cannot keep her lustrous eyes,
30   Or new Love pine at them beyond tomorrow.

4

Away! away! for I will fly to thee,
Not charioted by Bacchus and his pards,[4]
But on the viewless wings of Poesy,
Though the dull brain perplexes and retards:
35 Already with thee! tender is the night,
And haply the Queen-Moon is on her throne,
Clustered around by all her starry Fays;
But here there is no light,
Save what from heaven is with the breezes blown
40   Through verdurous glooms and winding mossy ways.

5

I cannot see what flowers are at my feet,
Nor what soft incense hangs upon the boughs,
But, in embalmèd darkness, guess each sweet
Wherewith the seasonable month endows
45 The grass, the thicket, and the fruit-tree wild;
White hawthorn, and the pastoral eglantine;
Fast fading violets covered up in leaves;
And mid-May's eldest child,
The coming musk-rose, full of dewy wine,
50   The murmurous haunt of flies on summer eves.

6

Darkling[5] I listen; and for many a time
I have been half in love with easeful Death,
Called him soft names in many a musèd rhyme,
To take into the air my quiet breath;
55 Now more than ever seems it rich to die,
To cease upon the midnight with no pain,
While thou art pouring forth thy soul abroad
In such an ecstasy!
Still wouldst thou sing, and I have ears in vain—
60   To thy high requiem become a sod.

---

4 Leopards drawing the chariot of Bacchus, god of wine.
5 In the darkness.

7

Thou wast not born for death, immortal Bird!
  No hungry generations tread thee down;
The voice I hear this passing night was heard
  In ancient days by emperor and clown:
65 Perhaps the selfsame song that found a path
    Through the sad heart of Ruth, when, sick for home,
      She stood in tears amid the alien corn:
        The same that oft-times hath
    Charmed magic casements, opening on the foam
70   Of perilous seas, in faery lands forlorn.

8

Forlorn! the very word is like a bell
  To toll me back from thee to my sole self!
Adieu! the fancy cannot cheat so well
  As she is famed to do, deceiving elf.
75 Adieu! adieu! thy plaintive anthem fades
    Past the near meadows, over the still stream,
      Up the hill side; and now 'tis buried deep
        In the next valley-glades:
    Was it a vision, or a waking dream?
80   Fled is that music:—Do I wake or sleep?

Ode on a Grecian Urn

1

Thou still unravished bride of quietness,
  Thou foster-child of silence and slow time,
Sylvan historian, who canst thus express
  A flowery tale more sweetly than our rhyme:
5 What leaf-fringed legend haunts about thy shape
    Of deities or mortals, or of both,
      In Tempe or the dales of Arcady? [1]
    What men or gods are these? What maidens loath?
What mad pursuit? What struggle to escape?
10   What pipes and timbrels? What wild ecstasy?

---

[1] The vale of Tempe and Arcady (Arcadia) in Greece are symbolic of pastoral beauty.

2

Heard melodies are sweet, but those unheard
  Are sweeter; therefore, ye soft pipes, play on;
Not to the sensual ear, but, more endeared,
  Pipe to the spirit ditties of no tone:
15 Fair youth, beneath the trees, thou canst not leave
  Thy song, nor ever can those trees be bare;
    Bold Lover, never, never canst thou kiss,
Though winning near the goal—yet, do not grieve;
    She cannot fade, though thou hast not thy bliss,
20   Forever wilt thou love, and she be fair!

3

Ah, happy, happy boughs! that cannot shed
  Your leaves, nor ever bid the Spring adieu;
And, happy melodist, unwearièd,
  Forever piping songs forever new;
25 More happy love! more happy, happy love!
  Forever warm and still to be enjoyed,
    Forever panting, and forever young;
All breathing human passion far above,
    That leaves a heart high-sorrowful and cloyed,
30   A burning forehead, and a parching tongue.

4

Who are these coming to the sacrifice?
  To what green altar, O mysterious priest,
Lead'st thou that heifer lowing at the skies,
  And all her silken flanks with garlands dressed?
35 What little town by river or sea shore,
  Or mountain-built with peaceful citadel,
    Is emptied of this folk, this pious morn?
And, little town, thy streets for evermore
  Will silent be; and not a soul to tell
40   Why thou art desolate, can e'er return.

5

O Attic[2] shape! Fair attitude! with brede[3]
  Of marble men and maidens overwrought,

---

[2] Grecian, especially Athenian.
[3] Embroidery.

With forest branches and the trodden weed;
   Thou, silent form, dost tease us out of thought
45 As doth eternity: Cold Pastoral!
      When old age shall this generation waste,
         Thou shalt remain, in midst of other woe
      Than ours, a friend to man, to whom thou say'st,
   "Beauty is truth, truth beauty,—that is all
50   Ye know on earth, and all ye need to know."

La Belle Dame Sans Merci

O, what can ail thee, knight-at-arms,
   Alone and palely loitering?
The sedge has wither'd from the lake,
   And no birds sing.

5 O, what can ail thee, knight-at-arms,
   So haggard and so woe-begone?
The squirrel's granary is full,
   And the harvest's done.

I see a lilly on thy brow,
10   With anguish moist and fever dew,
And on thy cheeks a fading rose
   Fast withereth too.

I met a lady in the meads,
   Full beautiful—a faery's child,
15 Her hair was long, her foot was light,
   And her eyes were wild.

I made a garland for her head,
   And bracelets too, and fragrant zone;
She look'd at me as she did love,
20   And made sweet moan.

I set her on my pacing steed,
   And nothing else saw all day long,
For sidelong would she bend and sing
   A faery's song.

25 She found me roots of relish sweet,
   And honey wild, and manna dew,

And sure in language strange she said
 "I love thee true."

 She took me to her elfin grot,
30 And there she wept and sigh'd full sore,
And there I shut her wild wild eyes
 With kisses four.

 And there she lullèd me asleep,
  And there I dream'd—Ah! woe betide!
35 The latest dream I ever dream'd
 On the cold hill side.

I saw pale kings and princes too,
 Pale warriors, death-pale were they all;
They cried, "La Belle Dame sans Merci
40 Hath thee in thrall!"

I saw their starved lips in the gloam,
 With horrid warning gapèd wide,
And I awoke, and found me here,
 On the cold hill's side.

45 And this is why I sojourn here,
 Alone and palely loitering,
Though the sedge is wither'd from the lake,
 And no birds sing.

Ode on Melancholy

I

No, no, go not to Lethe, neither twist
 Wolf's-bane, tight-rooted, for its poisonous wine;
Nor suffer thy pale forehead to be kiss'd
 By nightshade, ruby grape of Proserpine;[1]
5 Make not your rosary of yew-berries,
 Nor let the beetle,[2] nor the death-moth be
  Your mournful Psyche,[3] nor the downy owl

---

[1] Wife of the ruler of the underworld (Pluto).
[2] In Egypt, a symbol of rebirth placed in caskets.
[3] The soul, traditionally symbolized by the moth or butterfly.

A partner in your sorrow's mysteries;
　For shade to shade will come too drowsily,
10　　And drown the wakeful anguish of the soul.

II

But when the melancholy fit shall fall
　Sudden from heaven like a weeping cloud,
That fosters the droop-headed flowers all,
　And hides the green hill in an April shroud;
15 Then glut thy sorrow on a morning rose,
　Or on the rainbow of the salt sand-wave,
　　Or on the wealth of globèd peonies;
Or if thy mistress some rich anger shows,
　Emprison her soft hand, and let her rave,
20　　And feed deep, deep upon her peerless eyes.

III

She dwells with Beauty—Beauty that must die;
　And Joy, whose hand is ever at his lips
Bidding adieu; and aching Pleasure nigh,
　Turning to Poison while the bee-mouth sips:
25 Ay, in the very temple of Delight
　Veil'd Melancholy has her sovran shrine,
　　Though seen of none save him whose strenuous tongue
Can burst Joy's grape against his palate fine;
His soul shall taste the sadness of her might,
30　　And be among her cloudy trophies hung.

To Autumn

I

Season of mists and mellow fruitfulness,
　Close bosom-friend of the maturing sun;
Conspiring with him how to load and bless
　With fruit the vines that round the thatch-eves run;
5 To bend with apples the moss'd cottage-trees,
　And fill all fruit with ripeness to the core;
　　To swell the gourd, and plump the hazel shells
With a sweet kernel; to set budding more,
And still more, later flowers for the bees,
10 Until they think warm days will never cease,
　　For Summer has o'er-brimm'd their clammy cells.

II

Who hath not seen thee oft amid thy store?
  Sometimes whoever seeks abroad may find
Thee sitting careless on a granary floor,
15 Thy hair soft-lifted by the winnowing wind;
Or on a half-reap'd furrow sound asleep,
  Drows'd with the fume of poppies, while thy hook
    Spares the next swath and all its twinèd flowers:
And sometimes like a gleaner thou dost keep
20 Steady thy laden head across a brook;
  Or by a cyder-press, with patient look,
    Thou watchest the last oozings hours by hours.

III

Where are the songs of Spring? Ay, where are they?
  Think not of them, thou hast thy music too,—
25 While barrèd clouds bloom the soft-dying day,
  And touch the stubble-plains with rosy hue;
Then in a wailful choir the small gnats mourn
  Among the river sallows, borne aloft
    Or sinking as the light wind lives or dies;
30 And full-grown lambs loud bleat from hilly bourn;
  Hedge-crickets sing; and now with treble soft
  The red-breast whistles from a garden-croft;
    And gathering swallows twitter in the skies.

4

≈ A BRIEF HISTORY

The poems of England and America during the years of the Victorian era and the Industrial Revolution show simultaneous examples of experimentation and tradition. For a time American poetry imitates the traditional verse of England. Although the subject matter and imagery may change on the new world side of the Atlantic ocean, Emerson's *Concord Hymn* and Longfellow's *The Jewish Cemetery at Newport* sound as English as they do American. In this poetry, experience is formalized, elevated. In England Tennyson recalls the Greece of Homer in his *Ulysses* and *The Lotos Eaters*. Robert Browning recreates historical characters in the blank verse of his dramatic monologues. Walt Whitman charges into this tradition like a locomotive, a new American voice. Whitman's unrhymed free verse, arranged in parallel structure and energized with American speech patterns and slang, builds up a catalogue of images drawn from the technology and democracy of America. While Whitman supports his poetry on the two props of American speech and experience, Emily Dickinson finds another poetic voice in New England hymn meters and the New England countryside. She personifies death as a coachman, dying as the buzzing of a fly. Her deliberate use of half-rhymes, misunderstood in her day and considered an imperfection, adds to the distinctiveness of her verse and makes her seem especially modern to our ears. In England, Matthew Arnold experiments with rhymed free verse in *Dover Beach*. The rhythms of Matthew Arnold, however, flow with the regularity of scanned metrics, missing the deliberate common roughness often to be found in Whitman. Swinburne and Hopkins experiment with more complex rhythms. Hopkins, especially, looks backward to accentual verse, writing in what he referred to as "sprung rhythm." At the same time that these experiments are going on, A. E. Housman writes like a classicist in conventional stanzas. Housman's poems, their diction a mixture of the formal and colloquial, capture the English countryside while alluding to Ancient Greece and classical mythology.

RALPH WALDO EMERSON (1803–1882)

Concord Hymn

*Sung at the Completion of the Battle
Monument, July 4, 1837*

By the rude bridge that arched the flood,
    Their flag to April's breeze unfurled,
Here once the embattled farmers stood
    And fired the shot heard round the world.

5 The foe long since in silence slept;
    Alike the conqueror silent sleeps;
And Time the ruined bridge has swept
    Down the dark stream which seaward creeps.

On this green bank, by this soft stream,
10   We set to-day a votive stone;
That memory may their deed redeem,
    When, like our sires, our sons are gone.

Spirit, that made those heroes dare
    To die, and leave their children free,
15 Bid Time and Nature gently spare
    The shaft we raise to them and thee.

The Rhodora:

On Being Asked, Whence Is the Flower?
In May, when sea-winds pierced our solitudes,
I found the fresh Rhodora in the woods,
Spreading its leafless blooms in a damp nook,
To please the desert and the sluggish brook.
5 The purple petals, fallen in the pool,
Made the black water with their beauty gay;
Here might the red-bird come his plumes to cool,
And court the flower that cheapens his array.
Rhodora! if the sages ask thee why
10 This charm is wasted on the earth and sky,
Tell them, dear, that if eyes were made for seeing,
Then Beauty is its own excuse for being:
Why thou wert there, O rival of the rose!
I never thought to ask, I never knew;
15 But, in my simple ignorance, suppose
The self-same Power that brought me there brought you.

Hamatreya[1]

Bulkeley, Hunt, Willard, Hosmer, Meriam, Flint,[2]
Possessed the land which rendered to their toil
Hay, corn, roots, hemp, flax, apples, wool and wood.
Each of these landlords walked amidst his farm,
5 Saying, " 'Tis mine, my children's and my name's.
How sweet the west wind sounds in my own trees!
How graceful climb those shadows on my hill!
I fancy these pure waters and the flags
Know me, as does my dog: we sympathize;
10 And, I affirm, my actions smack of the soil."

Where are these men? Asleep beneath their grounds:
And strangers, fond as they, their furrows plough.
Earth laughs in flowers, to see her boastful boys
Earth-proud, proud of the earth which is not theirs;
15 Who steer the plough, but cannot steer their feet
Clear of the grave.
They added ridge to valley, brook to pond,
And sighed for all that bounded their domain;
"This suits me for a pasture; that's my park;
20 We must have clay, lime, gravel, granite-ledge,
And misty lowland, where to go for peat.
The land is well,—lies fairly to the south.
'Tis good, when you have crossed the sea and back,
To find the sitfast acres where you left them."
25 Ah! the hot owner sees not Death, who adds
Him to his land, a lump of mould the more.
Hear what the Earth says:—

EARTH SONG
"Mine and yours;
Mine, not yours.
30   Earth endures;
Stars abide—
Shine down in the old sea;
Old are the shores;
But where are old men?
35   I who have seen much,
Such have I never seen.

---

[1] A variant of Maitreya, a Hindu god.
[2] Early settlers of Concord.

"The lawyer's deed
Ran sure,
In tail,[3]
40   To them, and to their heirs
Who shall succeed,
Without fail,
Forevermore.

"Here is the land,
45   Shaggy with wood,
With its old valley,
Mound and flood.
But the heritors?—
Fled like the flood's foam.
50   The lawyer, and the laws,
And the kingdom,
Clean swept herefrom.

"They called me theirs,
Who so controlled me;
55   Yet every one
Wished to stay, and is gone,
How am I theirs,
If they cannot hold me,
But I hold them?"

60   When I heard the Earth-song
I was no longer brave;
My avarice cooled
Like lust in the chill of the grave.

Days

Daughters of Time, the hypocritic Days,
Muffled and dumb like barefoot dervishes,
And marching single in an endless file,
Bring diadems and fagots in their hands.
5 To each they offer gifts after his will,
Bread, kingdoms, stars, and sky that holds them all.
I, in my pleached garden, watched the pomp,
Forgot my morning wishes, hastily

---

[3] Entailed.

Took a few herbs and apples, and the Day
10 Turned and departed silent. I, too late,
Under her solemn fillet saw the scorn.

ELIZABETH BARRETT BROWNING (1806–1861)

On a Portrait of Wordsworth by B. R. Haydon[1]

Wordsworth upon Helvellyn! [2] Let the cloud
Ebb audibly along the mountain-wind
Then break against the rock, and show behind
The lowland valleys floating up to crowd
5 The sense with beauty. He with forehead bowed
And humble-lidded eyes, as one inclined
Before the sovran thought of his own mind,
And very meek with inspirations proud,
Takes here his rightful place as poet-priest
10 By the high altar, singing prayer and prayer
To the higher Heavens. A nobler vision free
Our Haydon's hand has flung out from the mist:
No portrait this, with Academic air!
This is the poet and his poetry.

Grief

I tell you, hopeless grief is passionless;
That only men incredulous of despair,
Half-taught in anguish, through the midnight air
Beat upward to God's throne in loud access
5 Of shrieking and reproach. Full desertness,
In souls as countries, lieth silent-bare
Under the blanching, vertical eye-glare
Of the absolute Heavens. Deep-hearted man, express
Grief for thy Dead in silence like to death—
10 Most like a monumental statue set
In everlasting watch and moveless woe
Till itself crumble to the dust beneath.
Touch it; the marble eyelids are not wet:
If it could weep, it could arise and go.

---

1 English painter, friend of Wordsworth.
2 A peak in the English Lake Country.

Sonnets from the Portuguese

SONNET 14

If thou must love me, let it be for nought
Except for love's sake only. Do not say,
"I love her for her smile—her look—her way
Of speaking gently,—for a trick of thought
5 That falls in well with mine, and certes brought
A sense of pleasant ease on such a day"—
For these things in themselves, Belovèd, may
Be changed, or change for thee,—and love, so wrought,
May be unwrought so. Neither love me for
10 Thine own dear pity's wiping my cheeks dry,—
A creature might forget to weep, who bore
Thy comfort long, and lose thy love thereby!
But love me for love's sake, that evermore
Thou may'st love on, through love's eternity.

SONNET 43

How do I love thee? Let me count the ways.
I love thee to the depth and breadth and height
My soul can reach, when feeling out of sight
For the ends of Being and ideal Grace.
5 I love thee to the level of everyday's
Most quiet need, by sun and candle-light.
I love thee freely, as men strive for Right;
I love thee purely, as they turn from Praise.
I love thee with the passion put to use
10 In my old griefs, and with my childhood's faith.
I love thee with a love I seemed to lose
With my lost saints,—I love thee with the breath,
Smiles, tears, of all my life!—and, if God choose,
I shall but love thee better after death.

HENRY WADSWORTH LONGFELLOW (1807–1882)

The Jewish Cemetery at Newport

How strange it seems! These Hebrews in their graves,
  Close by the street of this fair seaport town,
Silent beside the never-silent waves,
  At rest in all this moving up and down!

5 The trees are white with dust, that o'er their sleep
    Wave their broad curtains in the southwind's breath,
While underneath these leafy tents they keep
    The long, mysterious Exodus of Death.

And these sepulchral stones, so old and brown,
10   That pave with level flags their burial-place,
Seem like the tablets of the Law, thrown down
    And broken by Moses at the mountain's base.

The very names recorded here are strange,
    Of foreign accent, and of different climes;
15 Alvares and Rivera interchange
    With Abraham and Jacob of old times.

"Blessed be God! for he created Death!"
    The mourners said, "and Death is rest and peace";
Then added, in the certainty of faith,
20   "And giveth Life that nevermore shall cease."

Closed are the portals of their Synagogue,
    No Psalms of David now the silence break,
No Rabbi reads the ancient Decalogue
    In the grand dialect the Prophets spake.

25 Gone are the living, but the dead remain,
    And not neglected; for a hand unseen,
Scattering its bounty, like a summer rain,
    Still keeps their graves and their remembrance green.

How came they here? What burst of Christian hate,
30   What persecution, merciless and blind,
Drove o'er the sea—that desert desolate—
    These Ishmaels and Hagars of mankind?

They lived in narrow streets and lanes obscure,
    Ghetto and Judenstrass,[1] in mirk and mire;
35 Taught in the school of patience to endure
    The life of anguish and the death of fire.

---

[1] German for "Street of Jews."

All their lives long, with the unleavened bread
   And bitter herbs of exile and its fears,
The wasting famine of the heart they fed,
40   And slaked its thirst with marah[2] of their tears.

Anathema maranatha! [3] was the cry
   That rang from town to town, from street to street;
At every gate the accursed Mordecai[4]
   Was mocked and jeered, and spurned by Christian feet.

45 Pride and humiliation hand in hand
   Walked with them through the world wher'er they went;
Trampled and beaten were they as the sand,
   And yet unshaken as the continent.

For in the background figures vague and vast
50   Of patriarchs and of prophets rose sublime,
And all the great traditions of the Past
   They saw reflected in the coming time.

And thus forever with reverted look
   The mystic volume of the world they read,
55 Spelling it backward, like a Hebrew book,
   Till life became a Legend of the Dead.

But ah! what once has been shall be no more!
   The growing earth in travail and in pain
Brings forth its races, but does not restore,
60   And the dead nations never rise again.

Chaucer

An old man in a lodge within a park;
   The chamber walls depicted all around
   With portraitures of huntsman, hawk, and hound,
   And the hurt deer. He listeneth to the lark,
5 Whose song comes with the sunshine through the dark
   Of painted glass in leaden lattice bound;
   He listeneth and he laugheth at the sound,
   Then writeth in a book like any clerk.

---

2 "Bitter" in Hebrew.
3 A curse.
4 See the Old Testament book of Esther.

He is the poet of the dawn, who wrote
10   The Canterbury Tales, and his old age
     Made beautiful with song; and as I read
I hear the crowing cock, I hear the note
     Of lark and linnet, and from every page
     Rise odors of ploughed field or flowery mead.

The Cross of Snow

In the long, sleepless watches of the night
     A gentle face—the face of one long dead—[1]
     Looks at me from the wall, where round its head
     The night-lamp casts a halo of pale light.
5 Here in this room she died; and soul more white
     Never through martyrdom of fire was led
     To its repose; nor can in books be read
     The legend of a life more benedight.[2]
There is a mountain in the distant West
10   That, sun-defying, in its deep ravines
     Displays a cross of snow upon its side.
Such is the cross I wear upon my breast
     These eighteen years, through all the changing scenes
     And seasons, changeless since the day she died.

EDGAR ALLAN POE (1809–1849)

To Helen

Helen, thy beauty is to me
     Like those Nicèan barks of yore,
That gently, o'er a perfumed sea,
     The weary, way-worn wanderer bore
5   To his own native shore.

On desperate seas long wont to roam,
     Thy hyacinth hair, thy classic face,
Thy Naiad airs have brought me home
     To the glory that was Greece,
10 And the grandeur that was Rome.

---

[1] Frances Appleton, Longfellow's second wife, died of burns in 1861.
[2] Blessed.

Lo! in yon brilliant window-niche
   How statue-like I see thee stand,
   The agate lamp within thy hand!
Ah, Psyche, from the regions which
15   Are Holy Land!

The Raven

Once upon a midnight dreary, while I pondered, weak and weary,
Over many a quaint and curious volume of forgotten lore—
While I nodded, nearly napping, suddenly there came a tapping,
As of some one gently rapping, rapping at my chamber door.
5   " 'Tis some visiter," I muttered, "tapping at my chamber door—
                    Only this and nothing more."

Ah, distinctly I remember it was in the bleak December;
And each separate dying ember wrought its ghost upon the floor.
Eagerly I wished the morrow;—vainly I had sought to borrow
10 From my books surcease of sorrow—sorrow for the lost Lenore—
For the rare and radiant maiden whom the angels name Lenore—
                    Nameless *here* for evermore.

And the silken, sad, uncertain rustling of each purple curtain
Thrilled me—filled me with fantastic terrors never felt before;
15 So that now, to still the beating of my heart, I stood repeating
   " 'Tis some visiter entreating entrance at my chamber door—
Some late visiter entreating entrance at my chamber door;—
                    That it is and nothing more."

Presently my soul grew stronger; hesitating then no longer,
20 "Sir," said I, "or Madam, truly your forgiveness I implore;
But the fact is I was napping, and so gently you came rapping,
And so faintly you came tapping, tapping at my chamber door,
That I scarce was sure I heard you"—here I opened wide the
      door:—
                    Darkness there and nothing more.

25 Deep into that darkness peering, long I stood there wondering,
      fearing,
Doubting, dreaming dreams no mortal ever dared to dream before;
But the silence was unbroken, and the stillness gave no token,
And the only word there spoken was the whispered word, "Lenore?"
                    Merely this and nothing more.

30 Back into the chamber turning, all my soul within me burning,
　 Soon again I heard a tapping somewhat louder than before.
　 "Surely," said I, "surely that is something at my window lattice;
　 Let me see, then, what thereat is, and this mystery explore—
　 Let my heart be still a moment and this mystery explore;—
35 　　　　　　　　　　　　　　　'Tis the wind and nothing more!"

　 Open here I flung the shutter, when, with many a flirt and flutter
　 In there stepped a stately Raven of the saintly days of yore;
　 Not the least obeisance made he; not a minute stopped or stayed he;
　 But, with mien of lord or lady, perched above my chamber door—
40 Perched upon a bust of Pallas¹ just above my chamber door—
　　　　　　　　　　　　Perched, and sat, and nothing more.

　 Then this ebony bird beguiling my sad fancy into smiling,
　 By the grave and stern decorum of the countenance it wore,
　 "Though thy crest be short and shaven, thou," I said, "art sure no
　　　craven,
45 Ghastly grim and ancient Raven wandering from the Nightly shore—
　 Tell me what thy lordly name is on the Night's Plutonian² shore!
　　　　　　　　　　　Quoth the Raven "Nevermore."

　 Much I marvelled this ungainly fowl to hear discourse so plainly,
　 Though its answer little meaning—little relevancy bore;
50 For we cannot help agreeing that no living human being
　 Ever yet was blessed with seeing bird above his chamber door—
　 Bird or beast upon the sculptured bust above his chamber door,
　　　　　　　　　　　With such name as "Nevermore."

　 But the Raven, sitting lonely on the placid bust, spoke only
55 That one word, as if his soul in that one word he did outpour.
　 Nothing farther then he uttered—not a feather then he fluttered—
　 Till I scarcely more than muttered "Other friends have flown be-
　　　fore—
　 On the morrow *he* will leave me, as my Hopes have flown before."
　　　　　　　　　　　Then the bird said "Nevermore."

60 Startled at the stillness broken by reply so aptly spoken,
　 "Doubtless," said I, "what it utters is its only stock and store

---

¹ Pallas Athena was the Greek goddess of wisdom and the arts.
² Infernal. The Greek god Pluto ruled the underworld.

Caught from some unhappy master whom unmerciful Disaster
Followed fast and followed faster till his songs one burden bore—
Till the dirges of his Hope that melancholy burden bore
65   Of 'Never—nevermore.' "

But the Raven still beguiling all my fancy into smiling,
Straight I wheeled a cushioned seat in front of bird, and bust and
    door;
Then, upon the velvet sinking, I betook myself to linking
Fancy unto fancy, thinking what this ominous bird of yore—
70 What this grim, ungainly, ghastly, gaunt, and ominous bird of yore
                          Meant in croaking "Nevermore."

This I sat engaged in guessing, but no syllable expressing
To the fowl whose fiery eyes now burned into my bosom's core;
This and more I sat divining, with my head at ease reclining
75 On the cushion's velvet lining that the lamp light gloated o'er,
But whose velvet-violet lining with the lamp-light gloating o'er,
                    She shall press, ah, nevermore!

Then, methought, the air grew denser, perfumed from an unseen
    censer
Swung by Seraphim[3] whose foot-falls tinkled on the tufted floor.
80 "Wretch," I cried, "thy God hath lent thee—by these angels he hath
    sent thee
Respite—respite and nepenthe[4] from thy memories of Lenore;
Quaff, oh quaff this kind nepenthe and forget this lost Lenore!"
                    Quoth the Raven "Nevermore."

"Prophet!" said I, "thing of evil!—prophet still, if bird or devil!—
85 Whether Tempter sent, or whether tempest tossed thee here ashore,
Desolate yet all undaunted, on this desert land enchanted—
On this home by Horror haunted—tell me truly, I implore—
Is there—*is* there balm in Gilead?[5]—tell me—tell me, I implore!"
                    Quoth the Raven "Nevermore."

90 "Prophet!" said I, "thing of evil!—prophet still, if bird or devil!
By that Heaven that bends above us—by that God we both adore!—
Tell this soul with sorrow laden if, within the distant Aidenn,[6]

---

[3] Angels of the highest of the nine orders.
[4] A drug which induces forgetfulness and oblivion when drunk.
[5] Resin from evergreen trees in Palestine, used to heal wounds and ease pain.
[6] Eden.

It shall clasp a sainted maiden whom the angels name Lenore—
Clasp a rare and radiant maiden whom the angels name Lenore."
95   Quoth the Raven "Nevermore."

"Be that word our sign of parting, bird or fiend!" I shrieked,
    upstarting—
"Get thee back into the tempest and the Night's Plutonian shore!
Leave no black plume as a token of that lie thy soul hath spoken!
Leave my loneliness unbroken!—quit the bust above my door!
100 Take thy beak from out my heart, and take thy form from off my
    door!"
                              Quoth the Raven "Nevermore."

And the Raven, never flitting, still is sitting, *still* is sitting
On the pallid bust of Pallas just above my chamber door;
And his eyes have all the seeming of a demon's that is dreaming,
105 And the lamp-light o'er him streaming throws his shadow on the
    floor;
And my soul from out that shadow that lies floating on the floor
                              Shall be lifted—nevermore!

Annabel Lee

It was many and many a year ago,
        In a kingdom by the sea,
That a maiden there lived whom you may know
        By the name of Annabel Lee;—
5 And this maiden she lived with no other thought
        Than to love and be loved by me.

She was a child and *I* was a child,
        In this kingdom by the sea,
But we loved with a love that was more than love—
10   I and my Annabel Lee—
With a love that the wingèd seraphs of Heaven
        Coveted her and me.

And this was the reason that, long ago,
        In this kingdom by the sea,
15 A wind blew out of a cloud by night
        Chilling my Annabel Lee;
So that her highborn kinsmen came
        And bore her away from me,

To shut her up in a sepulchre
20   In this kingdom by the sea.

The angels, not half so happy in Heaven,
            Went envying her and me—
Yes!—that was the reason (as all men know,
            In this kingdom by the sea)
25 That the wind came out of the cloud chilling
            And killing my Annabel Lee.

But our love it was stronger by far than the love
      Of those who were older than we—
      Of many far wiser than we—
30 And neither the angels in Heaven above,
      Nor the demons down under the sea,
Can ever dissever my soul from the soul
      Of the beautiful Annabel Lee:—

For the moon never beams without bringing me dreams
35   Of the beautiful Annabel Lee;
And the stars never rise but I see the bright eyes
      Of the beautiful Annabel Lee;
And so, all the night-tide, I lie down by the side
Of my darling, my darling, my life and my bride,
40   In her sepulchre there by the sea—
      In her tomb by the side of the sea.

ALFRED, LORD TENNYSON (1809–1892)

Song

1

A spirit haunts the year's last hours
Dwelling amid these yellowing bowers.
      To himself he talks;
For at eventide, listening earnestly,
5 At his work you may hear him sob and sigh
      In the walks;
      Earthward he boweth the heavy stalks
Of the moldering flowers.
      Heavily hangs the broad sunflower
10   Over its grave i' the earth so chilly;
      Heavily hangs the hollyhock,
            Heavily hangs the tiger-lily.

2

The air is damp, and hushed, and close,
As a sick man's room when he taketh repose
15　　An hour before death;
My very heart faints and my whole soul grieves
At the moist rich smell of the rotting leaves,
　　And the breath
　Of the fading edges of box[1] beneath,
20　And the year's last rose.
　　　Heavily hangs the broad sunflower
　　　　Over its grave i' the earth so chilly;
　　　Heavily hangs the hollyhock,
　　　Heavily hangs the tiger-lily.

Ulysses

It little profits that an idle king,
By this still hearth, among these barren crags,
Matched with an aged wife, I mete and dole
Unequal laws unto a savage race,
5　That hoard, and sleep, and feed, and know not me.
I cannot rest from travel; I will drink
Life to the lees. All times I have enjoyed
Greatly, have suffered greatly, both with those
That loved me, and alone; on shore, and when
10　Through scudding drifts the rainy Hyades[1]
Vexed the dim sea: I am become a name;
For always roaming with a hungry heart
Much have I seen and known—cities of men
And manners, climates, councils, governments,
15　Myself not least, but honored of them all;
And drunk delight of battle with my peers,
Far on the ringing plains of windy Troy.
I am a part of all that I have met;
Yet all experience is an arch wherethrough
20　Gleams that untraveled world whose margin fades
For ever and for ever when I move.
How dull it is to pause, to make an end,
To rust unburnished, not to shine in use!

---

[1] Boxwood.

[1] A group of stars in the constellation Taurus, whose rise with the sun heralded the spring rains.

As though to breathe were life! Life piled on life
25 Were all too little, and of one to me
Little remains; but every hour is saved
From that eternal silence, something more,
A bringer of new things; and vile it were
For some three suns to store and hoard myself,
30 And this gray spirit yearning in desire
To follow knowledge like a sinking star,
Beyond the utmost bound of human thought.

This is my son, mine own Telemachus,
To whom I leave the scepter and the isle—
35 Well-loved of me, discerning to fulfil
This labor, by slow prudence to make mild
A rugged people, and through soft degrees
Subdue them to the useful and the good.
Most blameless is he, centered in the sphere
40 Of common duties, decent not to fail
In offices of tenderness, and pay
Meet adoration to my household gods,
When I am gone. He works his work, I mine.

There lies the port; the vessel puffs her sail;
45 There gloom the dark, broad seas. My mariners,
Souls that have toiled, and wrought, and thought with me—
That ever with a frolic welcome took
The thunder and the sunshine, and opposed
Free hearts, free foreheads—you and I are old;
50 Old age hath yet his honor and his toil.
Death closes all; but something ere the end,
Some work of noble note, may yet be done,
Not unbecoming men that strove with Gods.
The lights begin to twinkle from the rocks:
55 The long day wanes: the slow moon climbs: the deep
Moans round with many voices. Come, my friends,
'Tis not too late to seek a newer world.
Push off, and sitting well in order smite
The sounding furrows; for my purpose holds
60 To sail beyond the sunset, and the baths
Of all the western stars, until I die.
It may be that the gulfs will wash us down;
It may be we shall touch the Happy Isles,
And see the great Achilles, whom we knew.
65 Though much is taken, much abides; and though

We are not now that strength which in old days
Moved earth and heaven, that which we are, we are;
One equal temper of heroic hearts,
Made weak by time and fate, but strong in will
70 To strive, to seek, to find, and not to yield.

From **The Lotos-Eaters**

Choric Song

1

There is sweet music here that softer falls
Than petals from blown roses on the grass,
Or night-dews on still waters between walls
Of shadowy granite, in a gleaming pass;
5 Music that gentlier on the spirit lies,
Than tired eyelids upon tired eyes;
Music that brings sweet sleep down from the blissful skies.
Here are cool mosses deep,
And through the moss the ivies creep,
10 And in the stream the long-leaved flowers weep,
And from the craggy ledge the poppy hangs in sleep.

2

Why are we weighed upon with heaviness,
And utterly consumed with sharp distress,
While all things else have rest from weariness?
15 All things have rest: why should we toil alone,
We only toil, who are the first things,
And make perpetual moan,
Still from one sorrow to another thrown;
Nor ever fold our wings,
20 And cease from wanderings,
Nor steep our brows in slumber's holy balm;
Nor harken what the inner spirit sings,
"There is no joy but calm!"
Why should we only toil, the roof and crown of things?

Break, Break, Break

Break, break, break,
    On thy cold gray stones, O Sea!
And I would that my tongue could utter
    The thoughts that arise in me.

5 O well for the fisherman's boy,
    That he shouts with his sister at play!
O well for the sailor lad,
    That he sings in his boat on the bay!

And the stately ships go on
10   To their haven under the hill;
But O for the touch of a vanished hand,
    And the sound of a voice that is still!

Break, break, break
    At the foot of thy crags, O Sea!
15 But the tender grace of a day that is dead
    Will never come back to me.

The Splendor Falls on Castle Walls

The splendor falls on castle walls
    And snowy summits old in story:
The long light shakes across the lakes,
    And the wild cataract leaps in glory.
5 Blow, bugle, blow, set the wild echoes flying,
Blow, bugle; answer, echoes, dying, dying, dying.

O hark, O hear! how thin and clear,
    And thinner, clearer, farther going!
O sweet and far from cliff and scar
10   The horns of Elfland faintly blowing!
Blow, let us hear the purple glens replying:
Blow, bugle; answer, echoes, dying, dying, dying.

O love, they die in yon rich sky,
    They faint on hill or field or river;
15   Our echoes roll from soul to soul,
    And grow for ever and for ever.
Blow, bugle, blow, set the wild echoes flying,
And answer, echoes, answer, dying, dying, dying.

From **In Memoriam A. H. H.**

OBIIT, MDCCCXXXIII

1

I held it truth, with him who sings
    To one clear harp in divers tones,

That men may rise on stepping-stones
Of their dead selves to higher things.

5 But who shall so forecast the years
And find in loss a gain to match?
Or reach a hand through time to catch
The far-off interest of tears?

Let Love clasp Grief lest both be drowned,
10   Let darkness keep her raven gloss.
Ah, sweeter to be drunk with loss,
To dance with Death, to beat the ground,

Than that the victor Hours should scorn
The long result of love, and boast,
15   "Behold the man that loved and lost,
But all he was is overworn,"

7

Dark house, by which once more I stand
Here in the long unlovely street,
Doors, where my heart was used to beat
20 So quickly, waiting for a hand,

A hand that can be clasped no more—
Behold me, for I cannot sleep,
And like a guilty thing I creep
At earliest morning to the door.

25 He is not here; but far away
The noise of life begins again,
And ghastly through the drizzling rain
On the bald street breaks the blank day.

11

Calm is the morn without a sound,
30   Calm as to suit a calmer grief,
And only through the faded leaf
The chestnut pattering to the ground;

Calm and deep peace on this high wold,[1]
And on these dews that drench the furze,

---

[1] Upland plain.

35   And all the silvery gossamers
      That twinkle into green and gold;

      Calm and still light on yon great plain
          That sweeps with all its autumn bowers,
          And crowded farms and lessening towers,
40 To mingle with the bounding main;

      Calm and deep peace in this wide air,
          These leaves that redden to the fall,
          And in my heart, if calm at all,
      If any calm, a calm despair;

45 Calm on the seas, and silver sleep,
          And waves that sway themselves in rest,
          And dead calm in the noble breast
      Which heaves but with the heaving deep.

50

      Be near me when my light is low,
50   When the blood creeps, and the nerves prick
          And tingle; and the heart is sick,
      And all the wheels of being slow.

      Be near me when the sensuous frame
          Is racked with pangs that conquer trust;
55   And Time, a maniac scattering dust,
      And Life, a Fury slinging flame.

      Be near me when my faith is dry,
          And men the flies of latter spring,
          That lay their eggs, and sting and sing
60 And weave their petty cells and die.

      Be near me when I fade away,
          To point the term of human strife,
          And on the low dark verge of life
      The twilight of eternal day.

130

65 They voice is on the rolling air;
          I hear thee where the waters run;
          Thou standest in the rising sun,
      And in the setting thou art fair.

What are thou then? I cannot guess;
70　But though I seem in star and flower
　　To feel thee some diffusive power,
I do not therefore love thee less.

My love involves the love before;
　　My love is vaster passion now;
75　Though mixed with God and Nature thou,
I seem to love thee more and more.

Far off thou art, but ever nigh;
　　I have thee still, and I rejoice;
　　I prosper, circled with thy voice;
80 I shall not lose thee though I die.

The Eagle

Fragment

He clasps the crag with crooked hands;
Close to the sun in lonely lands,
Ringed with the azure world, he stands.

The wrinkled sea beneath him crawls;
5 He watches from his mountain walls,
And like a thunderbolt he falls.

Crossing the Bar

Sunset and evening star,
　　And one clear call for me!
And may there be no moaning of the bar,
　　When I put out to sea,

5 But such a tide as moving seems asleep,
　　Too full for sound and foam,
When that which drew from out the boundless deep
　　Turns again home.

Twilight and evening bell,
10　And after that the dark!
And may there be no sadness of farewell,
　　When I embark;

For though from out our bourne of Time and Place
 The flood may bear me far,
¹⁵ I hope to see my Pilot face to face
 When I have crossed the bar.

EDWARD FITZGERALD (1809–1883)

The Rubáiyát of Omar Khayyám of Naishápúr

1

Awake! for Morning in the Bowl of Night
Has flung the Stone that puts the Stars to Flight:
 And Lo! the Hunter of the East has caught
The Sultán's Turret in a Noose of Light.

2

Dreaming when Dawn's Left Hand was in the Sky
I heard a Voice within the Tavern cry,
 "Awake, my Little ones, and fill the Cup
Before Life's Liquor in its Cup be dry."

3

And, as the Cock crew, those who stood before
The Tavern shouted—"Open then the Door!
 You know how little while we have to stay,
And, once departed, may return no more."

4

Now the New Year reviving old Desires,
The thoughtful Soul to Solitude retires,
 Where the "White Hand of Moses" on the Bough
Puts out, and Jesus from the Ground suspires.

5

Irám indeed is gone with all its Rose,
And Jamshyd's Sev'n-ring'd Cup where no one knows;
 But still the Vine her ancient Ruby yields,
And still a Garden by the Water blows.

6

And David's Lips are lock't; but in divine
High piping Péhlevi, with "Wine! Wine! Wine!
　　Red Wine!"—the Nightingale cries to the Rose
That yellow Cheek of hers to incarnadine.

7

Come, fill the Cup, and in the Fire of Spring
The Winter Garment of Repentance fling:
　　The Bird of Time has but a little way
To fly—and Lo! the Bird is on the Wing.

8

And look—a thousand Blossoms with the Day
Woke—and a thousand scatter'd into Clay:
　　And this first Summer Month that brings the Rose
Shall take Jamshyd and Kaikobád away.

9

But come with old Khayyám, and leave the Lot
Of Kaikobád and Kaikhosrú forgot:
　　Let Rustum lay about him as he will,
Or Hátim Tai cry Supper—heed them not.

10

With me along some Strip of Herbage strown
That just divides the desert from the sown,
　　Where name of Slave and Sultán scarce is known,
And pity Sultán Máhmúd on his Throne.

11

Here with a Loaf of Bread beneath the Bough,
A Flask of Wine, a Book of Verse—and Thou
　　Beside me singing in the Wilderness—
And Wilderness is Paradise enow.

12

"How sweet is mortal Sovranty!"—think some:
Others—"How blest the Paradise to come!"
　　Ah, take the Cash in hand and wave the Rest;
Oh, the brave Music of a distant Drum!

13

Look to the Rose that blows about us—"Lo,
Laughing," she says, "into the World I blow:
  At once the silken Tassel of my Purse
Tear, and its Treasure on the Garden throw."

14

The Worldly Hope men set their Hearts upon
Turns Ashes— or it prospers; and anon,
  Like Snow upon the Desert's dusty Face
Lighting a little Hour or two—is gone.

15

And those who husbanded the Golden Grain,
And those who flung it to the Winds like Rain,
  Alike to no such aureate Earth are turn'd
As, buried once, Men want dug up again.

16

Think, in this batter'd Caravanserai
Whose doorways are alternate Night and Day,
  How Sultán after Sultán with his Pomp
Abode his Hour or two, and went his way.

17

They say the Lion and the Lizard keep
The Courts where Jamshyd gloried and drank deep:
  And Bahrám, that great Hunter—the Wild Ass
Stamps o'er his Head, and he lies fast asleep.

18

I sometimes think that never blows so red
The Rose as where some buried Caesar bled;
  That every Hyacinth the Garden wears
Dropt in its Lap from some once lovely Head.

19

And this delightful Herb whose tender Green
Fledges the River's Lip on which we lean—
  Ah, lean upon it lightly! for who knows
From what once lovely Lip it springs unseen!

20

Ah, my Belovéd, fill the Cup that clears
"To-day" of past Regrets and future Fears—
　　"To-morrow"? Why, To-morrow I may be
Myself with Yesterday's Sev'n Thousand Years.

21

Lo! some we loved, the loveliest and best
That Time and Fate of all their Vintage prest,
　　Have drunk their Cup a Round or two before
And one by one crept silently to Rest.

22

And we, that now make merry in the Room
They left, and Summer dresses in new Bloom,
　　Ourselves must we beneath the Couch of Earth
Descend, ourselves to make a Couch—for whom?

23

Ah, make the most of what we yet may spend.
Before we too into the Dust descend;
　　Dust into Dust, and under Dust, to lie,
Sans Wine, sans Song, sans Singer, and—sans End!

24

Alike for those who for "To-day" prepare,
And those that after a "To-morrow" stare,
　　A Muezzín from the Tower of Darkness cries
"Fools! your Reward is neither Here nor There!"

25

Why, all the Saints and Sages who discuss'd
Of the Two Worlds so learnedly, are thrust
　　Like foolish Prophets forth; their Words to Scorn
Are scatter'd, and their Mouths are stopt with Dust.

26

Oh, come with old Khayyám, and leave the Wise
To talk; one thing is certain, that Life flies;
　　One thing is certain, and the Rest is Lies;
The Flower that once has blown for ever dies.

27

Myself when young did eagerly frequent
Doctor and Saint, and heard great Argument
   About it and about: but evermore
Came out by the Same Door as in I went.

28

With them the Seed of Wisdom did I sow,
And with my own hand labour'd it to grow:
   And this was all the Harvest that I reap'd—
"I came like Water, and like Wind I go."

29

Into this Universe, and "why" not knowing,
Nor "whence", like Water willy-nilly flowing:
   And out of it, as Wind along the Waste,
I know not "whither", willy-nilly blowing.

30

What, without asking, hither hurried whence?
And, without asking, whither hurried hence!
   Another and another Cup to drown
The Memory of this Impertinence!

31

Up from Earth's Centre through the Seventh Gate
I rose, and on the Throne of Saturn sate,
   And many Knots unravel'd by the Road;
But not the Knot of Human Death and Fate.

32

There was a Door to which I found no Key:
There was a Veil past which I could not see:
   Some little Talk awhile of "Me" and "Thee"
There seemed—and then no more of "Thee" and "Me".

33

Then to the rolling Heav'n itself I cried,
Asking, "What Lamp had Destiny to guide
   Her little Children stumbling in the Dark?"
And—"A blind Understanding!" Heav'n replied.

34

Then to this earthen Bowl did I adjourn
My Lip the secret Well of Life to learn:
   And Lip to Lip it murmur'd—"While you live
Drink! for once dead you never shall return."

35

I think the Vessel, that with fugitive
Articulation answer'd, once did live,
   And merry-make; and the cold Lip I kiss'd
How many Kisses might it take—and give!

36

For in the Market-place, one Dusk of Day,
I watch'd the Potter thumping his wet Clay:
   And with its all obliterated Tongue
It murmur'd—"Gently, Brother, gently, pray!"

37

Ah, fill the Cup:—what boots it to repeat
How Time is slipping underneath our Feet:
   Unborn "To-morrow," and dead "Yesterday",
Why fret about them if "To-day" be sweet!

38

One Moment in Annihilation's Waste,
One Moment, of the Well of Life to taste—
   The Stars are setting and the Caravan
Starts for the Dawn of Nothing—Oh, make haste!

39

How long, how long, in infinite Pursuit
Of This and That endeavour and dispute?
   Better be merry with the fruitful Grape
Than sadden after none, or bitter, Fruit.

40

You know, my Friends, how long since in my House
For a new Marriage I did make Carouse:
   Divorced old barren Reason from my Bed,
And took the Daughter of the Vine to Spouse.

41

For "Is" and "Is-not" though with Rule and Line,
And "Up-and-down" without, I could define,
    I yet in all I only cared to know,
Was never deep in anything but—Wine.

42

And lately, by the Tavern Door agape,
Came stealing through the Dusk an Angel Shape
    Bearing a Vessel on his Shoulder; and
He bid me taste of it; and 'twas—the Grape!

43

The Grape that can with Logic absolute
The Two-and-Seventy jarring Sects confute:
    The subtle Alchemist that in a Trice
Life's leaden Metal into Gold transmute.

44

The mighty Mahmúd, the victorious Lord,
That all the misbelieving and black Horde
    Of Fears and Sorrows that infest the Soul
Scatters and slays with his enchanted Sword.

45

But leave the Wise to wrangle, and with me
The Quarrel of the Universe let be:
    And, in some corner of the Hubbub coucht,
Make Game of that which makes as much of Thee.

46

For in and out, above, about, below,
'Tis nothing but a Magic Shadow-show,
    Play'd in a Box whose Candle is the Sun,
Round which we Phantom Figures come and go.

47

And if the Wine you drink, the Lip you press,
End in the Nothing all Things end in—Yes—
    Then fancy while Thou art, Thou art but what
Thou shalt be—Nothing—Thou shalt not be less.

48

While the Rose blows along the River Brink,
With old Khayyám the Ruby Vintage drink:
    And when the Angel with his darker Draught
Draws up to Thee—take that, and do not shrink.

49

'Tis all a Chequer-board of Nights and Days
Where Destiny with Men for Pieces plays:
    Hither and thither moves, and mates, and slays,
And one by one back in the Closet lays.

50

The Ball no Question makes of Ayes and Noes,
But Right or Left as strikes the Player goes;
    And He that toss'd Thee down into the Field,
He knows about it all—HE knows—HE knows!

51

The Moving Finger writes; and, having writ,
Moves on: nor all thy Piety nor Wit
    Shall lure it back to cancel half a Line,
Nor all thy Tears wash out a Word of it.

52

And that inverted Bowl we call The Sky,
Whereunder crawling coop't we live and die,
    Lift not thy hands to "It" for help—for It
Rolls impotently on as Thou or I.

53

With Earth's first Clay They did the Last Man's knead,
And then of the Last Harvest sow'd the Seed:
    Yea, the first Morning of Creation wrote
What the Last Dawn of Reckoning shall read.

54

I tell Thee this—When, starting from the Goal,
Over the shoulders of the flaming Foal
    Of Heav'n Parwín and Mushtara they flung,
In my predestin'd Plot of Dust and Soul.

55

The Vine had struck a Fibre; which about
If clings my Being—let the Súfi flout;
  Of my Base Metal may be filed a Key,
That shall unlock the Door he howls without.

56

And this I know: whether the one True Light,
Kindle to Love, or Wrath consume me quite,
  One Glimpse of it within the Tavern caught
Better than in the Temple lost outright.

57

Oh Thou, who didst with Pitfall and with Gin
Beset the Road I was to wander in,
  Thou wilt not with Predestination round
Enmesh me, and impute my Fall to Sin?

58

Oh, Thou, who Man of baser Earth didst make,
And who with Eden didst devise the Snake;
  For all the Sin wherewith the Face of Man
Is blacken'd Man's Forgiveness give—and take!

KÚZA-NÁMA

59

Listen again. One Evening at the Close
Of Ramazán, ere the better Moon arose,
  In that old Potter's Shop I stood alone
With the clay Population round in Rows.

60

And, strange to tell, among that Earthen Lot
Some could articulate, while others not:
  And suddenly one more impatient cried—
"Who is the Potter, pray, and who the Pot?"

61

Then said another—"Surely not in vain
My Substance from the common Earth was ta'en,
  That He who subtly wrought me into Shape
Should stamp me back to common Earth again."

62

Another said—"Why, ne'er a peevish Boy,
Would break the Bowl from which he drank in Joy;
    Shall He that made the Vessel in pure Love
And Fancy, in an after Rage destroy!"

63

None answer'd this; but after Silence spake
A Vessel of a more ungainly Make:
    "They sneer at me for leaning all awry;
What! did the Hand then of the Potter shake?"

64

Said one—"Folks of a surly Tapster tell,
And daub his Visage with the Smoke of Hell;
    They talk of some strict Testing of us—Pish!
He's a Good Fellow, and 'twill all be well."

65

Then said another with a long-drawn Sigh,
"My Clay with long oblivion is gone dry:
    But, fill me with the old familiar Juice,
Methinks I might recover by-and-bye!"

66

So while the Vessels one by one were speaking,
One spied the little Crescent all were seeking:
    And then they jogg'd each other, "Brother! Brother!"
Hark to the Porter's Shoulder-knot a-creaking!"

67

Ah, with the Grape my fading Life provide,
And wash my Body whence the Life has died,
    And in a Windingsheet of Vine-leaf wrapt
So bury me by some sweet Garden-side.

68

That ev'n my buried Ashes such a Snare
Of Perfume shall fling up into the Air
    As not a True Believer passing by
But shall be overtaken unaware.

69

Indeed the Idols I have loved so long
Have done my Credit in Men's Eye much wrong;
　　Have drown'd my Honour in a shallow Cup,
And sold my Reputation for a Song.

70

Indeed, indeed, Repentance oft before
I swore—but was I sober when I swore?
　　And then and then came Spring, and Rose-in-hand
My thread-bare Penitence apieces tore.

71

And much as Wine has play'd the Infidel,
And robb'd me of my Robe of Honour—well,
　　I often wonder what the Vintners buy
One half so precious as the Goods they sell.

72

Alas, that Spring should vanish with the Rose!
That Youth's sweet-scented Manuscript shoud close!
　　The Nightingale that in the Branches sang,
Ah, whence, and whither flown again, who knows!

73

Ah Love! could thou and I with Fate conspire
To grasp this sorry Scheme of Things entire,
　　Would not we shatter it to bits—and then
Re-mould it nearer to the Heart's Desire!

74

Ah, Moon of my Delight who know'st no wane,
The Moon of Heav'n is rising once again:
　　How oft hereafter rising shall she look
Through this same Garden after me—in vain!

75

And when Thyself with shining Foot shall pass
Among the Guests Star-scatter'd on the Grass,
　　And in thy joyous Errand reach the Spot
Where I made one—turn down an empty Glass.

TAMÁM SHUD

ROBERT BROWNING (1812–1889)

My Last Duchess

Ferrara

That's my last duchess painted on the wall,
Looking as if she were alive. I call
That piece a wonder, now: Frà Pandolf's[1] hands
Worked busily a day, and there she stands.
5 Will't please you sit and look at her? I said
"Frà Pandolf" by design, for never read
Strangers like you that pictured countenance,
The depth and passion of its earnest glance,
But to myself they turned (since none puts by
10 The curtain I have drawn for you, but I)
And seemed as they would ask me, if they durst,
How such a glance came there; so, not the first
Are you to turn and ask thus. Sir, 'twas not
Her husband's presence only, called that spot
15 Of joy into the Duchess' cheek: perhaps
Frà Pandolf chanced to say "Her mantle laps
"Over my lady's wrist too much," or "Paint
"Must never hope to reproduce the faint
"Half-flush that dies along her throat": such stuff
20 Was courtesy, she thought, and cause enough
For calling up that spot of joy. She had
A heart—how shall I say?—too soon made glad,
Too easily impressed; she liked whate'er
She looked on, and her looks went everywhere.
25 Sir, 'twas all one! My favor at her breast,
The dropping of the daylight in the West,
The bough of cherries some officious fool
Broke in the orchard for her, the white mule
She rode with round the terrace—all and each
30 Would draw from her alike the approving speech,
Or blush, at least. She thanked men—good! but thanked
Somehow—I know not how—as if she ranked
My gift of a nine-hundred-years-old name
With anybody's gift. Who'd stoop to blame
35 This sort of trifling? Even had you skill
In speech—which I have not—to make your will

---

1 A fictitious artist, as is Claus of Innsbruck in the last line.

Quite clear to such an one, and say, "Just this
"Or that in you disgusts me; here you miss,
"Or there exceed the mark"—and if she let
40 Herself be lessoned so, nor plainly set
Her wits to yours, forsooth, and made excuse,
—E'en then would be some stooping; and I choose
Never to stoop. Oh sir, she smiled, no doubt,
Whene'er I passed her; but who passed without
45 Much the same smile? This grew; I gave commands;
Then all smiles stopped together. There she stands
As if alive. Will 't please you rise? We'll meet
The company below, then. I repeat,
The Count your master's known munificence
50 Is ample warrant that no just pretense
Of mine for dowry will be disallowed;
Though his fair daughter's self, as I avowed
At starting, is my object. Nay, we'll go
Together down, sir. Notice Neptune, though,
55 Taming a sea-horse, thought a rarity,
Which Claus of Innsbruck cast in bronze for me!

The Bishop Orders His Tomb at Saint Praxed's Church

Rome, 15—

Vanity, saith the preacher, vanity!
Draw round my bed: is Anselm keeping back?
Nephews[1]—sons mine . . . ah God, I know not! Well—
She, men would have to be your mother once,
5 Old Gandolf envied me, so fair she was!
What's done is done, and she is dead beside,
Dead long ago, and I am Bishop since,
And as she died so must we die ourselves,
And thence ye may perceive the world's a dream.
10 Life, how and what is it? As here I lie
In this state-chamber, dying by degrees,
Hours and long hours in the dead night, I ask
"Do I live, am I dead?" Peace, peace seems all.
Saint Praxed's ever was the church for peace;
15 And so, about this tomb of mine. I fought
With tooth and nail to save my niche, ye know:

---

[1] Euphemism for illegitimate sons.

—Old Gandolf cozened me, despite my care;
Shrewd was that snatch from out the corner South
He graced his carrion with, God curse the same!
20 Yet still my niche is not so cramped but thence
One sees the pulpit o' the epistle side,[2]
And somewhat of the choir, those silent seats,
And up into the aery dome where live
The angels, and a sunbeam's sure to lurk:
25 And I shall fill my slab of basalt there,
And 'neath my tabernacle take my rest,
With those nine columns round me, two and two,
The odd one at my feet where Anselm stands:
Peach-blossom marble all, the rare, the ripe
30 As fresh-poured red wine of a mighty pulse.
—Old Gandolf with his paltry onion-stone,
Put me where I may look at him! True peach,
Rosy and flawless: how I earned the prize!
Draw close: that conflagration of my church
35 —What then? So much was saved if aught were missed!
My sons, ye would not be my death? Go dig
The white-grape vineyard where the oil-press stood,
Drop water gently till the surface sink,
And if ye find . . . Ah God, I know not, I! . . .
40 Bedded in store of rotten fig-leaves soft,
And corded up in a tight olive-frail,
Some lump, ah God, of *lapis lazuli,*
Big as a Jew's head cut off at the nape,
Blue as a vein o'er the Madonna's breast . . .
45 Sons, all have I bequeathed you, villas, all,
That brave Frascati villa with its bath,
So, let the blue lump poise between my knees,
Like God the Father's globe on both his hands
Ye worship in the Jesu Church so gay,
50 For Gandolf shall not choose but see and burst!
Swift as a weaver's shuttle fleet our years:
Man goeth to the grave, and where is he?
Did I say basalt for my slab, sons? Black—
'Twas ever antique-black I meant! How else
55 Shall ye contrast my frieze to come beneath?
The bas-relief in bronze ye promised me,
Those Pans and Nymphs ye wot of, and perchance

---

2 The right-hand side, as one faces the altar.

Some tripod,[3] thyrsus,[4] with a vase or so,
The Saviour at his sermon on the mount,
60 Saint Praxed in a glory, and one Pan
Ready to twitch the Nymph's last garment off,
And Moses with the tables . . . but I know
Ye mark me not! What do they whisper thee,
Child of my bowels, Anselm? Ah, ye hope
65 To revel down my villas while I gasp
Bricked o'er with beggar's moldy travertine
Which Gandolf from his tomb-top chuckles at!
Nay, boys, ye love me—all of jasper, then!
'Tis jasper ye stand pledged to, lest I grieve
70 My bath must needs be left behind, alas!
One block, pure green as a pistachio nut,
There's plenty jasper somewhere in the world—
And have I not Saint Praxed's ear to pray
Horses for ye, and brown Greek manuscripts,
75 And mistresses with great smooth marbly limbs?
—That's if ye carve my epitaph aright,
Choice Latin, picked phrase, Tully's[5] every word,
No gaudy ware like Gandolf's second line—
Tully, my masters? Ulpian[6] serves his need!
80 And then how I shall lie through centuries,
And hear the blessed mutter of the mass,
And see God made and eaten all day long,
And feel the steady candle-flame, and taste
Good strong thick stupefying incense-smoke!
85 For as I lie here, hours of the dead night,
Dying in state and by such slow degrees,
I fold my arms as if they clasped a crook,
And stretch my feet forth straight as stone can point,
And let the bedclothes, for a mortcloth, drop
90 Into great laps and folds of sculptor's-work:
And as yon tapers dwindle, and strange thoughts
Grow, with a certain humming in my ears,
About the life before I lived this life,
And this life too, popes, cardinals, and priests,

---

[3] Three-legged stool used by the oracle at Delphi.
[4] Staff carried by Dionysus and his followers.
[5] Marcus Tullius Cicero, master of Latin prose style.
[6] Domitius Ulpianus, third century Roman jurist, noted for bad prose.

95 Saint Praxed at his sermon on the mount,[7]
   Your tall pale mother with her talking eyes,
   And new-found agate urns as fresh as day,
   And marble's language, Latin pure, discreet
   —Aha, ELUCESCEBAT[8] quoth our friend?
100 No Tully, said I, Ulpian at the best!
   Evil and brief hath been my pilgrimage.
   All *lapis,* all, sons! Else I give the Pope
   My villas! Will ye ever eat my heart?
   Ever your eyes were as a lizard's quick,
105 They glitter like your mother's for my soul,
   Or ye would heighten my impoverished frieze,
   Piece out its starved design, and fill my vase
   With grapes, and add a vizor and a Term,[9]
   And to the tripod you would tie a lynx
110 That in his struggle throws the thyrsus down,
   To comfort me on my entablature
   Whereon I am to lie till I must ask
   "Do I live, am I dead?" There, leave me, there!
   For ye have stabbed me with ingratitude
115 To death—ye wish it—God, ye wish it! Stone—
   Gritstone, a-crumble! Clammy squares which sweat
   As if the corpse they keep were oozing through—
   And no more *lapis* to delight the world!
   Well go! I bless ye. Fewer tapers there,
120 But in a row: and, going, turn your backs
   —Aye, like departing altar-ministrants,
   And leave me in my church, the church for peace,
   That I may watch at leisure if he leers—
   Old Gandolf, at me, from his onion-stone,
125 As still he envied me, so fair she was!

Home-Thoughts, from Abroad

1

   Oh, to be in England
   Now that April's there,

---

7 The bishop's failing mind attributes the Sermon on the Mount to Saint Praxed (a woman) instead of Christ.
8 "He was illustrious," an example of Ulpian Latin.
9 A mask and a bust on a pedestal.

And whoever wakes in England
Sees, some morning, unaware,
5 That the lowest boughs and the brushwood sheaf
Round the elm-tree bole are in tiny leaf,
While the chaffinch sings on the orchard bough
In England—now!

2

And after April, when May follows,
10 And the whitethroat builds, and all the swallows!
Hark, where my blossomed pear-tree in the hedge
Leans to the field and scatters on the clover
Blossoms and dewdrops—at the bent spray's edge—
That's the wise thrush; he sings each song twice over,
15 Lest you should think he never could recapture
The first fine careless rapture!
And though the fields look rough with hoary dew,
All will be gay when noontide wakes anew
The buttercups, the little children's dower
20 —Far brighter than this gaudy melon-flower!

Meeting at Night

1

The gray sea and the long black land;
And the yellow half-moon large and low;
And the startled little waves that leap
In fiery ringlets from their sleep,
5 As I gain the cove with pushing prow,
And quench its speed i' the slushy sand.

2

Then a mile of warm sea-scented beach;
Three fields to cross till a farm appears;
A tap at the pane, the quick sharp scratch
10 And blue spurt of a lighted match,
And a voice less loud, through its joys and fears,
Than the two hearts beating each to each!

Parting at Morning

Round the cape of a sudden came the sea,
And the sun looked over the mountain's rim:
And straight was a path of gold for him,
And the need of a world of men for me.

HENRY DAVID THOREAU (1817–1862)

Smoke

Light-wingèd Smoke, Icarian[1] bird,
Melting thy pinions in thy upward flight;
Lark without song, and messenger of dawn,
Circling above the hamlets as thy nest;
5 Or else, departing dream, and shadowy form
Of midnight vision, gathering up thy skirts;
By night star-veiling, and by day
Darkening the light and blotting out the sun;
Go thou my incense upward from this hearth,
10 And ask the gods to pardon this clear flame.

Haze

Woof of the sun, ethereal gauze,
Woven of Nature's richest stuffs,
Visible heat, air-water, and dry sea,
Last conquest of the eye;
5 Toil of the day displayed, sun-dust,
Aerial surf upon the shores of earth,
Ethereal estuary, frith[1] of light,
Breakers of air, billows of heat,
Fine summer spray on inland seas;
10 Bird of the sun, transparent-winged
Owlet of noon, soft-pinioned,
From heath or stubble rising without song;
Establish thy serenity o'er the fields.

---

[1] Refers to Icarus in Greek mythology.

[1] An estuary.

Epitaph on the World

Here lies the body of this world,
Whose soul alas to hell is hurled.
This golden youth long since was past,
Its silver manhood went as fast,
5 And iron age drew on at last;
'Tis vain its character to tell,
The several fates which it befell,
What year it died, when 'twill arise,
We only know that here it lies.

EMILY BRONTË (1818–1848)

No Coward Soul Is Mine

No coward soul is mine,
No trembler in the world's storm-troubled sphere:
   I see Heaven's glories shine,
And faith shines equal, arming me from fear.

5   O God within my breast,
Almighty, ever-present Deity!
   Life, that in me hast rest
As I, undying life, have power in Thee!

   Vain are the thousand creeds
10 That move men's hearts; unutterably vain;
   Worthless as withered weeds,
Or idlest froth amid the boundless main,

   To waken doubt in one
Holding so fast by Thy infinity,
15   So surely anchored on
The steadfast rock of immortality.

   With wide embracing love
Thy spirit animates eternal years,
   Pervades and broods above,
20 Changes, sustains, dissolves, creates, and rears.

   Though earth and moon were gone,
And suns and universes cease to be,
   And Thou wert left alone,
Every existence would exist in Thee.

25   There is not room for death,
    Nor atom that his might could render void:
      Since Thou are Being and Breath
    And what Thou art may never be destroyed.

HERMAN MELVILLE (1819–1891)

Buddha

*"For what is your life? It is even
a vapor that appeareth for a little
time and then vanisheth away."* [1]

Swooning swim to less and less,
    Aspirant to nothingness!
Sobs of the worlds, and dole of kinds
    That dumb endurers be—
5 Nirvana! absorb us in your skies,
    Annul us into thee.

WALT WHITMAN (1819–1892)

Out of the Cradle Endlessly Rocking

Out of the cradle endlessly rocking,
Out of the mocking-bird's throat, the musical shuttle,
Out of the Ninth-month midnight,
Over the sterile sands and the fields beyond, where the child leaving
    his bed wander'd alone, bareheaded, barefoot,
5 Down from the shower'd halo,
Up from the mystic play of shadows twining and twisting as if they
    were alive,
Out from the patches of briers and blackberries,
From the memories of the bird that chanted to me,
From your memories sad brother, from the fitful risings and fallings
    I heard,
10 From under that yellow half-moon late-risen and swollen as if with
    tears,
From those beginning notes of yearning and love there in the mist,
From the thousand responses of my heart never to cease,
From the myriad thence-arous'd words,
From the word stronger and more delicious than any,
15 From such as now they start the scene revisiting,

---

[1] James 4:14.

As a flock, twittering, rising, or overhead passing,
Borne hither, ere all eludes me, hurriedly,
A man, yet by these tears a little boy again,
Throwing myself on the sand, confronting the waves,
20 I, chanter of pains and joys, uniter of here and hereafter,
Taking all hints to use them, but swiftly leaping beyond them,
A reminiscence sing.

One Paumanok,[1]
When the lilac-scent was in the air and Fifth-month grass was grow-
      ing,
25 Up this seashore in some briers,
Two feather'd guests from Alabama, two together,
And their nest, and four light-green eggs spotted with brown,
And every day the he-bird to and fro near at hand,
And every day the she-bird crouch'd on her nest, silent, with bright
      eyes,
30 And every day I, a curious boy, never too close, never disturbing
      them,
Cautiously peering, absorbing, translating.

Shine! shine! shine!
Pour down your warmth, great sun!
While we bask, we two together.

35 *Two together!*
Winds blow south, or winds blow north,
Day come white, or night come black,
Home, or rivers and mountains from home,
Singing all time, minding no time,
40 *While we two keep together.*

Till of a sudden,
May-be kill'd, unknown to her mate,
One forenoon, the she-bird crouch'd not on the nest,
Nor return'd that afternoon, nor the next,
45 Nor ever appear'd again.

And thenceforward all summer in the sound of the sea,
And at night under the full of the moon in calmer weather,
Over the hoarse surging of the sea,
Or flitting from brier to brier by day,

---

[1] The Indian name for Long Island.

50 I saw, I heard at intervals the remaining one, the he-bird,
   The solitary guest from Alabama.

   Blow! blow! blow!
   Blow up sea-winds along Paumanok's shore;
   I wait and I wait till you blow my mate to me.

55 Yes, when the stars glisten'd,
   All night long on the prong of a moss-scallop'd stake,
   Down almost amid the slapping waves,
   Sat the lone singer wonderful causing tears.

   He call'd on his mate,
60 He pour'd forth the meanings which I of all men know.

   Yes my brother I know,
   The rest might not, but I have treasur'd every note,
   For more than once dimly down to the beach gliding,
   Silent, avoiding the moonbeams, blending myself with the shadows,
65 Recalling now the obscure shapes, the echoes, the sounds and sights
           after their sorts,
   The white arms out in the breakers tirelessly tossing,
   I, with bare feet, a child, the wind wafting my hair,
   Listen'd long and long.

   Listen'd to keep, to sing, now translating the notes,
70 Following you my brother.

   Soothe! soothe! soothe!
   Close on its wave soothes the wave behind,
   And again another behind embracing and lapping, every one close,
   But my love soothes not me, not me.

75 *Low hangs the moon, it rose late,*
   It is lagging—O I think it is heavy with love, with love.

   O madly the sea pushes upon the land,
   With love, with love.

   O night! do I not see my love fluttering out among the breakers?
80 *What is that little black thing I see there in the white?*

   Loud! loud! loud!
   Loud I call to you, my love!
   High and clear I shoot my voice over the waves,
   Surely you must know who is here, is here,
85 *You must know who I am, my love.*

Low-hanging moon!
What is that dusky spot in your brown yellow?
O it is the shape, the shape of my mate!
O moon do not keep her from me any longer.

90 *Land! land! O land!*
Whichever way I turn, O I think you could give me my mate back
again if you only would,
For I am almost sure I see her dimly whichever way I look.

O rising stars!
Perhaps the one I want so much will rise, will rise with some of you.

95 *O throat! O trembling throat!*
Sound clearer through the atmosphere!
Pierce the woods, the earth,
Somewhere listening to catch you must be the one I want.

Shake out carols!
100 *Solitary here, the night's carols!*
Carols of lonesome love! death's carols!
Carols under that lagging, yellow, waning moon!
O under that moon where she droops almost down into the sea!
O reckless despairing carols.

105 *But soft! sink low!*
Soft! let me just murmur,
And do you wait a moment you husky-nois'd sea,
For somewhere I believe I heard my mate responding to me,
So faint, I must be still, be still to listen,
110 *But not altogether still, for then she might not come immediately*
to me.

Hither my love!
Here I am! here!
With this just-sustain'd note I announce myself to you,
This gentle call is for you my love, for you.

115 *Do not be decoy'd elsewhere,*
That is the whistle of the wind, it is not my voice,
That is the fluttering, the fluttering of the spray,
Those are the shadows of leaves.

O darkness! O in vain!
120 *O I am very sick and sorrowful.*

O brown halo in the sky near the moon, drooping upon the sea!
O troubled reflection in the sea!
O throat! O throbbing heart!
And I singing uselessly, uselessly all the night.

125 *O past! O happy life! O songs of joy!*
In the air, in the woods, over fields,
Loved! loved! loved! loved! loved!
But my mate no more, no more with me!
We two together no more.

130 The aria sinking,
All else continuing, the stars shining,
The winds blowing, the notes of the bird continuous echoing,
With angry moans the fierce old mother incessantly moaning,
On the sands of Paumanok's shore gray and rustling,
135 The yellow half-moon enlarged, sagging down, drooping, the face of
the sea almost touching,
The boy ecstatic, with his bare feet the waves, with his hair the
atmosphere dallying,
The love in the heart long pent, now loose, now at last tumultuously
bursting,
The aria's meaning, the ears, the soul, swiftly depositing,
The strange tears down the cheeks coursing,
140 The colloquy there, the trio, each uttering,
The undertone, the savage old mother incessantly crying,
To the boy's soul's questions sullenly timing, some drown'd secret
hissing,
To the outsetting bard.

Demon or bird! (said the boy's soul,)
145 Is it indeed toward your mate you sing? or is it really to me?
For I, that was a child, my tongue's use sleeping, now I have heard
you,
Now in a moment I know what I am for, I awake,
And already a thousand singers, a thousand songs, clearer, louder
and more sorrowful than yours,
A thousand warbling echoes have started to life within me, never
to die.

150 O you singer solitary, singing by yourself, projecting me,
O solitary me listening, never more shall I cease perpetuating you,
Never more shall I escape, never more the reverberations,
Never more the cries of unsatisfied love be absent from me,

Never again leave me to be the peaceful child I was before what
    there in the night,
155 By the sea under the yellow and sagging moon,
The messenger there arous'd, the fire, the sweet hell within,
The unknown want, the destiny of me.

O give me the clew! (it lurks in the night here somewhere,)
O if I am to have so much, let me have more!

160 A word then, (for I will conquer it,)
The word final, superior to all,
Subtle, sent up—what is it?—I listen;
Are you whispering it, and have been all the time, you sea-waves?
Is that it from your liquid rims and wet sands?

165 Whereto answering, the sea,
Delaying not, hurrying not,
Whisper'd me through the night, and very plainly before daybreak,
Lisp'd to me the low and delicious word death,
And again death, death, death, death,
170 Hissing melodious, neither like the bird nor like my arous'd child's
    heart,
But edging near as privately for me rustling at my feet,
Creeping thence steadily up to my ears and leaving me softly all over,
Death, death, death, death, death.

Which I do not forget,
175 But fuse the song of my dusky demon and brother,
That he sang to me in the moonlight on Paumanok's gray beach,
With the thousand responsive songs at random,
My own songs awaked from that hour,
And with them the key, the word up from the waves,
180 The word of the sweetest song and all songs,
That strong and delicious word which, creeping to my feet,
(Or like some old crone rocking the cradle, swathed in sweet gar-
    ments, bending aside,)
The sea whisper'd me.

When I Heard the Learn'd Astronomer

When I heard the learn'd astronomer,
When the proofs, the figures, were ranged in columns before me,
When I was shown the charts and diagrams, to add, divide, and
    measure them,

When I sitting heard the astronomer where he lectured with much
    applause in the lecture-room,
5 How soon unaccountable I became tired and sick,
Till rising and gliding out I wander'd off by myself,
In the mystical moist night-air, and from time to time,
Look'd up in perfect silence at the stars.

Cavalry Crossing a Ford

A line in long array where they wind betwixt green islands,
They take a serpentine course, their arms flash in the sun—hark to
    the musical clank,
Behold the silvery river, in it the splashing horses loitering stop to
    drink,
Behold the brown-faced men, each group, each person a picture, the
    negligent rest on the saddles,
5 Some emerge on the opposite bank, others are just entering the ford
    —while,
Scarlet and blue and snowy white,
The guidon flags flutter gayly in the wind.

When Lilacs Last in the Dooryard Bloom'd[1]

1

When lilacs last in the dooryard bloom'd,
And the great star early droop'd in the western sky in the night,
I mourn'd, and yet shall mourn with ever-returning spring.

Ever-returning spring, trinity sure to me you bring,
5 Lilac blooming perennial and drooping star in the west,
And thought of him I love.

2

O powerful western fallen star!
O shades of night—O moody, tearful night!
O great star disappear'd—O the black murk that hides the star!
10 O cruel hands that hold me powerless—O helpless soul of me!
O harsh surrounding cloud that will not free my soul.

3

In the dooryard fronting an old farm-house near the white-wash'd
    palings,

---

[1] This poem is an elegy to Abraham Lincoln.

Stands the lilac-bush tall-growing with heart-shaped leaves of rich
   green,
With many a pointed blossom rising delicate, with the perfume
   strong I love,
15 With every leaf a miracle—and from this bush in the dooryard,
With delicate-color'd blossoms and heart-shaped leaves of rich green,
A sprig with its flower I break.

4

In the swamp in secluded recesses,
A shy and hidden bird is warbling a song,

20 Solitary the thrush,
The hermit withdrawn to himself, avoiding the settlements,
Sings by himself a song.

Song of the bleeding throat,
Death's outlet song of life, (for well dear brother I know,
25 If thou wast not granted to sing thou would'st surely die.)

5

Over the breast of the spring, the land, amid cities,
Amid lanes and through old woods, where lately the violets peep'd
   from the ground, spotting the gray debris,
Amid the grass in the fields each side of the lanes, passing the end-
   less grass,
Passing the yellow-spear'd wheat, every grain from its shroud in the
   dark-brown fields uprisen,
30 Passing the apple-tree blows of white and pink in the orchards,
Carrying a corpse to where it shall rest in the grave,
Night and day journeys a coffin.

6

Coffin that passes through lanes and streets,
Through day and night with the great cloud darkening the land,
35 With the pomp of the inloop'd flags with the cities draped in black,
With the show of the States themselves as of crape-veil'd women
   standing,
With processions long and winding and the flambeaus of the night,
With the countless torches lit, with the silent sea of faces and the un-
   bared heads,
With the waiting depot, the arriving coffin, and the sombre faces,
40 With dirges through the night, with the thousand voices rising strong
   and solemn.

With all the mournful voices of the dirges pour'd around the coffin,
The dim-lit churches and the shuddering organs—where amid these
    you journey,
With the tolling tolling bells' perpetual clang,
Here, coffin that slowly passes,
45 I give you my sprig of lilac.

7

(Nor for you, for one alone,
Blossoms and branches green to coffins all I bring,
For fresh as the morning, thus would I chant a song for you O sane
    and sacred death.

All over bouquets of roses,
50 O death, I cover you over with roses and early lilies,
But mostly and now the lilac that blooms the first,
Copious I break, I break the sprigs from the bushes,
With loaded arms I come, pouring for you,
For you and the coffins all of you O death.)

8

55 O western orb sailing the heaven,
Now I know what you must have meant as a month since I walk'd,
As I walk'd in silence the transparent shadowy night,
As I saw you had something to tell as you bent to me night after
    night,
As you droop'd from the sky low down as if to my side, (while the
    other stars all look'd on,)
60 As we wander'd together the solemn night, (for something I know
    not what kept me from sleep,)
As the night advanced, and I saw on the rim of the west how full
    you were of woe,
As I stood on the rising ground in the breeze in the cool transparent
    night,
As I watch'd where you pass'd and was lost in the netherward black
    of the night,
As my soul in its trouble dissatisfied sank, as where you sad orb,
65 Concluded, dropt in the night, and was gone.

9

Sing on there in the swamp,
O singer bashful and tender, I hear your notes, I hear your call,
I hear, I come presently, I understand you,
But a moment I linger, for the lustrous star has detain'd me,
70 The star my departing comrade holds and detains me.

10

O how shall I warble myself for the dead one there I loved?
And how shall I deck my song for the large sweet soul that has
    gone?
And what shall my perfume be for the grave of him I love?

Sea-winds blown from east and west,
75 Blown from the Eastern sea and blown from the Western sea, till
    there on the prairies meeting,
These and with these and the breath of my chant,
I'll perfume the grave of him I love.

11

O what shall I hang on the chamber walls?
And what shall the pictures be that I hang on the walls,
80 To adorn the burial-house of him I love?

Pictures of growing spring and farms and homes,
With the Fourth-month eve at sundown, and the gray smoke lucid
    and bright,
With floods of the yellow gold of the gorgeous, indolent, sinking sun,
    burning, expanding the air,
With the fresh sweet herbage under foot, and the pale green leaves
    of the trees prolific,
85 In the distance the flowing glaze, the breast of the river, with a wind-
    dapple here and there,
With ranging hills on the banks, with many a line against the sky,
    and shadows,
And the city at hand with dwellings so dense, and stacks of chimneys,
And all the scenes of life and the workshops, and the workmen
    homeward returning.

12

Lo, body and soul—this land,
90 My own Manhattan with spires, and the sparkling and hurrying tides,
    and the ships,
The varied and ample land, the South and the North in the light,
    Ohio's shores and flashing Missouri,
And ever the far-spreading prairies cover'd with grass and corn.

Lo, the most excellent sun so calm and haughty,
The violet and purple morn with just-felt breezes,
95 The gentle soft-born measureless light,

The miracle spreading bathing all, the fulfill'd noon,
The coming eve delicious, the welcome night and the stars,
Over my cities shining all, enveloping man and land.

13

Sing on, sing on you gray-brown bird,
100 Sing from the swamps, the recesses, pour your chant from the
bushes,
Limitless out of the dusk, out of the cedars and pines.

Sing on dearest brother, warble your reedy song,
Loud human song, with voice of uttermost woe.

O liquid and free and tender!
105 O wild and loose to my soul—O wondrous singer!
You only I hear—yet the star holds me, (but will soon depart,)
Yet the lilac with mastering odor holds me.

14

Now while I sat in the day and look'd forth,
In the close of the day with its light and the fields of spring, and the
farmers preparing their crops,
110 In the large unconscious scenery of my land with its lakes and
forests,
In the heavenly aerial beauty, (after the perturb'd winds and the
storms,)
Under the arching heavens of the afternoon swift passing, and the
voices of children and women.
The many-moving sea-tides, and I saw the ships how they sail'd,
And the summer approaching with richness, and the fields all busy
with labor,
115 And the infinite separate houses, how they all went on, each with its
meals and minutia of daily usages,
And the streets how their throbbings throbb'd, and the cities pent—
lo, then and there,
Falling upon them all and among them all, enveloping me with the
rest,
Appear'd the cloud, appear'd the long black trail,
And I knew death, its thought, and the sacred knowledge of death.

120 Then with the knowledge of death as walking one side of me,
And the thought of death close-walking the other side of me,
And I in the middle as with companions, and as holding the hands
of companions,

I fled forth to the hiding receiving night that talks not,
Down to the shores of the water, the path by the swamp in the
    dimness,
125 To the solemn shadowy cedars and ghostly pines so still.

And the singer so shy to the rest receiv'd me,
The gray-brown bird I know receiv'd us comrades three,
And he sang the carol of death, and a verse for him I love.

From deep secluded recesses,
130 From the fragrant cedars and the ghostly pines so still,
Came the carol of the bird.

And the charm of the carol rapt me,
As I held as if by their hands my comrades in the night,
And the voice of my spirit tallied the song of the bird.

135 *Come lovely and soothing death,*
  Undulate round the world, serenely arriving, arriving,
  In the day, in the night, to all, to each,
  Sooner or later delicate death.

  Prais'd be the fathomless universe,
140 *For life and joy, and for objects and knowledge curious,*
  And for love, sweet love—but praise! praise! praise!
  For the sure-enwinding arms of cool-enfolding death.

  Dark mother always gliding near with soft feet,
  Have none chanted for three a chant of fullest welcome?
145 *Then I chant it for thee, I glorify thee above all,*
  I bring thee a song that when thou must indeed come, come
    unfalteringly.

  Approach strong deliveress,
  When it is so, when thou hast taken them I joyously sing the dead,
  Lost in the loving floating ocean of thee,
150 *Laved in the flood of thy bliss O death.*

  From me to thee glad serenades,
  Dances for thee I propose saluting thee, adornments, and feastings for thee,
  And the sights of the open landscape and the high-spread sky are fitting,
  And life and the fields, and the huge and thoughtful night.

155 *The night in silence under many a star,*
The ocean shore and the husky whispering wave whose voice I know,
And the soul turning to thee O vast and well-veil'd death,
And the body gratefully nestling close to thee.

Over the tree-tops I float thee a song,
160 *Over the rising and sinking waves, over the myriad fields and the prairies*
wide,
Over the dense-pack'd cities all and the teeming wharves and ways,
I float this carol with joy, with joy to thee O death.

15

To the tally of my soul,
Loud and strong kept up the gray-brown bird,
165 With pure deliberate notes spreading filling the night.

Loud in the pines and cedars dim,
Clear in the freshness moist and the swamp-perfume,
And I with my comrades there in the night.

While my sight that was bound in my eyes unclosed,
170 As to long panoramas of visions.

And I saw askant the armies,
I saw as in noiseless dreams hundreds of battle-flags,
Borne through the smoke of the battles and pierc'd with missiles I
saw them,
And carried hither and yon through the smoke, and torn and
bloody,
175 And at last but a few shreds left on the staffs, (and all in silence,)
And the staffs all splinter'd and broken.

I saw battle-corpses, myriads of them,
And the white skeletons of young men, I saw them,
I saw the debris and debris of all the slain soldiers of the war,
180 But I saw they were not as was thought,
They themselves were fully at rest, they suffer'd not,
The living remain'd and suffer'd, the mother suffer'd,
And the wife and the child and the musing comrade suffer'd,
And the armies that remain'd suffer'd.

16

185 Passing the visions, passing the night,
Passing, unloosing the hold of my comrades' hands,
Passing the song of the hermit bird and the tallying song of my soul,
Victorious song, death's outlet song, yet varying ever-altering song,
As low and wailing, yet clear the notes, rising and falling, flooding
the night,
190 Sadly sinking and fainting, as warning and warning, and yet again
bursting with joy,
Covering the earth and filling the spread of the heaven,
As that powerful psalm in the night I heard from recesses,
Passing, I leave thee lilac with heart-shaped leaves,
I leave thee there in the door-yard, blooming, returning with spring.

195 I cease from my song for thee,
From my gaze on thee in the west, fronting the west, communing
with thee,
O comrade lustrous with silver face in the night.

Yet each to keep and all, retrievements out of the night,
The song, the wondrous chant of the gray-brown bird,
200 And the tallying chant, the echo arous'd in my soul,
With the lustrous and drooping star with the countenance full of
woe,
With the holders holding my hand nearing the call of the bird,
Comrades mine and I in the midst, and their memory ever to keep,
for the dead I loved so well,
For the sweetest, wisest soul of all my days and lands—and this for
his dear sake,
205 Lilac and star and bird twined with the chant of my soul,
There in the fragrant pines and the cedars dusk and dim.

A Noiseless Patient Spider

A noiseless patient spider,
I mark'd where on a little promontory it stood isolated,
Mark'd how to explore the vacant vast surrounding,
It launch'd forth filament, filament, filament, out of itself,
5 Ever unreeling down, ever tirelessly speeding them.

And you O my soul where you stand,
Surrounded, detached, in measureless oceans of space,
Ceaselessly musing, venturing, throwing, seeking the spheres to con-
nect them,
Till the bridge you will need be form'd, till the ductile anchor hold,
10 Till the gossamer thread you fling catch somewhere, O my soul.

The Dalliance of the Eagles

Skirting the river road, (my forenoon walk, my rest,)
Skyward in air a sudden muffled sound, the dalliance of the eagles,
The rushing amorous contact high in space together,
The clinching interlocking claws, a living, fierce, gyrating wheel,
5 Four beating wings, two beaks, a swirling mass tight grappling,
In tumbling turning clustering loops, straight downward falling,
Till o'er the river pois'd, the twain yet one, a moment's lull,
A motionless still balance in the air, then parting, talons loosing,
Upward again on slow-firm pinions slanting, their separate diverse
flight,
10 She hers, he his, pursuing.

MATTHEW ARNOLD (1822–1888)

Shakespeare

Others abide our question. Thou art free.
We ask and ask—thou smilest and art still,
Out-topping knowledge. For the loftiest hill,
Who to the stars uncrowns his majesty,

5 Planting his stedfast footsteps in the sea,
Making the heaven of heavens his dwelling-place,
Spares but the cloudy border of his base
To the foiled searching of mortality;

And thou, who didst the stars and sunbeams know,
10 Self-schooled, self-scanned, self-honored, self-secure,
Didst tread on earth unguessed at—better so!

All pains the immortal spirit must endure,
All weakness which impairs, all griefs which bow,
Find their sole speech in that victorious brow.

The Scholar-Gipsy[1]

Go, for they call you, shepherd, from the hill;
  Go, shepherd, and untie the wattled cotes! [2]
    No longer leave thy wistful flock unfed,
    Nor let thy bawling fellows rack their throats,
5   Nor the cropped herbage shoot another head.
      But when the fields are still,
    And the tired men and dogs all gone to rest,
    And only the white sheep are sometimes seen
    Cross and recross the strips of moon-blanched green,
10 Come, shepherd, and again begin the quest!

Here, where the reaper was at work of late—
  In this high field's dark corner, where he leaves
    His coat, his basket, and his earthen cruse,
    And in the sun all morning binds the sheaves,
15   Then here, at noon, comes back his stores to use—
      Here will I sit and wait,
    While to my ear from uplands far away
    The bleating of the folded flocks is borne,
    With distant cries of reapers in the corn—
20 All the live murmur of a summer's day.

Screened is this nook o'er the high, half-reaped field,
  And here till sundown, shepherd! will I be.
    Through the thick corn the scarlet poppies peep,

---

1 " 'There was very lately a lad in the University of Oxford, who was by his poverty forced to leave his studies there; and at last to join himself to a company of vagabond gipsies. Among these extravagant people, by the insinuating subtlety of his carriage, he quickly got so much of their love and esteem as that they discovered to him their mystery. After he had been a pretty while well exercised in the trade, there chanced to ride by a couple of scholars, who had formerly been of his acquaintance. They quickly spied out their old friend among the gipsies; and he gave them an account of the necessity which drove him to that kind of life, and told them that the people he went with were not such impostors as they were taken for, but that they had a traditional kind of learning among them, and could do wonders by the power of imagination, their fancy binding that of others: that himself had learned much of their art, and when he had compassed the whole secret, he intended, he said, to leave their company, and give the world an account of what he had learned.'—Glanvil's *Vanity of Dogmatizing,* 1661" [Arnold's note]

2 Sheepfolds made of woven boughs (wattles).

And round green roots and yellowing stalks I see
25   Pale pink convolvulus in tendrils creep;
    And air-swept lindens yield
Their scent, and rustle down their perfumed showers
Of bloom on the bent grass where I am laid,
And bower me from the August sun with shade;
30   And the eye travels down to Oxford's towers.

And near me on the grass lies Glanvil's book—
    Come, let me read the oft-read tale again!
    The story of the Oxford scholar poor,
Of pregnant parts and quick inventive brain,
35   Who, tired of knocking at preferment's door,
    One summer-morn forsook
His friends, and went to learn the gipsy-lore,
And roamed the world with that wild brotherhood,
And came, as most men deemed, to little good,
40   But came to Oxford and his friends no more.

But once, years after, in the country-lanes,
    Two scholars, whom at college erst he knew,
    Met him, and of his way of life enquired;
Whereat he answered, that the gipsy-crew,
45   His mates, had arts to rule as they desired
    The workings of men's brains,
And they can bind them to what thoughts they will.
    "And I," he said, "the secret of their art,
    When fully learned, will to the world impart;
50   But it needs heaven-sent moments for this skill."

This said, he left them, and returned no more.—
    But rumors hung about the country-side,
    That the lost Scholar long was seen to stray,
Seen by rare glimpses, pensive and tongue-tied,
55   In hat of antique shape, and cloak of gray.
    The same the gipsies wore.
Shepherds had met him on the Hurst[3] in spring;
    At some lone alehouse in the Berkshire moors,

---

[3] A hill near Oxford. All of the following place names (except those in the final two stanzas) refer to the environs of Oxford.

On the warm ingle-bench,[4] the smock-frocked boors[5]
60   Had found him seated at their entering,

But, 'mid their drink and clatter, he would fly.
   And I myself seem half to know thy looks,
     And put the shepherds, wanderer! on thy trace;
   And boys who in lone wheatfields scare the rooks
65   I ask if thou hast passed their quiet place;
       Or in my boat I lie
   Moored to the cool bank in the summer-heats,
     'Mid wide grass meadows which the sunshine fills,
     And watch the warm, green-muffled Cumner hills,
70   And wonder if thou haunt'st their shy retreats.

For most, I know, thou lov'st retired ground!
   Thee at the ferry Oxford riders blithe,
     Returning home on summer-nights, have met
   Crossing the stripling Thames at Bab-lock-hithe,
75   Trailing in the cool stream thy fingers wet,
       As the punt's rope chops round;
   And leaning backward in a pensive dream,
     And fostering in thy lap a heap of flowers
     Plucked in shy fields and distant Wychwood bowers,
80   And thine eyes resting on the moonlit stream.

And then they land, and thou art seen no more!
   Maidens, who from the distant hamlets come
     To dance around the Fyfield elm in May,
   Oft through the darkening fields have seen thee roam,
85   Or cross a stile into the public way.
       Oft thou hast given them store
  Of flowers—the frail-leafed, white anemone,
     Dark bluebells drenched with dews of summer eves,
     And purple orchises with spotted leaves—
90   But none hath words she can report of thee.

And, above Godstow Bridge, when hay-time's here
   In June, and many a scythe in sunshine flames,
     Men who through those wide fields of breezy grass
   Where black-winged swallows haunt the glittering Thames,

---

[4] Bench in the chimney corner.
[5] Rustics.

95   To bathe in the abandoned lasher[6] pass,
　　　Have often passed thee near
　　Sitting upon the river bank o'ergrown;
　　　Marked thine outlandish garb, thy figure spare,
　　　Thy dark vague eyes, and soft abstracted air—
100 But, when they came from bathing, thou wast gone!

　　At some lone homestead in the Cumner hills,
　　　Where at her open door the housewife darns,
　　　Thou hast been seen, or hanging on a gate
　　To watch the threshers in the mossy barns.
105　　Children, who early range these slopes and late
　　　　For cresses from the rills,
　　Have known thee eying, all an April-day,
　　　The springing pastures and the feeding kine;
　　　And marked thee, when the stars come out and shine,
110 Through the long dewy grass move slow away.

　　In autumn, on the skirts of Bagley Wood—
　　　Where most the gipsies by the turf-edged way
　　　Pitch their smoked tents, and every bush you see
　　With scarlet patches tagged and shreds of gray,
115　　Above the forest-ground called Thessaly—
　　　　The blackbird, picking food,
　　Sees thee, nor stops his meal, nor fears at all;
　　　So often has he known thee past him stray,
　　　Rapt, twirling in thy hand a withered spray,
120 And waiting for the spark from heaven to fall.

　　And once, in winter, on the causeway chill
　　　Where home through flooded fields foot-travelers go,
　　　Have I not passed thee on the wooden bridge,
　　Wrapped in thy cloak and battling with the snow,
125　　Thy face tow'rd Hinksey and its wintry ridge?
　　　　And thou hast climbed the hill,
　　And gained the white brow of the Cumner range;
　　　Turned once to watch, while thick the snowflakes fall,
　　　The line of festal light in Christ-Church hall—
130 Then sought thy straw in some sequestered grange.

---

6 Pool below a dam.

But what—I dream! Two hundred years are flown
   Since first thy story ran through Oxford halls,
      And the grave Glanvil did the tale inscribe
   That thou wert wandered from the studious walls
135   To learn strange arts, and join a gipsy-tribe;
         And thou from earth art gone
   Long since, and in some quiet churchyard laid—
      Some country-nook, where o'er thy unknown grave
      Tall grasses and white flowering nettles wave,
140 Under a dark, red-fruited yew-tree's shade.

   —No, no, thou hast not felt the lapse of hours!
   For what wears out the life of mortal men?
      'Tis that from change to change their being rolls;
   'Tis that repeated shocks, again, again,
145   Exhaust the energy of strongest souls
         And numb the elastic powers.
   Till having used our nerves with bliss and teen,[7]
      And tired upon a thousand schemes our wit,
      To the just-pausing Genius[8] we remit
150 Our worn-out life, and are—what we have been.

Thou hast not lived, why should'st thou perish, so?
   Thou hadst *one* aim, *one* business, *one* desire;
      Else wert thou long since numbered with the dead!
   Else hadst thou spent, like other men, thy fire!
155   The generations of thy peers are fled.
         And we ourselves shall go;
   But thou possessest an immortal lot,
      And we imagine thee exempt from age
      And living as thou liv'st on Glanvil's page,
160 Because thou hadst—what we, alas! have not.

For early didst thou leave the world, with powers
   Fresh, undiverted to the world without,
      Firm to their mark, not spent on other things;
   Free from the sick fatigue, the languid doubt,
165   Which much to have tried, in much been baffled, brings.
      O life unlike to ours!

---

[7] Sorrow.
[8] Protective spirit.

Who fluctuate idly without term or scope,
    Of whom each strives, nor knows for what he strives,
    And each half lives a hundred different lives;
170 Who wait like thee, but not, like thee, in hope.

Thou waitest for the spark from heaven! and we,
    Light half-believers of our casual creeds,
    Who never deeply felt, nor clearly willed,
    Whose insight never has borne fruit in deeds,
175   Whose vague resolves never have been fulfilled;
        For whom each year we see
    Breeds new beginnings, disappointments new;
        Who hesitate and falter life away,
        And lose tomorrow the ground won today—
180 Ah! do not we, wanderer! await it too?

Yes, we await it! but it still delays,
    And then we suffer! and amongst us one,[9]
        Who most has suffered, takes dejectedly
    His seat upon the intellectual throne;
185   And all his store of sad experience he
        Lays bare of wretched days;
    Tells us his misery's birth and growth and signs,
        And how the dying spark of hope was fed,
        And how the breast was soothed, and how the head,
190 And all his hourly varied anodynes.

This for our wisest! and we others pine,
    And wish the long unhappy dream would end,
        And waive all claim to bliss, and try to bear;
    With close-lipped patience for our only friend,
195   Sad patience, too near neighbor to despair—
        But none has hope like thine!
    Thou through the fields and through the woods dost stray,
        Roaming the countryside, a truant boy,
        Nursing thy project in unclouded joy,
200 And every doubt long blown by time away.

O born in days when wits were fresh and clear,
    And life ran gaily as the sparkling Thames;
        Before this strange disease of modern life,

---

9 Tennyson.

With its sick hurry, its divided aims,
205   Its head o'ertaxed, its palsied hearts, was rife—
     Fly hence, our contact fear!
Still fly, plunge deeper in the bowering wood!
   Averse, as Dido did with gesture stern
   From her false friend's approach in Hades turn,[10]
210 Wave us away, and keep thy solitude!

Still nursing the unconquerable hope,
   Still clutching the inviolable shade,
     With a free, onward impulse brushing through,
   By night, the silvered branches of the glade—
215   Far on the forest-skirts, where none pursue,
     On some mild pastoral slope
Emerge, and resting on the moonlit pales
   Freshen thy flowers as in former years
   With dew, or listen with enchanted ears,
220 From the dark dingles,[11] to the nightingales!

But fly our paths, our feverish contact fly!
   For strong the infection of our mental strife,
     Which, though it gives no bliss, yet spoils for rest;
   And we should win thee from thy own fair life,
225   Like us distracted, and like us unblest.
     Soon, soon thy cheer would die,
Thy hopes grow timorous, and unfixed thy powers,
   And thy clear aims be cross and shifting made;
   And then thy glad perennial youth would fade,
230 Fade, and grow old at last, and die like ours.

Then fly our greetings, fly our speech and smiles!
   —As some grave Tyrian trader, from the sea,
     Described at sunrise an emerging prow
   Lifting the cool-haired creepers stealthily,
235   The fringes of a southward-facing brow
     Among the Aegean isles;

---

[10] Dido, who had killed herself because of Aeneas, turned scornfully away from him when he visited Hades.
[11] Secluded valleys.

And saw the merry Grecian coaster come,
  Freighted with amber grapes, and Chian[12] wine,
  Green, bursting figs, and tunnies steeped in brine—
240 And knew the intruders on his ancient home,

The young light-hearted masters of the waves—
  And snatched his rudder, he shook out more sail;
  And day and night held on indignantly
O'er the blue Midland waters with the gale,
245 Betwixt the Syrtes[13] and soft Sicily,
    To where the Atlantic raves
  Outside the western straits; and unbent sails
    There, where down cloudy cliffs, through sheets of foam,
    Shy traffickers, the dark Iberians come;
250 And on the beach undid his corded bales.

Requiescat

Strew on her roses, roses,
  And never a spray of yew!
In quiet she reposes;
  Ah, would that I did too!

5 Her mirth the world required;
  She bathed it in smiles of glee.
But her heart was tired, tired,
  And now they let her be.

Her life was turning, turning,
10 In mazes of heat and sound.
But for peace her soul was yearning,
  And now peace laps her round.

Her cabined, ample spirit,
  It fluttered and failed for breath.
15 To-night it doth inherit
  The vasty hall of death.

---

[12] From the island of Chios.
[13] Gulf of Sidra, on the north coast of Africa.

Dover Beach

The sea is calm tonight.
The tide is full, the moon lies fair
Upon the straits;—on the French coast the light
Gleams and is gone; the cliffs of England stand,
5 Glimmering and vast, out in the tranquil bay.
Come to the window, sweet is the night-air!
Only, from the long line of spray
Where the sea meets the moon-blanched land,
Listen! you hear the grating roar
10 Of pebbles which the waves draw back, and fling,
At their return, up the high strand,
Begin, and cease, and then again begin,
With tremulous cadence slow, and bring
The eternal note of sadness in.

15 Sophocles long ago
Heard it on the Aegean, and it brought
Into his mind the turbid ebb and flow
Of human misery; we
Find also in the sound a thought,
20 Hearing it by this distant northern sea.

The Sea of Faith
Was once, too, at the full, and round earth's shore
Lay like the folds of a bright girdle furled.
But now I only hear
25 Its melancholy, long, withdrawing roar,
Retreating, to the breath
Of the night-wind, down the vast edges drear
And naked shingles of the world.

Ah, love, let us be true
30 To one another! for the world, which seems
To lie before us like a land of dreams,
So various, so beautiful, so new,
Hath really neither joy, nor love, nor light,
Nor certitude, nor peace, nor help for pain;
35 And we are here as on a darkling plain
Swept with confused alarms of struggle and flight,
Where ignorant armies clash by night.

DANTE GABRIEL ROSSETTI (1828–1882)

From **The House of Life**

A SONNET

A Sonnet is a moment's monument,—
   Memorial from the Soul's eternity
   To one dead deathless hour. Look that it be,
Whether for lustral [1] rite or dire portent,
5 Of its own arduous fullness reverent:
   Carve it in ivory or in ebony,
   As Day or Night may rule; and let Time see
Its flowering crest impearled and orient.

A Sonnet is a coin: its face reveals
10   The soul—its converse, to what Power 'tis due:—
Whether for tribute to the august appeals
   Of Life, or dower in Love's high retinue,
It serve; or, 'mid the dark wharf's cavernous breath,
In Charon's[2] palm it pay the toll to Death.

The Woodspurge

The wind flapped loose, the wind was still,
Shaken out dead from tree and hill:
I had walked on at the wind's will,—
I sat now, for the wind was still.

5 Between my knees my forehead was,—
My lips, drawn in, said not Alas!
My hair was over in the grass,
My naked ears heard the day pass.

My eyes, wide open, had the run
10 Of some ten weeds to fix upon;
Among those few, out of the sun,
The woodspurge flowered, three cups in one.

From perfect grief there need not be
Wisdom or even memory:
15 One thing then learnt remains to me,—
The woodspurge has a cup of three.

---

[1] Purifying.
[2] Charon received a coin for ferrying the dead across the Styx to Hades.

GEORGE MEREDITH (1828–1909)

From **Modern Love**

SONNET 1

By this he knew she wept with waking eyes:
That, at his hand's light quiver by her head,
The strange low sobs that shook their common bed
Were called into her with a sharp surprise,
5 And strangled mute, like little gaping snakes,
Dreadfully venomous to him. She lay
Stone-still, and the long darkness flowed away
With muffled pulses. Then, as midnight makes
Her giant heart of Memory and Tears
10 Drink the pale drug of silence, and so beat
Sleep's heavy measure, they from head to feet
Were moveless, looking through their dead black years,
By vain regret scrawled over the blank wall.
Like sculptured effigies they might be seen
15 Upon their marriage-tomb, the sword between;
Each wishing for the sword that severs all.

SONNET 17

At dinner, she is hostess, I am host.
Went the feast ever cheerfuller? She keeps
The Topic over intellectual deeps
In buoyancy afloat. They see no ghost.
5 With sparkling surface-eyes we ply the ball;
It is in truth a most contagious game:
HIDING THE SKELETON shall be its name.
Such play as this the devils might appal!
But here's the greater wonder; in that we,
10 Enamored of an acting naught can tire,
Each other, like true hypocrites, admire;
Warm-lighted looks, Love's ephemeridae,[1]
Shoot gayly o'er the dishes and the wine.
We waken envy of our happy lot.
15 Fast, sweet, and golden, shows the marriage-knot.
Dear guests, you now have seen Love's corpse-light shine.

---

[1] Short-lived May flies.

EMILY DICKINSON (1830–1886)

I Taste a Liquor Never Brewed (#214)

I taste a liquor never brewed—
From Tankards scooped in Pearl—
Not all the Vats upon the Rhine
Yield such an Alcohol!

5 Inebriate of Air—am I—
And Debauchee of Dew—
Reeling—thro endless summer days—
From inns of Molten Blue—

When "Landlords" turn the drunken Bee
10 Out of the Foxglove's door—
When Butterflies—renounce their "drams"—
I shall but drink the more!

Till Seraphs swing their snowy Hats—
And Saints—to windows run—
15 To see the little Tippler
Leaning against the—Sun—

There's a Certain Slant of Light (#258)

There's a certain Slant of light,
Winter Afternoons—
That oppresses, like the Heft
Of Cathedral Tunes—

5 Heavenly Hurt, it gives us—
We can find no scar,
But internal difference,
Where the Meanings, are—

None may teach it—Any—
10 'Tis the Seal Despair—
An imperial affliction
Sent us of the Air—

When it comes, the Landscape listens—
Shadows—hold their breath—
15 When it goes, 'tis like the Distance
On the look of Death—

Much Madness Is Divinest Sense (#435)

Much Madness is divinest Sense—
To a discerning Eye—
Much Sense—the starkest Madness—
'Tis the Majority
5 In this, as All, prevail—
Assent—and you are sane—
Demur—you're straightway dangerous—
And handled with a Chain—

Because I Could Not Stop for Death (#712)

Because I could not stop for Death—
He kindly stopped for me—
The Carriage held but just Ourselves—
And Immortality.

5 We slowly drove—He knew no haste
And I had put away
My labor and my leisure too,
For His Civility—

We passed the School, where Children strove
10 At Recess—in the Ring—
We passed the Fields of Gazing Grain—
We passed the Setting Sun—

Or rather—He passed Us—
The Dews drew quivering and chill—
15 For only Gossamer, my Gown—
My Tippet[1]—only Tulle—

We paused before a House that seemed
A Swelling of the Ground—
The Roof was scarcely visible—
20 The Cornice—in the Ground—

Since then—'tis Centuries—and yet
Feels shorter than the Day
I first surmised the Horses' Heads
Were toward Eternity—

---

[1] A short cape.

The Poets Light but Lamps (#883)

The Poets light but Lamps—
Themselves—go out—
The Wicks they stimulate—
If vital Light

5 Inhere as do the Suns—
Each Age a Lens
Disseminating their
Circumference—

I Never Saw a Moor (#1052)

I never saw a Moor—
I never saw the Sea—
Yet know I how the Heather looks
And what a Billow be.

5 I never spoke with God
Nor visited in Heaven—
Yet certain am I of the spot
As if the Checks were given—

The Bustle in a House (#1078)

The Bustle in a House
The Morning after Death
Is solemnest of industries
Enacted upon Earth—

5 The Sweeping up the Heart
And putting Love away
We shall not want to use again
Until Eternity.

Tell All the Truth but Tell It Slant (#1129)

Tell all the Truth but tell it slant—
Success in Circuit lies
Too bright for our infirm Delight
The Truth's superb surprise
5 As Lightning to the Children eased

With explanation kind
The Truth must dazzle gradually
Or every man be blind—

My Life Closed Twice Before its Close (#1732)

My life closed twice before its close—
It yet remains to see
If Immortality unveil
A third event to me

5 So huge, so hopeless to conceive
As these that twice befell.
Parting is all we know of heaven,
And all we need of hell.

To Make a Prairie it Takes a Clover and One Bee (#1755)

To make a prairie it takes a clover and one bee,
One clover, and a bee,
And revery.
The revery alone will do,
5 If bees are few.

CHRISTINA GEORGINA ROSSETTI (1830–1894)

Sleeping at Last

Sleeping at last, the trouble and tumult over,
    Sleeping at last, the struggle and horror past,
Cold and white, out of sight of friend and of lover,
      Sleeping at last.

5   No more a tired heart downcast or overcast,
No more pangs that wring or shifting fears that hover,
    Sleeping at last in a dreamless sleep locked fast.

Fast asleep. Singing birds in their leafy cover
    Cannot wake her, nor shake her the gusty blast.
10 Under the purple thyme and the purple clover
      Sleeping at last.

LEWIS CARROLL (1832–1898)

Jabberwocky

'Twas brillig, and the slithy toves
.   Did gyre and gimble in the wabe;
All mimsy were the borogoves,
  And the mome raths outgrabe.

5 "Beware the Jabberwock, my son!
  The jaws that bite, the claws that catch!
Beware the Jubjub bird, and shun
  The frumious Bandersnatch!"

He took his vorpal sword in hand
10   Long time the manxome foe he sought—
So rested he by the Tumtum tree,
  And stood awhile in thought.

And, as in uffish thought he stood,
  The Jabberwock, with eyes of flame,
15 Came whiffling through the tulgey wood,
  And burbled as it came!

One, two! One, two! And through and through
  The vorpal blade went snicker-snack!
He left it dead, and with its head
20   He went galumphing back.

"And hast thou slain the Jabberwock?
  Come to my arms, my beamish boy!
O frabjous day! Callooh! Callay!"
  He chortled in his joy.

25 'Twas brillig, and the slithy toves
  Did gyre and gimble in the wabe;
All mimsy were the borogoves,
  And the mome raths outgrabe.

ALGERNON CHARLES SWINBURNE (1837–1909)

From Atalanta in Calydon

CHORUS 1

When the hounds of spring are on winter's traces,
  The mother of months[1] in meadow or plain

---

[1] Diana or Artemis, goddess of the moon.

Fills the shadows and windy places
  With lisp of leaves and ripple of rain;
5 And the brown bright nightingale amorous
  Is half assuaged for Itylus,
  For the Thracian ships and the foreign faces,
  The tongueless vigil, and all the pain.[2]

Come with bows bent and with emptying of quivers,
10   Maiden most perfect, lady of light,
With a noise of winds and many rivers,
  With a clamor of waters, and with might;
Bind on thy sandals, O thou most fleet,
Over the splendor and speed of thy feet;
15 For the faint east quickens, the wan west shivers,
  Round the feet of the day and the feet of the night.

Where shall we find her, how shall we sing to her,
  Fold our hands round her knees, and cling?
O that man's heart were as fire and could spring to her.
20   Fire, or the strength of the streams that spring!
For the stars and the winds are unto her
As raiment, as songs of the harp-player;
For the risen stars and the fallen cling to her,
  And the southwest-wind and the west-wind sing.

25 For winter's rains and ruins are over,
  And all the season of snows and sins;
The days dividing lover and lover,
  The light that loses, the night that wins;
And time remembered is grief forgotten,
30 And frosts are slain and flowers begotten,
And in green underwood and cover
  Blossom by blossom the spring begins.

The full streams feed on flower of rushes,
  Ripe grasses trammel a traveling foot,
35 The faint fresh flame of the young year flushes
  From leaf to flower and flower to fruit;

---

[2] In Greek legend, Itylus was the son of Tereus, king of Thrace, and Procne. Tereus raped Philomela, sister of Procne, and cut out her tongue to conceal the deed. Philomela revealed the outrage to her sister by weaving a tapestry. Procne, in revenge, killed Itylus and served his flesh to Tereus. All three were transformed into birds by the gods; Tereus became the hawk, Procne the swallow, and Philomela the nightingale.

And fruit and leaf are as gold and fire,
And the oat[3] is heard above the lyre,
And the hoofed heel of a satyr crushes
40   The chestnut-husk at the chestnut-root.

And Pan by noon and Bacchus by night,
   Fleeter of foot than the fleet-foot kid,
Follows with dancing and fills with delight
   The Maenad and the Bassarid;[4]
45 And soft as lips that laugh and hide
The laughing leaves of the trees divide,
And screen from seeing and leave in sight
   The god pursuing, the maiden hid.

The ivy falls with the Bacchanal's hair
50   Over her eyebrows hiding her eyes;
The wild vine slipping down leaves bare
   Her bright breast shortening into sighs;
The wild vine slips with the weight of its leaves,
But the berried ivy catches and cleaves
55 To the limbs that glitter, the feet that scare
   The wolf that follows, the fawn that flies.

CHORUS 2

Before the beginning of years
   There came to the making of man
Time, with a gift of tears;
   Grief, with a glass that ran;
5 Pleasure, with pain for leaven;
   Summer, with flowers that fell;
Remembrance fallen from heaven,
   And madness risen from hell;
Strength without hands to smite;
10   Love that endures for a breath:
Night, the shadow of light,
   And life, the shadow of death.
And the high gods took in hand
   Fire, and the falling of tears,
15 And a measure of sliding sand
   From under the feet of the years;

---

3 Shepherd's pipe made of oat straws.
4 Maenad, Bassarid, and Bacchanal, in the next stanza, are all names for female followers of Bacchus.

And froth and drift of the sea;
   And dust of the laboring earth;
And bodies of things to be
20   In the houses of death and of birth;
And wrought with weeping and laughter,
   And fashioned with loathing and love
With life before and after
   And death beneath and above,
25 For a day and a night and a morrow,
   That his strength might endure for a span
With travail and heavy sorrow,
   The holy spirit of man.

From the winds of the north and the south
30   They gathered as unto strife;
They breathed upon his mouth,
   They filled his body with life;
Eyesight and speech they wrought
   For the veils of the soul therein,
35 A time for labor and thought,
   A time to serve and to sin;
They gave him light in his ways,
   And love, and a space for delight,
And beauty and length of days,
40   And night, and sleep in the night.
His speech is a burning fire;
   With his lips he travaileth;
In his heart is a blind desire,
   In his eyes foreknowledge of death;
45 He weaves, and is clothed with derision;
   Sows, and he shall not reap;
His life is a watch or a vision
   Between a sleep and a sleep.

The Garden of Proserpine[1]

Here, where the world is quiet;
   Here, where all trouble seems
Dead winds' and spent waves' riot

---

[1] Persephone, in Roman mythology Proserpine, the daughter of Zeus and Demeter, had been abducted by Hades (the Roman Pluto), god of the underworld, over which she ruled with him thereafter as his queen.

In doubtful dreams of dreams;
5 I watch the green field growing
For reaping folk and sowing,
For harvest-time and mowing,
A sleepy world of streams.

I am tired of tears and laughter,
10   And men that laugh and weep;
Of what may come hereafter
For men that sow to reap:
I am weary of days and hours,
Blown buds of barren flowers,
15 Desires and dreams and powers
And everything but sleep.

Here life has death for neighbor,
And far from eye or ear
Wan waves and wet winds labor,
20   Weak ships and spirits steer;
They drive adrift, and whither
They wot not who make thither;
But no such winds blow hither,
And no such things grow here.

25 No growth of moor or coppice,
No heather-flower or vine,
But bloomless buds of poppies,
Green grapes of Proserpine,
Pale beds of blowing rushes
30 Where no leaf blooms or blushes
Save this whereout she crushes
For dead men deadly wine.

Pale, without name or number,
In fruitless fields of corn,[2]
35 They bow themselves and slumber
All night till light is born;
And like a soul belated,
In hell and heaven unmated,
By cloud and mist abated
40   Comes out of darkness morn.

---

[2] Wheat.

Though one were strong as seven,
   He too with death shall dwell,
Nor wake with wings in heaven,
   Nor weep for pains in hell;
45 Though one were fair as roses;
His beauty clouds and closes;
And well though love reposes,
   In the end it is not well.

Pale, beyond porch and portal,
50   Crowned with calm leaves, she stands
Who gathers all things mortal
   With cold immortal hands;
Her languid lips are sweeter
Than love's who fears to greet her
55 To men that mix and meet her
   From many times and lands.

She waits for each and other,
   She waits for all men born;
Forgets the earth her mother,
60   The life of fruits and corn;
And spring and seed and swallow
Take wing for her and follow
Where summer song rings hollow
   And flowers are put to scorn.

65 There go the loves that wither,
   The old loves with wearier wings;
And all dead years draw thither,
   And all disastrous things;
Dead dreams of days forsaken,
70 Blind buds that snows have shaken,
Wild leaves that winds have taken,
   Red strays of ruined springs.

We are not sure of sorrow,
   And joy was never sure;
75 Today will die tomorrow;
   Time stoops to no man's lure,[3]
And love, grown faint and fretful,

---

[3] In falconry, the lure is a device used to recall the hawk to the falconer's wrist.

With lips but half regretful
Sighs, and with eyes forgetful
80   Weeps that no love endure.

From too much love of living,
   From hope and fear set free,
We thank with brief thanksgiving
   Whatever gods may be
85 That no life lives for ever;
That dead men rise up never;
That even the weariest river
   Winds somewhere safe to sea.

Then star nor sun shall waken,
90   Nor any change of light:
Nor sound of waters shaken,
   Nor any sound or sight:
Nor wintry leaves nor vernal,
Nor days nor things diurnal;
95 Only the sleep eternal
   In an eternal night.

THOMAS HARDY (1840–1928)

The Ruined Maid

"O 'Melia, my dear, this does everything crown!
Who could have supposed I should meet you in Town?
And whence such fair garments, such prosperi-ty?"—
"O didn't you know I'd been ruined?" said she.

5 —"You left us in tatters, without shoes or socks,
Tired of digging potatoes, and spudding up docks;[1]
And now you've gay bracelets and bright feathers three!"—
"Yes: that's how we dress when we're ruined," said she.

—"At home in the barton[2] you said 'thee' and 'thou,'
10 And 'thik oon,' and 'theäs oon,' and 't'other'; but now
Your talking quite fits 'ee for high compa-ny!"—
"Some polish is gained with one's ruin," said she.

---

[1] Digging up weeds.
[2] Farmyard.

—"Your hands were like paws then, your face blue and bleak
But now I'm bewitched by your delicate cheek,
15 And your little gloves fit as on any la-dy!"—
"We never do work when we're ruined," said she.

—"You used to call home-life a hag-ridden dream,
And you'd sigh, and you'd sock; but at present you seem
To know not of megrims[3] or melancho-ly!"—
20 "True. One's pretty lively when ruined," said she.

—"I wish I had feathers, a fine sweeping gown,
And a delicate face, and could strut about Town!"—
"My dear—a raw country girl, such as you be,
Cannot quite expect that. You ain't ruined," said she.

Neutral Tones

We stood by a pond that winter day,
And the sun was white, as though chidden of God,
And a few leaves lay on the starving sod;
　　　—They had fallen from an ash, and were gray.

5 Your eyes on me were as eyes that rove
Over tedious riddles of years ago;
And some words played between us to and fro
　　　On which lost the more by our love.

The smile on your mouth was the deadest thing
10 Alive enough to have strength to die;
And a grin of bitterness swept thereby
　　　Like an ominous bird a-wing. . . .

Since then, keen lessons that love deceives,
And wrings with wrong, have shaped to me
15 Your face, and the God-curst sun, and a tree,
　　　And a pond edged with grayish leaves.

The Man He Killed

"Had he and I but met
　　By some old ancient inn,
We should have sat us down to wet
　　Right many a nipperkin![1]

---

[3] Low spirits.
[1] About a half-pint.

5   "But ranged as infantry,
      And staring face to face,
I shot at him as he at me,
      And killed him in his place.

      "I shot him dead because—
10   Because he was my foe,
Just so: my foe of course he was;
      That's clear enough; although

      "He thought he'd 'list, perhaps,
      Off-hand like—just as I—
15 Was out of work—had sold his traps—
      No other reason why.

      "Yes; quaint and curious war is!
      You shoot a fellow down
You'd treat if met where any bar is,
20   Or help to half-a-crown."

The Convergence of the Twain

(*Lines on the loss of the "Titanic"*)

1

      In a solitude of the sea
      Deep from human vanity,
And the Pride of Life that planned her, stilly couches she.

2

      Steel chambers, late the pyres
5   Of her salamandrine fires,
Cold currents thrid, and turn to rhythmic tidal lyres.

3

      Over the mirrors meant
      To glass the opulent
The sea-worm crawls—grotesque, slimed, dumb, indifferent.

4

      Jewels in joy designed
      To ravish the sensuous mind
Lie lightless, all their sparkles bleared and black and blind.

5

Dim moon-eyed fishes near
Gaze at the gilded gear
15 And query: 'What does this vaingloriousness down here?'. . .

6

Well: while was fashioning
This creature of cleaving wing,
The Immanent Will that stirs and urges everything

7

Prepared a sinister mate
20   For her—so gaily great—
A Shape of Ice, for the time far and dissociate.

8

And as the smart ship grew
In stature, grace, and hue,
In shadowy silent distance grew the Iceberg too.

9

25   Alien they seemed to be:
No mortal eye could see
The intimate welding of their later history.

10

Or sign that they were bent
By paths coincident
30 On being anon twin halves of one august event,

11

Till the Spinner of the Years
Said 'Now!' And each one hears,
And consummation comes, and jars two hemispheres.

Channel Firing

That night your great guns, unawares,
Shook all our coffins as we lay,
And broke the chancel window-squares,
We thought it was the Judgment-day

5 And sat upright. While drearisome
Arose the howl of wakened hounds:

The mouse let fall the altar-crumb,
The worms drew back into the mounds,

The glebe cow[1] drooled. Till God called, "No;
10 It's gunnery practice out at sea
Just as before you went below;
The world is as it used to be:

"All nations striving strong to make
Red war yet redder. Mad as hatters
15 They do no more for Christès sake
Than you who are helpless in such matters.

"That this is not the judgment-hour
For some of them's a blessed thing,
For if it were they'd have to scour
20 Hell's floor for so much threatening . . .

"Ha, ha. It will be warmer when
I blow the trumpet (if indeed
I ever do; for you are men,
And rest eternal sorely need)."

25 So down we lay again. "I wonder,
Will the world ever saner be,"
Said one, "than when He sent us under
In our indifferent century!"

And many a skeleton shook his head.
30 "Instead of preaching forty year,"
My neighbor Parson Thirdly said,
"I wish I had stuck to pipes and beer."

Again the guns disturbed the hour,
Roaring their readiness to avenge,
35 As far inland as Stourton Tower,
And Camelot, and starlit Stonehenge.[2]

---

1 Cow pastured in the parson's meadow.
2 Stourton Tower commemorates King Alfred's ninth-century victory over the Danes. Camelot is the legendary site of King Arthur's court. Stonehenge is the mysterious, pre-Celtic monument on Salisbury Plain.

GERARD MANLEY HOPKINS (1844–1889)

Heaven—Haven

A Nun Takes the Veil

I have desired to go
    Where springs not fail,
To fields where flies no sharp and sided hail
And a few lilies blow.

5   And I have asked to be
        Where no storms come,
Where the green swell is in the havens dumb,
    And out of the swing of the sea.

Pied Beauty

Glory be to God for dappled things—
    For skies of couple-color as a brinded cow;
        For rose-moles all in stipple upon trout that swim;
Fresh-firecoal chestnut-falls; finches' wings;
5   Landscape plotted and pieced—fold, fallow, and plough;
        And áll trádes, their gear and tackle and trim.
All things counter, original, spare, strange;
    Whatever is fickle, freckled (who knows how?)
        With swift, slow; sweet, sour; adazzle, dim;
10 He fathers-forth whose beauty is past change:
                    Praise him.

Spring and Fall

To a young child

Márgarét, are you gríeving
Over Goldengrove unleaving?
Leáves, líke the things of man, you
With your fresh thoughts care for, can you?
5 Áh! ás the heart grows older
It will come to such sights colder
By and by, nor spare a sigh
Though worlds of wanwood leafmeal lie;
And yet you wíll weep and know why.
10 Now no matter, child, the name:
Sórrow's spríngs áre the same.
Nor mouth had, no nor mind, expressed

What heart heard of, ghost guessed:
It ís the blight man was born for,
15 It is Margaret you mourn for.

(Carrion Comfort[1])

Not, I'll not, carrion comfort, Despair, not feast on thee;
Not untwist—slack they may be—these last strands of man
In me ór, most weary, cry *I can no more*. I can;
Can something, hope, wish day come, not choose not to be.

5 But ah, but O thou terrible, why wouldst thou rude on me
Thy wring-world right foot rock? lay a lionlimb against me? scan
With darksome devouring eyes my bruisèd bones? and fan,
O in turns of tempest, me heaped there; me frantic to avoid thee and
    flee?

Why? That my chaff might fly; my grain lie, sheer and clear.
10 Nay in all that toil, that coil, since (seems) I kissed the rod,
Hand rather, my heart lo! lapped strength, stole joy, would laugh,
    chéer.
Cheer whom though? the hero whose heaven-handling flung me, fóot
    tród
Me? or me that fought him? O which one? is it each one? That
    night, that year
Of now done darkness I wretch lay wrestling with (my God!) my
    God.

No Worst, There Is None

No worst, there is none. Pitched past pitch of grief,
More pangs will, schooled at forepangs, wilder wring.
Comforter, where, where is your comforting?
Mary, mother of us, where is your relief?
5 My cries heave, herds-long,[1] huddle in a main, a chief
woe, world-sorrow; on an age-old anvil wince and sing—
Then lull, then leave off. Fury had shrieked "No ling-
ering! Let me be fell: force I must be brief."
O the mind, mind has mountains; cliffs of fall
10 Frightful, sheer, no-man-fathomed. Hold them cheap

---

1 The title was added by Robert Bridges.

1 Like the successive cries of a herd of lost sheep.

May who ne'er hung there. Nor does long our small
Durance deal with that steep or deep. Here! creep,
Wretch, under a comfort serves in a whirlwind: all
Life death does end and each day dies with sleep.

A. E. HOUSMAN (1859–1936)

From **A Shropshire Lad**

LOVELIEST OF TREES, THE CHERRY NOW

Loveliest of trees, the cherry now
Is hung with bloom along the bough,
And stands about the woodland ride
Wearing white for Eastertide.

5 Now, of my threescore years and ten,
Twenty will not come again,
And take from seventy springs a score,
It only leaves me fifty more.

And since to look at things in bloom
10 Fifty springs are little room,
About the woodlands I will go
To see the cherry hung with snow.

WHEN I WAS ONE-AND-TWENTY

When I was one-and-twenty
  I heard a wise man say,
"Give crowns and pounds and guineas
  But not your heart away;
5 Give pearls away and rubies
  But keep your fancy free."
But I was one-and-twenty,
  No use to talk to me.

When I was one-and-twenty
10   I heard him say again,
"The heart out of the bosom
  Was never given in vain;
'Tis paid with sighs a plenty
  And sold for endless rue."
15 And I am two-and-twenty,
  And oh, 'tis true, 'tis true.

TO AN ATHLETE DYING YOUNG

The time you won your town the race
We chaired you through the market-place;
Man and boy stood cheering by,
And home we brought you shoulder-high.

5 To-day, the road all runners come,
Shoulder-high we bring you home,
And set you at your threshold down,
Townsman of a stiller town.

Smart lad, to slip betimes away
10 From fields where glory does not stay
And early though the laurel grows
It withers quicker than the rose.

Eyes the shady night has shut
Cannot see the record cut,
15 And silence sounds no worse than cheers
After earth has stopped the ears:

Now you will not swell the rout
Of lads that wore their honors out,
Runners whom renown outran
20 And the name died before the man.

So set, before its echoes fade,
The fleet foot on the sill of shade,
And hold to the low lintel up
The still-defended challenge-cup.

25 And round that early-laurelled head
Will flock to gaze the strengthless dead,
And find unwithered on its curls
The garland briefer than a girl's.

FROM FAR, FROM EVE AND MORNING

From far, from eve and morning
  And yon twelve-winded sky,
The stuff of life to knit me
  Blew hither: here am I.

5 Now—for a breath I tarry
   Nor yet disperse apart—
Take my hand quick and tell me,
   What have you in your heart.

Speak now, and I will answer;
10   How shall I help you, say;
Ere to the wind's twelve quarters
   I take my endless way.

WITH RUE MY HEART IS LADEN

With rue my heart is laden
   For golden friends I had,
For many a rose-lipt maiden
   And many a lightfoot lad.

5 By brooks too broad for leaping
   The lightfoot boys are laid;
The rose-lipt girls are sleeping
   In fields where roses fade.

"TERENCE, THIS IS STUPID STUFF ..."

   "Terence, this is stupid stuff:
You eat your victuals fast enough;
There can't be much amiss, 'tis clear,
To see the rate you drink your beer.
5 But oh, good Lord, the verse you make,
It gives a chap the belly-ache.
The cow, the old cow, she is dead;
It sleeps well, the hornèd head:
We poor lads, 'tis our turn now
10 To hear such tunes as killed the cow.
Pretty friendship 'tis to rhyme
Your friends to death before their time
Moping melancholy mad:
Come, pipe a tune to dance to, lad."

15   Why, if 'tis dancing you would be,
There's brisker pipes than poetry.
Say, for what were hop-yards meant,
Or why was Burton built on Trent? [1]

---

[1] A town noted for its breweries.

Oh many a peer of England brews
20 Livelier liquor than the Muse,
And malt does more than Milton can
To justify God's ways to man.
Ale, man, ale's the stuff to drink
For fellows whom it hurts to think:
25 Look into the pewter pot
To see the world as the world's not.
And faith, 'tis pleasant till 'tis past:
The mischief is that 'twill not last.
Oh I have been to Ludlow fair
30 And left my necktie God knows where,
And carried half-way home, or near,
Pints and quarts of Ludlow beer:
Then the world seemed none so bad,
And I myself a sterling lad;
35 And down in lovely muck I've lain,
Happy till I woke again.
Then I saw the morning sky:
Heigho, the tale was all a lie;
The world, it was the old world yet,
40 I was I, my things were wet,
And nothing now remained to do
But begin the game anew.

Therefore, since the world has still
Much good, but much less good than ill,
45 And while the sun and moon endure
Luck's a chance, but trouble's sure,
I'd face it as a wise man would,
And train for ill and not for good.
'Tis true, the stuff I bring for sale
50 Is not so brisk a brew as ale:
Out of a stem that scored the hand
I wrung it in a weary land.
But take it: if the smack is sour,
The better for the embittered hour;
55 It should do good to heart and head
When your soul is in my soul's stead;
And I will friend you, if I may,
In the dark and cloudy day.

There was a king reigned in the East:
60 There, when kings will sit to feast,

They get their fill before they think
With poisoned meat and poisoned drink.
He gathered all that springs to birth
From the many-venomed earth;
65 First a little, thence to more,
He sampled all her killing store;
An easy, smiling, seasoned sound,
Sate the king when healths went round.
They put arsenic in his meat
70 And stared aghast to watch him eat;
They poured strychnine in his cup
And shook to see him drink it up:
They shook, they stared as white's their shirt:
Them it was their poison hurt.
75 —I tell the tale that I heard told.
Mithridates,[2] he died old.

---

[2] King of Pontus in the first century B.C., who made himself immune to certain
poisons by taking them frequently in small doses.

5

⌒ A BRIEF HISTORY

Looking at Ireland's Yeats, we have an example of a poet trained in romantic conventional verse who evolves into a modern poet. Keeping his sense of form and structure, Yeats modernizes his verse in part by changing his imagery. In contrast to the mythological *Leda and the Swan,* for instance, his *Irish Airman* flies and dies in a sky of war and machinery. In *The Second Coming* Yeats creates a modern beast slouching toward a symbolic Bethlehem to compete with the traditional Christian message of hope and redemption. In America, Edward Arlington Robinson uses conventional verse forms to write about a changing American character. Robert Frost also writes in conventional verse forms, but his diction sounds distinctly American. Many of his rural New England poems raise familiar country images—for instance *Stopping by Woods*—to the level of symbolism. A new-world American character comes through in poems as traditional as the sonnet (*Once by the Pacific*) and as elaborate as the conceit (*Design*). Another American poet, Wallace Stevens, attaches dazzling tropical imagery and exotic language to established conventional blank verse. William Carlos Williams creates a poetry of clean flashing imagery and free-verse rhythms. Ezra Pound and H.D. demand that concise images replace the sometimes drawn-out metrics and language of accentual-syllabic verse. Their poetry often appeals to direct visual experience and relies on the reader to draw the subtle comparisons that give such poems meaning. T. S. Eliot combines a striking imagery with historical and mythological allusions. He experiments with combinations of traditional verse and modern experience. His tired, middle-aged Prufrock, for instance, yearns in a free verse poem—sometimes rhymed, sometimes not—after the grace and elegance of a bygone civilization.

WILLIAM BUTLER YEATS (1865–1939)

The Lake Isle of Innisfree

I will arise and go now, and go to Innisfree,
And a small cabin build there, of clay and wattles[1] made:
Nine bean-rows will I have there, a hive for the honey-bee,
And live alone in the bee-loud glade.

5 And I shall have some peace there, for peace comes dropping slow,
Dropping from the veils of the morning to where the cricket sings;
There midnight's all a glimmer, and noon a purple glow,
And evening full of the linnet's wings.

I will arise and go now, for always night and day
10 I hear lake water lapping with low sounds by the shore;
While I stand on the roadway, or on the pavements gray,
I hear it in the deep heart's core.

When You Are Old

When you are old and gray and full of sleep,
And nodding by the fire, take down this book,
And slowly read, and dream of the soft look
Your eyes had once, and of their shadows deep;

5 How many loved your moments of glad grace,
And loved your beauty with love false or true,
But one man loved the pilgrim soul in you,
And loved the sorrows of your changing face;

And bending down beside the glowing bars,
10 Murmur, a little sadly, how Love fled
And paced upon the mountains overhead
And hid his face amid a crowd of stars.

The Folly of Being Comforted

One that is ever kind said yesterday:
"Your well-belovèd's hair has threads of gray,
And little shadows come about her eyes;
Time can but make it easier to be wise

---

[1] Rods woven with twigs to form a wall or roof.

5 Though now it seem impossible, and so
All that you need is patience."
Heart cries, "No,

I have not a crumb of comfort, not a grain.
Time can but make her beauty over again:
Because of that great nobleness of hers
10 The fire that stirs about her, when she stirs,
Burns but more clearly. O she had not these ways
When all the wild summer was in her gaze."

O heart! O heart! if she'd but turn her head,
You'd know the folly of being comforted.

Easter 1916[1]

I have met them at close of day
Coming with vivid faces
From counter or desk among gray
Eighteenth-century houses.
5 I have passed with a nod of the head
Or polite meaningless words,
Or have lingered awhile and said
Polite meaningless words,
And thought before I had done
10 Of a mocking tale or a gibe
To please a companion
Around the fire at the club,
Being certain that they and I
But lived where motley is worn:
15 All changed, changed utterly:
A terrible beauty is born.

That woman's days were spent
In ignorant good will,
Her nights in argument
20 Until her voice grew shrill.
What voice more sweet than hers
When, young and beautiful,
She rode to harriers?
This man had kept a school
25 And rode our wingèd horse;

---

[1] Date of Irish Nationalist uprising.

This other his helper and friend
Was coming into his force;
He might have won fame in the end,
So sensitive his nature seemed,
30 So daring and sweet his thought.
This other man I had dreamed
A drunken, vainglorious lout.
He had done most bitter wrong
To some who are near my heart,
35 Yet I number him in the song;
He, too, has resigned his part
In the casual comedy;
He, too, has been changed in his turn,
Transformed utterly:
40 A terrible beauty is born.

Hearts with one purpose alone
Through summer and winter seem
Enchanted to a stone
To trouble the living stream.
45 The horse that comes from the road,
The rider, the birds that range
From cloud to tumbling cloud,
Minute by minute they change;
A shadow of cloud on the stream
50 Changes minute by minute;
A horse-hoof slides on the brim,
And a horse plashes within it;
The long-legged moor-hens dive,
And hens to moor-cocks call;
55 Minute by minute they live:
The stone's in the midst of all.

Too long a sacrifice
Can make a stone of the heart.
O when may it suffice?
60 That is Heaven's part, our part
To murmur name upon name,
As a mother names her child
When sleep at last has come
On limbs that had run wild.
65 What is it but nightfall?
No, no, not night but death;
Was it needless death after all?

For England may keep faith
For all that is done and said.
70 We know their dream; enough
To know they dreamed and are dead;
And what if excess of love
Bewildered them till they died?
I write it out in a verse—
75 MacDonagh and MacBride
And Connolly and Pearse
Now and in time to be,
Wherever green is worn,
Are changed, changed utterly:
80 A terrible beauty is born.

The Wild Swans at Coole

The trees are in their autumn beauty,
The woodland paths are dry,
Under the October twilight the water
Mirrors a still sky;
5 Upon the brimming water among the stones
Are nine-and-fifty swans.

The nineteenth autumn has come upon me
Since I first made my count;
I saw, before I had well finished,
10 All suddenly mount
And scatter wheeling in great broken rings
Upon their clamorous wings.

I have looked upon those brilliant creatures,
And now my heart is sore.
15 All's changed since I, hearing at twilight,
The first time on this shore,
The bell-beat of their wings above my head,
Trod with a lighter tread.

Unwearied still, lover by lover,
20 They paddle in the cold
Companionable streams or climb the air;
Their hearts have not grown old;
Passion or conquest, wander where they will,
Attend upon them still.

25 But now they drift on the still water,
    Mysterious, beautiful;
    Among what rushes will they build,
    By what lake's edge or pool
    Delight men's eyes when I awake some day
30 To find they have flown away?

An Irish Airman Foresees His Death[1]

I know that I shall meet my fate
Somewhere among the clouds above;
Those that I fight I do not hate,
Those that I guard I do not love;
5 My country is Kiltartan Cross,[2]
My countrymen Kiltartan's poor,
No likely end could bring them loss
Or leave them happier than before.
Nor law, nor duty bade me fight,
10 Nor public men, nor cheering crowds,
A lonely impulse of delight
Drove to this tumult in the clouds;
I balanced all, brought all to mind,
The years to come seemed waste of breath,
15 A waste of breath the years behind
In balance with this life, this death.

The Second Coming

Turning and turning in the widening gyre
The falcon cannot hear the falconer;
Things fall apart; the centre cannot hold;
Mere anarchy is loosed upon the world,
5 The blood-dimmed tide is loosed, and everywhere
The ceremony of innocence is drowned;
The best lack all conviction, while the worst
Are full of passionate intensity.

Surely some revelation is at hand;
10 Surely the Second Coming is at hand.

---

[1] Major Robert Gregory, son of Yeats's friend and patroness Lady Augusta Gregory, was killed in action in 1918.
[2] Kiltartan is an Irish village near Coole Park, the estate of the Gregorys.

The Second Coming! Hardly are those words out
When a vast image out of *Spiritus Mundi*[1]
Troubles my sight: somewhere in sands of the desert
A shape with lion body and the head of a man,
15 A gaze blank and pitiless as the sun,
Is moving its slow thighs, while all about it
Reel shadows of the indignant desert birds.
The darkness drops again; but now I know
That twenty centuries of stony sleep
20 Were vexed to nightmare by a rocking cradle,
And what rough beast, its hour come round at last,
Slouches towards Bethlehem to be born?

Leda and the Swan[1]

A sudden blow: the great wings beating still
Above the staggering girl, her thighs caressed
By the dark webs, her nape caught in his bill,
He holds her helpless breast upon his breast.

5 How can those terrified vague fingers push
The feathered glory from her loosening thighs?
And how can body, laid in that white rush,
But feel the strange heart beating where it lies?

A shudder in the loins engenders there
10 The broken wall, the burning roof and tower[2]
And Agamemnon dead.
                              Being so caught up,
So mastered by the brute blood of the air,
Did she put on his knowledge with his power
Before the indifferent beak could let her drop?

Sailing to Byzantium

1

That is no country for old men. The young
In one another's arms, birds in the trees

---

1 Soul of the universe.

1 In Greek mythology Leda was ravished by Zeus, in the form of a swan.
2 The fall of Troy. Agamemnon was murdered by his wife Clytemnestra upon his
return home from Troy.

—Those dying generations—at their song,
The salmon-falls, the mackerel-crowded seas,
5 Fish, flesh, or fowl, commend all summer long
Whatever is begotten, born, and dies.
Caught in that sensual music all neglect
Monuments of unageing intellect.

2

An aged man is but a paltry thing,
10 A tattered coat upon a stick, unless
Soul clap its hands and sing, and louder sing
For every tatter in its mortal dress,
Nor is there singing school but studying
Monuments of its own magnificence;
15 And therefore I have sailed the seas and come
To the holy city of Byzantium.

3

O sages standing in God's holy fire
As in the gold mosaic of a wall,
Come from the holy fire, perne in a gyre,[1]
20 And be the singing-masters of my soul.
Consume my heart away; sick with desire
And fastened to a dying animal
It knows not what it is; and gather me
Into the artifice of eternity.

4

25 Once out of nature I shall never take
My bodily form from any natural thing,
But such a form as Grecian goldsmiths make
Of hammered gold and gold enamelling
To keep a drowsy Emperor awake;
30 Or set upon a golden bough to sing
To lords and ladies of Byzantium
Of what is past, or passing, or to come.

Among School Children

1

I walk through the long schoolroom questioning;
A kind old nun in a white hood replies;
The children learn to cipher and to sing,

To study reading-books and histories,
5 To cut and sew, be neat in everything
In the best modern way—the children's eyes
In momentary wonder stare upon
A sixty-year-old smiling public man.

2

I dream of a Ledaean body,[1] bent
10 Above a sinking fire, a tale that she
Told of a harsh reproof, or trivial event
That changed some childish day to tragedy—
Told, and it seemed that our two natures blent
Into a sphere from youthful sympathy,
15 Or else, to alter Plato's parable,
Into the yolk and white of the one shell.

3

And thinking of that fit of grief or rage
I look upon one child or t'other there
And wonder if she stood so at that age—
20 For even daughters of the swan can share
Something of every paddler's heritage—
And had that color upon cheek or hair,
And thereupon my heart is driven wild:
She stands before me as a living child.

4

25 Her present image floats into the mind—
Did Quattrocento finger fashion it
Hollow of cheek as though it drank the wind
And took a mess of shadows for its meat?
And I though never of Ledaean kind
30 Had pretty plumage once—enough of that,
Better to smile on all that smile, and show
There is a comfortable kind of old scarecrow.

5

What youthful mother, a shape upon her lap
Honey of generation had betrayed,
35 And that must sleep, shriek, struggle to escape
As recollection or the drug decide,
Would think her son, did she but see that shape

---

[1] Like Leda, the daughter of Helen of Troy.

With sixty or more winters on its head,
A compensation for the pang of his birth,
40 Or the uncertainty of his setting forth?

6

Plato thought nature but a spume that plays
Upon a ghostly paradigm of things;
Solider Aristotle played the taws
Upon the bottom of a king of kings;
45 World-famous golden-thighed Pythagoras
Fingered upon a fiddle-stick or strings
What a star sang and careless Muses heard:
Old clothes upon old sticks to scare a bird.

7

Both nuns and mothers worship images,
50 But those the candles light are not as those
That animate a mother's reveries,
But keep a marble or a bronze repose.
And yet they too break hearts—O Presences
That passion, piety or affection knows,
55 And that all heavenly glory symbolize—
O self-born mockers of man's enterprise;

8

Labor is blossoming or dancing where
The body is not bruised to pleasure soul,
Nor beauty born out of its own despair,
60 Nor blear-eyed wisdom out of midnight oil.
O chestnut-tree, great-rooted blossomer,
Are you the leaf, the blossom or the bole?
O body swayed to music, O brightening glance,
How can we know the dancer from the dance?

After Long Silence

Speech after long silence; it is right,
All other lovers being estranged or dead,
Unfriendly lamplight hid under its shade,
The curtains drawn upon unfriendly night,
5 That we descant and yet again descant
Upon the supreme theme of Art and Song:
Bodily decrepitude is wisdom; young
We loved each other and were ignorant.

Lapis Lazuli[1]

(For Harry Clifton)

I have heard that hysterical women say
They are sick of the palette and fiddle-bow,
Of poets that are always gay,
For everybody knows or else should know
5 That if nothing drastic is done
Aeroplane and Zeppelin will come out,
Pitch like King Billy bomb-balls in
Until the town lie beaten flat.

All perform their tragic play,
10 There struts Hamlet, there is Lear,
That's Ophelia, that Cordelia;
Yet they, should the last scene be there,
The great stage curtain about to drop,
If worthy their prominent part in the play,
15 Do not break up their lines to weep.
They know that Hamlet and Lear are gay;
Gaiety transfiguring all that dread.
All men have aimed at, found and lost;
Black out; Heaven blazing into the head:
20 Tragedy wrought to its uttermost.
Though Hamlet rambles and Lear rages,
And all the drop-scenes drop at once
Upon a hundred thousand stages,
It cannot grow by an inch or an ounce.

25 On their own feet they came, or on shipboard,
Camelback, horseback, ass-back, mule-back,
Old civilizations put to the sword.
Then they and their wisdom went to rack:
No handiwork of Callimachus,[2]
30 Who handled marble as if it were bronze,
Made draperies that seemed to rise
When sea-wind swept the corner, stands;
His long lamp-chimney shaped like the stem
Of a slender palm, stood but a day;

---

[1] A deep-blue semi-precious stone.
[2] Greek sculptor of the fifth century B.C.

35 All things fall and are built again,
   And those that build them again are gay.

   Two Chinamen, behind them a third,
   Are carved in lapis lazuli,
   Over them flies a long-legged bird,
40 A symbol of longevity;
   The third, doubtless a serving-man,
   Carries a musical instrument.

   Every discoloration of the stone,
   Every accidental crack or dent,
45 Seems a water-course or an avalanche,
   Or lofty slope where it still snows
   Though doubtless plum or cherry-branch
   Sweetens the little half-way house
   Those Chinamen climb towards, and I
50 Delight to imagine them seated there;
   There, on the mountain and the sky,
   On all the tragic scene they stare.
   One asks for mournful melodies;
   Accomplished fingers begin to play.
55 Their eyes mid many wrinkles, their eyes,
   Their ancient, glittering eyes, are gay.

Politics

"In our time the destiny of man presents its meaning in political terms."—
THOMAS MANN

   How can I, that girl standing there,
   My attention fix
   On Roman or on Russian
   Or on Spanish politics?
5 Yet here's a travelled man that knows
   What he talks about,
   And there's a politician
   That has read and thought,
   And maybe what they say is true
10 Of war and war's alarms,
   But O that I were young again
   And held her in my arms!

ERNEST DOWSON (1867–1900)

Non sum qualis eram bonae sub regno Cynarae[1]

Last night, ah, yesternight, betwixt her lips and mine
There fell thy shadow, Cynara! thy breath was shed
Upon my soul between the kisses and the wine;
And I was desolate and sick of an old passion,
5   Yea, I was desolate and bowed my head:
I have been faithful to thee, Cynara! in my fashion.

All night upon mine heart I felt her warm heart beat,
Night-long within mine arms in love and sleep she lay;
Surely the kisses of her bought red mouth were sweet;
10 But I was desolate and sick of an old passion,
    When I awoke and found the dawn was gray:
I have been faithful to thee, Cynara! in my fashion.

I have forgot much, Cynara! gone with the wind,
Flung roses, roses riotously with the throng,
15 Dancing, to put thy pale, lost lilies out of mind;
But I was desolate and sick of an old passion,
    Yea, all the time, because the dance was long:
I have been faithful to thee, Cynara! in my fashion.

I cried for madder music and for stronger wine,
20 But when the feast is finished and the lamps expire,
Then falls thy shadow, Cynara! the night is thine;
And I am desolate and sick of an old passion,
    Yea hungry for the lips of my desire:
I have been faithful to thee, Cynara! in my fashion.

EDWIN ARLINGTON ROBINSON (1869–1935)

Miniver Cheevy

Miniver Cheevy, child of scorn,
    Grew lean while he assailed the seasons;
He wept that he was ever born,
    And he had reasons.

---

[1] "I am not what I was under the reign of the good Cynara": Horace, *Odes* IV.i.

5 Miniver loved the days of old
   When swords were bright and steeds were prancing;
The vision of a warrior bold
   Would set him dancing.

   Miniver sighed for what was not,
10   And dreamed, and rested from his labors;
He dreamed of Thebes and Camelot,
   And Priam's neighbors.

Miniver mourned the ripe renown
   That made so many a name so fragrant;
15 He mourned Romance, now on the town,
   And Art, a vagrant.

Miniver loved the Medici,
   Albeit he had never seen one;
He would have sinned incessantly
20   Could he have been one.

Miniver cursed the commonplace
   And eyed a khaki suit with loathing;
He missed the medieval grace
   Of iron clothing.

25 Miniver scorned the gold he sought,
   But sore annoyed was he without it;
Miniver thought, and thought, and thought,
   And thought about it.

Miniver Cheevy, born too late,
30   Scratched his head and kept on thinking;
Miniver coughed, and called it fate,
   And kept on drinking.

For a Dead Lady

No more with overflowing light
Shall fill the eyes that now are faded,
Nor shall another's fringe with night
Their woman-hidden world as they did.
5 No more shall quiver down the days

The flowing wonder of her ways,
Whereof no language may requite
The shifting and the many-shaded.

The grace, divine, definitive,
10 Clings only as a faint forestalling;
The laugh that love could not forgive
Is hushed, and answers to no calling;
The forehead and the little ears
Have gone where Saturn keeps the years;
15 The breast where roses could not live
Has done with rising and with falling.

The beauty, shattered by the laws
That have creation in their keeping,
No longer trembles at applause,
20 Or over children that are sleeping;
And we who delve in beauty's lore
Know all that we have known before
Of what inexorable cause
Makes Time so vicious in his reaping.

Eros Turannos[1]

She fears him, and will always ask
    What fated her to choose him;
She meets in his engaging mask
    All reasons to refuse him;
5 But what she meets and what she fears
Are less than are the downward years,
Drawn slowly to the foamless weirs
    Of age, were she to lose him.

Between a blurred sagacity
10   That once had power to sound him,
And Love, that will not let him be
    The Judas[2] that she found him,
Her pride assuages her almost,
As if it were alone the cost.
15 He sees that he will not be lost,
    And waits and looks around him.

---

[1] Tyrannical Love.
[2] The disciple who betrayed Christ.

A sense of ocean and old trees
Envelopes and allures him;
Tradition, touching all he sees,
20   Beguiles and reassures him;
And all her doubts of what he says
Are dimmed with what she knows of days—
Till even prejudice delays
And fades, and she secures him.

25 The falling leaf inaugurates
The reign of her confusion;
The pounding wave reverberates
The dirge of her illusion;
And home, where passion lived and died,
30 Becomes a place where she can hide,
While all the town and harbor side
Vibrate with her seclusion.

We tell you, tapping on our brows,
The story as it should be,
35 As if the story of a house
Were told, or ever could be;
We'll have no kindly veil between
Her visions and those we have seen,
As if we guessed what hers have been,
40   Or what they are or would be.

Meanwhile we do no harm; for they
That with a god have striven,
Not hearing much of what we say,
Take what the god has given;
45 Though like waves breaking it may be,
Or like a changed familiar tree,
Or like a stairway to the sea
Where down the blind are driven.

Mr. Flood's Party

Old Eben Flood, climbing alone one night
Over the hill between the town below
And the forsaken upland hermitage
That held as much as he should ever know
5 On earth again of home, paused warily.
The road was his with not a native near;

And Eben, having leisure, said aloud,
For no man else in Tilbury Town to hear:

"Well, Mr. Flood, we have the harvest moon
10 Again, and we may not have many more;
The bird is on the wing, the poet says,[1]
And you and I have said it here before.
Drink to the bird." He raised up to the light
The jug that he had gone so far to fill,
15 And answered huskily: "Well, Mr. Flood,
Since you propose it, I believe I will."

Alone, as if enduring to the end
A valiant armor of scarred hopes outworn,
He stood there in the middle of the road
20 Like Roland's ghost winding a silent horn.[2]
Below him, in the town among the trees,
Where friends of other days had honored him,
A phantom salutation of the dead
Rang thinly till old Eben's eyes were dim.

25 Then, as a mother lays her sleeping child
Down tenderly, fearing it may awake,
He set the jug down slowly at his feet
With trembling care, knowing that most things break;
And only when assured that on firm earth
30 It stood, as the uncertain lives of men
Assuredly did not, he paced away,
And with his hand extended paused again:

"Well, Mr. Flood, we have not met like this
In a long time; and many a change has come
35 To both of us, I fear, since last it was
We had a drop together. Welcome home!"
Convivially returning with himself,
Again he raised the jug up to the light;
And with an acquiescent quaver said:
40 "Well, Mr. Flood, if you insist, I might.

---

[1] See stanza 7 of *The Rubáiyát of Omar Khayyám* (p. 244).
[2] In the medieval *Song of Roland*, the hero refuses to blow his horn for help at the Battle of Roncevaux and loses his life.

"Only a very little, Mr. Flood—
For auld lang syne. No more, sir; that will do."
So, for the time, apparently it did,
And Eben evidently thought so too;
45 For soon amid the silver loneliness
Of night he lifted up his voice and sang,
Secure, with only two moons listening,
Until the whole harmonious landscape rang—

"For auld lang syne." The weary throat gave out,
50 The last word wavered; and the song being done,
He raised again the jug regretfully
And shook his head, and was again alone.
There was not much that was ahead of him,
And there was nothing in the town below—
55 Where strangers would have shut the many doors
That many friends had opened long ago.

Karma[1]

Christmas was in the air and all was well
With him, but for a few confusing flaws
In divers of God's images. Because
A friend of his would neither buy nor sell,
5 Was he to answer for the axe that fell?
He pondered; and the reason for it was,
Partly, a slowly freezing Santa Claus
Upon the corner, with his beard and bell.

Acknowledging an improvident surprise,
10 He magnified a fancy that he wished
The friend whom he had wrecked were here again.
Not sure of that, he found a compromise;
And from the fulness of his heart he fished
A dime for Jesus who had died for men.

New England

Here where the wind is always north-north-east
And children learn to walk on frozen toes,

---

[1] In Buddhist philosophy, the cumulative results of a person's deeds in one stage of his existence, controlling his fate in the next.

Wonder begets an envy of all those
Who boil elsewhere with such a lyric yeast
5 Of love that you will hear them at a feast
Where demons would appeal for some repose,
Still clamoring where the chalice overflows
And crying wildest who have drunk the least.

Passion is here a soilure of the wits,
10 We're told, and Love a cross for them to bear;
Joy shivers in the corner where she knits
And Conscience always has the rocking-chair,
Cheerful as when she tortured into fits
The first cat that was ever killed by Care.

JAMES WELDON JOHNSON (1871–1938)

O Black and Unknown Bards

O black and unknown bards of long ago,
How came your lips to touch the sacred fire?
How, in your darkness, did you come to know
The power and beauty of the minstrel's lyre?
5 Who first from midst his bonds lifted his eyes?
Who first from out the still watch, lone and long,
Feeling the ancient faith of prophets rise
Within his dark-kept soul, burst into song?

Heart of what slave poured out such melody
10 As "Steal away to Jesus"? On its strains
His spirit must have nightly floated free,
Though still about his hands he felt his chains.
Who heard great "Jordan roll"? Whose starward eye
Saw chariot "swing low"? And who was he
15 That breathed that comforting, melodic sigh,
"Nobody knows de trouble I see"?
What merely living clod, what captive thing,
Could up toward God through all its darkness grope,
And find within its deadened heart to sing
20 These songs of sorrow, love and faith, and hope?
How did it catch that subtle undertone,
That note in music heard not with the ears?
How sound the elusive reed so seldom blown,
Which stirs the soul or melts the heart to tears?

25 Not that great German master[1] in his dream
    Of harmonies that thundered amongst the stars
    At the creation, ever heard a theme
    Nobler than "Go down, Moses." Mark its bars,
    How like a mighty trumpet-call they stir
30 The blood. Such are the notes that men have sung
    Going to valorous deeds; such tones there were
    That helped make history when Time was young.

    There is a wide, wide wonder in it all,
    That from degraded rest and servile toil
35 The fiery spirit of the seer should call
    These simple children of the sun and soil.
    O black slave singers, gone, forgot, unfamed,
    You—you alone, of all the long, long line
    Of those who've sung untaught, unknown, unnamed,
40 Have stretched out upward, seeking the divine.

    You sang not deeds of heroes or of kings;
    No chant of bloody war, no exulting paean
    Of arms-won triumphs; but your humble strings
    You touched in chord with music empyrean.
45 You sang far better than you knew; the songs
    That for your listeners' hungry hearts sufficed
    Still live—but more than this to you belongs:
    You sang a race from wood and stone to Christ.

ARTHUR GUITERMAN (1871–1943)

On the Vanity of Earthly Greatness

The tusks that clashed in mighty brawls
Of mastodons, are billiard balls.

The sword of Charlemagne the Just
Is ferric oxide, known as rust.

5 The grizzly bear whose potent hug
Was feared by all, is now a rug.

Great Caesar's bust is on the shelf,
And I don't feel so well myself.

---

[1] Beethoven.

WALTER DE LA MARE (1873–1956)

The Listeners

"Is there anybody there?" said the Traveller,
    Knocking on the moonlit door;
And his horse in the silence champed the grasses
    Of the forest's ferny floor:
5 And a bird flew up out of the turret,
    Above the Traveller's head:
And he smote upon the door again a second time;
    "Is there anybody there?" he said.
But no one descended to the Traveller;
10   No head from the leaf-fringed sill
Leaned over and looked into his grey eyes,
    Where he stood perplexed and still.
But only a host of phantom listeners
    That dwelt in the lone house then
15 Stood listening in the quiet of the moonlight
    To that voice from the world of men:
Stood thronging the faint moonbeams on the dark stair,
    That goes down to the empty hall,
Hearkening in an air stirred and shaken
20   By the lonely Traveller's call.
And he felt in his heart their strangeness,
    Their stillness answering his cry,
While his horse moved, cropping the dark turf,
    'Neath the starred and leafy sky;
25 For he suddenly smote on the door, even
    Louder, and lifted his head: —
"Tell them I came, and no one answered,
    That I kept my word," he said.
Never the least stir made the listeners,
30   Though every word he spake
Fell echoing through the shadowiness of the still house
    From the one man left awake:
Ay, they heard his foot upon the stirrup,
    And the sound of iron on stone,
35 And how the silence surged softly backward,
    When the plunging hoofs were gone.

AMY LOWELL (1874–1925)

Wind and Silver

Greatly shining,
The Autumn moon floats in the thin sky;
And the fish-ponds shake their backs and flash their dragon scales
As she passes over them.

ROBERT FROST (1874–1963)

Mending Wall

Something there is that doesn't love a wall,
That sends the frozen-ground-swell under it
And spills the upper boulders in the sun,
And makes gaps even two can pass abreast.
5 The work of hunters is another thing:
I have come after them and made repair
Where they have left not one stone on a stone,
But they would have the rabbit out of hiding,
To please the yelping dogs. The gaps I mean,
10 No one has seen them made or heard them made,
But at spring mending-time we find them there.
I let my neighbor know beyond the hill;
And on a day we meet to walk the line
And set the wall between us once again.
15 We keep the wall between us as we go.
To each the boulders that have fallen to each.
And some are loaves and some so nearly balls
We have to use a spell to make them balance:
'Stay where you are until our backs are turned!'
20 We wear our fingers rough with handling them.
Oh, just another kind of outdoor game,
One on a side. It comes to little more:
There where it is we do not need the wall:
He is all pine and I am apple orchard.
25 My apple trees will never get across
And eat the cones under his pines, I tell him.
He only says, 'Good fences make good neighbors.'
Spring is the mischief in me, and I wonder
If I could put a notion in his head:
30 '*Why* do they make good neighbors? Isn't it
Where there are cows? But here there are no cows,

Before I built a wall I'd ask to know
What I was walling in or walling out,
And to whom I was like to give offense.
35 Something there is that doesn't love a wall,
That wants it down.' I could say 'Elves' to him,
But it's not elves exactly, and I'd rather
He said it for himself. I see him there,
Bringing a stone grasped firmly by the top
40 In each hand, like an old-stone savage armed.
He moves in darkness as it seems to me,
Not of woods only and the shade of trees.
He will not go behind his father's saying,
And he likes having thought of it so well
45 He says again, 'Good fences make good neighbors.'

The Death of the Hired Man

Mary sat musing on the lamp-flame at the table
Waiting for Warren. When she heard his step,
She ran on tiptoe down the darkened passage
To meet him in the doorway with the news
5 And put him on his guard. "Silas is back."
She pushed him outward with her through the door
And shut it after her. "Be kind," she said.
She took the market things from Warren's arms
And set them on the porch, then drew him down
10 To sit beside her on the wooden steps.

"When was I ever anything but kind to him?
But I'll not have the fellow back," he said.
"I told him so last haying, didn't I?
If he left then, I said, that ended it.
15 What good is he? Who else will harbor him
At his age for the little he can do?
What help he is there's no depending on.
Off he goes always when I need him most.
He thinks he ought to earn a little pay,
20 Enough at least to buy tobacco with,
So he won't have to beg and be beholden.
'All right,' I say, 'I can't afford to pay
Any fixed wages, though I wish I could.'
'Someone else can.' 'Then someone else will have to.'
25 I shouldn't mind his bettering himself
If that was what it was. You can be certain,

When he begins like that, there's someone at him
Trying to coax him off with pocket money,—
In haying time, when any help is scarce.
30 In winter he comes back to us. I'm done."

"Sh! not so loud: he'll hear you," Mary said.

"I want him to: he'll have to soon or late."

"He's worn out. He's asleep beside the stove.
When I came up from Rowe's I found him here,
35 Huddled against the barn door fast asleep,
A miserable sight, and frightening, too—
You needn't smile—I didn't recognize him—
I wasn't looking for him—and he's changed.
Wait till you see."

                    "Where did you say he'd been?"

40 "He didn't say. I dragged him to the house,
And gave him tea and tried to make him smoke.
I tried to make him talk about his travels.
Nothing would do: he just kept nodding off."

"What did he say? Did he say anything?"

"But little."

45   "Anything? Mary, confess
He said he'd come to ditch the meadow for me."

"Warren!"

              "But did he? I just want to know."

"Of course he did. What would you have him say?
Surely you wouldn't grudge the poor old man
50 Some humble way to save his self-respect.
He added, if you really care to know,
He meant to clear the upper pasture, too.
That sounds like something you have heard before?
Warren, I wish you could have heard the way
55 He jumbled everything. I stopped to look
Two or three times—he made me feel so queer—
To see if he was talking in his sleep.
He ran on Harold Wilson—you remember—

The boy you had in haying four years since.
60 He's finished school, and teaching in his college.
Silas declares you'll have to get him back.
He says they two will make a team for work:
Between them they will lay this farm as smooth!
The way he mixed that in with other things.
65 He thinks young Wilson a likely lad, though daft
On education—you know how they fought
All through July under the blazing sun,
Silas up on the cart to build the load,
Harold along beside to pitch it on."

70 "Yes, I took care to keep well out of earshot."

"Well, those days trouble Silas like a dream.
You wouldn't think they would. How some things linger!
Harold's young college boy's assurance piqued him.
After so many years he still keeps finding
75 Good arguments he sees he might have used.
I sympathize. I know just how it feels
To think of the right thing to say too late.
Harold's associated in his mind with Latin.
He asked me what I thought of Harold's saying
80 He studied Latin, like the violin,
Because he liked it—that an argument!
He said he couldn't make the boy believe
He could find water with a hazel prong—
Which showed how much good school had ever done him.
85 He wanted to go over that. But most of all
He thinks if he could have another chance
To teach him how to build a load of hay—"

"I know, that's Silas' one accomplishment.
He bundles every forkful in its place,
90 And tags and numbers it for future reference,
So he can find and easily dislodge it
In the unloading. Silas does that well.
He takes it out in bunches like big birds' nests.
You never see him standing on the hay
95 He's trying to lift, straining to lift himself."

"He thinks if he could teach him that, he'd be
Some good perhaps to someone in the world.
He hates to see a boy the fool of books.

    Poor Silas, so concerned for other folk,
100 And nothing to look backward to with pride,
    And nothing to look forward to with hope,
    So now and never any different."

    Part of a moon was falling down the west,
    Dragging the whole sky with it to the hills.
105 Its light poured softly in her lap. She saw it
    And spread her apron to it. She put out her hand
    Among the harp-like morning-glory strings,
    Taut with the dew from garden bed to eaves,
    As if she played unheard some tenderness
110 That wrought on him beside her in the night.
    "Warren," she said, "he has come home to die:
    You needn't be afraid he'll leave you this time."

    "Home," he mocked gently.

                   "Yes, what else but home?
    It all depends on what you mean by home.
115 Of course he's nothing to us, any more
    Than was the hound that came a stranger to us
    Out of the woods, worn out upon the trail."

    "Home is the place where, when you have to go there,
    They have to take you in."

                  "I should have called it
120 Something you somehow haven't to deserve."

    Warren leaned out and took a step or two,
    Picked up a little stick, and brought it back
    And broke it in his hand and tossed it by.
    "Silas has better claim on us you think
125 Than on his brother? Thirteen little miles
    As the road winds would bring him to his door.
    Silas has walked that far no doubt to-day.
    Why doesn't he go there? His brother's rich,
    A somebody—director in the bank."

    "He never told us that."

130   "We know it though."

    "I think his brother ought to help, of course.
    I'll see to that if there is need. He ought of right

To take him in, and might be willing to—
He may be better than appearances.
135 But have some pity on Silas. Do you think
If he had any pride in claiming kin
Or anything he looked for from his brother,
He'd keep so still about him all this time?"

"I wonder what's between them."

                                "I can tell you.
140 Silas is what he is—we wouldn't mind him—
But just the kind that kinsfolk can't abide.
He never did a thing so very bad.
He don't know why he isn't quite as good
As anybody. Worthless though he is,
145 He won't be made ashamed to please his brother."

"*I* can't think Si ever hurt anyone."

"No, but he hurt my heart the way he lay
And rolled his old head on that sharp-edged chair-back.
He wouldn't let me put him on the lounge.
150 You must go in and see what you can do.
I made the bed up for him there tonight.
You'll be surprised at him—how much he's broken.
His working days are done; I'm sure of it."

"I'd not be in a hurry to say that."

155 "I haven't been. Go, look, see for yourself.
But, Warren, please remember how it is:
He's come to help you ditch the meadow.
He has a plan. You mustn't laugh at him.
He may not speak of it, and then he may.
160 I'll sit and see if that small sailing cloud
Will hit or miss the moon."

                                It hit the moon.
Then there were three there, making a dim row,
The moon, the little silver cloud, and she.

Warren returned—too soon, it seemed to her,
165 Slipped to her side, caught up her hand and waited.
"Warren?" she questioned.

                                "Dead," was all he answered.

The Road Not Taken

Two roads diverged in a yellow wood,
And sorry I could not travel both
And be one traveler, long I stood
And looked down one as far as I could
5 To where it bent in the undergrowth;

Then took the other, as just as fair,
And having perhaps the better claim,
Because it was grassy and wanted wear;
Though as for that, the passing there
10 Had worn them really about the same,

And both that morning equally lay
In leaves no step had trodden black.
Oh, I kept the first for another day!
Yet knowing how way leads on to way,
15 I doubted if I should ever come back.

I shall be telling this with a sigh
Somewhere ages and ages hence:
Two roads diverged in a wood, and I—
I took the one less traveled by,
20 And that has made all the difference.

The Oven Bird

There is a singer everyone has heard,
Loud, a mid-summer and a mid-wood bird,
Who makes the solid tree trunks sound again.
He says that leaves are old and that for flowers
5 Mid-summer is to spring as one to ten.
He says the early petal-fall is past,
When pear and cherry bloom went down in showers
On sunny days a moment overcast;
And comes that other fall we name the fall.
10 He says the highway dust is over all.
The bird would cease and be as other birds
But that he knows in singing not to sing.
The question that he frames in all but words
Is what to make of a diminished thing.

Birches

When I see birches bend to left and right
Across the lines of straighter darker trees,
I like to think some boy's been swinging them.
But swinging doesn't bend them down to stay
5 As ice-storms do. Often you must have seen them
Loaded with ice a sunny winter morning
After a rain. They click upon themselves
As the breeze rises, and turn many-colored
As the stir cracks and crazes their enamel.
10 Soon the sun's warmth makes them shed crystal shells
Shattering and avalanching on the snowcrust—
Such heaps of broken glass to sweep away
You'd think the inner dome of heaven had fallen.
They are dragged to the withered bracken by the load,
15 And they seem not to break; though once they are bowed
So low for long, they never right themselves:
You may see their trunks arching in the woods
Years afterwards, trailing their leaves on the ground
Like girls on hands and knees that throw their hair
20 Before them over their heads to dry in the sun.
But I was going to say when Truth broke in
With all her matter-of-fact about the ice-storm,
I should prefer to have some boy bend them
As he went out and in to fetch the cows—
25 Some boy too far from town to learn baseball,
Whose only play was what he found himself,
Summer or winter, and could play alone.
One by one he subdued his father's trees
By riding them down over and over again
30 Until he took the stiffness out of them,
And not one but hung limp, not one was left
For him to conquer. He learned all there was
To learn about not launching out too soon
And so not carrying the tree away
35 Clear to the ground. He always kept his poise
To the top branches, climbing carefully
With the same pains you use to fill a cup
Up to the brim, and even above the brim.
Then he flung outward, feet first, with a swish,
40 Kicking his way down through the air to the ground.
So was I once myself a swinger of birches.
And so I dream of going back to be.

It's when I'm weary of considerations,
And life is too much like a pathless wood
45 Where your face burns and tickles with the cobwebs
Broken across it, and one eye is weeping
From a twig's having lashed across it open.
I'd like to get away from earth awhile
And then come back to it and begin over.
50 May no fate willfully misunderstand me
And half grant what I wish and snatch me away
Not to return. Earth's the right place for love:
I don't know where it's likely to go better.
I'd like to go by climbing a birch tree,
55 And climb black branches up a snow-white trunk,
Toward heaven, till the tree could bear no more,
But dipped its top and set me down again.
That would be good both going and coming back.
One could do worse than be a swinger of birches.

"Out, Out—" [1]

The buzz-saw snarled and rattled in the yard
And made dust and dropped stove-length sticks of wood,
Sweet-scented stuff when the breeze drew across it.
And from there those that lifted eyes could count
5 Five mountain ranges one behind the other
Under the sunset far into Vermont.
And the saw snarled and rattled, snarled and rattled,
As it ran light, or had to bear a load.
And nothing happened: day was all but done.
10 Call it a day, I wish they might have said
To please the boy by giving him the half hour
That a boy counts so much when saved from work.
His sister stood beside them in her apron
To tell them "Supper." At the word, the saw,
15 As if to prove saws knew what supper meant,
Leaped out at the boy's hand, or seemed to leap—
He must have given the hand. However it was,
Neither refused the meeting. But the hand!
The boy's first outcry was a rueful laugh,
20 As he swung toward them holding up the hand
Half in appeal, but half as if to keep

---

[1] An allusion to *Macbeth*, Act 5, Scene 5.

The life from spilling. Then the boy saw all—
Since he was old enough to know, big boy
Doing a man's work, though a child at heart—
25 He saw all spoiled. "Don't let him cut my hand off—
The doctor, when he comes. Don't let him, sister!"
So. But the hand was gone already.
The doctor put him in the dark of ether.
He lay and puffed his lips out with his breath.
30 And then—the watcher at his pulse took fright.
No one believed. They listened at his heart.
Little—less—nothing!—and that ended it.
No more to build on there. And they, since they
Were not the one dead, turned to their affairs.

Fire and Ice

Some say the world will end in fire,
Some say in ice.
From what I've tasted of desire
I hold with those who favor fire.
5 But if it had to perish twice,
I think I know enough of hate
To say that for destruction ice
Is also great
And would suffice

Stopping by Woods on a Snowy Evening

Whose woods these are I think I know.
His house is in the village, though;
He will not see me stopping here
To watch his woods fill up with snow.

5 My little horse must think it queer
To stop without a farmhouse near
Between the woods and frozen lake
The darkest evening of the year.

He gives his harness bells a shake
10 To ask if there is some mistake.
The only other sound's the sweep
Of easy wind and downy flake.

The woods are lovely, dark, and deep,
But I have promises to keep,
15 And miles to go before I sleep,
And miles to go before I sleep.

Once by the Pacific

The shattered water made a misty din.
Great waves looked over others coming in,
And thought of doing something to the shore
That water never did to land before.
5 The clouds were low and hairy in the skies,
Like locks blown forward in the gleam of eyes.
You could not tell, and yet it looked as if
The shore was lucky in being backed by cliff,
The cliff in being backed by continent;
10 It looked as if a night of dark intent
Was coming, and not only a night, an age.
Someone had better be prepared for rage.
There would be more than ocean-water broken
Before God's last *Put out the Light* was spoken.

Departmental

An ant on the tablecloth
Ran into a dormant moth
Of many times his size.
He showed not the least surprise.
5 His business wasn't with such.
He gave it scarcely a touch,
And was off on his duty run.
Yet if he encountered one
Of the hive's enquiry squad
10 Whose work is to find out God
And the nature of time and space,
He would put him onto the case.
Ants are a curious race;
One crossing with hurried tread
15 The body of one of their dead
Isn't given a moment's arrest—
Seems not even impressed.
But he no doubt reports to any
With whom he crosses antennae,

20 And they no doubt report
   To the higher-up at court.
   Then word goes forth in Formic:
   "Death's come to Jerry McCormic,
   Our selfless forager Jerry.
25 Will the special Janızary
   Whose office it is to bury
   The dead of the commissary
   Go bring him home to his people.
   Lay him in state on a sepal.
30 Wrap him for shroud in a petal.
   Embalm him with ichor of nettle.
   This is the word of your Queen."
   And presently on the scene
   Appears a solemn mortician;
35 And taking formal position
   With feelers calmly atwiddle,
   Seizes the dead by the middle,
   And heaving him high in air,
   Carries him out of there.
40 No one stands round to stare.
   It is nobody else's affair.

   It couldn't be called ungentle.
   But how thoroughly departmental.

Design

   I found a dimpled spider, fat and white,
   On a white heal-all, holding up a moth
   Like a white piece of rigid satin cloth—
   Assorted characters of death and blight
5 Mixed ready to begin the morning right,
   Like the ingredients of a witches' broth—
   A snow-drop spider, a flower like a froth,
   And dead wings carried like a paper kite.

   What had that flower to do with being white,
10 The wayside blue and innocent heal-all?
   What brought the kindred spider to that height,
   Then steered the white moth thither in the night?
   What but design of darkness to appall?—
   If design govern in a thing so small.

The Draft Horse

With a lantern that wouldn't burn
In too frail a buggy we drove
Behind too heavy a horse
Through a pitch-dark limitless grove.

5 And a man came out of the trees
And took our horse by the head
And reaching back to his ribs
Deliberately stabbed him dead.

The ponderous beast went down
10 With a crack of a broken shaft.
And the night drew through the trees
In one long invidious draft.

The most unquestioning pair
That ever accepted fate
15 And the least disposed to ascribe
Any more than we had to to hate,

We assumed that the man himself
Or someone he had to obey
Wanted us to get down
20 And walk the rest of the way.

In Winter in the Woods Alone

In winter in the woods alone
Against the trees I go.
I mark a maple for my own
And lay the maple low.

5 At four o'clock I shoulder ax,
And in the afterglow
I link a line of shadowy tracks
Across the tinted snow.

I see for Nature no defeat
10 In one tree's overthrow
Or for myself in my retreat
For yet another blow.

EDWARD THOMAS (1878–1917)

Birds' Nests

The summer nests uncovered by autumn wind,
Some torn, others dislodged, all dark,
Everyone sees them: low or high in tree,
Or hedge, or single bush, they hang like a mark.

5 Since there's no need of eyes to see them with
I cannot help a little shame
That I missed most, even at eye's level, till
The leaves blew off and made the seeing no game.

'Tis a light pang. I like to see the nests
10 Still in their places, now first known,
At home and by far roads. Boys knew them not,
Whatever jays and squirrels may have done.

And most I like the winter nests deep-hid
That leaves and berries fell into:
15 Once a dormouse dined there on hazel-nuts,
And grass and goose-grass seeds found soil and grew.

The Gypsy

A fortnight before Christmas Gypsies were everywhere:
Vans were drawn up on wastes, women trailed to the fair.
"My gentleman," said one, "you've got a lucky face."
"And you've a luckier," I thought, "if such a grace
5 And impudence in rags are lucky." "Give a penny
For the poor baby's sake." "Indeed I have not any
Unless you can give change for a sovereign, my dear."
"Then just half a pipeful of tobacco can you spare?"
I gave it. With that much victory she laughed content.
10 I should have given more, but off and away she went
With her baby and her pink sham flowers to rejoin
The rest before I could translate to its proper coin
Gratitude for her grace. And I paid nothing then,
As I pay nothing now with the dipping of my pen
15 For her brother's music when he drummed the tambourine
And stamped his feet, which made the workmen passing grin,
While his mouth-organ changed to a rascally Bacchanal dance
"Over the hills and far away." This and his glance
Outlasted all the fair, farmer, and auctioneer,
20 Cheap-jack, balloon-man, drover with crooked stick, and steer,

Pig, turkey, goose, and duck, Christmas corpses to be.
Not even the kneeling ox had eyes like the Romany.
That night he peopled for me the hollow wooded land,
More dark and wild than stormiest heavens, that I searched and
    scanned
25 Like a ghost new-arrived. The gradations of the dark
Were like an underworld of death, but for the spark
In the Gypsy boy's black eyes as he played and stamped his tune,
"Over the hills and far away," and a crescent moon.

CARL SANDBURG (1878–1967)

Early Copper

A slim and singing copper girl,
They lived next to the earth for her sake
And the yellow corn was in their faces
And the copper curve of prairie sunset.

5   In her April eyes bringing
Corn tassels shining from Duluth and Itasca,
From La Crosse to Keokuk and St. Louis, to the Big Muddy,
The yellow-hoofed Big Muddy meeting the Father of Waters,
In her eyes corn rows running to the prairie ends,
10 In her eyes copper men living next to the earth for her sake.

Fog

The fog comes
on little cat feet.

It sits looking
over harbor and city
5 on silent haunches
and then moves on.

Cool Tombs

When Abraham Lincoln was shoveled into the tombs, he forgot the
    copperheads and the assassin . . . in the dust, in the cool tombs.
And Ulysses Grant lost all thought of con men and Wall Street, cash
    and collateral turned ashes . . . in the dust, in the cool tombs.
Pocahontas' body, lovely as a poplar, sweet as a red haw in Novem-
    ber or a pawpaw in May, did she wonder? does she remember?
    . . . in the dust, in the cool tombs?

Take any streetful of people buying clothes and groceries, cheering
a hero or throwing confetti and blowing tin horns ... tell me if
the lovers are losers ... tell me if any get more than the lovers
... in the dust ... in the cool tombs.

WALLACE STEVENS (1879–1955)

Sunday Morning

1

Complacencies of the peignoir, and late
Coffee and oranges in a sunny chair,
And the green freedom of a cockatoo
Upon a rug mingle to dissipate
5 The holy hush of ancient sacrifice.
She dreams a little, and she feels the dark
Encroachment of that old catastrophe,
As a calm darkens among water-lights.
The pungent oranges and bright, green wings
10 Seem things in some procession of the dead,
Winding across wide water, without sound.
The day is like wide water, without sound,
Stilled for the passing of her dreaming feet
Over the seas, to silent Palestine,
15 Dominion of the blood and sepulchre.

2

Why should she give her bounty to the dead?
What is divinity if it can come
Only in silent shadows and in dreams?
Shall she not find in comforts of the sun,
20 In pungent fruit and bright, green wings, or else
In any balm or beauty of the earth,
Things to be cherished like the thought of heaven?
Divinity must live within herself:
Passions of rain, or moods in falling snow;
25 Grievings in loneliness, or unsubdued
Elations when the forest blooms; gusty
Emotions on wet roads on autumn nights;
All pleasures and all pains, remembering
The bough of summer and the winter branch.
30 These are the measures destined for her soul.

3

Jove in the clouds had his inhuman birth.
No mother suckled him, no sweet land gave
Large-mannered motions to his mythy mind
He moved among us, as a muttering king,
35 Magnificent, would move among his hinds
Until our blood, commingling, virginal,
With heaven, brought such requital to desire
The very hinds discerned it, in a star.
Shall our blood fail? Or shall it come to be
40 The blood of paradise? And shall the earth
Seem all of paradise that we shall know?
The sky will be much friendlier then than now,
A part of labor and a part of pain,
And next in glory to enduring love,
45 Not this dividing and indifferent blue.

4

She says, "I am content when wakened birds,
Before they fly, test the reality
Of misty fields, by their sweet questionings;
But when the birds are gone, and their warm fields
50 Return no more, where, then, is paradise?"
There is not any haunt of prophecy,
Nor any old chimera of the grave,
Neither the golden underground, nor isle
Melodious, where spirits gat them home,
55 Nor visionary south, nor cloudy palm
Remote on heaven's hill, that has endured
As April's green endures; or will endure
Like her remembrance of awakened birds,
Or her desire for June and evening, tipped
60 By the consummation of the swallow's wings.

5

She says, "But in contentment I still feel
The need of some imperishable bliss."
Death is the mother of beauty; hence from her,
Alone, shall come fulfilment to our dreams
65 And our desires. Although she strews the leaves
Of sure obliteration on our paths,
The path sick sorrow took, the many paths
Where triumph rang its brassy phrase, or love

Whispered a little out of tenderness,
70 She makes the willow shiver in the sun
For maidens who were wont to sit and gaze
Upon the grass, relinquished to their feet.
She causes boys to pile new plums and pears
On disregarded plate. The maidens taste
75 And stray impassioned in the littering leaves.

6

Is there no change of death in paradise?
Does ripe fruit never fall? Or do the boughs
Hang always heavy in that perfect sky,
Unchanging, yet so like our perishing earth,
80 With rivers like our own that seek for seas
They never find, the same receding shores
That never touch with inarticulate pang?
Why set the pear upon those river-banks
Or spice the shores with odors of the plum?
85 Alas, that they should wear our colors there,
The silken weavings of our afternoons,
And pick the strings of our insipid lutes!
Death is the mother of beauty, mystical,
Within whose burning bosom we devise
90 Our earthly mothers waiting, sleeplessly.

7

Supple and turbulent, a ring of men
Shall chant in orgy on a summer morn
Their boisterous devotion to the sun,
Not as a god, but as a god might be,
95 Naked among them, like a savage source.
Their chant shall be a chant of paradise,
Out of their blood, returning to the sky;
And in their chant shall enter, voice by voice,
The windy lake wherein their lord delights,
100 The trees, like serafin, and echoing hills,
That choir among themselves long afterward.
They shall know well the heavenly fellowship
Of men that perish and of summer morn.
And whence they came and whither they shall go
105 The dew upon their feet shall manifest.

8

She hears, upon that water without sound,
A voice that cries, "The tomb in Palestine
Is not the porch of spirits lingering.
It is the grave of Jesus, where he lay."
110 We live in an old chaos of the sun,
Or old dependency of day and night,
Or island solitude, unsponsored, free,
Of that wide water, inescapable.
Deer walk upon our mountains, and the quail
115 Whistle about us their spontaneous cries;
Sweet berries ripen in the wilderness;
And, in the isolation of the sky,
At evening, casual flocks of pigeons make
Ambiguous undulations as they sink.
120 Downward to darkness, on extended wings.

Anecdote of the Jar

I placed a jar in Tennessee,
And round it was, upon a hill.
It made the slovenly wilderness
Surround that hill.

5 The wilderness rose up to it,
And sprawled around, no longer wild.
The jar was round upon the ground
And tall and of a port in air.

It took dominion everywhere.
10 The jar was gray and bare.
It did not give of bird or bush,
Like nothing else in Tennessee.

Thirteen Ways of Looking at a Blackbird

I

Among twenty snowy mountains,
The only moving thing
Was the eye of the blackbird.

II

I was of three minds,
5 Like a tree
In which there are three blackbirds.

III

The blackbird whirled in the autumn winds.
It was a small part of the pantomime.

IV

A man and a woman
10 Are one.
A man and a woman and a blackbird
Are one.

V

I do not know which to prefer,
The beauty of inflections,
15 Or the beauty of innuendoes,
The blackbird whistling
Or just after.

VI

Icicles filled the long window
With barbaric glass.
20 The shadow of the blackbird
Crossed it, to and fro.
The mood
Traced in the shadow
An indecipherable cause.

VII

25 O thin men of Haddam,[1]
Why do you imagine golden birds?
Do you not see how the blackbird
Walks around the feet
Of the women about you?

VIII

30 I know noble accents
And lucid, inescapable rhythms;
But I know, too,
That the blackbird is involved
In what I know.

IX

35 When the blackbird flew out of sight,
It marked the edge
Of one of many circles.

---

[1] A town in Connecticut; Stevens liked its name.

X

At the sight of blackbirds
Flying in a green light,
40 Even the bawds of euphony
Would cry out sharply.

XI

He rode over Connecticut
In a glass coach.
Once, a fear pierced him,
45 In that he mistook
The shadow of his equipage
For blackbirds.

XII

The river is moving.
The blackbird must be flying.

XIII

50 It was evening all afternoon.
It was snowing
And it was going to snow.
The blackbird sat
In the cedar-limbs.

The Snow Man

One must have a mind of winter
To regard the frost and the boughs
Of the pine-trees crusted with snow;

And have been cold a long time
5 To behold the junipers shagged with ice,
The spruces rough in the distant glitter

Of the January sun; and not to think
Of any misery in the sound of the wind,
In the sound of a few leaves,

10 Which is the sound of the land
Full of the same wind
That is blowing in the same bare place

For the listener, who listens in the snow,
And, nothing himself, beholds
15 Nothing that is not there and the nothing that is.

The Emperor of Ice-Cream

Call the roller of big cigars,
The muscular one, and bid him whip
In kitchen cups concupiscent curds.
Let the wenches dawdle in such dress
5 As they are used to wear, and let the boys
Bring flowers in last month's newspapers.
Let be be finale of seem.
The only emperor is the emperor of ice-cream.

Take from the dresser of deal,
10 Lacking the three glass knobs, that sheet
On which she embroidered fantails once
And spread it so as to cover her face.
If her horny feet protrude, they come
To show how cold she is, and dumb.
15 Let the lamp affix its beam.
The only emperor is the emperor of ice-cream.

The Idea of Order at Key West

She sang beyond the genius of the sea.
The water never formed to mind or voice,
Like a body wholly body, fluttering
Its empty sleeves; and yet its mimic motion
5 Made constant cry, caused constantly a cry,
That was not ours although we understood,
Inhuman, of the veritable ocean.

The sea was not a mask. No more was she.
The song and water were not medleyed sound
10 Even if what she sang was what she heard,
Since what she sang was uttered word by word.
It may be that in all her phrases stirred
The grinding water and the gasping wind;
But it was she and not the sea we heard.

15 For she was the maker of the song she sang.
The ever-hooded, tragic-gestured sea
Was merely a place by which she walked to sing.
Whose spirit is this? we said, because we knew
It was the spirit that we sought and knew
20 That we should ask this often as she sang.

If it was only the dark voice of the sea
That rose, or even colored by many waves;
If it was only the outer voice of sky
And cloud, of the sunken coral water-walled,
25 However clear, it would have been deep air,
The heaving speech of air, a summer sound
Repeated in a summer without end
And sound alone. But it was more than that,
More even than her voice, and ours, among
30 The meaningless plungings of water and the wind,
Theatrical distances, bronze shadows heaped
On high horizons, mountainous atmospheres
Of sky and sea.
                        It was her voice that made
35 The sky acutest at its vanishing.
She measured to the hour its solitude.
She was the single artificer of the world
In which she sang. And when she sang, the sea,
Whatever self it had, became the self
40 That was her song, for she was the maker. Then we,
As we beheld her striding there alone,
Knew that there never was a world for her
Except the one she sang and, singing, made.

Ramon Fernandez,[1] tell me, if you know,
45 Why, when the singing ended and we turned
Toward the town, tell why the glassy lights,
The lights in the fishing boats at anchor there,
As the night descended, tilting in the air,
Mastered the night and portioned out the sea,
50 Fixing emblazoned zones and fiery poles,
Arranging, deepening, enchanting night.

Oh! Blessed rage for order, pale Ramon,
The maker's rage to order words of the sea,
Words of the fragrant portals, dimly-starred,
55 And of ourselves and of our origins,
In ghostlier demarcations, keener sounds.

---

[1] Does not refer to an actual person.

Peter Quince at the Clavier

I

Just as my fingers on these keys
Make music, so the selfsame sounds
On my spirit make a music, too.

Music is feeling, then, not sound;
5 And thus it is that what I feel,
Here in this room, desiring you,

Thinking of your blue-shadowed silk,
Is music. It is like the strain
Waked in the elders by Susanna.

10 Of a green evening, clear and warm,
She bathed in her still garden, while
The red-eyed elders watching, felt

The basses of their beings throb
In witching chords, and their thin blood
15 Pulse pizzicati of Hosanna.

II

In the green water, clear and warm,
Susanna lay.
She searched
The touch of springs,
20 And found
Concealed imaginings,
She sighed,
For so much melody.

Upon the bank, she stood
25 In the cool
Of spent emotions.
She felt, among the leaves,
The dew
Of old devotions.

30 She walked upon the grass,
Still quavering.
The winds were like her maids,
On timid feet,

Fetching her woven scarves,
35 Yet wavering.

A breath upon her hand
Muted the night.
She turned—
A cymbal crashed,
40 And roaring horns.

III

Soon, with a noise like tambourines,
Came her attendant Byzantines.

They wondered why Susanna cried
Against the elders by her side;

45 And as they whispered, the refrain
Was like a willow swept by rain.

Anon, their lamps' uplifted flame
Revealed Susanna and her shame.

And then, the simpering Byzantines
50 Fled, with a noise like tambourines.

IV

Beauty is momentary in the mind—
The fitful tracing of a portal;
But in the flesh it is immortal.

The body dies; the body's beauty lives.
55 So evenings die, in their green going,
A wave, interminably flowing.
So gardens die, their meek breath scenting
The cowl of winter, done repenting.
So maidens die, to the auroral
60 Celebration of a maiden's choral.
Susanna's music touched the bawdy strings
Of those white elders; but, escaping,
Left only Death's ironic scraping.
Now, in its immortality, it plays
65 On the clear viol of her memory,
And makes a constant sacrament of praise.

JAMES STEPHENS (1882–1950)

The Wind

The wind stood up, and gave a shout;
He whistled on his fingers, and

Kicked the withered leaves about,
And thumped the branches with his hand,

5 And said he'll kill, and kill, and kill;
And so he will! And so he will!

WILLIAM CARLOS WILLIAMS (1883–1963)

The Young Housewife

At ten A.M. the young housewife
moves about in negligee behind
the wooden walls of her husband's house.
I pass solitary in my car.

5 Then again she comes to the curb
to call the ice-man, fish-man, and stands
shy, uncorseted, tucking in
stray ends of hair, and I compare her
to a fallen leaf.

10 The noiseless wheels of my car
rush with a crackling sound over
dried leaves as I bow and pass smiling.

The Red Wheelbarrow

so much depends
upon

a red wheel
barrow

5 glazed with rain
water

beside the white
chickens.

The Yachts

contend in a sea which the land partly encloses
shielding them from the too heavy blows
of an ungoverned ocean which when it chooses

tortures the biggest hulls, the best man knows
5 to pit against its beatings, and sinks them pitilessly.
Mothlike in mists, scintillant in the minute

brilliance of cloudless days, with broad bellying sails
they glide to the wind tossing green water
from their sharp prows while over them the crew crawls

10 ant like, solicitously grooming them, releasing,
making fast as they turn, lean far over and having
caught the wind again, side by side, head for the mark.

In a well guarded arena of open water surrounded by
lesser and greater craft which, sycophant, lumbering
15 and flittering follow them, they appear youthful, rare

as the light of a happy eye, live with the grace
of all that in the mind is fleckless, free and
naturally to be desired. Now the sea which holds them

is moody, lapping their glossy sides, as if feeling
20 for some slightest flaw but fails completely.
Today no race. Then the wind comes again. The yachts

move, jockeying for a start, the signal is set and they
are off. Now the waves strike at them but they are too
well made, they slip through, though they take in canvas.

25 Arms with hands grasping seek to clutch at the prows.
Bodies thrown recklessly in the way are cut aside.
It is a sea of faces about them in agony, in despair

until the horror of the race dawns staggering the mind,
the whole sea become an entanglement of watery bodies
30 lost to the world bearing what they cannot hold. Broken,

beaten, desolate, reaching from the dead to be taken up
they cry out, failing, failing! their cries rising
in waves still as the skillful yachts pass over.

The Dance

In Breughel's great picture, The Kermess,[1]
the dancers go round, they go round and
around, the squeal and the blare and the
tweedle of bagpipes, a bugle and fiddles
5 tipping their bellies (round as the thick-
sided glasses whose wash they impound)
their hips and their bellies off balance
to turn them. Kicking and rolling about
the Fair Grounds, swinging their butts, those
10 shanks must be sound to bear up under such
rollicking measures, prance as they dance
in Breughel's great picture, The Kermess.

E. J. PRATT (1883–1964)

The Prize Cat

Pure blood domestic, guaranteed,
Soft-mannered, musical in purr,
The ribbon had declared the breed,
Gentility was in the fur.

5 Such feline culture in the gads[1]
No anger ever arched her back—
What distance since those velvet pads
Departed from the leopard's track!

And when I mused how Time had thinned
10 The jungle strains within the cells,
How human hands had disciplined
Those prowling optic parallels;

I saw the generations pass
Along the reflex of a spring,
15 A bird had rustled in the grass,
The tab had caught it on the wing;

Behind the leap so furtive-wild
Was such ignition in the gleam,
I thought an Abyssinian child
20 Had cried out in the whitethroat's scream.

---

1 Peter Breughel (1525?–1569), Flemish painter. "Kermess" means "fair."
1 Claws.

D. H. LAWRENCE (1885–1930)

Piano

Softly, in the dusk, a woman is singing to me;
Taking me back down the vista of years, till I see
A child sitting under the piano, in the boom of the tingling strings
And pressing the small, poised feet of a mother who smiles as she
    sings.

5 In spite of myself, the insidious mastery of song
Betrays me back, till the heart of me weeps to belong
To the old Sunday evenings at home, with winter outside
And hymns in the cozy parlor, the tinkling piano our guide.

So now it is vain for the singer to burst into clamor
10 With the great black piano appassionato. The glamour
Of childish days is upon me, my manhood is cast
Down in the flood of remembrance, I weep like a child for the past.

Snake

A snake came to my water-trough
On a hot, hot day, and I in pajamas for the heat,
To drink there.

In the deep, strange-scented shade of the great dark carob-tree
5 I came down the steps with my pitcher
And must wait, must stand and wait, for there he was at the trough
    before me.

He reached down from a fissure in the earth-wall in the gloom
And trailed his yellow-brown slackness soft-bellied down, over the
    edge of the stone trough
And rested his throat upon the stone bottom,
10 And where the water had dripped from the tap, in a small clearness,
He sipped with his straight mouth,
Softly drank through his straight gums, into his slack long body,
Silently.

Someone was before me at my water-trough,
15 And I, like a second comer, waiting.

He lifted his head from his drinking, as cattle do,
And looked at me vaguely, as drinking cattle do,

And flickered his two-forked tongue from his lips, and mused a
    moment,
And stooped and drank a little more,
20 Being earth-brown, earth-golden from the burning bowels of the
    earth
On the day of Sicilian July, with Etna smoking.

The voice of my education said to me
He must be killed,
For in Sicily the black, black snakes are innocent, the gold are
    venomous.

25 And voices in me said, If you were a man
You would take a stick and break him now, and finish him off.

But must I confess how I liked him,
How glad I was he had come like a guest in quiet, to drink at my
    water-trough
And depart peaceful, pacified, and thankless,
30 Into the burning bowels of this earth?

Was it cowardice, that I dared not kill him?
Was it perversity, that I longed to talk to him?
Was it humility, to feel so honored?
I felt so honored.

35 And yet those voices:
If you were not afraid, you would kill him!

And truly I was afraid, I was most afraid,
But even so, honored still more
That he should seek my hospitality
40 From out the dark door of the secret earth.

He drank enough
And lifted his head, dreamily, as one who has drunken,
And flickered his tongue like a forked night on the air, so black,
Seeming to lick his lips,
45 And looked round like a god, unseeing, into the air,
And slowly turned his head,
And slowly, very slowly, as if thrice adream,
Proceeded to draw his slow length curving round
And climb again the broken bank of my wall-face.

50 And as he put his head into that dreadful hole,
And as he slowly drew up, snake-easing his shoulders, and entered
    farther,
A sort of horror, a sort of protest against his withdrawing into that
    horrid black hole,
Deliberately going into the blackness, and slowly drawing himself
    after,
Overcame me now his back was turned.

55 I looked round, I put down my pitcher,
I picked up a clumsy log
And threw it at the water-trough with a clatter.

I think it did not hit him,
But suddenly that part of him that was left behind convulsed in un-
    dignified haste
60 Writhed like lightning, and was gone
Into the black hole, the earth-lipped fissure in the wall-front,
At which, in the intense still noon, I stared with fascination.

And immediately I regretted it.
I thought how paltry, how vulgar, what a mean act!
65 I despised myself and the voices of my accursed human education.

And I thought of the albatross
And I wished he would come back, my snake.

For he seemed to me again like a king,
Like a king in exile, uncrowned in the underworld,
70 Now due to be crowned again.

And so, I missed my chance with one of the lords
Of life.
And I have something to expiate;
A pettiness.

EZRA POUND (1885–1972)

The Garden

En robe de parade.
SAMAIN[1]

Like a skein of loose silk blown against a wall
She walks by the railing of a path in Kensington Gardens,

---

[1] "Dressed for state;" Albert Samain (1858–1900) was a French symbolist.

And she is dying piece-meal
    of a sort of emotional anæmia.

5 And round about there is a rabble
Of the filthy, sturdy, unkillable infants of the very poor.
They shall inherit the earth.

In her is the end of breeding.
Her boredom is exquisite and excessive.
10 She would like some one to speak to her,
And is almost afraid that I
    will commit that indiscretion.

Salutation

O generation of the thoroughly smug
    and thoroughly uncomfortable,
I have seen fishermen picnicking in the sun,
I have seen them with untidy families,
5 I have seen their smiles full of teeth
    and heard ungainly laughter.
And I am happier than you are,
And they were happier than I am;
And the fish swim in the lake
10   and do not even own clothing.

In a Station of the Metro

The apparition of these faces in the crowd;
Petals on a wet, black bough.

Dance Figure

For the Marriage in Cana of Galilee

Dark eyed,
O woman of my dreams,
Ivory sandalled,
There is none like thee among the dancers,
5 None with swift feet.
I have not found thee in the tents,
In the broken darkness.
I have not found thee at the well-head
Among the women with pitchers.

10 Thine arms are as a young sapling under the bark;
Thy face as a river with lights.

White as an almond are thy shoulders;
As new almonds stripped from the husk.
They guard thee not with eunuchs;
15 Not with bars of copper.

Gilt turquoise and silver are in the place of thy rest.
A brown robe, with threads of gold woven in
        patterns, hast thou gathered about thee,
O Nathat-Ikanaie, 'Tree-at-the-river'.

As a rillet among the sedge are thy hands upon me;
20 Thy fingers a frosted stream.

Thy maidens are white like pebbles;
Their music about thee!

There is none like thee among the dancers;
None with swift feet.

L'Art, 1910

Green arsenic smeared on an egg-white cloth,
Crushed strawberries! Come, let us feast our eyes.

The Tea Shop

The girl in the tea shop
                Is not so beautiful as she was,
The August has worn against her.
She does not get up the stairs so eagerly;
5 Yes, she also will turn middle-aged,
And the glow of youth that she spread about us
                As she brought us our muffins
Will be spread about us no longer.
                She also will turn middle-aged.

Ancient Music

Winter is icumen in,
Lhude sing Goddamm,
Raineth drop and staineth slop,

And how the wind doth ramm!
5   Sing : Goddamm.
Skiddeth bus and sloppeth us,
An ague hath my ham.
Freezeth river, turneth liver,
      Damn you, sing : Goddamm.
10 Goddamm, Goddamm, 'tis why I am, Goddamm,
      So 'gainst the winter's balm.
Sing goddamm, damm, sing Goddamm,
Sing goddamm, sing goddamm, DAMM.

The River-Merchant's Wife: A Letter

While my hair was still cut straight across my forehead
I played about the front gate, pulling flowers.
You came by on bamboo stilts, playing horse,
You walked about my seat, playing with blue plums.
5 And we went on living in the village of Chokan:
Two small people, without dislike or suspicion.

At fourteen I married My Lord you.
I never laughed, being bashful.
Lowering my head, I looked at the wall.
10 Called to, a thousand times, I never looked back.

At fifteen I stopped scowling,
I desired my dust to be mingled with yours
Forever and forever and forever.
Why should I climb the look out?

15 At sixteen you departed,
You went into far Ku-to-yen, by the river of swirling eddies,
And you have been gone five months.
The monkeys make sorrowful noise overhead.

You dragged your feet when you went out.
20 By the gate now, the moss is grown, the different mosses,
Too deep to clear them away!
The leaves fall early this autumn, in wind.
The paired butterflies are already yellow with August
Over the grass in the West garden;
25 They hurt me. I grow older.

If you are coming down through the narrows of the river Kiang,
Please let me know beforehand,
And I will come out to meet you
        As far as Cho-fu-Sa.

                By *Rihaku*[1]

These Fought in Any Case[1]

These fought in any case,
and some believing,
         pro domo,[2] in any case . . .

Some quick to arm,
5 some for adventure,
  some from fear of weakness,
  some from fear of censure,
  some for love of slaughter, in imagination,
  learning later . . .
10 some in fear, learning love of slaughter;

Died some, pro patria,
        non "dulce" non "et decor" [3] . . .
walked eye-deep in hell
believing in old men's lies, then unbelieving
15 came home, home to a lie,
  home to many deceits,
  home to old lies and new infamy;
  usury age-old and age-thick
  and liars in public places.

20 Daring as never before, wastage as never before.
  Young blood and high blood,
  fair cheeks, and fine bodies;

  fortitude as never before

---

[1] Rihaku is a transcription of the Japanese form of the name of the great Chinese poet Li Po (701–762).

[1] Section IV from "E. P. Ode pour L'Election de Son Sépulcre" ("E. P. Ode on the Selection of His Tomb").

[2] "For homeland."

[3] An ironic allusion to the famous line of Horace: "Dulce et decorum est pro patria mori" ("It is sweet and fitting to die for one's country").

frankness as never before,
25 disillusions as never told in the old days,
hysterias, trench confessions,
laughter out of dead bellies.

FRANCES CORNFORD (1886–1960)

The Watch

I wakened on my hot, hard bed,
Upon the pillow lay my head;
Beneath the pillow I could hear
My little watch was ticking clear.
5 I thought the throbbing of it went
Like my continual discontent.
I thought it said in every tick:
I am so sick, so sick, so sick.
O death, come quick, come quick, come quick,
10 Come quick, come quick, come quick, come quick!

H. D. (HILDA DOOLITTLE) (1886–1961)

Heat

O wind, rend open the heat,
cut apart the heat,
rend it to tatters.

Fruit cannot drop
5 through this thick air—
fruit cannot fall into heat
that presses up and blunts
the points of pears
and rounds the grapes.

10 Cut the heat—
plough through it,
turning it on either side
of your path.

Sea Rose

Rose, harsh rose,
marred and with stint of petals,
meagre flower, thin,
sparse of leaf,

5 more precious
than a wet rose,
single on a stem—
you are caught in the drift.

Stunted, with small leaf,
10 you are flung on the sand,
you are lifted
in the crisp sand
that drives in the wind.

Can the spice-rose
15 drip such acrid fragrance
hardened in a leaf?

Oread

Whirl up, sea—
whirl your pointed pines,
splash your great pines
on our rocks,
5 hurl your green over us,
cover us with your pools of fir.

SIEGFRIED SASSOON (1886–1967)

Base Details

If I were fierce, and bald, and short of breath,
    I'd live with scarlet Majors at the Base,
And speed glum heroes up the line to death.
    You'd see me with my puffy petulant face,
5 Guzzling and gulping in the best hotel,
    Reading the Roll of Honor. "Poor young chap,"
I'd say—"I used to know his father well;
    Yes, we've lost heavily in this last scrap."
And when the war is done and youth stone dead,
10 I'd toddle safely home and die—in bed.

RUPERT BROOKE (1887–1915)

The Soldier

If I should die, think only this of me:
That there's some corner of a foreign field

That is for ever England. There shall be
In that rich earth a richer dust concealed;
5 A dust whom England bore, shaped, made aware,
Gave, once, her flowers to love, her ways to roam,
A body of England's breathing English air,
Washed by the rivers, blest by suns of home.

And think, this heart, all evil shed away,
10 A pulse in the eternal mind, no less
Gives somewhere back the thoughts by England given;
Her sights and sounds; dreams happy as her day;
And laughter, learnt of friends; and gentleness,
In hearts at peace, under an English heaven.

EDWIN MUIR (1887–1959)

Childhood

Long time he lay upon the sunny hill,
  To his father's house below securely bound.
Far off the silent, changing sound was still,
  With the black islands lying thick around.

5 He saw each separate height, each vaguer hue,
  Where the massed islands rolled in mist away,
And though all ran together in his view
  He knew that unseen straits between them lay.

Often he wondered what new shores were there.
10 In thought he saw the still light on the sand,
The shallow water clear in tranquil air,
  And walked through it in joy from strand to strand.

Over the sound a ship so slow would pass
  That in the black hill's gloom it seemed to lie.
15 The evening sound was smooth like sunken glass,
  And time seemed finished ere the ship passed by.

Grey tiny rocks slept round him where he lay,
  Moveless as they, more still as evening came,
The grasses threw straight shadows far away,
20 And from the house his mother called his name.

The Animals

They do not live in the world,
Are not in time and space.
From birth to death hurled
No word do they have, not one
5 To plant a foot upon,
Were never in any place.

For with names the world was called
Out of the empty air,
With names was built and walled,
10 Line and circle and square,
Dust and emerald;
Snatched from deceiving death
By the articulate breath.

But these have never trod
15 Twice the familiar track,
Never never turned back
Into the memoried day.
All is new and near
In the unchanging Here
20 Of the fifth great day of God,
That shall remain the same,
Never shall pass away.

On the sixth day we came.

The Brothers

Last night I watched my brothers play,
The gentle and the reckless one,
In a field two yards away.
For half a century they were gone
5 Beyond the other side of care
To be among the peaceful dead.
Even in a dream how could I dare
Interrogate that happiness
So wildly spent yet never less?
10 For still they raced about the green
And were like two revolving suns;
A brightness poured from head to head,

So strong I could not see their eyes
Or look into their paradise.
15 What were they doing, the happy ones?
Yet where I was they once had been.

I thought, How could I be so dull,
Twenty thousand days ago,
Not to see they were beautiful?
20 I asked them, Were you really so
As you are now, that other day?
And the dream was soon away.

For then we played for victory
And not to make each other glad.
25 A darkness covered every head,
Frowns twisted the original face,
And through that mask we could not see
The beauty and the buried grace.

I have observed in foolish awe
30 The dateless mid-days of the law
And seen indifferent justice done
By everyone on everyone.
And in a vision I have seen
My brothers playing on the green.

The Horses

Barely a twelvemonth after
The seven days war that put the world to sleep,
Late in the evening the strange horses came.
By then we had made our covenant with silence,
5 But in the first few days it was so still
We listened to our breathing and were afraid.
On the second day
The radios failed; we turned the knobs; no answer.
On the third day a warship passed us, heading north,
10 Dead bodies piled on the deck. On the sixth day
A plane plunged over us into the sea. Thereafter
Nothing. The radios dumb;
And still they stand in corners of our kitchens,
And stand, perhaps, turned on, in a million rooms
15 All over the world. But now if they should speak,
If on a sudden they should speak again,
If on the stroke of noon a voice should speak,

We would not listen, we would not let it bring
That old bad world that swallowed its children quick
20 At one great gulp. We would not have it again.
Sometimes we think of the nations lying asleep,
Curled blindly in impenetrable sorrow,
And then the thought confounds us with its strangeness.
The tractors lie about our fields; at evening
25 They look like dank sea-monsters couched and waiting.
We leave them where they are and let them rust:
"They'll molder away and be like other loam."
We make our oxen drag our rusty plows,
Long laid aside. We have gone back
Far past our fathers' land.
30
                              And then, that evening
Late in the summer the strange horses came.
We heard a distant tapping on the road,
A deepening drumming; it stopped, went on again
And at the corner changed to hollow thunder.
35 We saw the heads
Like a wild wave charging and were afraid.
We had sold our horses in our fathers' time
To buy new tractors. Now they were strange to us
As fabulous steeds set on an ancient shield
40 Or illustrations in a book of knights.
We did not dare go near them. Yet they waited,
Stubborn and shy, as if they had been sent
By an old command to find our whereabouts
And that long-lost archaic companionship.
45 In the first moment we had never a thought
That they were creatures to be owned and used.
Among them were some half a dozen colts
Dropped in some wilderness of the broken world,
Yet new as if they had come from their own Eden.
50 Since then they have pulled our plows and borne our loads,
But that free servitude still can pierce our hearts.
Our life is changed; their coming our beginning.

ROBINSON JEFFERS (1887–1962)

Divinely Superfluous Beauty

The storm-dances of gulls, the barking game of seals,
Over and under the ocean . . .

Divinely superfluous beauty
Rules the games, presides over destinies, makes trees grow
5 And hills tower, waves fall.
The incredible beauty of joy
Stars with fire the joining of lips, O let our loves too
Be joined, there is not a maiden
Burns and thirsts for love
10 More than my blood for you, by the shore of seals while the wings
Weave like a web in the air
Divinely superfluous beauty.

Love the Wild Swan

"I hate my verses, every line, every word.
Oh pale and brittle pencils ever to try
One grass-blade's curve, or the throat of one bird
That clings to twig, ruffled against white sky.
5 Oh cracked and twilight mirrors ever to catch
One color, one glinting flash, of the splendor of things.
Unlucky hunter, Oh bullets of wax,
. The lion beauty, the wild-swan wings, the storm of the wings."
—This wild swan of a world is no hunter's game.
10 Better bullets than yours would miss the white breast,
Better mirrors than yours would crack in the flame.
Does it matter whether you hate your . . . self? At least
Love your eyes that can see, your mind that can
Hear the music, the thunder of the wings. Love the wild swan.

Cassandra[1]

The mad girl with the staring eyes and long white fingers
Hooked in the stones of the wall,
The storm-wrack hair and the screeching mouth: does it matter,
    Cassandra,
Whether the people believe
5 Your bitter fountain? Truly men hate the truth; they'd liefer
Meet a tiger on the road.
Therefore the poets honey their truth with lying; but religion-
Venders and political men

---

[1] Princess of Troy, gifted with the power of prophecy but doomed never to be believed.

Pour from the barrel, new lies on the old, and are praised for kindly
10 Wisdom. Poor bitch, be wise.
No: you'll still mumble in a corner a crust of truth, to men
And gods disgusting.—You and I, Cassandra.

MARIANNE MOORE (1887–1972)

Poetry

I, too, dislike it: there are things that are important beyond all this
    fiddle.
   Reading it, however, with a perfect contempt for it, one discovers
       in
  it after all, a place for the genuine.
     Hands that can grasp, eyes
5   that can dilate, hair that can rise
       if it must, these things are important not because a

high-sounding interpretation can be put upon them but because they
       are
  useful. When they become so derivative as to become unintelligble,
   the same thing may be said for all of us, that we
10   do not admire what
     we cannot understand: the bat
       holding on upside down or in quest of something to

eat, elephants pushing, a wild horse taking a roll, a tireless wolf
       under
  a tree, the immovable critic twitching his skin like a horse that
     feels a flea, the base-
15   ball fan, the statistician—
     nor is it valid
       to discriminate against "business documents and

school-books";[1] all these phenomena are important. One must make
    a distinction
  however: when dragged into prominence by half poets, the result
    is not poetry,

---

[1] Moore's note cites the Diary of Tolstoy: "poetry is everything with the exception of business documents and school books."

20   nor till the poets among us can be
           "literalists of
              the imagination" [2]—above
                 insolence and triviality and can present

      for inspection, "imaginary gardens with real toads in them," shall we
           have
25   it. In the meantime, if you demand on the one hand,
           the raw material of poetry in
              all its rawness and
              that which is on the other hand
                 genuine, you are interested in poetry.

A Grave

Man looking into the sea,
taking the view from those who have as much right to it as you have
      to yourself,
it is human nature to stand in the middle of a thing,
but you cannot stand in the middle of this;
 5 the sea has nothing to give but a well excavated grave.
The firs stand in a procession, each with an emerald turkey-foot at the
      top,
reserved as their contours, saying nothing;
repression, however, is not the most obvious characteristic of the sea;
the sea is a collector, quick to return a rapacious look.
10 There are others besides you who have worn that look—
whose expression is no longer a protest; the fish no longer investigate
      them
for their bones have not lasted:
men lower nets, unconscious of the fact that they are desecrating a
      grave,
and row quickly away—the blades of the oars
15 moving together like the feet of water-spiders as if there were no such
      thing as death.
The wrinkles progress among themselves in a phalanx—beautiful
      under networks of foam,
and fade breathlessly while the sea rustles in and out of the seaweed;
the birds swim through the air at top speed, emitting catcalls as
      heretofore—
the tortoise-shell scourges about the feet of the cliffs, in motion be-
      neath them;
20 and the ocean, under the pulsation of lighthouses and noise of bell-
      buoys,

---

[2] From Yeats, *Ideas of Good and Evil.*

advances as usual, looking as if it were not that ocean in which
dropped things are bound to sink—
in which if they turn and twist, it is neither with volition nor consciousness.

The Mind is an Enchanting Thing

is an enchanted thing
      like the glaze on a
katydid-wing
            subdivided by sun
5   till the nettings are legion.
Like Gieseking[1] playing Scarlatti;[2]

like the apteryx-awl [3]
      as a beak, or the
kiwi's rain-shawl
10   of haired feathers, the mind
            feeling its way as though blind,
walks along with its eyes on the ground.

It has memory's ear
      that can hear without
15 having to hear.
            Like the gyroscope's fall,
            truly unequivocal
because trued by regnant certainty,

it is a power of
20   strong enchantment. It
is like the dove-
            neck animated by
            sun; it is memory's eye;
it's conscientious inconsistency.

25 It tears off the veil; tears
            the temptation, the
mist the heart wears,
            from its eyes,—if the heart
            has a face; it takes apart
30 dejection. It's fire in the dove-neck's

---

[1] Walter Gieseking (1895–1956), eminent German pianist.
[2] Domenico Scarlatti (1685–1757), Italian composer of brilliant keyboard sonatas.
[3] A apteryx is a flightless bird with a long, slender beak resembling the shape of an awl.

iridescence; in the
    inconsistencies
of Scarlatti.
       Unconfusion submits
35 its confusion to proof; it's
not a Herod's oath[4] that cannot change.

T. S. ELIOT (1888–1965)

The Love Song of J. Alfred Prufrock

S'io credesse che mia risposta fosse
A persona che mai tornasse al mondo,
Questa fiamma staria senza piu scosse.
Ma perciocche giammai di questo fondo
Non torno vivo alcun, s'i'odo il vero,
Senza tema d'infamia ti rispondo.[1]

Let us go then, you and I,
When the evening is spread out against the sky
Like a patient etherized upon a table;
Let us go, through certain half-deserted streets,
5 The muttering retreats
Of restless nights in one-night cheap hotels
And sawdust restaurants with oyster-shells:
Streets that follow like a tedious argument
Of insidious intent
10 To lead you to an overwhelming question . . .

Oh, do not ask, "What is it?"
Let us go and make our visit.

In the room the women come and go
Talking of Michelangelo.

15 The yellow fog that rubs its back upon the window-panes
The yellow smoke that rubs its muzzle on the window-panes

---

4 See Matthew 2:1–16.

1 "If I thought that my response were given to one who would ever return to the
world, this flame would move no more. But since never from this depth has man
returned alive, if what I hear is true, without fear of infamy I answer thee." In
Dante's *Inferno* these words are addressed to the poet by the spirit of Guido da
Montefeltro.

Licked its tongue into the corners of the evening,
Lingered upon the pools that stand in drains,
Let fall upon its back the soot that falls from chimneys,
20 Slipped by the terrace, made a sudden leap,
And seeing that it was a soft October night,
Curled once about the house, and fell asleep.

And indeed there will be time
For the yellow smoke that slides along the street,
25 Rubbing its back upon the window-panes;
There will be time, there will be time
To prepare a face to meet the faces that you meet;
There will be time to murder and create,
And time for all the works and days of hands
30 That lift and drop a question on your plate;
Time for you and time for me,
And time yet for a hundred indecisions,
And for a hundred visions and revisions,
Before the taking of a toast and tea.

35 In the room the women come and go
Talking of Michelangelo.

And indeed there will be time
To wonder, "Do I dare?" and, "Do I dare?"
Time to turn back and descend the stair,
40 With a bald spot in the middle of my hair—
[They will say: "How his hair is growing thin!"]
My morning coat, my collar mounting firmly to the chin,
My necktie rich and modest, but asserted by a simple pin—
[They will say: "But how his arms and legs are thin!"]
45 Do I dare
Disturb the universe?
In a minute there is time
For decisions and revisions which a minute will reverse.

For I have known them all already, known them all:
50 Have known the evenings, mornings, afternoons,
I have measured out my life with coffee spoons;
I know the voices dying with a dying fall
Beneath the music from a farther room.
    So how should I presume?

55 And I have known the eyes already, known them all—
The eyes that fix you in a formulated phrase,
And when I am formulated, sprawling on a pin,
When I am pinned and wriggling on the wall,
Then how should I begin
60 To spit out all the butt-ends of my days and ways?
 And how should I presume?

And I have known the arms already, known them all—
Arms that are braceleted and white and bare
[But in the lamplight, downed with light brown hair!]
65 Is it perfume from a dress
That makes me so digress?
Arms that lie along a table, or wrap about a shawl.
 And should I then presume?
 And how should I begin?

    . . . . .

70 Shall I say, I have gone at dusk through narrow streets
And watched the smoke that rises from the pipes
Of lonely men in shirt-sleeves, leaning out of windows? . . .

I should have been a pair of ragged claws
Scuttling across the floors of silent seas.

    . . . . .

75 And the afternoon, the evening, sleeps so peacefully!
Smoothed by long fingers,
Asleep . . . tired . . . or it malingers,
Stretched on the floor, here beside you and me.
Should I, after tea and cakes and ices,
80 Have the strength to force the moment to its crisis?
But though I have wept and fasted, wept and prayed,
Though I have seen my head [grown slightly bald] brought in upon a
 platter,
I am no prophet—and here's no great matter;
I have seen the moment of my greatness flicker,
85 And I have seen the eternal Footman hold my coat, and snicker,
And in short, I was afraid.

And would it have been worth it, after all,
After the cups, the marmalade, the tea,
Among the porcelain, among some talk of you and me,
90 Would it have been worth while,

To have bitten off the matter with a smile,
To have squeezed the universe into a ball
To roll it toward some overwhelming question,
To say: "I am Lazarus, come from the dead,
95 Come back to tell you all, I shall tell you all"—
If one, settling a pillow by her head,
    Should say: "That is not what I meant at all.
That is not it, at all."

And would it have been worth it, after all,
100 Would it have been worth while,
After the sunsets and the dooryards and the sprinkled streets,
After the novels, after the teacups, after the skirts that trail along the
    floor—
And this, and so much more?—
It is impossible to say just what I mean!
105 But as if a magic lantern threw the nerves in patterns on a screen:
Would it have been worth while
If one, settling a pillow or throwing off a shawl,
And turning toward the window, should say:
    "That is not it at all,
110   That is not what I meant, at all."

          . . . . .

No! I am not Prince Hamlet, nor was meant to be;
Am an attendant lord, one that will do
To swell a progress, start a scene or two,
Advise the prince; no doubt, an easy tool,
115 Deferential, glad to be of use,
Politic, cautious, and meticulous;
Full of high sentence, but a bit obtuse;
At times, indeed, almost ridiculous—
Almost, at times, the Fool.

120 I grow old . . . I grow old . . .
I shall wear the bottoms of my trousers rolled.

Shall I part my hair behind? Do I dare to eat a peach?
I shall wear white flannel trousers, and walk upon the beach.
I have heard the mermaids singing, each to each.

125 I do not think that they will sing to me.

I have seen them riding seaward on the waves
Combing the white hair of the waves blown back
When the wind blows the water white and black.

We have lingered in the chambers of the sea
130 By sea-girls wreathed with seaweed red and brown
Till human voices wake us, and we drown.

Preludes

1

The winter evening settles down
With smell of steaks in passageways.
Six o'clock.
The burnt-out ends of smoky days.
5 And now a gusty shower wraps
The grimy scraps
Of withered leaves about your feet
And newspapers from vacant lots;
The showers beat
10 On broken blinds and chimney-pots,
And at the corner of the street
A lonely cab-horse steams and stamps.
And then the lighting of the lamps.

2

The morning comes to consciousness
15 Of faint stale smells of beer
From the sawdust-trampled street
With all its muddy feet that press
To early coffee-stands.
With the other masquerades
20 That time resumes,
One thinks of all the hands
That are raising dingy shades
In a thousand furnished rooms.

3

You tossed a blanket from the bed,
25 You lay upon your back, and waited;
You dozed, and watched the night revealing
The thousand sordid images
Of which your soul was constituted;

They flickered against the ceiling.
30 And when all the world came back
And the light crept up between the shutters
And you heard the sparrows in the gutters,
You had such a vision of the street
As the street hardly understands;
35 Sitting along the bed's edge, where
You curled the papers from your hair,
Or clasped the yellow soles of feet
In the palms of both soiled hands.

4

His soul stretched tight across the skies
40 That fade behind a city block,
Or trampled by insistent feet
At four and five and six o'clock;
And short square fingers stuffing pipes,
And evening newspapers, and eyes
45 Assured of certain certainties,
The conscience of a blackened street
Impatient to assume the world.

I am moved by fancies that are curled
Around these images, and cling:
50 The notion of some infinitely gentle
Infinitely suffering thing.

Wipe your hand across your mouth, and laugh;
The worlds revolve like ancient women
Gathering fuel in vacant lots.

Sweeney Among the Nightingales

ὤμοι, πέπληγμαι καιρίαν πληγὴν ἔσω.[1]

Apeneck Sweeney spreads his knees
Letting his arms hang down to laugh,
The zebra stripes along his jaw
Swelling to maculate giraffe.

---

[1] From Aeschylus' Agamemnon: "Oh, I have been struck deep with a deadly blow."

5 The circles of the stormy moon
Slide westward toward the River Plate,[2]
Death and the Raven[3] drift above
And Sweeney guards the hornèd gate.[4]

Gloomy Orion[5] and the Dog[6]
10 Are veiled; and hushed the shrunken seas;
The person in the Spanish cape
Tries to sit on Sweeney's knees

Slips and pulls the table cloth
Overturns a coffee-cup,
15 Reorganized upon the floor
She yawns and draws a stocking up;

The silent man in mocha brown
Sprawls at the window-sill and gapes;
The waiter brings in oranges
20 Bananas figs and hothouse grapes;

The silent vertebrate in brown
Contracts and concentrates, withdraws;
Rachel *née* Rabinovitch
Tears at the grapes with murderous paws;

25 She and the lady in the cape
Are suspect, thought to be in league;
Therefore the man with heavy eyes
Declines the gambit, shows fatigue,

Leaves the room and reappears
30 Outside the window, leaning in,
Branches of wistaria
Circumscribe a golden grin;

---

2 Rio de la Plata in South America.
3 The constellation Corvus.
4 Through the gates of ivory, in Greek mythology, come dreams that are pleasant
but untrue; through the gates of horn, dreams that are unpleasant but true.
5 An equatorial constellation.
6 The dog-star Sirius, near Orion.

The host with someone indistinct
Converses at the door apart,
35 The nightingales are singing near
The Convent of the Sacred Heart,

And sang within the bloody wood
When Agamemnon cried aloud,
And let their liquid siftings fall
40 To stain the stiff dishonored shroud.

Rhapsody on a Windy Night

Twelve o'clock.
Along the reaches of the street
Held in a lunar synthesis,
Whispering lunar incantations
5 Dissolve the floors of memory
And all its clear relations
Its divisions and precisions,
Every street-lamp that I pass
Beats like a fatalistic drum,
10 And through the spaces of the dark
Midnight shakes the memory
As a madman shakes a dead geranium.

Half-past one,
The street-lamp sputtered,
15 The street-lamp muttered,
The street-lamp said, "Regard that woman
Who hesitates toward you in the light of the door
Which opens on her like a grin.
You see the border of her dress
20 Is torn and stained with sand,
And you see the corner of her eye
Twists like a crooked pin."

The memory throws up high and dry
A crowd of twisted things;
25 A twisted branch upon the beach
Eaten smooth, and polished
As if the world gave up
The secret of its skeleton,
Stiff and white.

30 A broken spring in a factory yard,
   Rust that clings to the form that the strength has left
   Hard and curled and ready to snap.

   Half-past two,
   The street-lamp said,
35 "Remark the cat which flattens itself in the gutter,
   Slips out its tongue
   And devours a morsel of rancid butter."
   So the hand of the child, automatic,
   Slipped out and pocketed a toy that was running along the quay.
40 I could see nothing behind that child's eye.
   I have seen eyes in the street
   Trying to peer through lighted shutters,
   And a crab one afternoon in a pool,
   An old crab with barnacles on his back,
45 Gripped the end of a stick which I held him.

   Half-past three,
   The lamp sputtered,
   The lamp muttered in the dark.
   The lamp hummed:
50 "Regard the moon,
   La lune ne garde aucune rancune,[1]
   She winks a feeble eye,
   She smiles into corners.
   She smooths the hair of the grass.
55 The moon has lost her memory.

   A washed-out smallpox cracks her face,
   Her hand twists a paper rose,
   That smells of dust and eau de Cologne,
   She is alone
60 With all the old nocturnal smells
   That cross and cross across her brain."
   The reminiscence comes
   Of sunless dry geraniums
   And dust in crevices,
65 Smells of chestnuts in the streets,
   And female smells in shuttered rooms,
   And cigarettes in corridors
   And cocktail smells in bars.

---

[1] "The moon holds no grudge," a quotation from the French symbolist poet Laforgue.

The lamp said,
70 "Four o'clock,
Here is the number on the door.
Memory!
You have the key,
The little lamp spreads a ring on the stair.
75 Mount.
The bed is open; the tooth-brush hangs on the wall,
Put your shoes at the door, sleep, prepare for life."

The last twist of the knife.

La Figlia Che Piange[1]

O quam te memorem virgo ...[2]

Stand on the highest pavement of the stair—
Lean on a garden urn—
Weave, weave the sunlight in your hair—
Clasp your flowers to you with a pained surprise—
5 Fling them to the ground and turn
With a fugitive resentment in your eyes:
But weave, weave the sunlight in your hair.

So I would have had him leave,
So I would have had her stand and grieve,
10 So he would have left
As the soul leaves the body torn and bruised,
As the mind deserts the body it has used.
I should find
Some way incomparably light and deft,
15 Some way we both should understand,
Simple and faithless as a smile and shake of the hand.

She turned away, but with the autumn weather
Compelled my imagination many days,
Many days and many hours:
20 Her hair over her arms and her arms full of flowers.
And I wonder how they should have been together!
I should have lost a gesture and a pose.
Sometimes these cogitations still amaze
The troubled midnight and the noon's repose.

---

[1] "The girl who weeps."
[2] Aeneas' words to Venus in disguise: "O maiden how shall I recall you?"

Marina[1]

Quis hic locus, quae regio, quae mundi plaga? [2]

What seas what shores what gray rocks and what islands
What water lapping the bow
And scent of pine and the woodthrush singing through the fog
What images return
5 O my daughter.

Those who sharpen the tooth of the dog, meaning
Death
Those who glitter with the glory of the hummingbird, meaning
Death
10 Those who sit in the sty of contentment, meaning
Death
Those who suffer the ecstasy of the animals, meaning
Death

Are become unsubstantial, reduced by a wind,
15 A breath of pine, and the woodsong fog
By this grace dissolved in place
What is this face, less clear and clearer
The pulse in the arm, less strong and stronger—
Given or lent? more distant than stars and nearer than the eye

20 Whispers and small laughter between leaves and hurrying feet
Under sleep, where all the waters meet.

Bowsprit cracked with ice and paint cracked with heat.
I made this, I have forgotten
And remember.
25 The rigging weak and the canvas rotten
Between one June and another September.
Made this unknowing, half conscious, unknown, my own.
The garboard strake[3] leaks, the seams need calking.
This form, this face, this life

---

1 The daughter of Pericles and Thaisa, in Shakespeare's *Pericles, Prince of Tyre.*
Marina, born at sea, is later lost to her father. He finds her after many years
have passed, a young woman whose virtuous character has triumphed over
numerous perils.
2 From Seneca's tragedy *Hercules Furens*: "What place is this, what region, what
shore of the world?"
3 The first line of planking laid upon a ship's keel.

³⁰ Living to live in a world of time beyond me; let me
Resign my life for this life, my speech for that unspoken,
The awakened, lips parted, the hope, the new ships.

What seas what shores what granite islands towards my timbers
And woodthrush calling through the fog
35 My daughter.

Journey of the Magi

"A cold coming we had of it,
Just the worst time of the year
For a journey, and such a long journey:
The ways deep and the weather sharp,
5 The very dead of winter." [1]
And the camels galled, sore-footed, refractory,
Lying down in the melting snow.
There were times we regretted
The summer palaces on slopes, the terraces,
10 And the silken girls bringing sherbet.
Then the camel men cursing and grumbling
And running away, and wanting their liquor and women,
And the night-fires going out, and the lack of shelters,
And the cities hostile and the towns unfriendly
15 And the villages dirty and charging high prices:
A hard time we had of it.
At the end we preferred to travel all night,
Sleeping in snatches,
With the voices singing in our ears, saying
20 That this was all folly.
Then at dawn we came down to a temperate valley,
Wet, below the snow line, smelling of vegetation;
With a running stream and a water-mill beating the darkness,
And three trees on the low sky,
25 And an old white horse galloped away in the meadow.
Then we came to a tavern with vine-leaves over the lintel,
Six hands at an open door dicing for pieces of silver,
And feet kicking the empty wine-skins.
But there was no information, and so we continued
30 And arrived at evening, not a moment too soon
Finding the place; it was (you may say) satisfactory.

---

[1] Adapted from a 17th-century sermon of Lancelot Andrewes.

All this was a long time ago, I remember,
And I would do it again, but set down
This set down
35 This: were we led all that way for
Birth or Death? There was a Birth, certainly,
We had evidence and no doubt. I had seen birth and death,
But had thought they were different; this Birth was
Hard and bitter agony for us, like Death, our death.
40 We returned to our places, these Kingdoms,
But no longer at ease here, in the old dispensation,
With an alien people clutching their gods.
I should be glad of another death.

6

∿ A BRIEF HISTORY

When Archibald MacLeish writes in *Ars Poetica* that a poem "must not mean/but be," he is asserting in one more way the canon of the imagist movement. E. E. Cummings adds to direct imagery an easy, offhanded American diction and a lyrical typographical play: lower-casing all words, dividing lines in unexpected places. Dylan Thomas, like Marianne Moore before him, explores the possibilities of syllabic verse; others, like Robert Graves, Philip Larkin, and Yvor Winters maintain a commitment to traditional verse. W. H. Auden enriches traditional forms with ingenious modern variations. The spontaneity and technical iconoclasm of Whitman's verse surfaces in the lines of Ferlinghetti and Ginsberg. Both compose poems seemingly out of the raw experience of the street, offering little if any acknowledgment to the tradition of formal verse—although in *A Supermarket in California,* Ginsberg makes allusions to classical mythology as easily as any classical poet would do. Many poets experiment at various times with accentual, syllabic, or accentual-syllabic verse. Poets like Richard Wilbur and Thom Gunn remain basically formal, serious about traditional demands. Robert Lowell and Theodore Roethke at various periods explore formal verse and the looser free verse forms. John Berryman raises diction and syntax almost to the level of a new rhetoric. An amalgam of many styles exists simultaneously. One of the usual characteristics of modern poetry remains a concern for clarity of image—in both formal and informal verse—and some-times a confessional lyricism in which the poet becomes obsessed with self-exploration. The social concerns of some writers create a verse where the message or the sincerity of the experience is expected to take precedence over any technical apparatus, such as the brilliance of a metaphor or the deliberate control of language. Meanwhile modern poetry is being fed from new sources and strengths: the vision and vocabulary of a rising generation of black poets, a surge of poetry by women questioning conventional wisdom.

JOHN CROWE RANSOM (1888–1974)

Bells for John Whiteside's Daughter

There was such speed in her little body,
And such lightness in her footfall,
It is no wonder her brown study
Astonishes us all.

5 Her wars were bruited in our high window.
We looked among orchard trees and beyond
Where she took arms against her shadow,
Or harried unto the pond

The lazy geese, like a snow cloud
10 Dripping their snow on the green grass,
Tricking and stopping, sleepy and proud,
Who cried in goose, Alas,

For the tireless heart within the little
Lady with rod that made them rise
15 From their noon apple-dreams and scuttle
Goose-fashion under the skies!

But now go the bells, and we are ready,
In one house we are sternly stopped
To say we are vexed at her brown study,
20 Lying so primly propped.

Old Mansion

As an intruder I trudged with careful innocence
To mask in decency a meddlesome stare,
Passing the old house often on its eminence,
Exhaling my foreign weed on its weighted air.

5 Here age seemed newly imaged for the historian
After his monstrous châteaux on the Loire,
A beauty not for depicting by old vulgarian
Reiterations which gentle readers abhor.

Each time of seeing I absorbed some other feature
10 Of a house whose legend could in no wise be brief
Nor ignoble, for it expired as sweetly as Nature,
With her tinge of oxidation on autumn leaf.

It was a Southern manor. One need hardly imagine
Towers, white monoliths, or even ivied walls;
15 But sufficient state if its peacock *was* a pigeon;
Where no courts held, but grave rites and funerals.

Indeed, not distant, possibly not external
To the property, were tombstones, where the catafalque
Had carried their dead; and projected a note too charnel
20 But for the honeysuckle on its intricate stalk.

Stability was the character of its rectangle
Whose line was seen in part and guessed in part
Through trees. Decay was the tone of old brick and shingle.
Green blinds dragging frightened the watchful heart

25 To assert: "Your mansion, long and richly inhabited,
Its exits and entrances suiting the children of man,
Will not forever be thus, O man, exhibited,
And one had best hurry to enter it if one can."

And at last with my happier angel's own temerity,
30 Did I clang their brazen knocker against the door,
To beg their dole of a look, in simple charity,
Or crumbs of history dropping from their great store.

But it came to nothing—and may so gross denial,
Which has been deplored duly with a beating of the breast,
35 Never shorten the tired historian, loyal
To acknowledge defeat and discover a new quest—

The old mistress was ill, and sent my dismissal
By one even more wrappered and lean and dark
Than that warped concierge and imperturbable vassal
40 Who bids you begone from her master's Gothic park.

Emphatically, the old house crumbled; the ruins
Would litter, as already the leaves, this petted sward;
And no annalist went in to the lord or the peons;
The antiquary would finger the bits of shard.

45 But on retreating I saw myself in the token,
How loving from my foreign weed the feather curled
On the languid air; and I went with courage shaken
To dip, alas, into some unseemlier world.

Piazza Piece

—I am a gentleman in a dustcoat trying
To make you hear. Your ears are soft and small
And listen to an old man not at all,
They want the young men's whispering and sighing.
5 But see the roses on your trellis dying
And hear the spectral singing of the moon;
For I must have my lovely lady soon,
I am a gentleman in a dustcoat trying.

—I am a lady young in beauty waiting
10 Until my truelove comes, and then we kiss.
But what grey man among the vines is this
Whose words are dry and faint as in a dream?
Back from my trellis, Sir, before I scream!
I am a lady young in beauty waiting.

Spectral Lovers

By night they haunted a thicket of April mist,
Out of that black ground suddenly come to birth,
Else angels lost in each other and fallen on earth.
Lovers they knew they were, but why unclasped, unkissed?
5 Why should two lovers be frozen apart in fear?
And yet they were, they were.

Over the shredding of an April blossom
Scarcely her fingers touched him, quick with care,
Yet of evasions even she made a snare.
10 The heart was bold that clanged within her bosom,
The moment perfect, the time stopped for them,
Still her face turned from him.

Strong were the batteries of the April night
And the stealthy emanations of the field;
15 Should the walls of her prison undefended yield
And open her treasure to the first clamorous knight?
"This is the mad moon, and shall I surrender all?
If he but ask it I shall."

And gesturing largely to the moon of Easter,
20 Mincing his steps and swishing the jubilant grass,
Beheading some field-flowers that had come to pass,

He had reduced his tributaries faster
Had not considerations pinched his heart
Unfitly for his art.

25 "Do I reel with the sap of April like a drunkard?
Blessed is he that taketh this richest of cities:
But it is so stainless the sack were a thousand pities.
This is that marble fortress not to be conquered,
Lest its white peace in the black flame turn to tinder
30 And an unutterable cinder."

They passed me once in April, in the mist,
No other season is it when one walks and discovers
Two tall and wandering, like spectral lovers,
White in the season's moon-gold and amethyst,
35 Who touch quick fingers fluttering like a bird
Whose songs shall never be heard.

EDNA ST. VINCENT MILLAY (1892–1950)

First Fig

My candle burns at both ends;
    It will not last the night;
But ah, my foes, and oh, my friends—
    It gives a lovely light!

Love Is Not All: It Is Not Meat nor Drink

Love is not all; it is not meat nor drink
Nor slumber nor a roof against the rain;
Nor yet a floating spar to men that sink
And rise and sink and rise and sink again;
5 Love can not fill the thickened lung with breath,
Nor clean the blood, nor set the fractured bone;
Yet many a man is making friends with death
Even as I speak, for lack of love alone.
It well may be that in a difficult hour,
10 Pinned down by pain and moaning for release,
Or nagged by want past resolution's power,
I might be driven to sell your love for peace,
Or trade the memory of this night for food.
It well may be. I do not think I would.

What Lips My Lips Have Kissed, and Where, and Why

What lips my lips have kissed, and where, and why,
I have forgotten, and what arms have lain
Under my head till morning; but the rain
Is full of ghosts tonight, that tap and sigh
5 Upon the glass and listen for reply,
And in my heart there stirs a quiet pain
For unremembered lads that not again
Will turn to me at midnight with a cry.
Thus in the winter stands the lonely tree,
10 Nor knows what birds have vanished one by one,
Yet knows its boughs more silent than before:
I cannot say what loves have come and gone,
I only know that summer sang in me
A little while, that in me sings no more.

ARCHIBALD MacLEISH (1892–1982)

Ars Poetica

A poem should be palpable and mute
As a globed fruit,

Dumb
As old medallions to the thumb,

5 Silent as the sleeve-worn stone
Of casement ledges where the moss has grown—

A poem should be wordless
As the flight of birds.

A poem should be motionless in time
10 As the moon climbs,

Leaving, as the moon releases
Twig by twig the night-entangled trees,

Leaving, as the moon behind the winter leaves
Memory by memory the mind—

15 A poem should be motionless in time
As the moon climbs.

A poem should be equal to:
Not true.

For all the history of grief
20 An empty doorway and a maple leaf.

For love
The leaning grasses and two lights above the sea—

A poem should not mean
But be.

You, Andrew Marvell [1]

And here face down beneath the sun
And here upon earth's noonward height
To feel the always coming on
The always rising of the night:

5 To feel creep up the curving east
The earthy chill of dusk and slow
Upon those under lands the vast
And ever climbing shadow grow

And strange at Ecbatan[2] the trees
10 Take leaf by leaf the evening strange
The flooding dark about their knees
The mountains over Persia change

And now at Kermanshah[3] the gate
Dark empty and the withered grass
15 And through the twilight now the late
Few travelers in the westward pass

And Baghdad darken and the bridge
Across the silent river gone
And through Arabia the edge
20 Of evening widen and steal on

And deepen on Palmyra's[4] street
The wheel rut in the ruined stone

---

1 The allusion is to Marvell's "To His Coy Mistress."
2 Ecbatana, ancient Persian city, modern Hamadan.
3 City in western Iran.
4 Ancient city in Syria.

And Lebanon fade out and Crete
High through the clouds and overblown

25 And over Sicily the air
Still flashing with the landward gulls
And loom and slowly disappear
The sails above the shadowy hulls

And Spain go under and the shore
30 Of Africa the gilded sand
And evening vanish and no more
The low pale light across that land

Nor now the long light on the sea:

And here face downward in the sun
35 To feel how swift how secretly
The shadow of the night comes on . . .

WILFRED OWEN (1893–1918)

Strange Meeting

It seemed that out of battle I escaped
Down some profound dull tunnel, long since scooped
Through granites which titanic wars had groined.
Yet also there encumbered sleepers groaned,
5 Too fast in thought or death to be bestirred.
Then, as I probed them, one sprang up, and stared
With piteous recognition in fixed eyes,
Lifting distressful hands as if to bless.
And by his smile, I knew that sullen hall,
10 By his dead smile I knew we stood in Hell.
With a thousand pains that vision's face was grained;
Yet no blood reached there from the upper ground,
And no guns thumped, or down the flues made moan.
"Strange friend," I said, "here is no cause to mourn."
15 "None," said the other, "save the undone years,
The hopelessness. Whatever hope is yours,
Was my life also; I went hunting wild
After the wildest beauty in the world,
Which lies not calm in eyes, or braided hair,
20 But mocks the steady running of the hour,
And if it grieves, grieves richlier than here.

For of my glee might many men have laughed,
And of my weeping something had been left,
Which must die now. I mean the truth untold,
25 The pity of war, the pity war distilled.
Now men will go content with what we spoiled,
Or, discontent, boil bloody, and be spilled.
They will be swift with swiftness of the tigress.
None will break ranks, though nations trek from progress.
30 Courage was mine, and I had mystery,
Wisdom was mine, and I had mastery:
To miss the march of this retreating world
Into vain citadels that are not walled.
Then, when much blood had clogged their chariot-wheels,
35 I would go up and wash them from sweet wells,
Even with truths that lie too deep for taint.
I would have poured my spirit without stint
But not through wounds; not on the cess of war.
Foreheads of men have bled where no wounds were.
40 I am the enemy you killed, my friend.
I knew you in this dark: for so you frowned
Yesterday through me as you jabbed and killed.
I parried; but my hands were loath and cold.
Let us sleep now. . . ."

Dulce et Decorum Est[1]

Bent double, like old beggars under sacks,
Knock-kneed, coughing like hags, we cursed through sludge,
Till on the haunting flares we turned our backs
And towards our distant rest began to trudge.
5 Men marched asleep. Many had lost their boots
But limped on, blood-shod. All went lame; all blind;
Drunk with fatigue; deaf even to the hoots
Of tired, outstripped Five-Nines that dropped behind.

Gas! Gas! Quick, boys!—An ecstasy of fumbling,
10 Fitting the clumsy helmets just in time;
But someone still was yelling out and stumbling
And flound'ring like a man in fire or lime . . .
Dim, through the misty panes and thick green light,
As under a green sea, I saw him drowning.

---

1 Horace: "Dulce et decorum est pro patria mori" ("It is sweet and fitting to die for one's country").

¹⁵ In all my dreams, before my helpless sight,
He plunges at me, guttering, choking, drowning.

If in some smothering dreams you too could pace
Behind the wagon that we flung him in,
And watch the white eyes writhing in his face,
²⁰ His hanging face, like a devil's sick of sin;
If you could hear, at every jolt, the blood
Come gargling from the froth-corrupted lungs,
Obscene as cancer, bitter as the cud
Of vile, incurable sores on innocent tongues,—
²⁵ My friend, you would not tell with such high zest
To children ardent for some desperate glory,
The old Lie: Dulce et decorum est
Pro patria mori.

Anthem for Doomed Youth

What passing-bells for these who die as cattle?
   Only the monstrous anger of the guns.
   Only the stuttering rifles' rapid rattle
Can patter out their hasty orisons.
⁵ No mockeries now for them; no prayers nor bells,
   Nor any voice of mourning save the choirs—
The shrill, demented choirs of wailing shells;
   And bugles calling for them from sad shires.

What candles may be held to speed them all?
¹⁰   Not in the hands of boys, but in their eyes
Shall shine the holy glimmers of good-byes.
   The pallor of girls' brows shall be their pall;
Their flowers the tenderness of patient minds,
And each slow dusk a drawing-down of blinds.

DOROTHY PARKER (1893–1967)

Résumé

Razors pain you;
Rivers are damp;
Acids stain you;
And drugs cause cramp.
⁵ Guns aren't lawful;
Nooses give;
Gas smells awful;
You might as well live.

E. E. CUMMINGS (1894–1963)

the Cambridge ladies who live in furnished souls

the Cambridge ladies who live in furnished souls
are unbeautiful and have comfortable minds
(also, with the church's protestant blessings
daughters, unscented shapeless spirited)
5 they believe in Christ and Longfellow, both dead,
are invariably interested in so many things—
at the present writing one still finds
delighted fingers knitting for the is it Poles?
perhaps. While permanent faces coyly bandy
10 scandal of Mrs. N and Professor D
. . . . the Cambridge ladies do not care, above
Cambridge if sometimes in its box of
sky lavender and cornerless, the
moon rattles like a fragment of angry candy

may i feel said he

may i feel said he
(i'll squeal said she
just once said he)
it's fun said she

5 (may i touch said he
how much said she
a lot said he)
why not said she

(let's go said he
10 not too far said she
what's too far said he
where you are said she)

may i stay said he
(which way said she
15 like this said he
if you kiss said she

may i move said he
is it love said she)
if you're willing said he
20 (but you're killing said she

but it's life said he
but your wife said she
now said he)
ow said she

25 (tiptop said he
don't stop said she
oh no said he)
go slow said she

(cccome?said he
30 ummm said she)
you're divine!said he
(you are Mine said she)

All in green went my love riding

All in green went my love riding
on a great horse of gold
into the silver dawn.

four lean hounds crouched low and smiling
5 the merry deer ran before.

Fleeter be they than dappled dreams
the swift sweet deer
the red rare deer.

Four red roebuck at a white water
10 the cruel bugle sang before.

Horn at hip went my love riding
riding the echo down
into the silver dawn.

four lean hounds crouched low and smiling
15 the level meadows ran before.

Softer be they than slippered sleep
the lean lithe deer
the fleet flown deer.

Four fleet does at a gold valley
20 the famished arrow sang before.

Bow at belt went my love riding
riding the mountain down
into the silver dawn.

four lean hounds crouched low and smiling
25 the sheer peaks ran before.

Paler be they than daunting death
the sleek slim deer
the tall tense deer.

Four tall stags at a green mountain
30 the lucky hunter sang before.

All in green went my love riding
on a great horse of gold
into the silver dawn.

four lean hounds crouched low and smiling
35 my heart fell dead before.

in Just-

in Just-
spring   when the world is mud-
luscious the little
lame balloonman

5 whistles   far   and wee

and eddieandbill come
running from marbles and
piracies and it's
spring

10 when the world is puddle-wonderful

the queer
old balloonman whistles
far   and   wee
and bettyandisbel come dancing

15 from hop-scotch and jump-rope and

it's
spring
and
    the

20   goat-footed
balloonMan   whistles
far
and
wee

Buffalo Bill 's

Buffalo Bill 's
defunct
      who used to
      ride a watersmooth-silver
5   stallion
and break onetwothreefourfive pigeonsjustlikethat
                                  Jesus

he was a handsome man
                    and what i want to know is
10 how do you like your blueeyed boy
Mister Death

my sweet old etcetera

my sweet old etcetera
aunt lucy during the recent

war could and what
is more did tell you just
5 what everybody was fighting

for,
my sister

isabel created hundreds
(and
10 hundreds) of socks not to
mention shirts fleaproof earwarmers

etcetera wristers etcetera, my
mother hoped that

i would die etcetera
15 bravely of course my father used
to become hoarse talking about how it was
a privilege and if only he
could meanwhile my

self etcetera lay quietly
20 in the deep mud et

cetera
(dreaming,
et
    cetera, of
25 Your smile
eyes knees and of your Etcetera)

i sing of Olaf glad and big

i sing of Olaf glad and big
whose warmest heart recoiled at war:
a conscientious object-or

his wellbelovèd colonel(trig
 5 westpointer most succinctly bred)
took erring Olaf soon in hand;
but—though an host of overjoyed
noncoms(first knocking on the head
him)do through icy waters roll
10 that helplessness which others stroke
with brushes recently employed
anent this muddy toiletbowl,
while kindred intellects evoke
allegiance per blunt instruments—
15 Olaf(being to all intents
a corpse and wanting any rag
upon what God unto him gave)
responds, without getting annoyed
"I will not kiss your f.ing flag"

20 straightway the silver bird looked grave
(departing hurriedly to shave)

but—though all kinds of officers
(a yearning nation's blueeyed pride)

their passive prey did kick and curse
25 until for wear their clarion
voices and boots were much the worse,
and egged the firstclassprivates on
his rectum wickedly to tease
by means of skilfully applied
30 bayonets roasted hot with heat—
Olaf(upon what were once knees)
does almost ceaselessly repeat
"there is some s. I will not eat"

our president,being of which
35 assertions duly notified
threw the yellowsonofabitch
into a dungeon,where he died

Christ(of His mercy infinite)
i pray to see;and Olaf,too

40 preponderatingly because
unless statistics lie he was
more brave than me:more blond than you.

ROBERT GRAVES (1895–1985)

Down, Wanton, Down!

Down, wanton, down! Have you no shame
That at the whisper of Love's name,
Or Beauty's, presto! up you raise
Your angry head and stand at gaze?

5 Poor bombard-captain, sworn to reach
The ravelin and effect a breach—
Indifferent what you storm or why,
So be that in the breach you die!

Love may be blind, but Love at least
10 Knows what is man and what mere beast;
Or Beauty wayward, but requires
More delicacy from her squires.

Tell me, my witless, whose one boast
Could be your staunchness at the post,

15 When were you made a man of parts
  To think fine and profess the arts?

  Will many-gifted Beauty come
  Bowing to your bald rule of thumb,
  Or Love swear loyalty to your crown?
20 Be gone, have done! Down, wanton, down!

The Villagers and Death

  The Rector's pallid neighbor at The Firs,
  Death, did not flurry the parishioners.
  Yet from a weight of superstitious fears
  Each tried to lengthen his own term of years.
5 He was congratulated who combined
  Toughness of flesh and weakness of the mind
  In consequential rosiness of face.
  This dull and not ill-mannered populace
  Pulled off their caps to Death, as they slouched by,
10 But rumored him both atheist and spy.
  All vowed to outlast him (though none ever did)
  And hear the earth drum on his coffin-lid.
  Their groans and whispers down the village street
  Soon soured his nature, which was never sweet.

LOUISE BOGAN (1897–1970)

The Crossed Apple

  I've come to give you fruit from out my orchard,
  Of wide report.
  I have trees there that bear me many apples
  Of every sort:

5 Clear, streakèd; red and russet; green and golden;
  Sour and sweet.
  This apple's from a tree yet unbeholden,
  Where two kinds meet,—

  So that this side is red without a dapple,
10 And this side's hue
  Is clear and snowy. It's a lovely apple.
  It is for you.

Within are five black pips as big as peas,
As you will find,
15 Potent to breed you five great apple trees
Of varying kind:

To breed you wood for fire, leaves for shade,
Apples for sauce.
Oh, this is a good apple for a maid,
20 It is a cross,

Fine on the finer, so the flesh is tight,
And grained like silk.
Sweet Burning gave the red side, and the white
Is Meadow Milk.

25 Eat it; and you will taste more than the fruit:
The blossom, too,
The sun, the air, the darkness at the root,
The rain, the dew,

The earth we came to, and the time we flee,
30 The fire and the breast.
I claim the white part, maiden, that's for me.
You take the rest.

The Dragonfly

You are made of almost nothing
But of enough
To be great eyes
And diaphanous double vans;
5 To be ceaseless movement,
Unending hunger
Grappling love.

Link between water and air,
Earth repels you.
10 Light touches you only to shift into iridescence
Upon your body and wings.

Twice-born, predator,
You split into the heat.
Swift beyond calculation or capture
15 You dart into the shadow
Which consumes you.

You rocket into the day.
But at last, when the wind flattens the grasses,
For you, the design and purpose stop.

20 And you fall
With the other husks of summer.

HART CRANE (1899–1932)

My Grandmother's Love Letters

There are no stars to-night
But those of memory.
Yet how much room for memory there is
In the loose girdle of soft rain.

5 There is even room enough
For the letters of my mother's mother,
Elizabeth,
That have been pressed so long
Into a corner of the roof
10 That they are brown and soft,
And liable to melt as snow.

Over the greatness of such space
Steps must be gentle.
It is all hung by an invisible white hair.
15 It trembles as birch limbs webbing the air.

And I ask myself:

"Are your fingers long enough to play
Old keys that are but echoes:
Is the silence strong enough
20 To carry back the music to its source
And back to you again
As though to her?"

Yet I would lead my grandmother by the hand
Through much of what she would not understand;
25 And so I stumble. And the rain continues on the roof
With such a sound of gently pitying laughter.

Proem: To Brooklyn Bridge

How many dawns, chill from his rippling rest
The seagull's wings shall dip and pivot him,
Shedding white rings of tumult, building high
Over the chained bay waters Liberty—

5 Then, with inviolate curve, forsake our eyes
As apparitional as sails that cross
Some page of figures to be filed away;
—Till elevators drop us from our day . . .

I think of cinemas, panoramic sleights
10 With multitudes bent toward some flashing scene
Never disclosed, but hastened to again,
Foretold to other eyes on the same screen;

And Thee, across the harbor, silver-paced
As though the sun took steps of thee, yet left
15 Some motion ever unspent in thy stride,—
Implicitly thy freedom staying thee!

Out of some subway scuttle, cell or loft
A bedlamite speeds to thy parapets,
Tilting there momently, shrill shirt ballooning,
20 A jest falls from the speechless caravan.

Down Wall, from girder into street noon leaks,
A rip-tooth of the sky's acetylene;
All afternoon the cloud-flown derricks turn . . .
Thy cables breathe the North Atlantic still.

25 And obscure as that heaven of the Jews,
Thy guerdon . . . Accolade thou dost bestow
Of anonymity time cannot raise;
Vibrant reprieve and pardon thou dost show.

O harp and altar, of the fury fused,
30 (How could mere toil align thy choiring strings!)
Terrific threshold of the prophet's pledge,
Prayer of pariah, and the lover's cry,—

Again the traffic lights that skim thy swift
Unfractioned idiom, immaculate sigh of stars,
35 Beading thy path—condense eternity:
And we have seen night lifted in thine arms.

Under thy shadow by the piers I waited;
Only in darkness is thy shadow clear.
The City's fiery parcels all undone,
40 Already snow submerges an iron year . . .

O Sleepless as the river under thee,
Vaulting the sea, the prairies' dreaming sod,
Unto us lowliest sometime sweep, descend
And of the curveship lend a myth to God.

ALLEN TATE (1899–1979)

Ode to the Confederate Dead

Row after row with strict impunity
The headstones yield their names to the element,
The wind whirrs without recollection;
In the riven troughs the splayed leaves
5 Pile up, of nature the casual sacrament
To the seasonal eternity of death;
Then driven by the fierce scrutiny
Of heaven to their election in the vast breath,
They sough the rumor of mortality.

10 Autumn is desolation in the plot
Of a thousand acres where these memories grow
From the inexhaustible bodies that are not
Dead, but feed the grass row after rich row.
Think of the autumns that have come and gone!
15 Ambitious November with the humors of the year,
With a particular zeal for every slab,
Staining the uncomfortable angels that rot
On the slabs, a wing chipped here, an arm there:
The brute curiosity of an angel's stare
20 Turns you, like them, to stone,
Transforms the heaving air
Till plunged to a heavier world below

You shift your sea-space blindly
Heaving, turning like the blind crab.

25   Dazed by the wind, only the wind
The leaves flying, plunge

You know who have waited by the wall
The twilight certainty of an animal,
Those midnight restitutions of the blood
30 You know—the immitigable pines, the smoky frieze
Of the sky, the sudden call: you know the rage,
The cold pool left by the mounting flood,
Of muted Zeno and Parmenides.[1]
You who have waited for the angry resolution
35 Of those desires that should be yours tomorrow,
You know the unimportant shrift of death
And praise the vision
And praise the arrogant circumstance
Of those who fall
40 Rank upon rank, hurried beyond decision—
Here by the sagging gate, stopped by the wall.

Seeing, seeing only the leaves
Flying, plunge and expire

Turn your eyes to the immoderate past,
45 Turn to the inscrutable infantry rising
Demons out of the earth—they will not last.
Stonewall, Stonewall, and the sunken fields of hemp,
Shiloh, Antietam, Malvern Hill, Bull Run.
Lost in that orient of the thick and fast
50 You will curse the setting sun.

Cursing only the leaves crying
Like an old man in a storm

You hear the shout, the crazy hemlocks point
With troubled fingers to the silence which
55 Smothers you, a mummy, in time.

---

[1] Zeno and Parmenides: Greek philosophers of the Eleatic School, who held that
change is illusion.

                    The hound bitch
Toothless and dying, in a musty cellar
Hears the wind only.

                    Now that the salt of their blood
60 Stiffens the saltier oblivion of the sea,
Seals the malignant purity of the flood,
What shall we who count our days and bow
Our heads with a commemorial woe
In the ribboned coats of grim felicity,
65 What shall we say of the bones, unclean,
Whose verdurous anonymity will grow?

The ragged arms, the ragged heads and eyes
Lost in these acres of the insane green?
The gray lean spiders come, they come and go;
70 In a tangle of willows without light
The singular screech-owl's tight
Invisible lyric seeds the mind
With the furious murmur of their chivalry.

                    We shall say only the leaves
75   Flying, plunge and expire

We shall say only the leaves whispering
In the improbable mist of nightfall
That flies on multiple wing:
Night is the beginning and the end
80 And in between the ends of distraction
Waits mute speculation, the patient curse
That stones the eyes, or like the jaguar leaps
For his own image in a jungle pool, his victim.

What shall we say who have knowledge
85 Carried to the heart? Shall we take the act
To the grave? Shall we, more hopeful, set up the grave
In the house? The ravenous grave?

                    Leave now
The shut gate and the decomposing wall:
90 The gentle serpent, green in the mulberry bush,
Riots with his tongue through the hush—
Sentinel of the grave who counts us all!

JANET LEWIS (1899–   )

Girl Help

Mild and slow and young,
She moves about the room,
And stirs the summer dust
With her wide broom.

5 In the warm, lofted air,
Soft lips together pressed,
Soft wispy hair,
She stops to rest.

And stops to breathe,
10 Amid the summer hum,
The great white lilac bloom
Scented with days to come.

YVOR WINTERS (1900–1968)

The Slow Pacific Swell

Far out of sight forever stands the sea,
Bounding the land with pale tranquillity.
When a small child, I watched it from a hill
At thirty miles or more. The vision still
5 Lies in the eye, soft blue and far away;
The rain has washed the dust from April day;
Paint-brush and lupine lie against the ground;
The wind above the hill-top has the sound
Of distant water in unbroken sky;
10 Dark and precise the little steamers ply—
Firm in direction they seem not to stir.
That is illusion. The artificer
Of quiet, distance holds me in a vise
And holds the ocean steady to my eyes.

15 Once when I rounded Flattery, the sea
Hove its loose weight like sand to tangle me
Upon the washing deck, to crush the hull;
Subsiding, dragged flesh at the bone. The skull
Felt the retreating wash of dreaming hair.
20 Half drenched in dissolution, I lay bare.

I scarcely pulled myself erect; I came
Back slowly, slowly knew myself the same.
That was the ocean. From the ship we saw
Gray whales for miles: the long sweep of the jaw,
25 The blunt head plunging clean above the wave.
And one rose in a tent of sea and gave
A darkening shudder; water fell away;
The whale stood shining, and then sank in spray.

A landsman, I. The sea is but a sound.
30 I would be near it on a sandy mound,
And hear the steady rushing of the deep
While I lay stinging in the sand with sleep.
I have lived inland long. The land is numb.
It stands beneath the feet, and one may come
35 Walking securely, till the sea extends
Its limber margin, and precision ends.
By night a chaos of commingling power,
The whole Pacific hovers hour by hour.
The slow Pacific swell stirs on the sand,
40 Sleeping to sink away, withdrawing land,
Heaving and wrinkled in the moon, and blind;
Or gathers seaward, ebbing out of mind.

To the Moon

Goddess of poetry,
Maiden of icy stone
With no anatomy,
Between us two alone
5 Your light falls thin and sure
On all that I propound.

Your service I have found
To be no sinecure;
For I must still inure
10 My words to what I find,
Though it should leave me blind
Ere I discover how.

What brings me here? Old age.
Here is the written page.
15 What is your pleasure now?

At the San Francisco Airport

To my daughter, 1954

This is the terminal: the light
Gives perfect vision, false and hard;
The metal glitters, deep and bright.
Great planes are waiting in the yard—
5 They are already in the night.

And you are here beside me, small,
Contained and fragile, and intent
On things that I but half recall—
Yet going whither you are bent.
10 I am the past, and that is all.

But you and I in part are one:
The frightened brain, the nervous will,
The knowledge of what must be done,
The passion to acquire the skill
15 To face that which you dare not shun.

The rain of matter upon sense
Destroys me momently. The score:
There comes what will come. The expense
Is what one thought, and something more—
20 One's being and intelligence.

This is the terminal, the break.
Beyond this point, on lines of air,
You take the way that you must take;
And I remain in light and stare—
25 In light, and nothing else, awake.

ROBERT FRANCIS (1901–   )

Catch

Two boys uncoached are tossing a poem together,
Overhand, underhand, backhand, sleight of hand, every hand,
Teasing with attitudes, latitudes, interludes, altitudes,
High, make him fly off the ground for it, low, make him stoop,
5 Make him scoop it up, make him as-almost-as-possible miss it,
Fast, let him sting from it, now, now fool him slowly,
Anything, everything tricky, risky, nonchalant,

Anything under the sun to outwit the prosy,
Over the tree and the long sweet cadence down,
10 Over his head, make him scramble to pick up the meaning,
And now, like a posy, a pretty one plump in his hands.

STEVIE SMITH (1902–1972)

Not Waving but Drowning

Nobody heard him, the dead man,
But still he lay moaning:
I was much further out than you thought
And not waving but drowning.

5 Poor chap, he always loved larking
And now he's dead
It must have been too cold for him his heart gave way,
They said.

Oh, no no no, it was too cold always
10 (Still the dead one lay moaning)
I was much too far out all my life
And not waving but drowning.

KENNETH FEARING (1902–1961)

Dirge

1–2–3 was the number he played but today the number came 3–2–1;
Bought his Carbide at 30 and it went to 29; had the favorite at
   Bowie but the track was slow—

O executive type, would you like to drive a floating-power, knee-
   action, silk-upholstered six? Wed a Hollywood star? Shoot the
   course in 58? Draw to the ace, king, jack?

O fellow with a will who won't take no, watch out for three cigarettes on the same, single match; O democratic voter born in
   August under Mars, beware of liquidated rails—

5 Denouement to denouement, he took a personal pride in the certain,
   certain way he lived his own, private life,
But nevertheless, they shut off his gas; nevertheless, the bank fore-
   closed; nevertheless, the landlord called; nevertheless, the radio
   broke,

And twelve o'clock arrived just once too often,
Just the same he wore one gray tweed suit, bought one straw hat,
drank one straight Scotch, walked one short step, took one long
look, drew one deep breath,
Just one too many,

10 And wow he died as wow he lived,
Going whop to the office and blooie home to sleep and biff got mar-
ried and bam had children and oof got fired,
Zowie did he live and zowie did he die,

With who the hell are you at the corner of his casket, and where the
hell're we going on the right-hand silver knob, and who the hell
cares walking second from the end with an American Beauty
wreath from why the hell not,

Very much missed by the circulation staff of the New York Evening
Post; deeply, deeply mourned by the B.M.T.
15 Wham, Mr. Roosevelt; pow, Sears Roebuck; awk, big dipper; bop,
summer rain;
Bong, Mr., bong, Mr., bong, Mr., bong.

LANGSTON HUGHES (1902–1967)

The Negro Speaks of Rivers

I've known rivers:
I've known rivers ancient as the world and older than the flow of
human blood in human veins.

My soul has grown deep like the rivers.

I bathed in the Euphrates when dawns were young.
5 I built my hut near the Congo and it lulled me to sleep.

I looked upon the Nile and raised the pyramids above it.
I heard the singing of the Mississippi when Abe Lincoln went down
to New Orleans, and I've seen its muddy bosom turn all golden
in the sunset.

I've known rivers:
Ancient, dusky rivers.

10 My soul has grown deep like the rivers.

I, Too

I, too, sing America.

I am the darker brother.
They send me to eat in the kitchen
When company comes,
5 But I laugh,
And eat well,
And grow strong.

Tomorrow,
I'll be at the table
10 When company comes.
Nobody'll dare
Say to me,
"Eat in the kitchen,"
Then.

15 Besides,
They'll see how beautiful I am
And be ashamed—

I, too, am America.

Old Walt

Old Walt Whitman
Went finding and seeking,
Finding less than sought
Seeking more than found,
5 Every detail minding
Of the seeking or the finding.

Pleasured equally
In seeking as in finding,
Each detail minding,
10 Old Walt went seeking
And finding.

Harlem

What happens to a dream deferred?

Does it dry up
like a raisin in the sun?
Or fester like a sore—
5 And then run?
Does it stink like rotten meat?
Or crust and sugar over—
like a syrupy sweet?

Maybe it just sags
10 like a heavy load.

Or does it explode?

COUNTEE CULLEN (1903–1946)

For a Lady I Know

She even thinks that up in heaven
Her class lies late and snores,
While poor black cherubs rise at seven
To do celestial chores.

Heritage

(For Harold Jackman)

What is Africa to me:
Copper sun or scarlet sea,
Jungle star or jungle track,
Strong bronzed men, or regal black
5 Women from whose loins I sprang
When the birds of Eden sang?
One three centuries removed
From the scenes his fathers loved,
Spicy grove, cinnamon tree,
10 *What is Africa to me?*

So I lie, who all day long
Want no sound except the song
Sung by wild barbaric birds
Goading massive jungle herds,

15 Juggernauts of flesh that pass
　　Trampling tall defiant grass
　　Where young forest lovers lie,
　　Plighting troth beneath the sky.
　　So I lie, who always hear,
20 Though I cram against my ear
　　Both my thumbs, and keep them there,
　　Great drums throbbing through the air.
　　So I lie, whose fount of pride,
　　Dear distress, and joy allied,
25 Is my somber flesh and skin,
　　With the dark blood dammed within
　　Like great pulsing tides of wine
　　That, I fear, must burst the fine
　　Channels of the chafing net
30 Where they surge and foam and fret.

　　Africa? A book one thumbs
　　Listlessly, till slumber comes.
　　Unremembered are her bats
　　Circling through the night, her cats
35 Crouching in the river reeds,
　　Stalking gentle flesh that feeds
　　By the river brink; no more
　　Does the bugle-throated roar
　　Cry that monarch claws have leapt
40 From the scabbards where they slept.
　　Silver snakes that once a year
　　Doff the lovely coats you wear,
　　Seek no covert in your fear
　　Lest a mortal eye should see;
45 What's your nakedness to me?
　　Here no leprous flowers rear
　　Fierce corollas in the air;
　　Here no bodies sleek and wet,
　　Dripping mingled rain and sweat,
50 Tread the savage measures of
　　Jungle boys and girls in love.
　　What is last year's snow to me,
　　Last year's anything? The tree
　　Budding yearly must forget
55 How its past arose or set—
　　Bough and blossom, flower, fruit,
　　Even what shy bird with mute

Wonder at her travail there,
Meekly labored in its hair.
60 *One three centuries removed*
From the scenes his fathers loved,
Spicy grove, cinnamon tree,
What is Africa to me?

So I lie, who find no peace
65 Night or day, no slight release
From the unremittent beat
Made by cruel padded feet
Walking through my body's street.
Up and down they go, and back,
70 Treading out a jungle track.
So I lie, who never quite
Safely sleep from rain at night—
I can never rest at all
When the rain begins to fall;
75 Like a soul gone mad with pain
I must match its weird refrain;
Ever must I twist and squirm,
Writhing like a baited worm,
While its primal measures drip
80 Through my body, crying, "Strip!
Doff this new exuberance.
Come and dance the Lover's Dance!"
In an old remembered way
Rain works on me night and day.

85 Quaint, outlandish heathen gods
Black men fashion out of rods,
Clay, and brittle bits of stone,
In a likeness like their own,
My conversion came high-priced;
90 I belong to Jesus Christ,
Preacher of humility;
Heathen gods are naught to me.

Father, Son, and Holy Ghost,
So I make an idle boast;
95 Jesus of the twice-turned cheek,
Lamb of God, although I speak
With my mouth thus, in my heart
Do I play a double part.

Ever at Thy glowing altar
100 Must my heart grow sick and falter,
Wishing He I served were black,
Thinking then it would not lack
Precedent of pain to guide it,
Let who would or might deride it;
105 Surely then this flesh would know
Yours had borne a kindred woe.
Lord, I fashion dark gods, too,
Daring even to give You
Dark despairing features where,
110 Crowned with dark rebellious hair,
Patience wavers just so much as
Mortal grief compels, while touches
Quick and hot, of anger, rise
To smitten cheek and weary eyes.
115 Lord, forgive me if my need
Sometimes shapes a human creed.
All day long and all night through,
One thing only must I do;
Quench my pride and cool my blood,
120 *Lest I perish in the flood.*
Lest a hidden ember set
Timber that I thought was wet
Burning like the dryest flax,
Melting like the merest wax,
125 *Lest the grave restore its dead.*
Not yet has my heart or head
In the least way realized
They and I are civilized.

EARLE BIRNEY (1904–   )

Anglosaxon Street

Dawndrizzle ended   dampness steams from
blotching brick and   blank plasterwaste
Faded housepatterns   hoary and finicky
unfold stuttering   stick like a phonograph

5 Here is a ghetto   gotten for goyim
O with care denuded   of nigger and kike
No coonsmell rankles   reeks only cellarrot
attar of carexhaust   catcorpse and cookinggrease
Imperial hearts   heave in this haven

¹⁰ Cracks across windows   are welded with slogans
There'll Always Be An England   enhances geraniums
and V's for a Victory   vanquish the housefly

Ho! with climbing sun   march the bleached beldames
festooned with shopping bags   farded flatarched
¹⁵ bigthewed Saxonwives   stepping over buttrivers
waddling back wienerladen   to suckle smallfry

Hoy! with sunslope   shrieking over hydrants
flood from learninghall   the lean fingerlings
Nordic nobblecheeked   not all clean of nose
²⁰ leaping Commandowise   into leprous lanes

What! after whistleblow!   spewed from wheelboat
after daylong doughtiness   dire handplay
in sewertrench or sandpit   come Saxonthegns
Junebrown Jutekings   jawslack for meat

²⁵ Sit after supper   on smeared doorsteps
not humbly swearing   hatedeeds on Huns
profiteers politicians   pacifists Jews

Then by twobit magic   to muse in movie
unlock picturehoard   or lope to alehall
³⁰ soaking bleakly   in beer skittleless
Home again to hotbox   and humid husbandhood
in slumbertrough adding   sleepily to Anglekin

Alongside in lanenooks   carling and leman
caterwaul and clip   careless of Saxonry
³⁵ with moonglow and haste   and a higher heartbeat

Slumbers now slumtrack   unstinks cooling
waiting brief for milkmaid   mornstar and worldrise

Twenty-Third Flight

Lo as I pause in the alien vale of the airport
fearing ahead the official ambush
a voice languorous and strange as these winds of Oahu
calleth my name and I turn to be quoited in orchids
5 and amazed with a kiss perfumed and soft as the *lei*

Straight from a travel poster thou steppest
thy arms like mangoes for smoothness
o implausible shepherdess for this one aging sheep
and leadest me through the righteous paths of the Customs
10 in a mist of my own wild hopes
Yea though I walk through the valley of Immigration
I fear no evil   for thou art a vision beside me
and my name is correctly spelled
and I shall dwell in the Hawaiian Village Hotel
15 where thy kindred prepareth a table before me
Thou restorest my baggage   and by limousine leadest me
to where I may lie on coral sands by a stream-lined pool

Nay but thou stayest not?
Thou anointest not my naked head with oil?
20 O shepherdess of Flight Number Twenty-three only
thou hastenest away on thy long brown legs to enchant
thy fellow-members in Local Five of the Greeters' Union
or that favored professor of Commerce mayhap
who leadeth thee into higher courses in Hotel Management
25 O nubile goddess of the Kaiser Training Programme
is it possible that tonight my cup runneth not over
and that I shall sit in the still pastures of the lobby
whilst thou leadest another old ram in garlands past me
and   bland as papaya   appearest not to remember me?
30 And that I shall lie by the waters of Waikiki   and want?

The Bear on the Delhi Road

Unreal   tall as a myth
by the road the Himalayan bear
is beating the brilliant air
with his crooked arms
5 About him two men   bare
spindly as locusts   leap

One pulls on a ring
in the great soft nose   His mate
flicks   flicks with a stick
10 up at the rolling eyes

They have not led him here
down from the fabulous hills

to this bald alien plain
and the clamorous world   to kill
15 but simply to teach him to dance

They are peaceful both   these spare
men of Kashmir   and the bear
alive is their living   too
If   far on the Delhi way
20 around him galvanic they dance
it is merely to wear   wear
from his shaggy body the tranced
wish forever to stay
only an ambling bear
25 four-footed in berries

It is no more joyous for them
in this hot dust to prance
out of reach of the praying claws
sharpened to paw for ants
30 in the shadows of deodars
It is not easy to free
myth from reality
or rear this fellow up
to lurch   lurch with them
35 in the tranced dancing of men

From the Hazel Bough

He met a lady
    on a lazy street
hazel eyes
    and little plush feet

5 her legs swam by
    like lovely trout
eyes were trees
    where boys leant out

hands in the dark and
10   a river side
round breasts rising
    with the finger's tide

she was plump as a finch
 and live as a salmon
15 gay as silk and
 proud as a Brahmin

they winked when they met
 and laughed when they parted
never took time
20 to be brokenhearted

but no man sees
 where the trout lie now
or what leans out
 from the hazel bough

RICHARD EBERHART (1904–   )

The Fury of Aerial Bombardment

You would think the fury of aerial bombardment
Would rouse God to relent; the infinite spaces
Are still silent. He looks on shock-pried faces.
History, even, does not know what is meant.

5 You would feel that after so many centuries
God would give man to repent; yet he can kill
As Cain could, but with multitudinous will,
No farther advanced than in his ancient furies.

Was man made stupid to see his own stupidity?
10 Is God by definition indifferent, beyond us all?
Is the eternal truth man's fighting soul
Wherein the Beast ravens in its own avidity?

Of Van Wettering I speak, and Averill,
Names on a list, whose faces I do not recall
15 But they are gone to early death, who late in school
Distinguished the belt feed lever from the belt holding pawl.

On a Squirrel Crossing the Road in Autumn, in New England

It is what he does not know,
Crossing the road under the elm trees,
About the mechanism of my car,

About the Commonwealth of Massachusetts,
5 About Mozart, India, Arcturus,

That wins my praise. I engage
At once in whirling squirrel-praise.

He obeys the orders of nature
Without knowing them.
10 It is what he does not know
That makes him beautiful.
Such a knot of little purposeful nature!

I who can see him as he cannot see himself
Repose in the ignorance that is his blessing.

15 It is what man does not know of God
Composes the visible poem of the world.
     . . . Just missed him!

LOUIS MacNEICE (1907–1963)

London Rain

The rain of London pimples
The ebony street with white
And the neon-lamps of London
Stain the canals of night
5 And the park becomes a jungle
In the alchemy of night.

My wishes turn to violent
Horses black as coal—
The randy mares of fancy,
10 The stallions of the soul—
Eager to take the fences
That fence about my soul.

Across the countless chimneys
The horses ride and across
15 The country to the channel
Where warning beacons toss,
To a place where God and No-God
Play at pitch and toss.

Whichever wins I am happy
20 For God will give me bliss
But No-God will absolve me
From all I do amiss
And I need not suffer conscience
If the world was made amiss.

25 Under God we can reckon
On pardon when we fall
But if we are under No-God
Nothing will matter at all,
Adultery and murder
30 Will count for nothing at all.

So reinforced by logic
As having nothing to lose
My lust goes riding horseback
To ravish where I choose,
35 To burgle all the turrets
Of beauty as I choose.

But now the rain gives over
Its dance upon the town
Logic and lust together
40 Come dimly tumbling down,
And neither God nor No-God
Is either up or down.

The argument was wilful,
The alternatives untrue,
45 We need no metaphysics
To sanction what we do
Or to muffle us in comfort
From what we did not do.

Whether the living river
50 Began in bog or lake,
The world is what was given,
The world is what we make.
And we only can discover
Life in the life we make.

55 So let the water sizzle
Upon the gleaming slates,

There will be sunshine after
When the rain abates
And rain returning duly
60 When the sun abates.

My wishes now come homeward,
Their gallopings in vain,
Logic and lust are quiet
And again it starts to rain;
65 Falling asleep I listen
To the falling London rain.

Sunday Morning

Down the road someone is practicing scales,
The notes like little fishes vanish with a wink of tails,
Man's heart expands to tinker with his car
For this is Sunday morning, Fate's great bazaar;
5 Regard these means as ends, concentrate on this Now,
And you may grow to music or drive beyond Hindhead anyhow,
Take corners on two wheels until you go so fast
That you can clutch a fringe or two of the windy past,
That you can abstract this day and make it to the week of time
10 A small eternity, a sonnet self-contained in rhyme.
But listen, up the road, something gulps, the church spire
Opens its eight bells out, skulls' mouths which will not tire
To tell how there is no music or movement which secures
Escape from the weekday time. Which deadens and endures.

W. H. AUDEN (1907–1973)

The Unknown Citizen

*(To JS/07/M/378
This Marble Monument
Is Erected by the State)*

He was found by the Bureau of Statistics to be
One against whom there was no official complaint,
And all the reports on his conduct agree
That, in the modern sense of an old-fashioned word, he was a saint,
5 For in everything he did he served the Greater Community.
Except for the War till the day he retired
He worked in a factory and never got fired,

But satisfied his employers, Fudge Motors Inc.
Yet he wasn't a scab or odd in his views,
10 For his Union reports that he paid his dues,
(Our report on his Union shows it was sound)
And our Social Psychology workers found
That he was popular with his mates and liked a drink.
The Press are convinced that he bought a paper every day
15 And that his reactions to advertisements were normal in every way.
Policies taken out in his name prove that he was fully insured,
And his Health-card shows he was once in hospital but left it cured.
Both Producers Research and High-Grade Living declare
He was fully sensible to the advantages of the Instalment Plan
20 And had everything necessary to the Modern Man,
A phonograph, a radio, a car, and a frigidaire.
Our researchers into Public Opinion are content
That he held the proper opinions for the time of year;
When there was peace, he was for peace; when there was war, he
went.
25 He was married and added five children to the population,
Which our Eugenist says was the right number for a parent of his
generation,
And our teachers report that he never interfered with their educa-
tion.
Was he free? Was he happy? The question is absurd:
Had anything been wrong, we should certainly have heard.

Musée des Beaux Arts[1]

About suffering they were never wrong,
The Old Masters: how well they understood
Its human position; how it takes place
While someone else is eating or opening a window or just walking
dully along;
5 How, when the aged are reverently, passionately waiting
For the miraculous birth, there always must be
Children who did not specially want it to happen, skating
On a pond at the edge of the wood:
They never forgot
10 That even the dreadful martyrdom must run its course
Anyhow in a corner, some untidy spot

---

[1] The Museum of Fine Arts, in Brussels.

Where the dogs go on with their doggy life and the torturer's horse
Scratches its innocent behind on a tree.

In Brueghel's *Icarus*,[2] for instance: how everything turns away
15 Quite leisurely from the disaster; the plowman may
Have heard the splash, the forsaken cry,
But for him it was not an important failure; the sun shone
As it had to on the white legs disappearing into the green
Water; and the expensive delicate ship that must have seen
20 Something amazing, a boy falling out of the sky,
Had somewhere to get to and sailed calmly on.

In Memory of W. B. Yeats

(d. January, 1939)

1

He disappeared in the dead of winter:
The brooks were frozen, the airports almost deserted,
And snow disfigured the public statues;
The mercury sank in the mouth of the dying day.
5 What instruments we have agree
The day of his death was a dark cold day.

Far from his illness
The wolves ran on through the evergreen forests,
The peasant river was untempted by the fashionable quays;
10 By mourning tongues
The death of the poet was kept from his poems.

But for him it was his last afternoon as himself,
An afternoon of nurses and rumors;
The provinces of his body revolted,
15 The squares of his mind were empty,
Silence invaded the suburbs,
The current of his feeling failed; he became his admirers.

Now he is scattered among a hundred cities
And wholly given over to unfamiliar affections,
20 To find his happiness in another kind of wood

---

[2] Icarus, in Greek myth, flew too close to the sun on wings of wax, fell into the
sea and drowned. In Brueghel's painting Icarus is a peripheral figure.

And be punished under a foreign code of conscience.
The words of a dead man
Are modified in the guts of the living.

But in the importance and noise of tomorrow
25 When the brokers are roaring like beasts on the floor of the Bourse,[1]
And the poor have the sufferings to which they are fairly accus-
    tomed,
And each in the cell of himself is almost convinced of his freedom,
A few thousand will think of this day
As one thinks of a day when one did something slightly unusual.
30 What instruments we have agree
The day of his death was a dark cold day.

2

You were silly like us; your gift survived it all:
The parish of rich women, physical decay,
Yourself. Mad Ireland hurt you into poetry.
35   Now Ireland has her madness and her weather still,
For poetry makes nothing happen: it survives
In the valley of its making where executives
Would never want to tamper, flows on south
From ranches of isolation and the busy griefs,
40   Raw towns that we believe and die in; it survives,
A way of happening, a mouth.

3

Earth, receive an honored guest:
William Yeats is laid to rest.
Let the Irish vessel lie
45   Emptied of its poetry.

In the nightmare of the dark
All the dogs of Europe bark,
And the living nations wait,
Each sequestered in its hate;

50   Intellectual disgrace
Stares from every human face,
And the seas of pity lie
Locked and frozen in each eye.

---

[1] The Paris stock exchange.

Follow, poet, follow right
55   To the bottom of the night,
With your unconstraining voice
Still persuade us to rejoice;

With the farming of a verse
Make a vineyard of the curse,
60   Sing of human unsuccess
In a rapture of distress;

In the deserts of the heart
Let the healing fountain start,
In the prison of his days
65   Teach the free man how to praise.

Epitaph on a Tyrant

Perfection, of a kind, was what he was after,
And the poetry he invented was easy to understand;
He knew human folly like the back of his hand,
And was greatly interested in armies and fleets;
5 When he laughed, respectable senators burst with laughter,
And when he cried the little children died in the streets.

As I Walked Out One Evening

As I walked out one evening,
    Walking down Bristol Street,
The crowds upon the pavement
    Were fields of harvest wheat.

5 And down by the brimming river
    I heard a lover sing
Under an arch of the railway:
    "Love has no ending.

"I'll love you dear, I'll love you
10   Till China and Africa meet,
And the river jumps over the mountain
    And the salmon sing in the street.

"I'll love you till the ocean
    Is folded and hung up to dry,

15 And the seven stars go squawking
      Like geese about the sky.

  The years shall run like rabbits,
      For in my arms I hold
  The Flower of the Ages,
20   And the first love of the world."

  But all the clocks in the city
      Began to whirr and chime:
  "O let not Time deceive you,
      You cannot conquer Time.

25 "In the burrows of the Nightmare
      Where Justice naked is,
  Time watches from the shadow
      And coughs when you would kiss.

  "In headaches and in worry
30   Vaguely life leaks away,
  And Time will have his fancy
      Tomorrow or to-day.

  "Into many a green valley
      Drifts the appalling snow;
35 Time breaks the threaded dances
      And the diver's brilliant bow.

  "O plunge your hands in water,
      Plunge them in up to the wrist;
  Stare, stare in the basin
40   And wonder what you've missed.

  "The glacier knocks in the cupboard,
      The desert sighs in the bed,
  And the crack in the tea-cup opens
      A lane to the land of the dead.

45 "Where the beggars raffle the banknotes
      And the Giant is enchanting to Jack,
  And the Lily-white Boy is a Roarer,
      And Jill goes down on her back.

"O look, look in the mirror,
50   O look in your distress;
Life remains a blessing
    Although you cannot bless.

"O stand, stand at the window
    As the tears scald and start;
55 You shall love your crooked neighbor
    With your crooked heart."

It was late, late in the evening,
    The lovers they were gone;
The clocks had ceased their chiming,
60   And the deep river ran on.

THEODORE ROETHKE (1908–1963)

Root Cellar

Nothing would sleep in that cellar, dank as a ditch,
Bulbs broke out of boxes hunting for chinks in the dark,
Shoots dangled and drooped,
Lolling obscenely from mildewed crates,
5 Hung down long yellow evil necks, like tropical snakes.
And what a congress of stinks!—
Roots ripe as old bait,
Pulpy stems, rank, silo-rich,
Leaf-mold, manure, lime, piled against slippery planks.
10 Nothing would give up life:
Even the dirt kept breathing a small breath.

The Waking

I wake to sleep, and take my waking slow.
I feel my fate in what I cannot fear.
I learn by going where I have to go.

We think by feeling. What is there to know?
5 I hear my being dance from ear to ear.
I wake to sleep, and take my waking slow.

Of those so close beside me, which are you?
God bless the Ground! I shall walk softly there,
And learn by going where I have to go.

10 Light takes the Tree; but who can tell us how?
The lowly worm climbs up a winding stair;
I wake to sleep, and take my waking slow.

Great Nature has another thing to do
To you and me; so take the lively air,
15 And, lovely, learn by going where to go.

This shaking keeps me steady. I should know.
What falls away is always. And is near.
I wake to sleep, and take my waking slow.
I learn by going where I have to go.

Dolor

I have known the inexorable sadness of pencils,
Neat in their boxes, dolor of pad and paper-weight,
All the misery of manilla folders and mucilage,
Desolation in immaculate public places,
5 Lonely reception room, lavatory, switchboard,
The unalterable pathos of basin and pitcher,
Ritual of multigraph, paper-clip, comma,
Endless duplication of lives and objects.
And I have seen dust from the walls of institutions,
10 Finer than flour, alive, more dangerous than silica,
Sift, almost invisible, through long afternoons of tedium,
Dropping a fine film on nails and delicate eyebrows,
Glazing the pale hair, the duplicate gray standard faces.

I Knew a Woman

I knew a woman, lovely in her bones,
When small birds sighed, she would sigh back at them;
Ah, when she moved, she moved more ways than one:
The shapes a bright container can contain!
5 Of her choice virtues only gods should speak,
Or English poets who grew up on Greek
(I'd have them sing in chorus, cheek to cheek).

How well her wishes went! She stroked my chin,
She taught me Turn, and Counter-turn, and Stand;
10 She taught me Touch, that undulant white skin;
I nibbled meekly from her proffered hand;
She was the sickle; I, poor I, the rake,

Coming behind her for her pretty sake
(But what prodigious mowing we did make).

15 Love likes a gander, and adores a goose:
Her full lips pursed, the errant note to seize;
She played it quick, she played it light and loose;
My eyes, they dazzled at her flowing knees;
Her several parts could keep a pure repose,
20 Or one hip quiver with a mobile nose
(She moved in circles, and those circles moved).

Let seed be grass, and grass turn into hay:
I'm martyr to a motion not my own;
What's freedom for? To know eternity.
25 I swear she cast a shadow white as stone.
But who would count eternity in days?
These old bones live to learn her wanton ways:
(I measure time by how a body sways).

In a Dark Time

In a dark time, the eye begins to see,
I meet my shadow in the deepening shade;
I hear my echo in the echoing wood—
A lord of nature weeping to a tree.
5 I live between the heron and the wren,
Beasts of the hill and serpents of the den.

What's madness but nobility of soul
At odds with circumstance? The day's on fire!
I know the purity of pure despair,
10 My shadow pinned against a sweating wall.
That place among the rocks—is it a cave,
Or winding path? The edge is what I have.

A steady storm of correspondences!
A night flowing with birds, a ragged moon,
15 And in broad day the midnight come again!
A man goes far to find out what he is—
Death of the self in a long, tearless night,
All natural shapes blazing unnatural light.

Dark, dark my light, and darker my desire.
20 My soul, like some heat-maddened summer fly,

Keeps buzzing at the sill. Which I is *I*?
A fallen man, I climb out of my fear.
The mind enters itself, and God the mind,
And one is One, free in the tearing wind.

My Papa's Waltz

The whiskey on your breath
Could make a small boy dizzy;
But I hung on like death:
Such waltzing was not easy.

5 We romped until the pans
Slid from the kitchen shelf;
My mother's countenance
Could not unfrown itself.

The hand that held my wrist
10 Was battered on one knuckle;
At every step you missed
My right ear scraped a buckle.

You beat time on my head
With a palm caked hard by dirt,
15 Then waltzed me off to bed
Still clinging to your shirt.

The Meadow Mouse

1

In a shoe box stuffed in an old nylon stocking
Sleeps the baby mouse I found in the meadow,
Where he trembled and shook beneath a stick
Till I caught him up by the tail and brought him in,
5 Cradled in my hand,
A little quaker, the whole body of him trembling,
His absurd whiskers sticking out like a cartoon-mouse,
His feet like small leaves,
Little lizard-feet,
10 Whitish and spread wide when he tried to struggle away,
Wriggling like a minuscule puppy.

Now he's eaten his three kinds of cheese and drunk from his bottle-
cap watering-trough—

So much he just lies in one corner,
His tail curled under him, his belly big
15 As his head; his bat-like ears
Twitching, tilting toward the least sound.

Do I imagine he no longer trembles
When I come close to him?
He seems no longer to tremble.

2

20 But this morning the shoe-box house on the back porch is empty.
Where has he gone, my meadow mouse,
My thumb of a child that nuzzled in my palm?—
To run under the hawk's wing,
Under the eye of the great owl watching from the elm-tree,
25 To live by courtesy of the shrike, the snake, the tom-cat.

I think of the nestling fallen into the deep grass,
The turtle gasping in the dusty rubble of the highway,
The paralytic stunned in the tub, and the water rising,—
All things innocent, hapless, forsaken.

STEPHEN SPENDER (1909–   )

I Think Continually of Those Who Were Truly Great

I think continually of those who were truly great.
Who, from the womb, remembered the soul's history
Through corridors of light where the hours are suns
Endless and singing. Whose lovely ambition
5 Was that their lips, still touched with fire,
Should tell of the Spirit clothed from head to foot in song.
And who hoarded from the Spring branches
The desired falling across their bodies like blossoms.

What is precious is never to forget
10 The essential delight of the blood drawn from ageless springs
Breaking through rocks in worlds before our earth.
Never to deny its pleasure in the morning simple light
Nor its grave evening demand for love.
Never to allow gradually the traffic to smother
15 With noise and fog the flowering of the spirit.

Near the snow, near the sun, in the highest fields
See how these names are fêted by the waving grass

And by the streamers of white cloud
And whispers of wind in the listening sky.
20 The names of those who in their lives fought for life
Who wore at their hearts the fire's center.
Born of the sun they traveled a short while towards the sun,
And left the vivid air signed with their honor.

The Express

After the first powerful, plain manifesto
The black statement of pistons, without more fuss
But gliding like a queen, she leaves the station.
Without bowing and with restrained unconcern
5 She passes the houses which humbly crowd outside,
The gasworks, and at last the heavy page
Of death, printed by gravestones in the cemetery.
Beyond the town, there lies the open country
Where, gathering speed, she acquires mystery,
10 The luminous self-possession of ships on ocean.
It is now she begins to sing—at first quite low
Then loud, and at last with a jazzy madness—
The song of her whistle screaming at curves,
Of deafening tunnels, brakes, innumerable bolts.
15 And always light, aerial, underneath,
Retreats the elate metre of her wheels.
Steaming through metal landscape on her lines,
She plunges new eras of white happiness,
Where speed throws up strange shapes, broad curves
20 And parallels clean like trajectories from guns.
At last, further than Edinburgh or Rome,
Beyond the crest of the world, she reaches night
Where only a low stream-line brightness
Of phosphorus on the tossing hills is light.
25 Ah, like a comet through flame, she moves entranced,
Wrapt in her music no bird song, no, nor bough
Breaking with honey buds, shall ever equal.

A. M. KLEIN (1902–1972)

The Rocking Chair

It seconds the crickets of the province. Heard
in the clean lamplit farmhouses of Quebec,—
wooden,—it is no less a national bird;
and rivals, in its cage, the mere stuttering clock.

5 To its time, the evenings are rolled away;
and in its peace the pensive mother knits
contentment to be worn by her family,
grown-up, but still cradled by the chair in which she sits.

It is also the old man's pet, pair to his pipe,
10 the two aids of his arithmetic and plans,
plans rocking and puffing into market-shape;
and it is the toddler's game and dangerous dance.
Moved to the verandah, on summer Sundays, it is,
among the hanging plants, the girls, the boy-friends,
15 sabbatical and clumsy, like the white haloes
dangling above the blue serge suits of the young men.

It has a personality of its own;
is a character (like that old drunk Lacoste,
exhaling amber, and toppling on his pins);
20 it is alive; individual; and no less
an identity than those about it. And
it is tradition. Centuries have been flicked
from its arcs, alternately flicked and pinned.
It rolls with the gait of St. Malo.[1] It is act

25 and symbol, symbol of this static folk
which moves in segments, and returns to base,—
a sunken pendulum: *invoke, revoke;*
loosed yon, leashed hither, motion on no space.
O, like some Anjou[2] ballad, all refrain,
30 which turns about its longing, and seems to move
to make a pleasure out of repeated pain,
its music moves, as if always back to a first love.

Lone Bather

Upon the ecstatic diving board the diver,
poised for parabolas, lets go
lets go his manshape to become a bird.
Is bird, and topsy-turvy
5 the pool floats overhead, and the white tiles snow

their crazy hexagons. Is dolphin. Then
is plant with lilies bursting from his heels.

---

[1] A seaport in Brittany.
[2] A former province of western France.

Himself, suddenly mysterious and marine,
bobs up a merman leaning on his hills.

10 Plashes and plays alone the deserted pool;
as those, is free, who think themselves unseen.
He rolls in his heap of fruit,
he slides his belly over
the melonrinds of water, curved and smooth and green.
15 Feels good: and trains, like little acrobats
his echoes dropping from the galleries;
circles himself over a rung of water;
swims fancy and gay; taking a notion, hides
under the satins of his great big bed,—
20 and then comes up to float until he thinks
the ceiling at his brow, and nowhere any sides.

His thighs are a shoal of fishes: scattered: he
turns with many gloves of greeting
towards the sunnier water and the tiles.

25 Upon the tiles he dangles from his toes
lazily the eight reins of his ponies.

An afternoon, far from the world
a street sound throws like a stone, with paper, through the glass.
Up, he is chipped enamel, grained with hair.
30 The gloss of his footsteps follows him to the showers,
the showers, and the male room, and the towel
which rubs the bird, the plant, the dolphin back again
personable plain.

ELIZABETH BISHOP (1911–1979)

The Fish

I caught a tremendous fish
and held him beside the boat
half out of water, with my hook
fast in a corner of his mouth.
5 He didn't fight.
He hadn't fought at all.
He hung a grunting weight,
battered and venerable
and homely. Here and there

10 his brown skin hung in strips
   like ancient wall-paper,
   and its pattern of darker brown
   was like wall-paper:
   shapes like full-blown roses
15 stained and lost through age.
   He was speckled with barnacles,
   fine rosettes of lime,
   and infested
   with tiny white sea-lice,
20 and underneath two or three
   rags of green weed hung down.
   While his gills were breathing in
   the terrible oxygen
   —the frightening gills,
25 fresh and crisp with blood,
   that can cut so badly—
   I thought of the coarse white flesh
   packed in like feathers,
   the big bones and the little bones,
30 the dramatic reds and blacks
   of his shiny entrails,
   and the pink swim-bladder
   like a big peony.
   I looked into his eyes
35 which were far larger than mine
   but shallower, and yellowed,
   the irises backed and packed
   with tarnished tinfoil
   seen through the lenses
40 of old scratched isinglass.
   They shifted a little, but not
   to return my stare.
   —It was more like the tipping
   of an object toward the light.
45 I admired his sullen face,
   the mechanism of his jaw,
   and then I saw
   that from his lower lip
   —if you could call it a lip—
50 grim, wet, and weapon-like,
   hung five old pieces of fish-line,
   or four and a wire leader
   with the swivel still attached,

with all their five big hooks
55 grown firmly in his mouth.
A green line, frayed at the end
where he broke it, two heavier lines,
and a fine black thread
still crimped from the strain and snap
60 when it broke and he got away.
Like medals with their ribbons
frayed and wavering,
a five-haired beard of wisdom
trailing from his aching jaw.
65 I stared and stared
and victory filled up
the little rented boat,
from the pool of bilge
where oil had spread a rainbow
70 around the rusted engine
to the bailer rusted orange,
the sun-cracked thwarts,
the oarlocks on their strings,
the gunnels—until everything
75 was rainbow, rainbow, rainbow!
And I let the fish go.

Sandpiper

The roaring alongside he takes for granted,
and that every so often the world is bound to shake.
He runs, he runs to the south, finical, awkward,
in a state of controlled panic, a student of Blake.

5 The beach hisses like fat. On his left, a sheet
of interrupting water comes and goes
and glazes over his dark and brittle feet.
He runs, he runs straight through it, watching his toes.

—Watching, rather, the spaces of sand between them,
10 where (no detail too small) the Atlantic drains
rapidly backwards and downwards. As he runs,
he stares at the dragging grains.

The world is a mist. And then the world is
minute and vast and clear. The tide
15 is higher or lower. He couldn't tell you which.
His beak is focussed; he is preoccupied,

looking for something, something, something.
Poor bird, he is obsessed!
The millions of grains are black, white, tan, and gray,
20 mixed with quartz grains, rose and amethyst.

In the Waiting Room

In Worcester, Massachusetts,
I went with Aunt Consuelo
to keep her dentist's appointment
and sat and waited for her
5 in the dentist's waiting room.
It was winter. It got dark
early. The waiting room
was full of grown-up people,
arctics and overcoats,
10 lamps and magazines.
My aunt was inside
what seemed like a long time
and while I waited I read
the *National Geographic*
15 (I could read) and carefully
studied the photographs:
The inside of a volcano,
black, and full of ashes;
then it was spilling over
20 in rivulets of fire.
Osa and Martin Johnson
dressed in riding breeches,
laced boots, and pith helmets.
A dead man slung on a pole
25 —"Long Pig," the caption said.
Babies with pointed heads
wound round and round with string;
black, naked women with necks
wound round and round with wire
30 like the necks of light bulbs.
Their breasts were horrifying.
I read it right straight through.
I was too shy to stop.
And then I looked at the cover:
35 the yellow margins, the date.

Suddenly, from inside,
came an *oh!* of pain

—Aunt Consuelo's voice—
not very loud or long.
40 I wasn't at all surprised;
even then I knew she was
a foolish, timid woman.
I might have been embarrassed,
but wasn't. What took me
45 completely by surprise
was that it was *me:*
my voice, in my mouth.
Without thinking at all
I was my foolish aunt,
50 I—we—were falling, falling,
our eyes glued to the cover
of the *National Geographic,*
February, 1918.
I said to myself: three days
55 and you'll be seven years old.
I was saying it to stop
the sensation of falling off
the round, turning world
into cold, blue-black space.
60 But I felt: you are an *I,*
you are an *Elizabeth,*
you are one of *them.*
Why should you be one, too?
I scarcely dared to look
65 to see what it was I was.
I gave a sidelong glance
—I couldn't look any higher—
at shadowy gray knees,
trousers and skirts and boots
70 and different pairs of hands
lying under the lamps.
I knew that nothing stranger
had ever happened, that nothing
stranger could ever happen.

75 Why should I be my aunt,
or me, or anyone?
What similarities—
boots, hands, the family voice
I felt in my throat, or even
80 the *National Geographic*
and those awful hanging breasts—

held us all together
or made us all just one?
How—I didn't know any
85 word for it—how "unlikely" . . .
How had I come to be here,
like them, and overhear
a cry of pain that could have
got loud and worse but hadn't?

90 The waiting room was bright
and too hot. It was sliding
beneath a big black wave,
another, and another.

Then I was back in it.
95 The War was on. Outside,
in Worcester, Massachusetts,
were night and slush and cold,
and it was still the fifth
of February, 1918.

IRVING LAYTON (1912–   )

Party at Hydra[1]

For Marianne

The white cormorants shaped like houses stare down at you.
A Greek Chagall [2] perched them there on the crooked terraces.
The steep ascent is through a labyrinth of narrow streets
Cobbled with huge stones that speak only Arvanitika.[3]
5 A surfeit of wisdom has made the stars above you eternally silent.
Many are ambushed by the silence and many never find their way
To the house where the perpetual party is going on.
If you are on the lookout for monsters or demons
You will not find their legs sprawled out in the terraces.
10 They are all assembled at the house threshing one another
With extracts from diaries whose pages fly open releasing beetles
That crawl along the grapevines and disappear into a night of ears.
Though only one head can be seen, several monsters have seven
And some have three and some no more than two. Beware of the one
15 Headed monster with an aspirin in his hand who'll devour you instead.

---

[1] An island in the Aegean Sea.
[2] Marc Chagall (b. 1887), famous for his dreamlike paintings.
[3] An Albanian language.

You know the number of heads each has by the small sucking winds
They make as they dissolve the salads and meats on their plates. So
Listen carefully holding a lighted incense stick for a talisman.
A rutting woman lets her smile float on your glass of punch.
20 You scoop it up to hand back to her on a soaked slice of lemonpeel.
A poet announces to everyone not listening he has begun a new poem.
He hears a spider growling at him from a suntanned cleavage
And at once pierces it with a metaphor using its blood for glue.
A married man discourses tenderly on love and poultices.
25 It is almost dark when a goddess appears beside you.
She guides your hand under her white robe and murmurs
"The sweat of invalids in medicine bottles is not love
And wisdom is love that has lost one of its testicles.
Desire is love's lubricant yet love is no wheel spinning in a groove.
30 Love resides neither in the body nor in the soul
But is a volatile element reconciling spirit to flesh.
Love is the holy seal of their interpenetration and unity
When they come together in the perfect moment of fusion.
If you wish to know more about love listen to the crickets on the moon
35 And emulate the silent shining of the stars but do not become one."
When she vanishes your hand is a river you swim in forever.

Berry Picking

Silently my wife walks on the still wet furze
Now darkgreen the leaves are full of metaphors
Now lit up is each tiny lamp of blueberry.
The white nails of rain have dropped and the sun is free.

5 And whether she bends or straightens to each bush
To find the children's laughter among the leaves
Her quiet hands seem to make the quiet summer hush—
Berries or children, patient she is with these.

I only vex and perplex her; madness, rage
10 Are endearing perhaps put down upon the page;
Even silence daylong and sullen can then
Enamour as restraint or classic discipline.

So I envy the berries she puts in her mouth,
The red and succulent juice that stains her lips;
15 I shall never taste that good to her, nor will they
Displease her with a thousand barbarous jests.

How they lie easily for her hand to take,
Part of the unoffending world that is hers;
Here beyond complexity she stands and stares
20 And leans her marvellous head as if for answers.

No more the easy soul my childish craft deceives
Nor the simpler one for whom yes is always yes;
No, now her voice comes to me from a far way off
Though her lips are redder than the raspberries.

DYLAN THOMAS (1914–1953)

A Refusal to Mourn the Death, by Fire, of a Child in London

Never until the mankind making
Bird beast and flower
Fathering and all humbling darkness
Tells with silence the last light breaking
5 And the still hour
Is come out of the sea tumbling in harness

And I must enter again the round
Zion of the water bead
And the synagogue of the ear of corn
10 Shall I let pray the shadow of a sound
Or sow my salt seed
In the least valley of sackcloth to mourn

The majesty and burning of the child's death.
I shall not murder
15 The mankind of her going with a grave truth
Nor blaspheme down the stations of the breath
With any further
Elegy of innocence and youth.

Deep with the first dead lies London's daughter,
20 Robed in the long friends,
The grains beyond age, the dark veins of her mother,
Secret by the unmourning water
Of the riding Thames.
After the first death, there is no other.

In My Craft or Sullen Art

In my craft or sullen art
Exercised in the still night
When only the moon rages
And the lovers lie abed
5 With all their griefs in their arms,
I labor by singing light
Not for ambition or bread
Or the strut and trade of charms
On the ivory stages
10 But for the common wages
Of their most secret heart.

Not for the proud man apart
From the raging moon I write
On these spindrift pages
15 Nor for the towering dead
With their nightingales and psalms
But for the lovers, their arms
Round the griefs of the ages,
Who pay no praise or wages
20 Nor heed my craft or art.

Fern Hill

Now as I was young and easy under the apple boughs
About the lilting house and happy as the grass was green,
    The night above the dingle starry,
      Time let me hail and climb
5   Golden in the heydays of his eyes,
And honored among wagons I was prince of the apple towns
And once below a time I lordly had the trees and leaves
      Trail with daisies and barley
    Down the rivers of the windfall light.

10 And as I was green and carefree, famous among the barns
About the happy yard and singing as the farm was home,
    In the sun that is young once only,
      Time let me play and be
    Golden in the mercy of his means,
15 And green and golden I was huntsman and herdsman, the calves
Sang to my horn, the foxes on the hills barked clear and cold,
      And the sabbath rang slowly
    In the pebbles of the holy streams.

All the sun long it was running, it was lovely, the hay
20 Fields high as the house, the tunes from the chimneys, it was air
And playing, lovely and watery
And fire green as grass.
And nightly under the simple stars
As I rode to sleep the owls were bearing the farm away,
25 All the moon long I heard, blessed among stables, the night-jars
Flying with the ricks, and the horses
Flashing into the dark.

And then to awake, and the farm, like a wanderer white
With the dew, come back, the cock on his shoulder: it was all
Shining, it was Adam and maiden,
The sky gathered again
And the sun grew round that very day.
So it must have been after the birth of the simple light
In the first, spinning place, the spellbound horses walking warm
35 Out of the whinnying green stable
On to the fields of praise.

And honored among foxes and pheasants by the gay house
Under the new made clouds and happy as the heart was long,
In the sun born over and over,
I ran my heedless ways,
My wishes raced through the house high hay
And nothing I cared, at my sky blue trades, that time allows
In all his tuneful turning so few and such morning songs
Before the children green and golden
45 Follow him out of grace,

Nothing I cared, in the lamb white days, that time would take me
Up to the swallow thronged loft by the shadow of my hand,
In the moon that is always rising,
Nor that riding to sleep
50 I should hear him fly with the high fields
And wake to the farm forever fled from the childless land.
Oh as I was young and easy in the mercy of his means,
Time held me green and dying
Though I sang in my chains like the sea.

Do Not Go Gentle into That Good Night

Do not go gentle into that good night,
Old age should burn and rave at close of day;
Rage, rage against the dying of the light.

Though wise men at their end know dark is right,
5 Because their words had forked no lightning they
Do not go gentle into that good night.

Good men, the last wave by, crying how bright
Their frail deeds might have danced in a green bay,
Rage, rage against the dying of the light.

10 Wild men who caught and sang the sun in flight,
And learn, too late, they grieved it on its way,
Do not go gentle into that good night.

Grave men, near death, who see with blinding sight
Blind eyes could blaze like meteors and be gay,
15 Rage, rage against the dying of the light.

And you, my father, there on the sad height,
Curse, bless, me now with your fierce tears, I pray.
Do not go gentle into that good night.
Rage, rage against the dying of the light.

RANDALL JARRELL (1914–1965)

The Death of the Ball Turret Gunner

From my mother's sleep I fell into the State,
And I hunched in its belly till my wet fur froze.
Six miles from earth, loosed from its dream of life,
I woke to black flak and the nightmare fighters.
5 When I died they washed me out of the turret with a hose.

Nestus Gurley

Sometimes waking, sometimes sleeping,
Late in the afternoon, or early
In the morning, I hear on the lawn,
On the walk, on the lawn, the soft quick step,
5 The sound half song, half breath: a note or two
That with a note or two would be a tune.
It is Nestus Gurley.

It is an old
Catch or snatch or tune
10 In the Dorian mode: the mode of the horses
That stand all night in the fields asleep

Or awake, the mode of the cold
Hunter, Orion, wheeling upside-down,
All space and stars, in cater-cornered Heaven.
15 When, somewhere under the east,
The great march begins, with birds and silence;
When, in the day's first triumph, dawn
Rides over the houses, Nestus Gurley
Delivers to me my lot.

20 As the sun sets, I hear my daughter say:
"He has four routes and makes a hundred dollars."
Sometimes he comes with dogs, sometimes with children,
Sometimes with dogs and children.
He collects, today.
25 I hear my daughter say:
"Today Nestus has got on his derby."
And he says, after a little: "It's two-eighty."
"How could it be two-eighty?"
"Because this month there're five Sundays: it's two-eighty."

30 He collects, delivers. Before the first, least star
Is lost in the paling east; at evening
While the soft, side-lit, gold-leafed day
Lingers to see the stars, the boy Nestus
Delivers to me the Morning Star, the Evening Star
35 —Ah no, only the Morning *News*, the Evening *Record*
Of what I have done and what I have not done
Set down and held against me in the Book
Of Death, on paper yellowing
Already, with one morning's sun, one evening's sun.

40 Sometimes I only dream him. He brings then
News of a different morning, a judgment not of men.
The bombers have turned back over the Pole,
Having met a star. . . . I look at that new year
And, waking, think of our Moravian Star
45 Not lit yet, and the pure beeswax candle
With its red flame-proofed paper pompom
Not lit yet, and the sweetened
Bun we brought home from the love-feast, still not eaten,
And the song the children sang: *O Morning Star—*

50 And at this hour, to the dew-hushed drums
Of the morning, Nestus Gurley
Marches to me over the lawn; and the cat Elfie,

Furred like a musk-ox, coon-tailed, gold-leaf-eyed,
Looks at the paper boy without alarm
55 But yawns, and stretches, and walks placidly
Across the lawn to his ladder, climbs it, and begins to purr.

I let him in,
Go out and pick up from the grass the paper hat
Nestus has folded: this tricorne fit for a Napoleon
60 Of our days and institutions, weaving
Baskets, being bathed, receiving
Electric shocks, Rauwolfia. . . . I put it on
—Ah no, only unfold it.
There is dawn inside; and I say to no one
65 About—
          it is a note or two
That with a note or two would—
                       say to no one
About nothing: "He delivers dawn."

70 When I lie coldly
—Lie, that is, neither with coldness nor with warmth—
In the darkness that is not lit by anything,
In the grave that is not lit by anything
Except our hope: the hope
75 That is not proofed against anything, but pure
And shining as the first, least star
That is lost in the east on the morning of Judgment—
May I say, recognizing the step
Or tune or breath. . . .
80   recognizing the breath,
May I say, "It is Nestus Gurley."

JOHN BERRYMAN (1914–1972)

A Professor's Song

(. . rabid or dog-dull.) Let me tell you how
The Eighteenth Century couplet ended. Now
Tell me. Troll me the sources of that Song—
Assigned last week—by Blake. Come, come along,
5 Gentlemen. (Fidget and huddle, do. Squint soon.)
I want to end these fellows all by noon.

"That deep romantic chasm"—an early use;
The word is from the French, by our abuse
Fished out a bit. (Red all your eyes. O when?)

¹⁰ "A poet is a man speaking to men":
But I am then a poet, am I not?—
Ha ha. The radiator, please. Well, what?

Alive now—no—Blake would have written prose,
But movement following movement crisply flows,
¹⁵ So much the better, better the much so,
As burbleth Mozart. Twelve. The class can go.
Until I meet you, then, in Upper Hell
Convulsed, foaming immortal blood: farewell.

Dream Song #14

Life, friends, is boring. We must not say so.
After all, the sky flashes, the great sea yearns,
we ourselves flash and yearn,
and moreover my mother told me as a boy
5 (repeatingly) "Ever to confess you're bored
means you have no

Inner Resources." I conclude now I have no
inner resources, because I am heavy bored.
Peoples bore me,
¹⁰ literature bores me, especially great literature,
Henry bores me, with his plights & gripes
as bad as achilles,

who loves people and valiant art, which bores me.
And the tranquil hills, & gin, look like a drag
¹⁵ and somehow a dog
has taken itself & its tail considerably away
into mountains or sea or sky, leaving
behind: me, wag.

DUDLEY RANDALL (1914–   )

Ballad of Birmingham

(On the bombing of a church in Birmingham, Alabama, 1963)

"Mother dear, may I go downtown
Instead of out to play,
And march the streets of Birmingham
In a Freedom March today?"

5 "No, baby, no, you may not go,
  For the dogs are fierce and wild,
  And clubs and hoses, guns and jails
  Aren't good for a little child."

  "But, mother, I won't be alone.
10 Other children will go with me,
  And march the streets of Birmingham
  To make our country free."

  "No, baby, no, you may not go,
  For I fear those guns will fire.
15 But you may go to church instead
  And sing in the children's choir."

  She has combed and brushed her night-dark hair,
  And bathed rose petal sweet,
  And drawn white gloves on her small brown hands,
20 And white shoes on her feet.

  The mother smiled to know her child
  Was in the sacred place,
  But that smile was the last smile
  To come upon her face.

25 For when she heard the explosion,
  Her eyes grew wet and wild.
  She raced through the streets of Birmingham
  Calling for her child.

  She clawed through bits of glass and brick,
30 Then lifted out a shoe.
  "O, here's the shoe my baby wore,
  But, baby, where are you?"

HENRY REED (1914–   )

Lessons of the War

TO ALAN MICHELL
Vixi duellis nuper idoneus
Et militavi non sine gloria[1]

---

[1] From a poem of Horace, with the word "puellis" (girls) altered to "duellis" (battles). "Of late I have lived capably amongst battles and I have served not without glory."

NAMING OF PARTS

Today we have naming of parts. Yesterday,
We had daily cleaning. And tomorrow morning,
We shall have what to do after firing. But today,
Today we have naming of parts. Japonica
5 Glistens like coral in all of the neighboring gardens,
     And today we have naming of parts.

This is the lower sling swivel. And this
Is the upper sling swivel, whose use you will see,
When you are given your slings. And this is the piling swivel,
10 Which in your case you have not got. The branches
Hold in the gardens their silent, eloquent gestures,
     Which in our case we have not got.

This is the safety-catch, which is always released
With an easy flick of the thumb. And please do not let me
15 See anyone using his finger. You can do it quite easy
If you have any strength in your thumb. The blossoms
Are fragile and motionless, never letting anyone see
     Any of them using their finger.

And this you can see is the bolt. The purpose of this
20 Is to open the breech, as you see. We can slide it
Rapidly backwards and forwards: we call this
Easing the spring. And rapidly backwards and forwards
The early bees are assaulting and fumbling the flowers:
     They call it easing the Spring.

25 They call it easing the Spring: it is perfectly easy
If you have any strength in your thumb: like the bolt,
And the breech, and the cocking-piece, and the point of balance,
Which in our case we have not got; and the almond-blossom
Silent in all of the gardens and the bees going backwards and for-
     wards,
30   For today we have naming of parts.

JUDGING DISTANCES

Not only how far away, but the way that you say it
Is very important. Perhaps you may never get
The knack of judging a distance, but at least you know
How to report on a landscape: the central sector,
5 The right of arc and that, which we had last Tuesday,
     And at least you know

That maps are of time, not place, so far as the army
Happens to be concerned—the reason being,
Is one which need not delay us. Again, you know
10 There are three kinds of tree, three only, the fir and the poplar,
And those which have bushy tops to; and lastly
    That things only seem to be things.

A barn is not called a barn, to put it more plainly,
Or a field in the distance, where sheep may be safely grazing.
15 You must never be over-sure. You must say, when reporting:
At five o'clock in the central sector is a dozen
Of what appear to be animals; whatever you do,
    Don't call the bleeders *sheep*.

I am sure that's quite clear; and suppose, for the sake of example,
20 The one at the end, asleep, endeavors to tell us
What he sees over there to the west, and how far away,
After first having come to attention. There to the west,
On the fields of summer the sun and the shadows bestow
    Vestments of purple and gold.

25 The still white dwellings are like a mirage in the heat,
And under the swaying elms a man and a woman
Lie gently together. Which is, perhaps, only to say
That there is a row of houses to the left of arc,
And that under some poplars a pair of what appear to be humans
30   Appear to be loving.

Well that, for an answer, is what we might rightly call
Moderately satisfactory only, the reason being,
Is that two things have been omitted, and those are important.
The human beings, now: in what direction are they,
35 And how far away, would you say? And do not forget
    There may be dead ground in between.

There may be dead ground in between; and I may not have got
The knack of judging a distance; I will only venture
A guess that perhaps between me and the apparent lovers,
40 (Who, incidentally, appear by now to have finished,)
At seven o'clock from the houses, is roughly a distance
    Of about one year and a half.

UNARMED COMBAT

In due course of course you will all be issued with
Your proper issue; but until tomorrow,
You can hardly be said to need it; and until that time,
We shall have unarmed combat. I shall teach you
5 The various holds and rolls and throws and breakfalls
     Which you may sometimes meet.

And the various holds and rolls and throws and breakfalls
Do not depend on any sort of weapon,
But only on what I might coin a phrase and call
10 The ever-important question of human balance,
And the ever-important need to be in a strong
     Position at the start.

There are many kinds of weakness about the body
Where you would least expect, like the ball of the foot.
15 But the various holds and rolls and throws and breakfalls
Will always come in useful. And never be frightened
To tackle from behind: it may not be clean to do so,
     But this is global war.

So give them all you have, and always give them
20 As good as you get; it will always get you somewhere.
(You may not know it, but you can tie a Jerry
Up without rope; it is one of the things I shall teach you.)
Nothing will matter if only you are ready for him.
     The readiness is all.

25 *The readiness is all.* How can I help but feel
I have been here before? But somehow then,
I was the tied-up one. How to get out
Was always then my problem. And even if I had
A piece of rope I was always the sort of person
30   Who threw the rope aside.

And in my time I have given them all I had,
Which was never as good as I got, and it got me nowhere.
And the various holds and rolls and throws and breakfalls
Somehow or other I always seemed to put
35 In the wrong place. And as for war, my wars
     Were global from the start.

Perhaps I was never in a strong position,
Or the ball of my foot got hurt, or I had some weakness
Where I had least expected. But I think I see your point.
40 While awaiting a proper issue, we must learn the lesson
Of the ever-important question of human balance.
     It is courage that counts.

Things may be the same again; and we must fight
Not in the hope of winning but rather of keeping
45 Something alive: so that when we meet our end,
It may be said that we tackled wherever we could,
That battle-fit we lived, and though defeated,
     Not without glory fought.

WILLIAM STAFFORD (1914–   )

At the Un-National Monument Along the Canadian Border

This is the field where the battle did not happen,
where the unknown soldier did not die.
This is the field where grass joined hands,
Where no monument stands,
5 and the only heroic thing is the sky.

Birds fly here without any sound,
unfolding their wings across the open.
No people killed—or were killed—on this ground
hallowed by neglect and an air so tame
10 that people celebrate it by forgetting its name.

Traveling Through the Dark

Traveling through the dark I found a deer
dead on the edge of the Wilson River road.
It is usually best to roll them into the canyon:
that road is narrow; to swerve might make more dead.

By glow of the tail-light I stumbled back of the car
and stood by the heap, a doe, a recent killing;
she had stiffened already, almost cold.
I dragged her off; she was large in the belly.

My fingers touching her side brought me the reason—
her side was warm; her fawn lay there waiting,
alive, still, never to be born.
Beside that mountain road I hesitated.

The car aimed ahead its lowered parking lights;
under the hood purred the steady engine.
15 I stood in the glare of the warm exhaust turning red;
around our group I could hear the wilderness listen.

I thought hard for us all—my only swerving—
then pushed her over the edge into the river.

P. K. PAGE (1916–   )

The Stenographers

After the brief bivouac of Sunday,
their eyes, in the forced march of Monday to Saturday,
hoist the white flag, flutter in the snow storm of paper,
haul it down and crack in the midsun of temper.

5 In the pause between the first draft and the carbon
they glimpse the smooth hours when they were children—
the ride in the ice-cart, the ice-man's name,
the end of the route and the long walk home;

remember the sea where floats at high tide
10 were sea marrows growing on the scatter-green vine
or spools of gray toffee, or wasps' nests on water;
remember the sand and the leaves of the country.

Bell rings and they go and the voice draws their pencil
like a sled across snow; when its runners are frozen
15 rope snaps and the voice then is pulling no burden
but runs like a dog on the winter of paper.

Their climates are winter and summer—no wind
for the kites of their hearts—no wind for a flight;
a breeze at the most, to tumble them over
20 and leave them like rubbish—the boy-friends of blood.

In the inch of the noon as they move they are stagnant.
The terrible calm of the noon is their anguish;
the lip of the counter, the shapes of the straws
like icicles breaking their tongues are invaders.

25 Their beds are their oceans—salt water of weeping
the waves that they know—the tide before sleep;
and fighting to drown they assemble their sheep
in columns and watch them leap desks for their fences
and stare at them with their own mirror-worn faces.

30 In the felt of the morning the calico minded,
sufficiently starched, insert papers, hit keys,
efficient and sure as their adding machines;
yet they weep in the vault, they are taut as net curtains
stretched upon frames. In their eyes I have seen
35 the pin men of madness in marathon trim
race round the track of the stadium pupil.

Schizophrenic

Nobody knew when it would start again—
the extraordinary beast go violent in her blood;
nobody knew the virtue of her need
to shape her face to the giant in her brain.

5 Certainly friends were sympathetic, kind,
gave her small handkerchiefs and showed her tricks,
built her life to a sort of 'pick-up sticks'
simplification—as if she were a child.

Malleable she wore her lustre nails
10 daily like a debutante and smoked,
watching the fur her breath made as they joked,
caught like a wind in the freedom of their sails.

While always behind her face, the giant's face
struggled to break the matte mask of her skin—
15 and, turned about at last, be looking in—
tranquilly *in* to that imprisoned place.

Strong for the dive he dived one day at tea—
the cakes like flowers, the cups dreamy with cream—
he saw the window a lake and with a scream
20 nobody heard, shot by immediacy

he forced the contours of her features out.
Her tea-time friends were statues as she passed,
pushed, but seemingly drawn towards the glass;

her tea-time friends were blind, they did not see
25 the violence of his struggle to get free,
and deaf, and deaf, they did not hear his shout.

The waters of his lake were sharp and cold—
splashed and broke, triangular on the floor
after the dive from his imagined shore
30 in a land where all the inhabitants are old.

GWENDOLYN BROOKS (1917–   )

The Bean Eaters

They eat beans mostly, this old yellow pair.
Dinner is a casual affair.
Plain chipware on a plain and creaking wood,
Tin flatware.

5 Two who are Mostly Good.
Two who have lived their day,
But keep on putting on their clothes
And putting things away.

And remembering . . .
10 Remembering, with twinklings and twinges,
As they lean over the beans in their rented back room that is full of
       beads and receipts and dolls and clothes, tobacco crumbs, vases
       and fringes.

We Real Cool

The Pool Players.
Seven at the Golden Shovel.

We real cool. We
Left school. We

5 Lurk late. We
Strike straight. We

Sing sin. We
Thin gin. We

Jazz June. We
10 Die soon.

ROBERT LOWELL (1917–1977)

Mr. Edwards and the Spider

I saw the spiders marching through the air,
    Swimming from tree to tree that mildewed day
        In latter August when the hay

Came creaking to the barn. But where
5   The wind is westerly,
Where gnarled November makes the spiders fly
Into the apparitions of the sky,
They purpose nothing but their ease and die
Urgently beating east to sunrise and the sea;

10   What are we in the hands of the great God?
It was in vain you set up thorn and briar
      In battle array against the fire
      And treason crackling in your blood;
         For the wild thorns grow tame
15   And will do nothing to oppose the flame;
Your lacerations tell the losing game
You play against a sickness past your cure
How will the hands be strong? How will the heart endure?

A very little thing, a little worm,
20   Or hourglass-blazoned spider, it is said,
      Can kill a tiger. Will the dead
      Hold up his mirror and affirm
         To the four winds the smell
And flash of his authority? It's well
25   If God who holds you to the pit of hell,
Much as one holds a spider, will destroy,

Baffle and dissipate your soul. As a small boy
      On Windsor Marsh, I saw the spider die
      When thrown into the bowels of fierce fire:
30   There's no long struggle, no desire
         To get up on its feet and fly—
            It stretches out its feet
And dies. This is the sinner's last retreat;
Yes, and no strength exerted on the heat
35   Then sinews the abolished will, when sick
And full of burning, it will whistle on a brick.

But who can plumb the sinking of that soul?
      Josiah Hawley, picture yourself cast
      Into a brick-kiln where the blast
40   Fans your quick vitals to a coal—
            If measured by a glass,

How long would it seem burning! Let there pass
A minute, ten, ten trillion; but the blaze
Is infinite, eternal: this is death,
45 To die and know it. This is the Black Widow, death.

Skunk Hour

For Elizabeth Bishop

Nautilus Island's hermit
heiress still lives through winter in her Spartan cottage;
her sheep still graze above the sea.
Her son's a bishop. Her farmer
5 is first selectman in our village;
she's in her dotage.

Thirsting for
the hierarchic privacy ·
of Queen Victoria's century,
10 she buys up all
the eyesores facing her shore,
and lets them fall.

The season's ill—
we've lost our summer millionaire,
15 who seemed to leap from an L. L. Bean
catalogue. His nine-knot yawl
was auctioned off to lobstermen.
A red fox stain covers Blue Hill.

And now our fairy
20 decorator brightens his shop for fall;
his fishnet's filled with orange cork,
orange, his cobbler's bench and awl;
there is no money in his work,
he'd rather marry.

25 One dark night,
my Tudor Ford climbed the hill's skull;
I watched for love-cars. Lights turned down,
they lay together, hull to hull,
where the graveyard shelves on the town. . . .
30 My mind's not right.

A car radio bleats,
"Love, O careless Love. . . ." I hear
my ill-spirit sob in each blood cell,
as if my hand were at its throat. . . .
35 I myself am hell;
nobody's here—

only skunks, that search
in the moonlight for a bite to eat.
They march on their soles up Main Street:

40 white stripes, moonstruck eyes' red fire
under the chalk-dry and spar spire
of the Trinitarian Church.

I stand on top
of our back steps and breathe the rich air—
45 a mother skunk with her column of kittens swills the garbage pail.
She jabs her wedge-head in a cup
of sour cream, drops her ostrich tail,
and will not scare.

Water

It was a Maine lobster town—
each morning boatloads of hands
pushed off for granite
quarries on the islands,

5 and left dozens of bleak
white frame houses stuck
like oyster shells
on a hill of rock,

and below us, the sea lapped
10 the raw little match-stick
mazes of a weir,
where the fish for bait were trapped.

Remember? We sat on a slab of rock.
From this distance in time,
15 it seems the color
of iris, rotting and turning purpler,

but it was only
the usual gray rock
turning the usual green
20 when drenched by the sea.

The sea drenched the rock
at our feet all day,
and kept tearing away
flake after flake.

²⁵ One night you dreamed
 you were a mermaid clinging to a wharf-pile,
 and trying to pull
 off the barnacles with your hands.

 We wished our two souls
³⁰ might return like gulls
 to the rock. In the end,
 the water was too cold for us.

For the Union Dead

"Relinquunt Omnia Servare Rem Publican." 1

The old South Boston Aquarium stands
in a Sahara of snow now. Its broken windows are boarded.
The bronze weathervane cod has lost half its scales.
The airy tanks are dry.

5 Once my nose crawled like a snail on the glass;
 my hand tingled
 to burst the bubbles
 drifting from the noses of the cowed, compliant fish.

 My hand draws back. I often sigh still
¹⁰ for the dark downward and vegetating kingdom
 of the fish and reptile. One morning last March,
 I pressed against the new barbed and galvanized

 fence on the Boston Common. Behind their cage,
 yellow dinosaur steamshovels were grunting
¹⁵ as they cropped up tons of mush and grass
 to gouge their underworld garage.

 Parking spaces luxuriate like civic
 sandpiles in the heart of Boston.
 A girdle of orange, Puritan-pumpkin colored girders
²⁰ braces the tingling Statehouse,

 shaking over the excavations, as it faces Colonel Shaw
 and his bell-cheeked Negro infantry
 on St. Gaudens' shaking Civil War relief,
 propped by a plank splint against the garage's earthquake.

---

1 "They gave up all to serve the republic."

25 Two months after marching through Boston,
   half the regiment was dead;
   at the dedication,
   William James could almost hear the bronze Negroes breathe.

   Their monument sticks like a fishbone
30 in the city's throat.
   Its Colonel is as lean
   as a compass-needle.

   He has an angry wrenlike vigilance,
   a greyhound's gentle tautness;
35 he seems to wince at pleasure,
   and suffocate for privacy.

   He is out of bounds now. He rejoices in man's lovely,
   peculiar power to choose life and die—
   when he leads his black soldiers to death,
40 he cannot bend his back.

   On a thousand small town New England greens,
   the old white churches hold their air
   of sparse, sincere rebellion; frayed flags
   quilt the graveyards of the Grand Army of the Republic.

45 The stone statues of the abstract Union Soldier
   grow slimmer and younger each year—
   wasp-waisted, they doze over muskets
   and muse through their sideburns . . .

   Shaw's father wanted no monument
50 except the ditch,
   where his son's body was thrown
   and lost with his "niggers."

   The ditch is nearer.
   There are no statues for the last war here;
55 on Boylston Street, a commercial photograph
   shows Hiroshima boiling

   over a Mosler Safe, the "Rock of Ages"
   that survived the blast. Space is nearer.
   When I crouch to my television set,
60 the drained faces of Negro school-children rise like balloons.

Colonel Shaw
is riding on his bubble,
he waits
for the blessèd break.

65 The Aquarium is gone. Everywhere,
giant finned cars nose forward like fish;
a savage servility
slides by on grease.

MARGARET AVISON (1918–   )

A Nameless One

Hot in June a narrow winged
long-elbowed-thread-legged
living insect lived
and died within
5 the lodgers' second-floor bathroom here.

At six a.m.
wafting ceilingward,
no breeze but what it living made there;

at noon standing
10 still as a constellation of spruce needles
before the moment of
making it, whirling;

at four a
wilted flotsam, cornsilk, on the linoleum:

15 now that it is
over, I
look with new eyes
upon this room
adequate for one to
20 be, in.

Its insect-day
has threaded a needle
for me for my eyes dimming
over rips and tears and
25 thin places.

ALFRED PURDY (1918–   )

The Cariboo Horses

At 100 Mile House the cowboys ride in rolling
stagey cigarettes with one hand reining
restive equine rebels on a morning grey as stone
—so much like riding dangerous women
5   with whiskey coloured eyes—
such women as once fell dead with their lovers
with fire in their heads and slippery froth on thighs
—Beaver and Carrier women maybe or
           Blackfoot squaws far past the edge of this valley
10 on the other side of those two toy mountain ranges
          from the sunfierce plains beyond—

But only horses
          waiting in stables
hitched at taverns
15   standing at dawn
pastured outside the town with
jeeps and fords and chevvys and
busy muttering stake trucks rushing
importantly over roads of man's devising
20 over the safe known roads of the ranchers
families and merchants of the town—
          On the high prairie
are only horse and rider
          wind in dry grass
25 clopping in silence under the toy mountains
dropping sometimes and
          lost in the dry grass
          golden oranges of dung—
Only horses
30   no stopwatch memories or palace ancestors
not Kiangs hauling undressed stone in the Nile Valley
and having stubborn Egyptian tantrums or
Onagers racing thru Hither Asia and
the last Quagga screaming in African highlands
35   lost relatives of these
          whose hooves were thunder
the ghosts of horses battering thru the wind
whose names were the wind's common usage
whose life was the sun's
40   arriving here at chilly noon

in the gasoline smell of the
dust and waiting 15 minutes
at the grocer's—

Wilderness Gothic

Across Roblin Lake, two shores away,
they are sheathing the church spire
with new metal. Someone hangs in the sky
over there from a piece of rope,
5   hammering and fitting God's belly-scratcher,
working his way up along the spire
until there's nothing left to nail on—
Perhaps the workman's faith reaches beyond:
touches intangibles, wrestles with Jacob,
10 replacing rotten timber with pine thews,
pounds hard in the blue cave of the sky,
contends heroically with difficult problems of
gravity, sky navigation and mythopeia,
his volunteer time and labor donated to God,
15 minus sick benefits of course on a non-union job—

Fields around are yellowing into harvest,
nestling and fingering are sky and water borne,
death is yodeling quiet in green woodlots,
and bodies of three young birds have disappeared
20 in the sub-surface of the new county highway—

That picture is incomplete, part left out
that might alter the whole Dürer landscape:
gothic ancestors peer from medieval sky,
dour faces trapped in photograph albums escaping
25 to clop down iron roads with matched grays:
work-sodden wives groping inside their flesh
for what keeps moving and changing and flashing
beyond and past the long frozen Victorian day.
A sign of fire and brimstone? A two-headed calf
30 born in the barn last night? A sharp female agony?
An age and a faith moving into transition,
the dinner cold and new-baked bread a failure,
deep woods shiver and water drops hang pendant,
double yolked eggs and the house creaks a little—
35 Something is about to happen. Leaves are still.
Two shores away, a man hammering in the sky.
Perhaps he will fall.

MAY SWENSON (1919–   )

Question

Body my house
my horse my hound
what will I do
when you are fallen

5 Where will I sleep
How will I ride
What will I hunt

Where can I go
without my mount
10 all eager and quick
How will I know
in thicket ahead
is danger or treasure
when Body my good
15 bright dog is dead

How will it be
to lie in the sky
without roof or door
and wind for an eye

20 With cloud for shift
how will I hide?

ROBERT DUNCAN (1919–   )

**Often I Am Permitted to Return to a
Meadow**

as if it were a scene made-up by the mind,
that is not mine, but is a made place,

that is mine, it is so near to the heart,
an eternal pasture folded in all thought
5 so that there is a hall therein

that is a made place, created by light
wherefrom the shadows that are forms fall.

Wherefrom fall all architectures I am
I say are likenesses of the First Beloved
10 whose flowers are flames lit to the Lady.

She it is Queen Under The Hill
whose hosts are a disturbance of words within words
that is a field folded.

It is only a dream of the grass blowing
15 east against the source of the sun
in an hour before the sun's going down

whose secret we see in a children's game
of ring a round of roses told.

Often I am permitted to return to a meadow
20 as if it were a given property of the mind
that certain bounds hold against chaos,

that is a place of first permission,
everlasting omen of what is.

LAWRENCE FERLINGHETTI (1919–   )

In Goya's greatest scenes we seem to see

In Goya's greatest scenes we seem to see
                              the people of the world
         exactly at the moment when
               they first attained the title of
5   "suffering humanity"
         They writhe upon the page
                    in a veritable rage
                              of adversity
            Heaped up
10   groaning with babies and bayonets
                              under cement skies
         in an abstract landscape of blasted trees
            bent statues bats wings and beaks
                    slippery gibbets
15   cadavers and carnivorous cocks
         and all the final hollering monsters
               of the
                    "imagination of disaster"

they are so bloody real
20   it is as if they really still existed

And they do

Only the landscape is changed

They still are ranged along the roads
    plagued by legionnaires
25   false windmills and demented roosters
      They are the same people
             only further from home
      on freeways fifty lanes wide
          on a concrete continent
30   spaced with bland billboards
         illustrating imbecile illusions of happiness
    The scene shows fewer tumbrils
          but more maimed citizens
              in painted cars
35   and they have strange license plates
    and engines
        that devour America

The pennycandystore beyond the El

The pennycandystore beyond the El
is where I first
      fell in love
          with unreality
5 Jellybeans glowed in the semi-gloom
of that september afternoon
A cat upon the counter moved among
           the licorice sticks
      and tootsie rolls
10   and Oh Boy Gum

Outside the leaves were falling as they died

A wind had blown away the sun

A girl ran in
Her hair was rainy
15 Her breasts were breathless in the little room

Outside the leaves were falling
        and they cried
            Too soon! too soon!

HOWARD NEMEROV (1920–   )

The Goose Fish

On the long shore, lit by the moon
To show them properly alone,
Two lovers suddenly embraced
So that their shadows were as one.
5 The ordinary night was graced
For them by the swift tide of blood
That silently they took at flood,
And for a little time they prized
   Themselves emparadised.

10 Then, as if shaken by stage-fright
Beneath the hard moon's bony light,
They stood together on the sand
Embarrassed in each other's sight
But still conspiring hand in hand,
15 Until they saw, there underfoot,
As though the world had found them out,
The goose fish turning up, though dead,
   His hugely grinning head.

There in the china light he lay,
20 Most ancient and corrupt and gray
They hesitated at his smile,
Wondering what it seemed to say
To lovers who a little while
Before had thought to understand,
25 By violence upon the sand,
The only way that could be known
   To make a world their own.

It was a wide and moony grin
Together peaceful and obscene;
30 They knew not what he would express,
So finished a comedian
He might mean failure or success,
But took it for an emblem of
Their sudden, new and guilty love
35 To be observed by, when they kissed,
   That rigid optimist.

So he became their patriarch,
Dreadfully mild in the half-dark.
His throat that the sand seemed to choke,
40 His picket teeth, these left their mark
But never did explain the joke
That so amused him, lying there
While the moon went down to disappear
Along the still and tilted track
45   That bears the zodiac.

I Only Am Escaped Alone To Tell Thee

I tell you that I see her still
At the dark entrance of the hall.
One gas lamp burning near her shoulder
Shone also from her other side
5 Where hung the long inaccurate glass
Whose pictures were as troubled water.
An immense shadow had its hand
Between us on the floor, and seemed
To hump the knuckles nervously,
10 A giant crab readying to walk,
Or a blanket moving in its sleep.

You will remember, with a smile
Instructed by movies to reminisce,
How strict her corsets must have been,
15 How the huge arrangements of her hair
Would certainly betray the least
Impassionate displacement there.
It was no rig for dallying,
And maybe only marriage could
20 Derange that queenly scaffolding—
As when a great ship, coming home,
Coasts in the harbor, dropping sail
And loosing all the tackle that had laced
Her in the long lanes . . .
                                    I know
25 We need not draw this figure out
But all that whalebone came from whales
And all the whales lived in the sea,
In calm beneath the troubled glass,
Until the needle drew their blood.

30 I see her standing in the hall,
    Where the mirror's lashed to blood and foam,
    And the black flukes of agony
    Beat at the air till the light blows out.

RAYMOND SOUSTER (1921–   )

Young Girls

With night full of spring and stars we stand
here in this dark doorway and watch the young
girls pass, two, three together, hand in hand.
They are like flowers whose fragrance hasn't sprung

5 or awakened, whose bodies now dimly feel
the flooding, upward welling of the trees;
whose senses, caressed by the wind's soft fingers, reel
with a mild delirium that makes them ill at ease.

They lie awake at night unable to sleep

10 and walk the streets kindled by strange desires;
they steal lightning glances at us, unable to keep
control upon those subterranean fires.
We whistle after them, then laugh, for they
stiffen, not knowing what to do or say.

RICHARD WILBUR (1921–   )

In a Churchyard

That flower unseen, that gem of purest ray,
    Bright thoughts uncut by men:
Strange that you need but speak them, Thomas Gray,
    And the mind skips and dives beyond its ken,

5 Finding at once the wild supposèd bloom,
    Or in the imagined cave
Some pulse of crystal staving off the gloom
    As covertly as phosphorus in a grave.

Void notions proper to a buried head!

10 Beneath these tombstones here
Unseenness fills the sockets of the dead,
    Whatever to their souls may now appear;

And who but those unfathomably deaf
    Who quiet all this ground

15 Could catch, within the ear's diminished clef,
    A music innocent of time and sound?

What do the living hear, then, when the bell
Hangs plumb within the tower
Of the still church, and still their thoughts compel
20 Pure tollings that intend no mortal hour?

As when a ferry for the shore of death
Glides looming toward the dock,
Her engines cut, her spirits bating breath
As the ranked pilings narrow toward the shock,

25 So memory and expectation set
Some pulseless clangor free
Of circumstance, and charm us to forget
This twilight crumbling in the churchyard tree,

Those swifts or swallows which do not pertain,
30 Scuffed voices in the drive,
That light flicked on behind the vestry pane,
Till, unperplexed from all that is alive,

It shadows all our thought, balked imminence
Of uncommitted sound,
35 And still would tower at the sill of sense
Were not, as now, its honeyed abeyance crowned

With a mauled boom of summons far more strange
Than any stroke unheard,
Which breaks again with unimagined range
40 Through all reverberations of the word,

Pooling the mystery of things that are,
The buzz of prayer said,
The scent of grass, the earliest-blooming star,
These unseen gravestones, and the darker dead.

Exeunt

Piecemeal the summer dies;
At the field's edge a daisy lives alone;
   A last shawl of burning lies
      On the gray field-stone.

5   All cries are thin and terse;
The field has droned the summer's final mass;
   A cricket like a dwindled hearse
      Crawls from the dry grass.

Place Pigalle

Now homing tradesmen scatter through the streets
Toward suppers, thinking on improved conditions,
While evening, with a million simple fissions,
Takes up its warehouse watches, storefront beats,
5 By nursery windows its assigned positions.

Now at the corners of the Place Pigalle
Bright bars explode against the dark's embraces;
The soldiers come, the boys with ancient faces,
Seeking their ancient friends, who stroll and loll
10 Amid the glares and glass: electric graces.

The puppies are asleep, and snore the hounds;
But here wry hares, the soldier and the whore,
Mark off their refuge with a gaudy door,
Brazen at bay, and boldly out of bounds:
15 The puppies dream, the hounds superbly snore.

Ionized innocence: this pair reclines,
She on the table, he in a tilting chair,
With Arden ease; her eyes as pale as air
Travel his priestgoat face; his hand's thick tines
20 Touch the gold whorls of her Corinthian hair.

"Girl, if I love thee not, then let me die;
Do I not scorn to change my state with kings?
Your muchtouched flesh, incalculable, which wrings
Me so, now shall I gently seize in my
25 Desperate soldier's hands which kill all things."

Love Calls Us to the Things of This World

The eyes open to a cry of pulleys,
And spirited from sleep, the astounded soul
Hangs for a moment bodiless and simple
As false dawn.
5   Outside the open window
The morning air is all awash with angels.

Some are in bed-sheets, some are in blouses,
Some are in smocks: but truly there they are.
Now they are rising together in calm swells
10 Of halcyon feeling, filling whatever they wear
With the deep joy of their impersonal breathing;

Now they are flying in place, conveying
The terrible speed of their omnipresence, moving
And staying like white water; and now of a sudden
15 They swoon down into so rapt a quiet
That nobody seems to be there.
                                    The soul shrinks

    From all that it is about to remember,
From the punctual rape of every blessèd day,
20 And cries,
            "Oh, let there be nothing on earth but laundry,
Nothing but rosy hands in the rising steam
And clear dances done in the sight of heaven."

    Yet, as the sun acknowledges
25 With a warm look the world's hunks and colors,
The soul descends once more in bitter love
To accept the waking body, saying now
In a changed voice as the man yawns and rises,

    "Bring them down from their ruddy gallows;
30 Let there be clean linen for the backs of thieves;
Let lovers go fresh and sweet to be undone,
And the heaviest nuns walk in a pure floating
Of dark habits,
                keeping their difficult balance."

Year's-End

Now winter downs the dying of the year,
And night is all a settlement of snow;
From the soft street the rooms of houses show
A gathered light, a shapen atmosphere,
5 Like frozen-over lakes whose ice is thin
And still allows some stirring down within.

I've known the wind by water banks to shake
The late leaves down, which frozen where they fell
And held in ice as dancers in a spell
10 Fluttered all winter long into a lake;
Graved on the dark in gestures of descent,
They seemed their own most perfect monument.

There was perfection in the death of ferns
Which laid their fragile cheeks against the stone
15 A million years. Great mammoths overthrown
Composedly have made their long sojourns,
Like palaces of patience, in the gray
And changeless lands of ice. And at Pompeii

The little dog lay curled and did not rise
20 But slept the deeper as the ashes rose
And found the people incomplete, and froze
The random hands, the loose unready eyes
Of men expecting yet another sun
To do the shapely thing they had not done.

25 These sudden ends of time must give us pause.
We fray into the future, rarely wrought
Save in the tapestries of afterthought.
More time, more time. Barrages of applause
Come muffled from a buried radio.
30 The New-year bells are wrangling with the snow.

PHILIP LARKIN (1922–   )

Church Going

Once I am sure there's nothing going on
I step inside, letting the door thud shut.
Another church: matting, seats, and stone,
And little books; sprawlings of flowers, cut
5 For Sunday, brownish now; some brass and stuff
Up at the holy end; the small neat organ;
And a tense, musty, unignorable silence,
Brewed God knows how long. Hatless, I take off
My cycle-clips in awkward reverence,

10 Move forward, run my hand around the font.
From where I stand, the roof looks almost new—
Cleaned, or restored? Someone would know: I don't.
Mounting the lectern, I peruse a few
Hectoring large-scale verses, and pronounce
15 "Here endeth" much more loudly than I'd meant.
The echoes snigger briefly. Back at the door
I sign the book, donate an Irish sixpence,
Reflect the place was not worth stopping for.

Yet stop I did: in fact I often do,
20 And always end much at a loss like this,
Wondering what to look for; wondering, too,
When churches fall completely out of use
What we shall turn them into, if we shall keep
A few cathedrals chronically on show,

25 Their parchment, plate and pyx in locked cases,
   And let the rest rent-free to rain and sheep.
   Shall we avoid them as unlucky places?

   Or, after dark, will dubious women come
   To make their children touch a particular stone;
30 Pick simples for a cancer; or on some
   Advised night see walking a dead one?
   Power of some sort or other will go on
   In games, in riddles, seemingly at random;
   But superstition, like belief, must die,
35 And what remains when disbelief has gone?
   Grass, weedy pavement, brambles, buttress, sky,

   A shape less recognisable each week,
   A purpose more obscure. I wonder who
   Will be the last, the very last, to seek
40 This place for what it was; one of the crew
   That tap and jot and know what rood-lofts were?
   Some ruin-bibber, randy for antique,
   Or Christmas-addict, counting on a whiff
   Of gown-and-bands and organ-pipes and myrrh?
45 Or will he be my representative,

   Bored, uninformed, knowing the ghostly silt
   Dispersed, yet tending to this cross of ground
   Through suburb scrub because it held unspilt
   So long and equably what since is found
50 Only in separation—marriage, and birth,
   And death, and thoughts of these—for whom was built
   This special shell? For, though I've no idea
   What this accoutred frowsty barn is worth,
   It pleases me to stand in silence here;

55 A serious house on serious earth it is,
   In whose blent air all our compulsions meet,
   Are recognised, and robed as destinies,
   And that much never can be obsolete,
   Since someone will forever be surprising
60 A hunger in himself to be more serious,
   And gravitating with it to this ground,
   Which, he once heard, was proper to grow wise in,
   If only that so many dead lie round.

The Whitsun Weddings[1]

That Whitsun, I was late getting away:
   Not till about
One-twenty on the sunlit Saturday
Did my three-quarters-empty train pull out,
5 All windows down, all cushions hot, all sense
Of being in a hurry gone. We ran
Behind the backs of houses, crossed a street
Of blinding windscreens, smelt the fish-dock; thence
The river's level drifting breadth began,
10 Where sky and Lincolnshire and water meet.

All afternoon, through the tall heat that slept
   For miles inland,
A slow and stopping curve southwards we kept.
Wide farms went by, short-shadowed cattle, and
15 Canals with floatings of industrial froth;
A hothouse flashed uniquely: hedges dipped
And rose: and now and then a smell of grass
Displaced the reek of buttoned carriage-cloth
Until the next town, new and nondescript,
20 Approached with acres of dismantled cars.

At first, I didn't notice what a noise
   The weddings made
Each station that we stopped at: sun destroys
The interest of what's happening in the shade,
25 And down the long cool platforms whoops and skirls
I took for porters larking with the mails,
And went on reading. Once we started, though,
We passed them, grinning and pomaded, girls
In parodies of fashion, heels and veils,
30 All posed irresolutely, watching us go,

As if out on the end of an event
   Waving goodbye
To something that survived it. Struck, I leant
More promptly out next time, more curiously,
35 And saw it all again in different terms:
The fathers with broad belts under their suits
And seamy foreheads; mothers loud and fat;

---

[1] Whitsunday is the seventh Sunday after Easter.

An uncle shouting smut; and then the perms,
The nylon gloves and jewelry-substitutes,
40 The lemons, mauves and olive-ochers that

Marked off the girls unreally from the rest.
   Yes, from cafés
And banquet-halls up yards, and bunting-dressed
Coach-party annexes, the wedding-days
45 Were coming to an end. All down the line
Fresh couples climbed aboard: the rest stood round;
The last confetti and advice were thrown,
And, as we moved, each face seemed to define
Just what it saw departing; children frowned
50 At something dull; fathers had never known

Success so huge and wholly farcical;
   The women shared
The secret like a happy funeral;

While girls, gripping their handbags tighter, stared
55 At a religious wounding. Free at last,
And loaded with the sum of all they saw,
We hurried towards London, shuffling gouts of steam.
Now fields were building-plots, and poplars cast
Long shadows over major roads, and for
60 Some fifty minutes, that in time would seem

Just long enough to settle hats and say
   I nearly died,
A dozen marriages got under way.
They watched the landscape, sitting side by side
65 —An Odeon went past, a cooling tower,
And someone running up to bowl—and none
Thought of the others they would never meet
Or how their lives would all contain this hour.
I thought of London spread out in the sun,
70 Its postal districts packed like squares of wheat:

There we were aimed. And as we raced across
   Bright knots of rail
Past standing Pullmans, walls of blackened moss
Came close, and it was nearly done, this frail
75 Traveling coincidence; and what it held
Stood ready to be loosed with all the power

That being changed can give. We slowed again,
And as the tightened brakes took hold, there swelled
A sense of falling, like an arrow-shower
80 Sent out of sight, somewhere becoming rain.

JAMES DICKEY (1923–   )

The Heaven of Animals

Here they are. The soft eyes open.
If they have lived in a wood
It is a wood.
If they have lived on plains
5 It is grass rolling
Under their feet forever.

Having no souls, they have come,
Anyway, beyond their knowing.
Their instincts wholly bloom
10 And they rise.
The soft eyes open.

To match them, the landscape flowers,
Outdoing, desperately
Outdoing what is required:
15 The richest wood,
The deepest field.

For some of these,
It could not be the place
It is, without blood.
20 These hunt, as they have done
But with claws and teeth grown perfect,

More deadly than they can believe.
They stalk more silently,
And crouch on the limbs of trees,
25 And their descent
Upon the bright backs of their prey

May take years
In a sovereign floating of joy.
And those that are hunted
30 Know this as their life,
Their reward: to walk

Under such trees in full knowledge
Of what is in glory above them,
And to feel no fear,
35 But acceptance, compliance.
Fulfilling themselves without pain

At the cycle's center,
They tremble, they walk
Under the tree,
40 They fall, they are torn,
They rise, they walk again.

Buckdancer's Choice

So I would hear out those lungs,
The air split into nine levels,
Some gift of tongues of the whistler

In the invalid's bed: my mother,
5 Warbling all day to herself
The thousand variations of one song;

It is called Buckdancer's Choice.
For years, they have all been dying
Out, the classic buck-and-wing men

10 Of traveling minstrel shows;
With them also an old woman
Was dying of breathless angina,

Yet still found breath enough
To whistle up in my head
15 A sight like a one-man band,

Freed black, with cymbals at heel,
An ex-slave who thrivingly danced
To the ring of his own clashing light

Through the thousand variations of one song
20 All day to my mother's prone music,
The invalid's warbler's note,

While I crept close to the wall
Sock-footed, to hear the sounds alter,
Her tongue like a mockingbird's break

25 Through stratum after stratum of a tone
   Proclaiming what choices there are
   For the last dancers of their kind,

   For ill women and for all slaves
   Of death, and children enchanted at walls
30 With a brass-beating glow underfoot,

   Not dancing but nearly risen
   Through barnlike, theatrelike houses
   On the wings of the buck and wing.

DENISE LEVERTOV (1923–   )

Six Variations (part iii)

Shlup, shlup, the dog
as it laps up
water
makes intelligent
5 music, resting
now and then to take breath in irregular
measure.

Come into Animal Presence

Come into animal presence.
No man is so guileless as
the serpent. The lonely white
rabbit on the roof is a star
5 twitching its ears at the rain.
The llama intricately
folding its hind legs to be seated
not disdains but mildly
disregards human approval.
10 What joy when the insouciant
armadillo glances at us and doesn't
quicken its trotting
across the track into the palm brush.

What is this joy? That no animal
15 falters, but knows what it must do?
That the snake has no blemish,
that the rabbit inspects his strange surroundings

in white star-silence? The llama
rests in dignity, the armadillo
20 has some intention to pursue in the palm-forest.
Those who were sacred have remained so,
holiness does not dissolve, it is a presence
of bronze, only the sight that saw it
faltered and turned from it.
25 An old joy returns in holy presence.

What Were They Like?

1) Did the people of Viet Nam
use lanterns of stone?
2) Did they hold ceremonies
to reverence the opening of buds?
5 3) Were they inclined to rippling laughter?
4) Did they use bone and ivory,
jade and silver, for ornament?
5) Had they an epic poem?
6) Did they distinguish between speech and singing?

10 1) Sir, their light hearts turned to stone.
It is not remembered whether in gardens
stone lanterns illumined pleasant ways.
2) Perhaps they gathered once to delight in blossom,
but after the children were killed
15 there were no more buds.
3) Sir, laughter is bitter to the burned mouth.
4) A dream ago, perhaps. Ornament is for joy.
All the bones were charred.
5) It is not remembered. Remember,
20 most were peasants; their life
was in rice and bamboo.
When peaceful clouds were reflected in the paddies
and the water buffalo stepped surely along terraces,
maybe fathers told their sons old tales.
25 When bombs smashed the mirrors
there was time only to scream.
6) There is an echo yet, it is said,
of their speech which was like a song.
It is reported their singing resembled
30 the flight of moths in moonlight.
Who can say? It is silent now.

Losing Track

Long after you have swung back
away from me
I think you are still with me:

you come in close to the shore
5 on the tide
and nudge me awake the way

a boat adrift nudges the pier:
am I a pier
half-in half-out of the water?

10 and in the pleasure of that communion
I lose track,
the moon I watch goes down, the

tide swings you away before
I know I'm
15 alone again long since,

mud sucking at gray and black
timbers of me,
a light growth of green dreams drying.

LOUIS SIMPSON (1923–   )

My Father in the Night Commanding No

My father in the night commanding No
Has work to do. Smoke issues from his lips;
    He reads in silence.
The frogs are croaking and the streetlamps glow.

5 And then my mother winds the gramophone;
The Bride of Lammermoor begins to shriek—
    Or reads a story
About a prince, a castle, and a dragon.

The moon is glittering above the hill.
10 I stand before the gateposts of the King—
    So runs the story—
Of Thule, at midnight when the mice are still.

And I have been in Thule! It has come true—
The journey and the danger of the world,
15   All that there is
To bear and to enjoy, endure and do.

Landscapes, seascapes . . . where have I been led?
The names of cities—Paris, Venice, Rome—
      Held out their arms.
20 A feathered god, seductive, went ahead.

Here is my house. Under a red rose tree
A child is swinging; another gravely plays.
      They are not surprised
That I am here; they were expecting me.

25 And yet my father sits and reads in silence,
My mother sheds a tear, the moon is still,
      And the dark wind
Is murmuring that nothing ever happens.

Beyond his jurisdiction as I move
30 Do I not prove him wrong? And yet, it's true
      They will not change
There, on the stage of terror and of love.

The actors in that playhouse always sit
In fixed positions—father, mother, child
35   With painted eyes.
How sad it is to be a little puppet!

Their heads are wooden. And you once pretended
To understand them! Shake them as you will,
      They cannot speak.
40 Do what you will, the comedy is ended.

Father, why did you work? Why did you weep,
Mother? Was the story so important?
      "Listen!" the wind
Said to the children, and they fell asleep.

EDWARD FIELD (1924–   )

The Bride of Frankenstein

The Baron has decided to mate the monster,
to breed him perhaps,
in the interests of pure science, his only god.

So he goes up into his laboratory
5 which he has built in the tower of the castle
to be as near the interplanetary forces as possible,
and puts together the prettiest monster-woman you ever saw
with a body like a pin-up girl
and hardly any stitching at all
10 where he sewed on the head of a raped and murdered beauty queen.

He sets his liquids burping, and coils blinking and buzzing,
and waits for an electric storm to send through the equipment
the spark vital for life.
The storm breaks over the castle
15 and the equipment really goes crazy
like a kitchen full of modern appliances
as the lightning juice starts oozing right into that pretty corpse.

He goes to get the monster
so he will be right there when she opens her eyes,
20 for she might fall in love with the first thing she sees
as ducklings do.
That monster is already straining at his chains and slurping
ready to go right to it:
He has been well prepared for coupling
25 by his pinching leering keeper who's been saying for weeks,
"You gonna get a little nookie, kid,"
or "How do you go for some poontag, baby."
All the evil in him is focused on this one thing now
as he is led into her very presence.

30 She awakens slowly,
she bats her eyes,
she gets up out of the equipment,
and finally she stands in all her seamed glory,
a monster princess with a hairdo like a fright-wig,
35 lightning flashing in the background
like a halo and a wedding veil,
like a photographer snapping pictures of great moments.

She stands and stares with her electric eyes,
beginning to understand that in this life too
40 she was just another body to be raped.

The monster is ready to go:
He roars with joy at the sight of her,

so they let him loose and he goes right for those knockers.
And she starts screaming to break your heart
45 and you realize that she was just born:
In spite of her big tits she was just a baby.

But her instincts are right—
rather death than that green slobber:
She jumps off the parapet.
50 And then the monster's sex drive goes wild.
Thwarted, it turns to violence, demonstrating sublimation crudely,
and he wrecks the lab, those burping acids and buzzing coils,
overturning the control panel so the equipment goes off like a bomb,
the stone castle crumbling and crashing in the storm
55 destroying them all . . . perhaps.

Perhaps somehow the Baron got out of that wreckage of his dreams
with his evil intact if not his good looks
and more wicked than ever went on with his thrilling career.

And perhaps even the monster lived
60 to roam the earth, his desire still ungratified,
and lovers out walking in shadowy and deserted places
will see his shape loom up over them, their doom—
and children sleeping in their beds
will wake up in the dark night screaming
65 as his hideous body grabs them.

JOHN HAINES (1924–   )

If the Owl Calls Again

at dusk
from the island in the river,
and it's not too cold,

I'll wait for the moon
5 to rise,
then take wing and glide
to meet him.

We will not speak,
but hooded against the frost
10 soar above

the alder flats, searching
with tawny eyes.

And then we'll sit
in the shadowy spruce and
15 pick the bones
of careless mice,

while the long moon drifts
toward Asia
and the river mutters
20 in its icy bed.

And when morning climbs
the limbs
we'll part without a sound,

fulfilled, floating
25 homeward as
the cold world awakens.

DONALD JUSTICE (1925–   )

Here in Katmandu[1]

We have climbed the mountain,
There's nothing more to do.
It is terrible to come down
To the valley
5 Where, amidst many flowers,
One thinks of snow,

As, formerly, amidst snow,
Climbing the mountain,
One thought of flowers,
10 Tremulous, ruddy with dew,
In the valley.
One caught their scent coming down.

It is difficult to adjust, once down,
To the absence of snow.

---

[1] Capital of Nepal, west of Mt. Everest.

15 Clear days, from the valley,
   One looks up at the mountain.
   What else is there to do?
   Prayerwheels, flowers!

   Let the flowers
20 Fade, the prayerwheels run down.
   What have these to do
   With us who have stood atop the snow
   Atop the mountain,
   Flags seen from the valley?

25 It might be possible to live in the valley,
   To bury oneself among flowers,
   If one could forget the mountain,
   How, setting out before dawn,
   Blinded with snow,
30 One knew what to do.

   Meanwhile it is not easy here in Katmandu,
   Especially when to the valley
   That wind which means snow
   Elsewhere, but here means flowers,
35 Comes down,
   As soon it must, from the mountain.

Luxury

You are like a sun of the tropics
Peering through blinds

Drawn for siesta.
Already you teach me

5 The Spanish for sunflower.
You, alone on the clean sheet.

You, like the spilt moon.
You, like a star

Hidden by sun-goggles.
10 You shall have a thousand lovers.

You, spread here like butter,
Like doubloons, like flowers.

Anonymous Drawing

A delicate young Negro stands
With the reins of a horse clutched loosely in his hands;
So delicate, indeed, that we wonder if he can hold the spirited crea-
    ture beside him
Until the master shall arrive to ride him.
5 Already the animal's nostrils widen with rage or fear.
But if we imagine him snorting, about to rear,
This boy, who should know about such things better than we,
Only stands smiling, passive and ornamental, in a fantastic livery
Of ruffles and puffed breeches,
10 Watching the artist, apparently, as he sketches.
Meanwhile the petty lord who must have paid
For the artist's trip up from Perugia, for the horse, for the boy, for
    everything here, in fact, has been delayed,
Kept too long by his steward, perhaps, discussing
Some business concerning the estate, or fussing
15 Over the details of his impeccable toilet
With a manservant whose opinion is that any alteration at all would
    spoil it.
However fast he should come hurrying now
Over this vast greensward, mopping his brow
Clear of the sweat of the fine Renaissance morning, it would be too
    late:
20 The artist will have had his revenge for being made to wait,
A revenge not only necessary but right and clever—
Simply to leave him out of the scene forever.

KENNETH KOCH (1925–   )

Mending Sump

"Hiram, I think the sump is backing up.
The bathroom floor boards for above two weeks
Have seemed soaked through. A little bird, I think
Has wandered in the pipes, and all's gone wrong."
5 "Something there is that doesn't hump a sump,"
He said; and through his head she saw a cloud
That seemed to twinkle. "Hiram, well," she said,
"Smith is come home! I saw his face just now
While looking through your head. He's come to die
10 Or else to laugh, for hay is dried-up grass
When you're alone." He rose, and sniffed the air.
"We'd better leave him in the sump," he said.

ALLEN GINSBERG (1926–   )

A Supermarket in California

What thoughts I have of you tonight, Walt Whitman, for I walked down the sidestreets under the trees with a headache self-conscious looking at the full moon.

In my hungry fatigue, and shopping for images, I went into the neon fruit supermarket, dreaming of your enumerations!

What peaches and what penumbras! Whole families shopping at night! Aisles full of husbands! Wives in the avocados, babies in the tomatoes!—and you, Garcia Lorca,[1] what were you doing down by the watermelons?

I saw you, Walt Whitman, childless, lonely old grubber, poking among the meats in the refrigerator and eyeing the grocery boys.

5   I heard you asking questions of each: Who killed the pork chops? What price bananas? Are you my Angel?

I wandered in and out of the brilliant stacks of cans following you, and followed in my imagination by the store detective.

We strode down the open corridors together in our solitary fancy tasting artichokes, possessing every frozen delicacy, and never passing the cashier.

Where are we going, Walt Whitman? The doors close in an hour. Which way does your beard point tonight?

(I touch your book and dream of our odyssey in the supermarket and feel absurd.)

10   Will we walk all night through solitary streets? The trees add shade to shade, lights out in the houses, we'll both be lonely.

Will we stroll dreaming of the lost America of love past blue automobiles in driveways, home to our silent cottage?

Ah, dear father, graybeard, lonely old courage-teacher, what America did you have when Charon quit poling his ferry and you got out on a smoking bank and stood watching the boat disappear on the black waters of Lethe? [2]

---

[1] Federico García Lorca (1899–1936), Spanish poet and playwright. He was murdered at the start of the Spanish Civil War; his works were suppressed by the Franco government.

[2] Charon, in Greek myth, ferried the shades of the dead to Hades across Lethe, River of Forgetfulness.

In back of the real

railroad yard in San Jose
   I wandered desolate
in front of a tank factory
   and sat on a bench
5 near the switchman's shack.

A flower lay on the hay on
   the asphalt highway
—the dread hay flower
   I thought—It had a
10 brittle black stem and
   corolla of yellowish dirty
spikes like Jesus' inchlong
   crown, and a soiled
dry center cotton tuft
15   like a used shaving brush
that's been lying under
   the garage for a year.

Yellow, yellow flower, and
   flower of industry,
20 tough spikey ugly flower,
   flower nonetheless,
with the form of the great yellow
   Rose in your brain!
This is the flower of the World.

ROBERT CREELEY (1926–   )

Oh No

If you wander far enough
you will come to it
and when you get there
they will give you a place to sit

5 for yourself only, in a nice chair,
and all your friends will be there
with smiles on their faces
and they will likewise all have places.

Naughty Boy

When he brings home a whale,
she laughs and says, that's not for real.

And if he won the Irish sweepstakes,
she would say, where were you last night?

5 Where are you now, for that matter? Am
I always (she says) to be looking

at you? She says,
if I thought it would get any better I

would shoot you, you
10 nut, you. Then pats her hair

into place, and waits
for Uncle Jim's deep-fired, all-fat, real gone

whale steaks.

ROBERT BLY (1926–   )

Driving to Town Late to Mail a Letter

It is a cold and snowy night. The main street is deserted.
The only things moving are swirls of snow.
As I lift the mailbox door, I feel its cold iron.
There is a privacy I love in this snowy night.
5 Driving around, I will waste more time.

W. D. SNODGRASS (1926–   )

Mementos, 1

Sorting out letters and piles of my old
        Canceled checks, old clippings, and yellow note cards
That meant something once, I happened to find
        Your picture. *That* picture. I stopped there cold,
5 Like a man raking piles of dead leaves in his yard
        Who has turned up a severed hand.

Still, that first second, I was glad: you stand
        Just as you stood—shy, delicate, slender,
In that long gown of green lace netting and daisies

10   That you wore to our first dance. The sight of you stunned
Us all. Well, our needs were different, then,
    And our ideals came easy.

Then through the war and those two long years
Overseas, the Japanese dead in their shacks
15 Among dishes, dolls, and lost shoes; I carried
    This glimpse of you, there, to choke down my fear,
Prove it had been, that it might come back.
    That was before we got married.

—Before we drained out one another's force
20   With lies, self-denial, unspoken regret
And the sick eyes that blame; before the divorce
    And the treachery. Say it: before we met. Still,
I put back your picture. Someday, in due course,
    I will find that it's still there.

Lobsters in the Window

First, you think they are dead.
Then you are almost sure
One is beginning to stir.
Out of the crushed ice, slow
5 As the hands of a schoolroom clock,
He lifts his one great claw
And holds it over his head;
Now, he is trying to walk.

But like a run-down toy;
10 Like the backward crabs we boys
Splashed after in the creek,
Trapped in jars or a net,
And then took home to keep.
Overgrown, retarded, weak,
15 He is fumbling yet
From the deep chill of his sleep

As if, in a glacial thaw,
Some ancient thing might wake
Sore and cold and stiff
20 Struggling to raise one claw
Like a defiant fist;
Yet wavering, as if
Starting to swell and ache
With that thick peg in the wrist.

JOHN ASHBERY (1927–   )

City Afternoon

A veil of haze protects this
Long-ago afternoon forgotten by everybody
In this photograph, most of them now
Sucked screaming through old age and death.

5 If one could seize America
Or at least a fine forgetfulness
That seeps into our outline
Defining our volumes with a stain
That is fleeting too

10 But commemorates
Because it does define, after all:
Gray garlands, that threesome
Waiting for the light to change,
Air lifting the hair of one
15 Upside down in the reflecting pool.

Paradoxes and Oxymorons

This poem is concerned with language on a very plain level.
Look at it talking to you. You look out a window
Or pretend to fidget. You have it but you don't have it.
You miss it, it misses you. You miss each other.

5 The poem is sad because it wants to be yours, and cannot.
What's a plain level? It is that and other things,
Bringing a system of them into play. Play?
Well, actually, yes, but I consider play to be

A deeper outside thing, a dreamed role-pattern,
10 As in the division of grace these long August days
Without proof. Open-ended. And before you know
It gets lost in the steam and chatter of typewriters.

It has been played once more. I think you exist only
To tease me into doing it, on your level, and then you aren't there
15 Or have adopted a different attitude. And the poem
Has set me softly down beside you. The poem is you.

W. S. MERWIN (1927–   )

The River of Bees

In a dream I returned to the river of bees
Five orange trees by the bridge and
Beside two mills my house
Into whose courtyard a blind man followed
5 The goats and stood singing
Of what was older

Soon it will be fifteen years

He was old he will have fallen into his eyes

I took my eyes
10 A long way to the calendars
Room after room asking how shall I live

One of the ends is made of streets
One man processions carry through it
Empty bottles their
15 Image of hope
It was offered to me by name

Once once and once
In the same city I was born
Asking what shall I say

20 He will have fallen into his mouth
Men think they are better than grass

I return to his voice rising like a forkful of hay

He was old he is not real nothing is real
Nor the noise of death drawing water

25 We are the echo of the future

On the door it says what to do to survive
But we were not born to survive
Only to live

The Moths

It is cold here
In the steel grass
At the foot of the invisible statue
Made by the incurables and called
5 Justice

At a great distance
An audience of rubber tombstones is watching
The skulls of
The leaders
10 Strung on the same worm

Darkness moves up the nail

And I am returning to a night long since past
In which the rain is falling and
A crying comes from the stations
15 And near at hand a voice a woman's
In a jug under the wind
Is trying to sing

No one has shown her
Any statue and
20 The music keeps rising through her
Almost beginning and
The moths
Lie in the black grass waiting

DONALD PETERSEN (1928–   )

The Ballad of Dead Yankees

Where's Babe Ruth, the King of Swat,
Who rocked the heavens with his blows?
Grabowski, Pennock, and Malone—
Mother of mercy, where are those?

5 Where's Tony (Poosh 'em up) Lazzeri,
The quickest man that ever played?
Where's the gang that raised the roof
In the house that Colonel Ruppert made?

Where's Lou Gehrig, strong and shy,
10 Who never missed a single game?
Where's Tiny Bonham, where's Jake Powell
And many another peerless name?

Where's Steve Sundra, good but late,
Who for a season had his fling?
15 Where are the traded, faded ones?
Lord, can they tell us anything?

Where's the withered nameless dwarf
Who sold us pencils at the gate?
Hurled past the clamor of our cheers?
20 Gone to rest with the good and great?

Where's the swagger, where's the strut,
Where's the style that was the hitter?
Where's the pitcher's swanlike motion?
What in God's name turned life bitter?

25 For strong-armed Steve, who lost control
And weighed no more than eighty pounds,
No sooner benched than in his grave,
Where's the cleverness that confounds?

For Lou the man, erect and clean,
30 Wracked with a cruel paralysis,
Gone in his thirty-seventh year,
Where's the virtue that was his?

For nimble Tony, cramped in death,
God knows why and God knows how,
35 Shut in a dark and silent house,
Where's the squirrel quickness now?

For big brash Babe in an outsize suit,
Himself grown thin and hoarse with cancer,
Still autographing balls for boys,
40 Mother of mercy, what's the answer?

Is there a heaven with rainbow flags,
Silver trophies hung on walls,
A horseshoe grandstand, mobs of fans,
Webbed gloves and official balls?

45 Is there a power in judgment there
To stand behind the body's laws,
A stern-faced czar whose slightest word
Is righteous as Judge Kenesaw's?

And if there be no turnstile gate
50 At that green park, can we get in?
Is the game suspended or postponed,
And do the players play to win?

Mother of mercy, if you're there,
Pray to the high celestial czar
55 For all of these, the early dead,
Who've gone where no ovations are.

ANNE SEXTON (1928–1974)

Her Kind

I have gone out, a possessed witch,
haunting the black air, braver at night;
dreaming evil, I have done my hitch
over the plain houses, light by light:
5 lonely thing, twelve-fingered, out of mind.
A woman like that is not a woman, quite.
I have been her kind.

I have found the warm caves in the woods,
filled them with skillets, carvings, shelves,
10 closets, silks, innumerable goods;
fixed the suppers for the worms and the elves:
whining, rearranging the disaligned.
A woman like that is misunderstood.
I have been her kind.

15 I have ridden in your cart, driver,
waved my nude arms at villages going by,
learning the last bright routes, survivor
where your flames still bite my thigh
and my ribs crack where your wheels wind.
20 A woman like that is not ashamed to die.
I have been her kind.

Cinderella

You always read about it:
the plumber with twelve children
who wins the Irish Sweepstakes.
From toilets to riches.
5 That story.

Or the nursemaid,
some luscious sweet from Denmark
who captures the oldest son's heart.
From diapers to Dior.
10 That story.

Or a milkman who serves the wealthy,
eggs, cream, butter, yogurt, milk,
the white truck like an ambulance
who goes into real estate
15 and makes a pile.
From homogenized to martinis at lunch.

Or the charwoman
who is on the bus when it cracks up
and collects enough from the insurance.
20 From mops to Bonwit Teller.
That story.

Once
the wife of a rich man was on her deathbed
and she said to her daughter Cinderella:
25 Be devout. Be good. Then I will smile
down from heaven in the seam of a cloud.
The man took another wife who had
two daughters, pretty enough
but with hearts like blackjacks.
30 Cinderella was their maid.
She slept on the sooty hearth each night
and walked around looking like Al Jolson
Her father brought presents home from town,
jewels and gowns for the other women
35 but the twig of a tree for Cinderella.
She planted that twig on her mother's grave
and it grew to a tree where a white dove sat.
Whenever she wished for anything the dove

would drop it like an egg upon the ground.
40 The bird is important, my dears, so heed him.

Next came the ball, as you all know.
It was a marriage market.
The prince was looking for a wife.
All but Cinderella were preparing
45 and gussying up for the big event.
Cinderella begged to go too.
Her stepmother threw a dish of lentils
into the cinders and said: Pick them
up in an hour and you shall go.
50 The white dove brought all his friends;
all the warm wings of the fatherland came,
and picked up the lentils in a jiffy.
No, Cinderella, said the stepmother,
you have no clothes and cannot dance.
55 That's the way with stepmothers.

Cinderella went to the tree at the grave
and cried forth like a gospel singer:
Mama! Mama! My turtledove,
send me to the prince's ball!
60 The bird dropped down a golden dress
and delicate little gold slippers.
Rather a large package for a simple bird.
So she went. Which is no surprise.
Her stepmother and sisters didn't
65 recognize her without her cinder face
and the prince took her hand on the spot
and danced with no other the whole day.

As nightfall came she thought she'd better
get home. The prince walked her home
70 and she disappeared into the pigeon house
and although the prince took an axe and broke
it open she was gone. Back to her cinders.
These events repeated themselves for three days.
However on the third day the prince
75 covered the palace steps with cobbler's wax
and Cinderella's gold shoe stuck upon it.

Now he would find whom the shoe fit
and find his strange dancing girl for keeps

He went to their house and the two sisters
80 were delighted because they had lovely feet.
The eldest went into a room to try the slipper on
but her big toe got in the way so she simply
sliced it off and put on the slipper.
The prince rode away with her until the white dove
85 told him to look at the blood pouring forth.
That is the way with amputations.
They don't just heal up like a wish.
The other sister cut off her heel
but the blood told as blood will.
90 The prince was getting tired.
He began to feel like a shoe salesman.
But he gave it one last try.
This time Cinderella fit into the shoe
like a love letter into its envelope.

95 At the wedding ceremony
the two sisters came to curry favor
and the white dove pecked their eyes out.
Two hollow spots were left
like soup spoons.

100 Cinderella and the prince
lived, they say, happily ever after,
like two dolls in a museum case
never bother by diapers or dust,
never arguing over the timing of an egg,
105 never telling the same story twice,
never getting a middle-aged spread,
their darling smiles pasted on for eternity.
Regular Bobbsey Twins.
That story.

THOM GUNN (1929–)

Street Song

I am too young to grow a beard
But yes man it was me you heard
In dirty denim and dark glasses.
I look through everyone who passes
5 But ask him clear, I do not plead,
Keys lids acid and speed.

My grass is not oregano.
Some of it grew in Mexico.
You cannot guess the weed I hold,
10 Clara Green, Acapulco Gold,
Panama Red, you name it man,
Best on the street since I began.

My methedrine, my double-sun,
Will give you two lives in your one,
15 Five days of power before you crash.
At which time use these lumps of hash
—They burn so sweet, they smoke so smooth,
They make you sharper while they soothe.

Now here, the best I've got to show,
20 Made by a righteous cat I know.
Pure acid—it will scrape your brain,
And make it something else again.
Call it heaven, call it hell,
Join me and see the world I sell.

25 Join me, and I will take you there,
Your head will cut out from your hair
Into whichever self you choose.
With Midday Mick man you can't lose,
I'll get you anything you need.
30 *Keys lids acid and speed.*

The Discovery of the Pacific

They lean against the cooling car, backs pressed
Upon the dusts of a brown continent,
And watch the sun, now Westward of their West,
Fall to the ocean. Where it led they went.

5 Kansas to California. Day by day
They travelled emptier of the things they knew.
They improvised new habits on the way,
But lost the occasions, and then lost them too.

One night, no-one and nowhere, she had woken
10 To resin-smell and to the firs' slight sound,
And through their sleeping-bag had felt the broken
Tight-knotted surfaces of the naked ground.

Only his lean quiet body cupping hers
Kept her from it, the extreme chill. By degrees
15 She fell asleep. Around them in the firs
The wind probed, tiding through forked estuaries.

And now their skin is caked with road, the grime
Merely reflecting sunlight as it fails.
They leave their clothes among the rocks they climb,
20 Blunt leaves of iceplant nuzzle at their soles.

Now they stand chin-deep in the sway of ocean,
Firm West, two stringy bodies face to face,
And come, together, in the water's motion,
The full caught pause of their embrace.

Black Jackets

In the silence that prolongs the span
Rawly of music when the record ends,
    The red-haired boy who drove a van
In weekday overalls but, like his friends,

5   Wore cycle boots and jacket here
To suit the Sunday hangout he was in,
    Heard, as he stretched back from his beer,
Leather creak softly round his neck and chin.

    Before him, on a coal-black sleeve
10 Remote exertion had lined, scratched, and burned
    Insignia that could not revive
The heroic fall or climb where they were earned.

    On the other drinkers bent together,
Concocting selves for their impervious kit,
15   He saw it as no more than leather
Which, taut across the shoulders grown to it,

    Sent through the dimness of a bar
As sudden and anonymous hints of light
    As those that shipping give, that are
20 Now flickers in the Bay, now lost in night.

He stretched out like a cat, and rolled
The bitterish taste of beer upon his tongue,
    And listened to a joke being told:
The present was the things he stayed among.

25   If it was only loss he wore,
He wore it to assert, with fierce devotion,
    Complicity and nothing more.
He recollected his initiation,

    And one especially of the rites.
30 For on his shoulders they had put tattoos:
    The group's name on the left, The Knights,
And on the right the slogan Born To Lose.

ADRIENNE RICH (1929–   )

A Clock in the Square

This handless clock stares blindly from its tower,
Refusing to acknowledge any hour.
But what can one clock do to stop the game
When others go on striking just the same?
5 Whatever mite of truth the gesture held,

Time may be silenced but will not be stilled,
Nor we absolved by any one's withdrawing
From all the restless ways we must be going
And all the rings in which we're spun and swirled,
10 Whether around a clockface or a world.

Aunt Jennifer's Tigers

Aunt Jennifer's tigers prance across a screen,
Bright topaz denizens of a world of green.
They do not fear the men beneath the tree;
They pace in sleek chivalric certainty.

5 Aunt Jennifer's fingers fluttering through her wool
Find even the ivory needle hard to pull.
The massive weight of Uncle's wedding band
Sits heavily upon Aunt Jennifer's hand.

When Aunt is dead, her terrified hands will lie
10 Still ringed with ordeals she was mastered by.
The tigers in the panel that she made
Will go on prancing, proud and unafraid.

The Insusceptibles

Then the long sunlight lying on the sea
Fell, folded gold on gold; and slowly we
Took up our decks of cards, our parasols,
The picnic hamper and the sandblown shawls
5 And climbed the dunes in silence. There were two
Who lagged behind as lovers sometimes do,
And took a different road. For us the night
Was final, and by artificial light
We came indoors to sleep. No envy there
10 Of those who might be watching anywhere
The lustres of the summer dark, to trace
Some vagrant splinter blazing out of space.
No thought of them, save in a lower room
To leave a light for them when they should come.

Diving into the Wreck

First having read the book of myths,
and loaded the camera,
and checked the edge of the knife-blade,
I put on
5 the body-armor of black rubber
the absurd flippers
the grave and awkward mask.
I am having to do this
not like Cousteau with his
10 assiduous team
aboard the sun-flooded schooner
but here alone.

There is a ladder.
The ladder is always there
15 hanging innocently
close to the side of the schooner.
We know what it is for,
we who have used it.
otherwise
20 it is a piece of maritime floss
some sundry equipment.

I go down.
Rung after rung and still
25 the oxygen immerses me
the blue light
the clear atoms
of our human air.
I go down.
My flippers cripple me,
30 I crawl like an insect down the ladder
and there is no one
to tell me when the ocean
will begin.

First the air is blue and then
35 it is bluer and then green and then
black I am blacking out and yet
my mask is powerful
it pumps my blood with power
the sea is another story
40 the sea is not a question of power
I have to learn alone
to turn my body without force
in the deep element.

And now: it is easy to forget
45 what I came for
among so many who have always
lived here
swaying their crenellated fans
between the reefs
50 and besides
you breathe differently down here.

I came to explore the wreck.
The words are purposes.
The words are maps.
55 I came to see the damage that was done
and the treasures that prevail.
I stroke the beam of my lamp
slowly along the flank
of something more permanent
60 than fish or weed

the thing I came for:
the wreck and not the story of the wreck

the thing itself and not the myth
the drowned face always staring
65 toward the sun
the evidence of damage
worn by salt and sway into this threadbare beauty
the ribs of the disaster
curving their assertion
70 among the tentative haunters.

This is the place.
And I am here, the mermaid whose dark hair
streams black, the merman in his armored body.
We circle silently
75 about the wreck
we dive into the hold.
I am she: I am he
whose drowned face sleeps with open eyes
whose breasts still bear the stress
80 whose silver, copper, vermeil cargo lies
obscurely inside barrels
half-wedged and left to rot
we are the half-destroyed instruments
that once held to a course
85 the water-eaten log
the fouled compass

We are, I am, you are
by cowardice or courage
the one who find our way
90 back to this scene
carrying a knife, a camera
a book of myths
in which
our names do not appear.

TED HUGHES (1930–   )

Hawk Roosting

I sit in the top of the wood, my eyes closed.
Inaction, no falsifying dream
Between my hooked head and hooked feet:
Or in sleep rehearse perfect kills and eat.

5 The convenience of the high trees!
    The air's buoyancy and the sun's ray
    Are of advantage to me;
    And the earth's face upward for my inspection.

    My feet are locked upon the rough bark.
10 It took the whole of Creation
    To produce my foot, my each feather:
    Now I hold Creation in my foot

    Or fly up, and revolve it all slowly—
    I kill where I please because it is all mine.
15 There is no sophistry in my body:
    My manners are tearing off heads—

    The allotment of death.
    For the one path of my flight is direct
    Through the bones of the living.
20 No arguments assert my right:

    The sun is behind me.
    Nothing has changed since I began.
    My eye has permitted no change.
    I am going to keep things like this.

Pike

    Pike, three inches long, perfect
    Pike in all parts, green tigering the gold.
    Killers from the egg: the malevolent aged grin.
    They dance on the surface among the flies.

5 Or move, stunned by their own grandeur,
    Over a bed of emerald, silhouette
    Of submarine delicacy and horror.
    A hundred feet long in their world.

    In ponds, under the heat-struck lily pads—
10 Gloom of their stillness:
    Logged on last year's black leaves, watching upwards.
    Or hung in an amber cavern of weeds

    The jaw's hooked clamp and fangs
    Not to be changed at this date;

¹⁵ A life subdued to its instrument;
The gills kneading quietly, and the pectorals.

Three we kept behind glass,
Jungled in weed: three inches, four,
And four and a half: fed fry to them—
²⁰ Suddenly there were two. Finally one

With a sag belly and the grin it was born with.
And indeed they spare nobody.
Two, six pounds each, over two feet long,
High and dry and dead in the willow-herb—

²⁵ One jammed past its gills down the other's gullet:
The outside eye stared: as a vice locks—
The same iron in this eye
Though its film shrank in death.

A pond I fished, fifty yards across,
³⁰ Whose lilies and muscular tench
Had outlasted every visible stone
Of the monastery that planted them—

Stilled legendary depth:
It was as deep as England. It held
³⁵ Pike too immense to stir, so immense and old
That past nightfall I dared not cast

But silently cast and fished
With the hair frozen on my head
For what might move, for what eye might move.
⁴⁰ The still splashes on the dark pond,

Owls hushing the floating woods
Frail on my ear against the dream
Darkness beneath night's darkness had freed,
That rose slowly towards me, watching.

The Thought-Fox

I imagine this midnight moment's forest:
Something else is alive
Beside the clock's loneliness
And this blank page where my fingers move.

5 Through the window I see no star:
Something more near
Though deeper within darkness
Is entering the loneliness:

Cold, delicately as the dark snow,
10 A fox's nose touches twig, leaf;
Two eyes serve a movement, that now
And again now, and now, and now

Sets neat prints into the snow
Between trees, and warily a lame
15 Shadow lags by stump and in hollow
Of a body that is bold to come

Across clearings, an eye,
A widening deepening greenness,
Brilliantly, concentratedly,
20 Coming about its own business

Till, with a sudden sharp hot stink of fox
It enters the dark hole of the head.
The window is starless still; the clock ticks,
The page is printed.

GARY SNYDER (1930–   )

Before the Stuff Comes Down

Walking out of the "big E"
Dope store of the suburb,
              canned music plugging up your ears
              the wide aisles,
5   miles of wares
              from nowheres,

Suddenly it's California:
Live oak, brown grasses

Butterflies over the parking lot and the freeway
10 A Turkey Buzzard power in the blue air.

A while longer,
Still here.

DEREK WALCOTT (1930–   )

Sea Canes

Half my friends are dead.
I will make you new ones, said earth.
No, give me them back, as they were, instead,
with faults and all, I cried.

5 Tonight I can snatch their talk
from the faint surf's drone
through the canes, but I cannot walk

on the moonlit leaves of ocean
down that white road alone,
10 or float with the dreaming motion

of owls leaving earth's load.
O earth, the number of friends you keep
exceeds those left to be loved.

The sea-canes by the cliff flash green and silver;
15 they were the seraph lances of my faith,
but out of what is lost grows something stronger

that has the rational radiance of stone,
enduring moonlight, further than despair,
strong as the wind, that through dividing canes

20 brings those we love before us, as they were,
with faults and all, not nobler, just there.

A Far Cry from Africa

A wind is ruffling the tawny pelt
Of Africa. Kikuyu,[1] quick as flies,
Batten down the bloodstreams of the veldt.
Corpses are scattered through a paradise.
5 Only the worm, colonel of carrion, cries:
'Waste no compassion on these separate dead!'
Statistics justify and scholars seize
The salients of colonial policy.
What is that to the white child hacked in bed?
10 To savages, expendable as Jews?

---

1 A tribe in Kenya who rose against the European colonialists during the 1950s in
what Europeans called the Mau Mau Rebellion.

Threshed out by beaters, the long rushes break
In a white dust of ibises whose cries
Have wheeled since civilization's dawn
From the parched river or beast-teeming plain.
15 The violence of beast on beast is read
As natural law, but upright man
Seeks his divinity by inflicting pain.
Delirious as these worried beasts, his wars
Dance to the tightened carcass of a drum,
20 While he calls courage still that native dread
Of the white peace contracted by the dead.

Again brutish necessity wipes its hands
Upon the napkin of a dirty cause, again
A waste of our compassion, as with Spain,[2]
25 The gorilla wrestles with the superman.

I who am poisoned with the blood of both,
Where shall I turn, divided to the vein?
I who have cursed
The drunken officer of British rule, how choose
30 Between this Africa and the English tongue I love?
Betray them both, or give back what they give?
How can I face such slaughter and be cool?
How can I turn from Africa and live?

SYLVIA PLATH (1932–1963)

Ariel

Stasis in darkness.
Then the substanceless blue
Pour of tor and distances.

God's lioness,
5 How one we grow,
Pivot of heels and knees!—The furrow

Splits and passes, sister to
The brown arc
Of the neck I cannot catch,

---

2 A reference to the Spanish Civil War of 1936–39.

10 Nigger-eye
   Berries cast dark
   Hooks——

   Black sweet blood mouthfuls,
   Shadows.
15 Something else

   Hauls me through air——
   Thighs, hair;
   Flakes from my heels.

   White
20 Godiva, I unpeel——
   Dead hands, dead stringencies.

   And now I
   Foam to wheat, a glitter of seas.
   The child's cry

25 Melts in the wall.
   And I
   Am the arrow,

   The dew that flies
   Suicidal, at one with the drive
30 Into the red

   Eye, the cauldron of morning.

Morning Song

Love set you going like a fat gold watch.
The midwife slapped your footsoles, and your bald cry
Took its place among the elements.

Our voices echo, magnifying your arrival. New statue.
5 In a drafty museum, your nakedness
Shadows our safety. We stand round blankly as walls.

I'm no more your mother
Than the cloud that distils a mirror to reflect its own slow
Effacement at the wind's hand.

10 All night your moth-breath
Flickers among the flat pink roses. I wake to listen:
A far sea moves in my ear.

One cry, and I stumble from bed, cow-heavy and floral
In my Victorian nightgown.
15 Your mouth opens clean as a cat's. The window square

Whitens and swallows its dull stars. And now you try
Your handful of notes;
The clear vowels rise like balloons.

Medallion

By the gate with star and moon
Worked into the peeled orange wood
The bronze snake lay in the sun

Inert as a shoelace; dead
5 But pliable still, his jaw
Unhinged and his grin crooked,

Tongue a rose-colored arrow.
Over my hand I hung him.
His little vermilion eye

10 Ignited with a glassed flame
As I turned him in the light;
When I split a rock one time

The garnet bits burned like that.
Dust dulled his back to ochre
15 The way sun ruins a trout.

Yet his belly kept its fire
Going under the chainmail,
The old jewels smoldering there

In each opaque belly-scale:
20 Sunset looked at through milk glass.
And I saw white maggots coil

Thin as pins in the dark bruise
Where his innards bulged as if
He were digesting a mouse.

25 Knifelike, he was chaste enough,
   Pure death's-metal. The yardman's
   Flung brick perfected his laugh.

Metaphors

I'm a riddle in nine syllables,
An elephant, a ponderous house,
A melon strolling on two tendrils.
O red fruit, ivory, fine timbers!
5 This loaf's big with its yeasty rising.
Money's new-minted in this fat purse.
I'm a means, a stage, a cow in calf.
I've eaten a bag of green apples,
Boarded the train there's no getting off.

Daddy

You do not do, you do not do
Any more, black shoe
In which I have lived like a foot
For thirty years, poor and white,
5 Barely daring to breath or Achoo.

Daddy, I have had to kill you.
You died before I had time—
Marble-heavy, a bag full of God,
Ghastly statue with one gray toe
10 Big as a Frisco seal

And a head in the freakish Atlantic
Where it pours bean green over blue
In the waters off beautiful Nauset.
I used to pray to recover you.
15 Ach, du.

In the German tongue, in the Polish town
Scraped flat by the roller
Of wars, wars, wars.

But the name of the town is common.
20 My Polack friend

Says there are a dozen or two.
So I never could tell where you
Put your foot, your root,
I never could talk to you.
25 The tongue stuck in my jaw.

It stuck in a barb wire snare.
Ich, ich, ich, ich,
I could hardly speak.
I thought every German was you.
30 And the language obscene

An engine, an engine
Chuffing me off like a Jew.
A Jew to Dachau, Auschwitz, Belsen.
I began to talk like a Jew.
35 I think I may well be a Jew.

The snows of the Tyrol, the clear beer of Vienna
Are not very pure or true.
With my gypsy ancestress and my weird luck
And my Taroc pack and my Taroc pack
40 I may be a bit of a Jew.

I have always been scared of *you*,
With your Luftwaffe, your gobbledygoo.
And your neat moustache
And your Aryan eye, bright blue.
45 Panzer-man, panzer-man, O You—

Bit my pretty red heart in two.
I was ten when they buried you.
At twenty I tried to die
And get back, back, back to you.
50 I thought even the bones would do.

But they pulled me out of the sack,
And they stuck me together with glue,
And then I knew what to do.
I made a model of you,
55 A man in black with a Meinkampf look

And a love of the rack and the screw.
And I said I do, I do.
So daddy, I'm finally through.
The black telephone's off at the root,
60 The voices just can't worm through.

If I've killed one man, I've killed two—
The vampire who said he was you
And drank my blood for a year,
Seven years, if you want to know.
65 Daddy, you can lie back now.

There's a stake in your fat black heart
And the villagers never liked you.
They are dancing and stamping on you.
They always *knew* it was you.
70 Daddy, daddy, you bastard, I'm through.

ROBERT CLAYTON CASTO (1932–   )

The Salt Pork

This is about the summer and the wheels of sleep
and the man shot through with Adam and dying from the heart

who moves through the night upstairs along a flowered wall
and longs for kitchens in the immense and preoccupied night.

5 He is about to die tomorrow or next week
and longs for the thing they say he must not have—salt, salt.

A woman stands at the base of the stairs and she looks up:
he has nothing for salt but tears and his tears are like his flesh

big and white in the night and slow to hover and drop,
10 so she brings him in pity salt pork, gray woman as biting as salt.

Picture the two of them poised on that landing, bitter and old,
measuring each other like gods, after the humbug of years;

and though she has long since spun and spun from her discontent
and shifts like a larva now inside her webbed regret,

15 it is the gift that makes her a woman again and she wings

the silence out from her thighs by the movement of offering
to the floods and coagulations of his flesh the pork,

that he may taste salt things again with a wet white tongue
an inch before dying in summer, when sleep is our green cargo.

20 She knows after all and all the biting years, at last
she will please the both of them and he will be glad on the stairs

to receive at his lips the forbidden and quite lively flavor
of the sharp wife and the offering beyond old duty—it is

the ransom (lord) of Eden. He is glad like a child from his heart
25 and she knows at last from her own: because we are less than gods

we are holy, holy, holy.

ETHERIDGE KNIGHT (1933–   )

For Black Poets Who Think of Suicide

Black Poets should live—not leap
From steel bridges (like the white boys do).

Black Poets should *live*—not lay
Their necks on railroad tracks (like the white boys do).
5 Black Poets should seek, but not search
Too much in sweet dark caves
Or hunt for snipes down psychic trails—
(Like the white boys do).

For Black Poets belong to Black People.
10 Are the flutes of Black Lovers—Are
The organs of Black Sorrows—Are
The trumpets of Black Warriors.
Let all Black Poets die as trumpets,
And be buried in the dust of marching feet.

WENDELL BERRY (1934–   )

The Peace of Wild Things

When despair for the world grows in me
and I wake in the night at the least sound

in fear of what my life and my children's lives may be,
I go and lie down where the wood drake
5 rests in his beauty on the water, and the great heron feeds.
I come into the peace of wild things
who do not tax their lives with forethought
of grief. I come into the presence of still water.
And I feel above me the day-blind stars
10 waiting with their light. For a time
I rest in the grace of the world, and am free.

LEONARD COHEN (1934–   )

Elegy

Do not look for him
In brittle mountain streams:
They are too cold for any god;
And do not examine the angry rivers
5 For shreds of his soft body
Or turn the shore stones for his blood;
But in the warm salt ocean
He is descending through cliffs
Of slow green water
10 And the hovering colored fish
Kiss his snow-bruised body
And build their secret nests
In his fluttering winding-sheet.

The Bus

I was the last passenger of the day,
I was alone on the bus,
I was glad they were spending all that money
just getting me up Eighth Avenue.
5 Driver! I shouted, it's you and me tonight,
let's run away from this big city
to a smaller city more suitable to the heart,
let's drive past the swimming pools of Miami Beach,
you in the driver's seat, me several seats back,
10 but in the racial cities we'll change places
so as to show how well you've done up North,
and let us find ourselves some tiny American fishing village
in unknown Florida
and park right at the edge of the sand,

15 a huge bus pointing out,
   metallic, painted, solitary,
   with New York plates.

AMIRI BARAKA (LeROI JONES) (1934–   )

W.W.

Back home the black women are all beautiful,
and the white ones fall back, cutoff from 1000
years stacked booty, and Charles of the Ritz
where jooshladies turn into billy burke in blueglass
5 kicks. With wings, and jingly bew-teeful things.
The black women in Newark are fine. Even with all that grease
in their heads. I mean even the ones where the wigs
slide around, and they coming at you 75 degrees off course.
I could talk to them. Bring them around. To something.
10 Some kind of quick course, on the sidewalk, like Hey baby
why don't you take that thing off yo' haid. You look like
Miss Muffet in a runaway ugly machine. I mean. Like that.

MARK STRAND (1934–   )

The Dead

The graves grow deeper.
The dead are more dead each night.

Under the elms and the rain of leaves,
The graves grow deeper.

5 The dark folds of the wind
Cover the ground. The night is cold.

The leaves are swept against the stones.
The dead are more dead each night.

A starless dark embraces them.
10 Their faces dim.

We cannot remember them
Clearly enough. We never will.

The Tunnel

A man has been standing
in front of my house
for days. I peek at him
from the living room
5 window and at night,
unable to sleep,
I shine my flashlight
down on the lawn.
He is always there.

10 After a while
I open the front door
just a crack and order
him out of my yard.
He narrows his eyes
15 and moans. I slam
the door and dash back
to the kitchen, then up
to the bedroom, then down.

I weep like a schoolgirl
20 and make obscene gestures
through the window. I
write large suicide notes
and place them so he
can read them easily.
25 I destroy the living
room furniture to prove
I own nothing of value.

When he seems unmoved
I decide to dig a tunnel
30 to a neighboring yard.
I seal the basement off
from the upstairs with
a brickwall. I dig hard
and in no time the tunnel
35 is done. Leaving my pick
and shovel below,

I come out in front of a house
and stand there too tired to

move or even speak, hoping
40 someone will help me.
I feel I'm being watched
and sometimes I hear
a man's voice,
but nothing is done
45 and I have been waiting for days.

Keeping Things Whole

In a field
I am the absence
of field.

This is
5 always the case.
Wherever I am
I am what is missing.

When I walk
I part the air
10 and always
the air moves in
to fill the spaces
where my body's been.

We all have reasons
15 for moving.
I move
to keep things whole.

LUCILLE CLIFTON (1936–   )

in the inner city

in the inner city
or
like we call it
home
5 we think a lot about uptown
and the silent nights
and the houses straight as
dead men

and the pastel lights
¹⁰ and we hang on to our no place
happy to be alive
and in the inner city
or
like we call it
¹⁵ home

JOSEPH DE ROCHE (1938–   )

**Aunt Laura Moves Toward the Open
Grave of Her Father**

You are coming toward us
As if you have done this
Every day of your life.

You are stumbling. You are my
5 Aunt, our ignorant, old fool
And you are completely in

Black. We are, to put it plain,
Putting grandfather into
A hole in the ground. We are

¹⁰ Dry eyed as dry ice is cold.
We have made it clear to you
How much you did wrong, how much

Better we could have done al-
Most anything. Except this.
¹⁵ This perfection. This grief.

You are in black. You are moving
Toward us. You are wisdom,
The dark that stabs me at midnight

On any street because I
²⁰ Am who I am and we are violent
At the horrible, hard gates of

Paradise. You are an army
Of crepe, onyx. Like the wind
You move curtains of sorrow,

²⁵ Simplicity, toward us.
And I love you while Grandpa
Slips now from our fingers for

Ever and I take your hand
And we hold on together.

Blond

I am not going to invite you,
For once, into my life.

Others may call you beautiful
Or handsome, but not from my lips

5 Any praises. This is the way
It should be with strangers,

Always. What if your hair be
The hair that shines bright in

Dark places? So does the sun
10 In the eye of the storm and,

O, we are just winds flying
About you. But not from my

Lips will you hear a sharp
Cry in the street—some summons

15 To follow. What if I dodge you
All night? Loiter behind you?

What matter? Off you go!
Home to your cloister of ciphers!

I will not praise you. I sprawl,
20 Instead, on a splendor of pillows.

In the late guttering light,
Tilted to sleep, I am biting my lips.

MARGARET ATWOOD (1939–   )

It Is Dangerous to Read Newspapers

While I was building neat
castles in the sandbox,
the hasty pits were
filling with bulldozed corpses

5 and as I walked to the school
washed and combed, my feet
stepping on the cracks in the cement
detonated red bombs.

Now I am grownup
10 and literate, and I sit in my chair
as quietly as a fuse

and the jungles are flaming, the under-
brush is charged with soldiers,
the names on the difficult
15 maps go up in smoke.

I am the cause, I am a stockpile of chemical
toys, my body
is a deadly gadget,
I reach out in love, my hands are guns,
20 my good intentions are completely lethal.

Even my
passive eyes transmute
everything I look at to the pocked
black and white of a war photo,
25 how
can I stop myself

It is dangerous to read newspapers.

Each time I hit a key
on my electric typewriter,
30 speaking of peaceful trees

another village explodes.

AL YOUNG (1939–)

Lemons, Lemons

Hanging from fresh trees
or yellow against green
in a soft blaze of afternoon
while I eat dutifully
5 my cheese & apple lunch
or the coolness of twilight
in some of these California towns
I inhabited a lifetime ago

Hung that way
10 filled up with sunlight
like myself ripe with light
brown with light & ripe with shadow
the apple red & gold & green with it
cheese from the insides of
15 sun-loving cows

Sweet goldenness of light
& life itself
sunny at the core
lasting all day long
20 into night
into sleep
permeating dream shapes
forming tingly little words
my 2¢ squeezed out
25 photosynthetically
in hasty praise
of lemon/light

SEAMUS HEANEY (1939–)

Bogland

for T. P. Flanagan

We have no prairies
To slice a big sun at evening—
Everywhere the eye concedes to
Encroaching horizon,

5 Is wooed into the cyclops' eye[1]
Of a tarn. Our unfenced country
Is bog that keeps crusting
Between the sights of the sun.

They've taken the skeleton
10 Of the Great Irish Elk
Out of the peat, set it up
An astounding crate full of air.

Butter sunk under
More than a hundred years
15 Was recovered salty and white.
The ground itself is kind, black butter

Melting and opening underfoot,
Missing its last definition
By millions of years.
20 They'll never dig coal here,

Only the waterlogged trunks
Of great firs, soft as pulp.
Our pioneers keep striking
Inwards and downwards.

25 Every layer they strip
Seems camped on before.
The bogholes might be Atlantic seepage.
The wet centre is bottomless.

Waterfall

The burn drowns steadily in its own downpour,
A helter-skelter of muslin and glass
That skids to a halt, crashing up suds.

Simultaneous acceleration
5 And sudden braking; water goes over
Like villains dropped screaming to justice.

---

[1] In Homer's *Odyssey*, the Cyclops are one-eyed giants.

It appears an athletic glacier
Has reared into reverse: is swallowed up
And regurgitated through this long throat.

10 My eye rides over and downwards, falls with
Hurtling tons that slabber and spill,
Falls, yet records the tumult thus standing still.

Docker

There, in the corner, staring at his drink.
The cap juts like a gantry's crossbeam,
Cowling plated forehead and sledgehead jaw.
Speech is clamped in the lips' vice.

5 That fist would drop a hammer on a Catholic—
Oh yes, that kind of thing could start again;
The only Roman collar he tolerates
Smiles all round his sleek pint of porter.

Mosaic imperatives bang home like rivets;
10 God is a foreman with certain definite views

HENRY TAYLOR (1942–   )

Riding a One-Eyed Horse

One side of his world is always missing.
You may give it a casual wave of the hand
or rub it with your shoulder as you pass,
but nothing on his blind side ever happens.

5 Hundreds of trees slip past him into darkness,
drifting into a hollow hemisphere
whose sounds you will have to try to explain.
Your legs will tell him not to be afraid

if you learn never to lie. Do not forget
10 to turn his head and let what comes come seen:
he will jump the fences he has to if you swing
toward them from the side that he can see

and hold his good eye straight. The heavy dark
will stay beside you always; let him learn

15 to lean against it. It will steady him
    and see you safely through diminished fields.

NIKKI GIOVANNI (1943–   )

Nikki-Rosa

childhood remembrances are always a drag
if you're Black
you always remember things like living in Woodlawn[1]
with no inside toilet
5 and if you become famous or something
they never talk about how happy you were to have your mother
all to your self and
how good the water felt when you got your bath from one of those
big tubs that folk in chicago barbecue in
10 and somehow when you talk about home
it never gets across how much you
understood their feelings
as the whole family attended meetings about Hollydale[2]
and even though you remember
15 your biographers never understand
your father's pain as he sells his stock
and another dream goes
and though you're poor it isn't poverty that
concerns you
20 and though they fought a lot
it isn't your father's drinking that makes any difference
but only that everybody is together and you
and your sister have happy birthdays and very good christmasses
and I really hope no white person ever has cause to write about me
25 because they never understand Black love is Black wealth and they'll
probably talk about my hard childhood and never understand that
all the while I was quite happy.

LOUISE GLÜCK (1943–   )

Gratitude

Do not think I am not grateful for your small
kindness to me.
I like small kindnesses.

---

[1] A working-class suburb of Cincinnati.
[2] A subdivision of single-family homes, launched in the 1950s.

In fact I actually prefer them to the more
5 substantial kindness, that is always eying you,
like a large animal on a rug,
until your whole life reduces
to nothing but waking up morning after morning
cramped, and the bright sun shining on its tusks.

MICHAEL ONDAATJE (1945–   )

King Kong meets Wallace Stevens

Take two photographs—
Wallace Stevens and King Kong
(Is it significant that I eat bananas as I write this?)

Stevens is portly, benign, a white brush cut
5 striped tie. Businessman but
for the dark thick hands, the naked brain
the thought in him.

Kong is staggering
lost in New York streets again
10 a spawn of annoyed cars at his toes.
The mind is nowhere.
Fingers are plastic, electric under the skin.
He's at the call of Metro-Goldwyn-Mayer.

Meanwhile W. S. in his suit
15 is thinking chaos is thinking fences.
In his head the seeds of fresh pain
his exorcising,
the bellow of locked blood.

The hands drain from his jacket,
20 pose in the murderer's shadow.

Charles Darwin pays a visit, December 1971

View of the coast of Brazil.
A man stood up to shout
at the image of a sailing ship
which was a vast white bird from over the sea
5 and now ripping its claws into the ocean.
Faded hills of March

painted during the cold morning.
On board ship Charles Darwin sketched clouds.

One of these days the Prime Mover will
10 paint the Prime Mover out of his sky.
I want a . . . centuries being displaced
. . . faith.
'23rd of June, 1832.
He caught sixty-eight species
15   of a particularly minute beetle.'

The blue thick leaves who greeted him
animals unconscious of celebration
moved slowly into law.
Adam with a watch.
20 Look past and future, (I want a . . .),
ease our way out of the structures
this smell of the cogs
and diamonds we live in.

I am waiting for a new ship, so new
25 we will think the lush machine
an animal of God.
Weary from travelling over the air and the water
it will sink to its feet at our door.

Birth of Sound

At night the most private of a dog's long body groan.
It comes with his last stretch
in the dark corridor outside our room.
The children turn.
5 A window tries to split with cold
the other dog hoofing the carpet for lice.
We're all alone.

KENNETH SHERMAN (1950–   )

My Father Kept His Cats Well Fed

My father kept his cats well fed.
In back of the tailor shop
far from consumer eye
they'd stretch

5 on thick rolls of mohair,
   on new blue synthetics from Japan.

   And somehow he bought time
   to keep fresh milk in the saucepan,
   providing leftovers
10 from a hurried lunch.

   Between the measurements and complaints,
   between the clean sound of closing shears
   they were his own animal symphony
   purring at a conducted stroke
15 under the chin,
   behind the ear.

   The cats,
   they sang my father's praise
   in the fishbone throat of the coldest nights
20 where their lives, once lean,
   curled fat and secure

   and dreamt their gifted names:
   No-Neck, Schvartz, Kaatz, Rabinovitz . . .
   a regular *minyan*[1]
25 to greet his early mornings
   when snow outside
   dropped soft as padded paws
   and the shop was a museum hush.

   There they reclined,
30 impenetrable as sphinx,
   the curious engines of their soft throats
   running, their great eyes smouldering
   in the precious twilight of my father's day

   before the startling ring
35 and the long unwinding of curses
   and cloth.

---

[1] The quorum needed in order to conduct a Jewish public worship service.

INDEX OF TERMS

INDEX OF AUTHORS AND TITLES

INDEX OF FIRST LINES